*S. M. Miller* is Professor of Sociology at the Maxwell Graduate School and the Youth Development Center of Syracuse University. His writings on poverty and stratification in scholarly and popular journals, and his several books, are widely known.

# APPLIED SOCIOLOGY:
## OPPORTUNITIES AND PROBLEMS

# APPLIED

# SOCIOLOGY

## OPPORTUNITIES AND PROBLEMS

*Edited by*

*ALVIN W. GOULDNER*

*and*

*S. M. MILLER*

*For the* SOCIETY FOR THE STUDY OF SOCIAL PROBLEMS

THE FREE PRESS, *New York*

COLLIER–MACMILLAN LIMITED, *London*

Collier-Macmillan Canada, Ltd., Toronto, Ontario

*Second printing November 1966*

Library of Congress Catalog Card Number: 65–13396

# CONTRIBUTORS

KATHLEEN ARCHIBALD, Institute of International Studies, University of California, Berkeley

ROBERT BIERSTEDT, Chairman, Department of Sociology, New York University

WARREN BREED, Professor of Sociology, Newcomb College, Tulane University

JAMES W. CARPER, U. S. Department of Labor

NICHOLAS J. DEMERATH, Professor of Sociology, Washington University

MABEL A. ELLIOTT, Irene Heinz Given Professor of Sociology and Chairman of Department of Sociology, Chatham College.

WILLIAM M. EVAN, Associate Professor of Sociology and Industrial Management, Massachusetts Institute of Technology

ARNOLD S. FELDMAN, Associate Professor of Sociology, Northwestern University

NICHOLAS G. FOTION, State University at Buffalo, New York

WILLIAM GAMSON, Associate Professor of Sociology, University of Michigan

BURLEIGH B. GARDNER, Executive Director, Social Research, Inc.

DAVID GOLD, Chairman, Department of Sociology, University of California, Santa Barbara

ALVIN W. GOULDNER, Professor of Sociology, Washington University; Editor, TRANS-ACTION

SCOTT A. GREER, Professor of Sociology and Political Science; Director, Center for Metropolitan Studies, Northwestern University

LLEWELLYN GROSS, Chairman, Department of Sociology, State University of New York at Buffalo

WILLIAM F. HANDY, Washington University

JEROME HIMELHOCH, Professor of Sociology; Director, Vermont Youth Study, Goddard College

NEHEMIAH JORDAN, Institute for Defense Analysis

*v*

# Contributors

Ralph L. Kolodny, Boston Children's Service Association

Alfred McClung Lee, Professor of Sociology and Anthropology, Brooklyn College of the City University of New York

Ritchie P. Lowry, Senior Research Scientist and Chairman, Basic Studies Division, Special Operations Research Office, American University

Frank N. Magid, Executive Director, Frank N. Magid Associates

Delbert C. Miller, Professor of Sociology and Business Administration, Indiana University

S. M. Miller, Professor of Sociology, Maxwell Graduate School, and Senior Research Associate, Youth Development Center, Syracuse University

John Mogey, Chairman, Department of Sociology, Boston University

Wilbert E. Moore, Sociologist, Russell Sage Foundation

Jerome K. Myers, Professor of Sociology, Yale University

Frank W. Neff, Survey Research Center, University of Michigan

Donald J. Newman, Associate Professor of Social Work, University of Wisconsin

David J. Pittman, Professor of Sociology; Director, Social Science Institute, Washington University

Richard Robbins, Associate Professor of Sociology, Wheaton College

Vincent Rock, George Washington University

Hyman Rodman, Research Associate, Merrill-Palmer Institute

Eva Rosenfeld, Research Staff, Jewish Board of Guardians

Ralph G. Ross, Professor of Philosophy and Humanities; Chairman, Humanities Program, University of Minnesota

Clarence C. Sherwood, Director of Research, Action for Boston Community Development

Rita James Simon, Research Associate Professor, Institute of Communications Research, and Department of Sociology, University of Illinois

Gordon Streib, Chairman, Department of Sociology, Cornell University

Charles V. Willie, Associate Professor Sociology, Maxwell Graduate School, and Senior Research Associate, Youth Development Center, Syracuse University

Lewis Yablonsky, Professor of Sociology, San Fernando Valley State College

# Preface

THIS BOOK GIVES A VIEW OF THE DIVERSE USES TO which sociology is being put in the organizations and communities in which Americans now live.

In dealing with the practical uses of sociology in today's society, we present the work of people who are, in effect, branching out and pioneering new styles of sociology. What is presented then has the freshness and vividness of the living case rather than the case-hardened: work done by men who are making the new applied sociology rather than by those who are codifying the work of others. At many points, different viewpoints are presented because the clash of perspective is necessary in the development of usefulness.

The current war on poverty is only one of the many wars in which the pragmatic American spirit will surely reach out for the guidance of the new sciences of man. Certainly, the wars against war, discrimination, delinquency, addiction, and political apathy will, no less, compel us to mobilize and utilize the instruments of intelligence.

It is the historic mission of the social sciences to enable mankind to take possession of society. This is a big job and will take a long time. The works presented here are surely among the significant and tangible beginnings of this effort to bring society under control. Some of the papers re-examine fundamental assumptions of social policy (see the papers in Section V, and those by Breed, Robbins, and Greer); others study the goals of society (see Section VI); still others evaluate the performance of our institutions (Section III); and a number are devoted to the examination of the complex tie between society and those who study it in order to change it (Sections I, II, and IV).

*vii*

# Preface

This book is an official publication of the Society for the Study of Social Problems (SSSP), a national organization of sociologists with a special concern for the application of sociology to the large problems of today. Most of the papers, which were planned by Gouldner, as president, and Miller, as program chairman of SSSP, were given at the 1961 meetings of the society in St. Louis. We are grateful to the authors for their co-operation and patience in the long process of turning the papers into a cohesive book. We also appreciate the editorial assistance of Marcia Ecker and the clerical aid of Fern Freel, Crestline Littlefield, Janet Carlisle Bogdan, and Betty Saleem.

A. W. G.
S. M. M.

# ACKNOWLEDGMENTS

The publishers of the following journals have granted us permission to reprint material that appeared originally in their publications:

*Sociology and Social Research,* for the articles by Newman and by Pittman and Handy, which appeared in volume 6, no. 2, January, 1962.

*Human Organization* and the Society for Applied Anthropology, for the article by Rodman and Kolodny, which appeared in volume 23, no. 2, Summer, 1964.

*Journal of Intergroup Relations* and the National Association of Intergroup Relations Officials, for permitting the revision of the article by Robbins, which appeared in volume 2, no. 4, Autumn, 1961.

*Rassegna Italiana di Sociologia,* for the Lee article, which appeared originally in Italian in volume 2, 1961.

*Estudios de Sociologio,* for the Evan article, which appeared originally in Spanish in 1962.

*Social Problems,* the Journal of the Society for the Study of Social Problems, for the articles by Gouldner, Archibald, and Rosenfeld.

# Contents

*x i*

# Contents

# Contents

# APPLIED SOCIOLOGY:
## OPPORTUNITIES AND PROBLEMS

# Part I

# A CLINICAL APPROACH

# 1.   Explorations in
## Applied Social Science

ALVIN W. GOULDNER

Not so long ago the words "social engineer" were a term of opprobrium. They carried with them the suspicion that such a social scientist had somehow betrayed his vow of dispassionate objectivity and had sold his scientific heritage for a tasteless mess of popularity. This fastidious judgment was congenial to a stable society confident in the capacity of its established routines to cope with familiar tensions. It made sense also in a culture which had an unshaken belief in progress, rationality, and justice, and an optimistic faith that each new generation would automatically outdistance its predecessors.[7] As these assumptions no longer appear transparently self-evident, there emerge such pragmatic disciplines as disaster research, industrial sociology, military sociology, propaganda and communications research, and group dynamics—to mention only a few. Today, the growth of such organizations as HUMRO, RAND Corporation, The Air Forces Institute, and others, indicates the rapid transition to a more honorific and powerful place for the applied social sciences.

The applied social sciences have shifted for themselves, growing rapidly but in a trial-and-error fashion and with little assistance from the theorist. Traditionally, sociological theory has ministered to the needs of pure or basic researches, rather than to those of applied research. Indeed, the casual observer may almost think it a contradiction in terms to speak of a "methodology" of the applied social sciences. Yet the fact is that the applied social sciences are badly in want of such a methodology. For as a result of this deficiency, the very meaning and character of "applied social science" remain obscure and those concerned with it often reflexively reiterate received formulae.

A variety of dubious assumptions, some explicit and some tacit, are now commonly made concerning the nature of applied social science. Unless these assumptions are given serious inspection they may become sacred items of faith rather than serving as useful guides to work. They can harden into a professional catechism which compulsively shapes future activities in the applied social sciences in ways that prematurely preclude lines of development which could prove fruitful. In the pages that follow several such assumptions will be subjected to re-examination. These are: (a) that an applied social science is one which applies the principles of pure or basic disciplines to practical problems; (b) that there is only one type of applied social science; (c) that applied social scientists cannot specify ends or values for their clients; (d) that resistance to the practical utilization of social science derives mainly from the inadequacy of present-day research methods.

## Social Science: Pure and Applied

To begin with the first assumption, it is all too commonly held that an applied sociology is "nothing but" the application of generalizations, developed by pure sociology, to concrete and practical cases. For example, in a seminar at Chicago University in 1937, A. R. Radcliffe-Brown commented: "There is . . . a very close relationship between theoretical natural science and applied natural science. Applied science is still science . . . it consists of propositions, but it consists essentially in the application of the knowledge which belongs to theoretical science to the practical problems which are met with in the application of the arts."[1] Fifteen years later essentially the same conception of applied anthropology was advanced by Darryl Forde at The International Symposium on Anthropology.[6] Russell Newman's paper on "Applied Anthropometry,"[19] at the same meeting, was prefaced with an approving reference to Webster's dictionary definition of applied science as "using and adapting abstract principles and theory in connection with concrete problems, especially with a utilitarian aim."

Though much reiterated, it would seem that this conception of applied social science is misleading if not inaccurate. There are in present day sociology few validated laws or broad generalizations; nonetheless, as the above comments indicate, there is a great acceleration of applied social science. There seems to be no close correlation, therefore, between the development of generalizations by the pure disciplines and the multiplication of opportunities for, and varieties of, applied sociology. The applied sciences cannot be fruitfully regarded as springing Athena-like from the furrowed brow of the pure disciplines. Any metaphor which conceives of applied social science as the offspring, and of the basic disciplines as parents, is misleading. It obscures the point that the applied sciences often contribute as much to pure science as they receive from it.

Perhaps the truth of the matter is that the applied social scientist presently makes use of the *concepts* rather than the generalized propositions of pure social science. For example, anthropologists who have turned to applied endeavors often begin by asking themselves how the concept of "culture" can illuminate their particular problem. This would seem to be the point that George Foster makes in his account of research into Latin American health programs, when he comments, "The research problem was defined in the following general terms: how can the anthropological axiom—'in order to work with a people it is essential to understand their culture'—be translated into terms that would be meaningful to administrators."[7] In like manner, much of market research makes more use of the concept of "social class," to aid it in analyzing differential consuming habits, than it does of specific propositions about the behavior of social classes. Stated differently, applied social science seems to use "general orientations," which focus attention on patterns of behavior and belief that are systematically neglected by practical men, rather than using propositions which could generate specific hypotheses about this behavior.[15]

In the standard view of the relationship between applied and pure social science there is the tacit assumption that the development of the applied social sciences requires no special planning and theoretical analyses. It is assumed they possess no distinctive problems and that, with the maturation of the basic disciplines, all that will be required is to transfer their developments, like carrying bones from an old graveyard to a new one. It is in this vein that Goode and Hatt report that there is a "belief that science has best been able to achieve practical results when no goals other than those of science are considered. Those who hold this position maintain that if scientists are allowed to pursue problems dictated purely by theoretical concerns, the growth of science and hence the growth of its potential applications will be served."[9] The thought is scarcely entertained, how-

7

ever, that the applied and pure disciplines may have differences in their basic interests and thus in their very conceptual roots.

It is an open question whether all theoretical systems or conceptual schemes, in pure social science, have equal relevance and value for applied social science. An applied social science is above all concerned with the prediction and production of social and cultural change. As Thelen has suggested, an applied social science is a technology and, as such, requires "a set of principles useful to bring about change toward desired ends."[26] Eliot Chapple has, in fact, defined applied anthropology as "that aspect of anthropology which deals with the description of changes in human relations and in the isolation of the principles that control them. Perhaps it should also be emphasized that such a definition, by necessity, includes an examination of those factors which restrict the possibility of change in human organization."[3] There is little doubt that the central focus of all the applied social sciences is on the problem of social and cultural change.

In contrast, however, many of the current models of pure sociology have not developed an analysis of change, often having little or nothing to say about this. Applied social science requires concepts enabling it to deal with change, while much of pure social science today is oriented to the analysis of stable social structures in their equilibrium.[17] As a result, the objectives of applied social science often fail to articulate with, or derive little aid from, the models and concepts of pure social science. In this connection, there is a very instructive case in the work of Talcott Parsons, which reflects this disparity between the requirements of applied social science and current models of pure sociological theory.[20]

In Parsons' analysis of "The Problem of Controlled Institutional Change," a work in applied sociology, he attempts to develop a strategy for changing conquered Germany after World War II. In this article Parsons stresses the significance of "internal conflicts" in Germany as a tactical lever for the production of change. While the equilibrium model which Parsons normally uses in his pure theory ignores internal tensions, the problems of preparing a plan for changing German society apparently constrained Parsons to give this concept a much more salient position.

Moreover, in this same article much use is made of "class" concepts—e.g., in appraising the vulnerable position of the Junkers or in planning to modify the recruiting pattern of the German civil service—although such concepts are normally but little stressed in his pure equilibrium theory. There is, then, a strong suggestion in Parsons' work that the conceptual requirements of even his own efforts in applied sociology were not well served by his own model of pure theory.* It seems evident that the needs of an applied social science, which must above all cope with social change, are not met by all models of present-day pure theory. An applied social science cannot, therefore, be regarded as entailing the simple transfer of either the established propositions or the concepts of pure science to practical purposes. Even if a fully mature basic social science existed, the applied social sciences might still be handicapped if the former failed to be organized around concepts and models useful to the applied fields, and particularly if it failed to focus centrally on the problem of change.

The suspicion that the applied behavior sciences do suffer from this handicap grows stronger if attention is directed to one crucial case: namely, that what is probably the most successful of the applied psychologies, psychoanalysis, did not develop by way of transferring the established principles of pure academic psychology to clinical problems. It seems instead to have been marked, from its very inception, by conceptual and theoretical innovations.**

Let there be no mistake about the meaning here: it is *not* being said that applied social sciences should not use or have not used the general principles and concepts of the basic disciplines. They may and have done so where they could. The actual relation between applied and basic social science is an empirical problem; we need many detailed case histories describing these relations as they have developed. Such researches, however, would be sorely misguided if they accepted the pat assumption now current concerning these relations as their guiding hypothesis. The following may instead be regarded as more favored hypotheses: (a) Applied social scientists are more likely to use the concepts than the generalized propositions of their basic discipline. (b) Not all concepts or theoretical models of pure social science are equally useful to applied social scientists. (c) Applied social scientists will more likely borrow from their basic disciplines those concepts and theoretical models which aid them in understand-

---

* It needs to be pointed out, however, that Parsons' work on "The Problem of Controlled Institutional Change" was completed before the maturation of his equilibrium model. This, however, is not the case with respect to his interesting piece on " 'McCarthyism' and American Social Tension" (*The Yale Review*, Winter, 1955), which is also, I believe, vulnerable to a similar interpretation. Moreover, the former article on Germany was also clearly divergent from the pure voluntaristic model which Parsons had earlier formulated in his *Structure of Social Action*.

** Psychoanalysis of course established its own pure theoretical model of substantive psychology, but this was based upon and largely derived from its applied clinical interests. As Freud sometimes stressed, his pure theory derived from his practical experience as a clinician.

ing or producing changes. (d) When the basic discipline does not provide theoretical systems or concepts aiding the applied social scientist to deal with change, the latter will develop these himself.[5] These new concepts will, in turn, exert pressure to produce modifications in the theories of the basic disciplines.

What implications follow from this analysis of the relations between pure and applied social science? Among others, it would seem that any discouragement of applied social science on the ground that it should not run too far ahead of pure science, and that its own development should await prior conceptual maturation of the pure sciences, is ill-advised. The applied social scientist cannot assume that theoretical guidance and aid will always derive from the efforts of the pure social scientist; he must be trained and prepared to make his own theoretical innovations. For unless he does so, his work may be in some ways impeded—even if it is in other ways aided—by the pure scientist, and especially by the latter's inclination to neglect the theory of social change.

One such theoretical innovation already attributable to applied behavioral scientists is the concept of "resistance to change."[8, 11] This is a concept which has derived largely from the work of the Freudians in psychology and the Marxians in sociology, both of them pre-eminently applied disciplines. Similarly, it is notable that the concept of "informal organization" emerged out of work in applied industrial sociology, where it was employed to account for resistances to industrial change.* Thus, in the Western Electric study, Roethlisberger and Dickson comment that the social function of the informal organization among the "bank wiremen" served to "protect the group from outside interference by manifesting a strong resistance to change, or threat of change. . . ."[22]

Our analysis also has implications for the pure social scientist as well. Not only does it reinforce him in his efforts to develop a theory of social change, but it also specifically indicates one further way in which this can be done. It has been suggested that applied social scientists are constrained to develop concepts useful in the analysis of social change. It follows, then, that the pure social scientist may well derive some cues for the formulation of a theory of change by keeping abreast of and by making a close analysis of developments in applied fields. For by doing so, he may

* I am, of course, aware that the concept of the "informal group" is now widely regarded as a "rediscovery" of the concept of the "primary group." This, however, overstates the continuity between the two concepts and fails to take as problematic the *differences* between the two, differences which are significant precisely in the context of an applied sociology.

identify useful conceptual innovations which have "spontaneously" emerged there. Indeed, this already seems to have been done by Parsons, who has given a central place to the concept of "resistance to change" in his pure theory of social change.[21]

## Engineering and Clinical Sociology

There is a second key assumption which seems to shape the growth of the applied social sciences. While it is never explicitly stated, it is nonetheless of considerable influence. This assumption seems to be that there is but one type of, or one model for, applied social science. In the pages that follow the suggestion will be made that there are at least two significantly different models available for applied social science, the "engineering" and the "clinical," and an attempt will be made to clarify a few of their underlying differences.

The distinction between an engineering and a clinical approach can be considered initially by inspecting a typical case, derived from my own experience, of an engineering research in the social sciences. An industrial concern contracts with a "management consulting" firm to conduct an employee attitude survey among its own employees. The stated aims of this research are to determine whether employees are satisfied with their working conditions, hours, wages, or supervisors. By and large, the consulting firm consents to do this on the terms specified by the hiring company. In the end, the consultant conveys a report to the company which indicates the percentage of employees who are satisfied with their wages, their supervision, or their chances for promotion. Not uncommonly, this report may also include some recommendations for changes in the company's labor relations policies. Usually, the company management invites the consultant to a discussion concerning the implications of these findings. Then, after a decent interval, the report may be quietly interred in that great graveyard of creativity, the filing room. Although crudely outlined, this is probably a representative history of the engineering type of applied social research. It is often with such a case in mind that people discuss the "gap between research and policy-making."

Notice that in the above example the consulting "engineer" has conceived and completed his assignment largely in terms formulated by his client. The consultant has failed to ask himself just why it was that the company management requested this survey in the first place; what kinds of problems produced a felt need for such a research among the company people; and will these problems persist even after the proposed survey is successfully completed according to management's prescriptions?

Many industrial sociologists would concur in believing that, underlying a request for an employee attitude survey, there usually exist a number of vaguely sensed tensions. For example, there has probably been some attenuation of informal communication between management and the worker. In short, the employee attitude survey may well serve as a functional equivalent for informal networks of communication which have deteriorated.

Such a survey, however, usually does little to alert the client to the existence of this underlying problem. Still less does the survey mend the ruptured informal channels, however much it supplies reliable data about employee attitudes. Indeed, the survey now makes it easier to continue operation *despite* the breakdown in informal organization. To that extent, then, the survey paradoxically preserves the very tensions which brought it into existence.

Again, an employee survey may also be used as a way of outflanking the union, by making it seem that management is better (because "scientifically") informed than the union leaders about the workers' feelings. In this case, one of the tensions promoting the research was a cleavage between management and the union. Here, once again, the tension is in no way mitigated by the use of the survey. If anything, the union feels increasingly threatened as a result of the research, and labor-management tensions are heightened rather than curtailed.

In contrast with these procedures, we may take a recent study in applied anthropology as a case which approximates, if it does not fully conform to, the clinical model. This is a project reported by Alan Holmberg which involved an Indian community in Peru, Hacienda Vicos. "When we first began to work at Vicos," writes Holmberg, "we soon discovered that one of the principal causes of in-group strife among the Indians was disagreements and fights over the ownership of cattle. . . . In view of this, it occurred to us—as it had apparently not occurred to the Indians—that one of the best ways in which to solve this problem would be to initiate a program of branding. This was suggested to the Indian leaders who heartily agreed, as did the people themselves with whom we discussed this matter in a general assembly."[10]

Branding irons were then made and offers of assistance were advanced. At first few takers were found, whereupon the matter was again discussed with the Indian leaders. Only after the wealthier leaders themselves consented to have their own cattle branded did others follow suit. Finally, through this means, community disputes concerning ownership of cattle were eliminated.

Even from this brief account certain contrasts between the clinical and engineering models are already evident. Most importantly, the "clinicians" at Hacienda Vicos did not assume, as had the "engineers" in the management consulting firm, that their clients' own formulation of their problem could be taken at face value. Instead the clinicians took their clients' complaints and self-formulations as only one among a number of "symptoms" useful in helping them to arrive at their own diagnosis of the clients' problems. In the employee attitude study, the engineers studied what they were told to; at Hacienda Vicos, the clinicians made their own independent identification of the group's problems.

## The "Value-Free" Assumption

Although this is only one difference between the engineers and clinicians, it is an extremely significant one. It is significant, above all, because it makes us re-examine one of the most cherished assumptions guiding work in the applied social sciences. This is the assumption that social science, pure or applied, cannot formulate and specify ends for its client group. Legitimated by references to the conceptions of a "value-free" social science, which were advanced by Max Weber and John Stuart Mill, many applied social scientists have claimed that all they can properly do is to study the diverse consequences of different policies, or to suggest efficient means for the realization of ends already specified by their client.[25]

The important questions concerning this assumption are pragmatic ones: To what extent does it truly describe the work of applied social scientists? To what extent does it provide clear and unambiguous directives for their actual operations? Is this assumption likely to be as congenial to engineers as to clinicians? There are many problems which the applied social scientist confronts for which this assumption, treated as a directive, provides no solutions. And there are many operations in which the applied social scientist engages which this assumption, treated as a description, does not accurately portray.

For example, in the event of employment by a client whose values differ from those of the group whom the applied scientist is asked to change, with whose values and to whose ends shall the scientist conform? If the work of industrial sociologists exhibits little uncertainty in this matter, the work of applied anthropologists employed by colonial governments evi-

*13*

dences considerable uneasiness and perplexity.[5] Furthermore, suppose the client does not know what his values are, or suppose he does not know in what priority to order his values? As sociologists very well know, this is a cultural condition which is very likely to give rise to all manner of tensions for the client. Is the applied scientist to deny assistance in these matters, to refuse to help his client formulate his values and goals, under the justification that his is a value-free Science? And if he does aid his client in specifying his ends—as evidenced for example by the work at Hacienda Vicos— then is the scientist giving more than "lip service" to the postulate that he should not specify ends for his client?

Again, what of the client who pursues values which may be somewhat incompatible—e.g., desegregation vs. political stability?[28] Should not the applied social scientist somehow indicate that the client's own values may be somewhat incompatible and that this incompatibility may be generating tensions for him? And if the applied scientist does these things, is he not then influencing the values of his client group? If the postulate of a value-free social science is not an accurate description of what applied social scientists do, and, above all, if this postulate is not translatable into clear-cut, unambiguous, operational directives, facilitating the applied scientist's solution of his professional problems, then the postulate itself—if not operationally meaningless—would seem to be in need of considerable respecification. This is not to imply that the postulate, as presently formulated, is totally useless. For the postulate of a value-free social science may be most useful as an ideological mechanism. That is, it may successfully serve the social scientist as an instrument of status defense, deflecting the suspicions of client groups who fear that the social scientist wishes to impose his own values upon them and is a silent competitor for administrative power.[13]

In any event, engineers and clinicians among applied social scientists seem to differ with respect to their interpretation of the value-free postulate. The clinician is less likely to take his client's own values as given, and he establishes a relation with the client in which they may legitimately come up for re-examination in the light of their connection with the client's problems.

There are many other respects in which clinician and engineer apparently differ and, in the remaining space, only a few of these can be examined. It will have been noted that the "clinicians" at Hacienda Vicos carefully consulted with all who would be affected by their diagnosis and proposed remedy of that community's problems. In contrast, the management "engineers" conferred with only one segment of the group, namely, the top echelon; they did not consult with the workers.

One reason for this difference is the differing anticipations which clinicians and engineers have concerning client resistance to their findings, and their differing interpretations of the sources of this resistance. The engineer fatalistically assumes that resistance to his findings is not his legitimate problem and, at worst, is due to the present deficiencies of his own research methods. He expects that inevitable improvements in research methods will sooner or later dissipate this resistance.[16] The clinician, however, assumes that findings produced by even the most perfect research technologies will continue to meet with resistance. He assumes that this resistance is his problem and that he has a responsibility for coping with it.

## Assumptions Concerning Resistance

Without doubt inadequate research impairs the relations between applied social scientists and their clients, leading to many failures in the practical use of social science. But the client's resistance to social science findings is undoubtedly motivated by many considerations. Today no one is able to weight the various factors contributing to breakdowns in the scientist-client relationship. It is well known, however, that there are important cases where this breakdown cannot be attributed to the dereliction of the researcher or to the inadequacies of his research technology. This becomes evident when a research technology is employed in two comparable settings. In one case it is given successful application, and its findings are used by the client. In another very similar setting, however, this same research method will be employed but its findings are ignored and go unused. This seems to have been the case with personnel research which was successfully conducted and fully utilized by the Army Air Force during World War II, while the Navy made very little application of the personnel research which had been conducted for it.[23]

The experience of other applied disciplines also suggests, unfortunately, that the utilization of their findings is by no means entirely dependent upon their validity. It is noteworthy that physicians have sometimes been quite successful in securing acceptance of certain of their recommendations which were far from well validated and which, in fact, they themselves later rejected. For example, American doctors persuaded many parents to feed their infants on a rigorous and regular time schedule, say once every three hours, and even succeeded in diffusing this practice to certain parts of Latin America. Yet, later, the medical profession maintained that infants should be placed on a "demand schedule" and be fed as they wished. It seems evident that, in the case of personnel research, its scientific adequacy was not sufficient to secure its equal utilization in all cases, while the inadequacy of earlier infant feeding research was not sufficient to prevent its utilization.

Pure and applied scientists alike may be relied upon to improve their research technologies and, with this, the scope and reliability of their findings. By itself, however, this will not solve the utilization problem and will not automatically guarantee that these findings are successfully put to use. Applied social science does have to contend with a kind of client resistance which has nothing to do with the deficiencies of scientific research. As suggested by the situation at Hacienda Vicos, clinicians, unlike engineers, fully anticipate and systematically prepare to cope with such client resistance.

They never suppose that client resistance is solely, or even mainly, reinforced by the researcher's ignorance or incompetence. It is clear, for example, that we do know a great deal about certain fields, for example, about criminology and penology, not to speak of ethnic discrimination and prejudice. Nonetheless, it is also painfully clear that this knowledge is grudgingly put to use, if at all. Indeed, it may well be true, as some psychiatric clinicians avow, that the *nearer* the social scientist approaches to the nerve centers of his client's problems, the more resistant the client becomes.

There are many reasons for resistance to the findings of social research, other than those residing in the defects of the research itself. One reason may be, as the Freudians and others have insisted, that the client actually derives certain satisfactions or gains from his disturbances. As a result, he is not entirely and single-mindedly ready to accept knowledge which exerts pressure to remedy these problems. Another reason may be that the research itself may serve as one or another form of defense mechanism. In brief, the client sometimes undertakes a research so that he does *not* have to solve certain problems, and so that he need *not* change. In this case, the very conduct of research provides participation in a problem-solving ceremonial. It is a ritual particularly pleasing to the consciences of men reared in a rational tradition. Moreover, it provides a publicly evident token of the client's good faith and of his sincere interest in resolving the problem. But it does not inevitably entail the client's commitment to the conclusions of the research, or to the recommendations for change which may be proposed.

Kenneth Burke, a gifted sociologist who obstinately calls himself a literary critic, has termed this pattern of resistance the "Hamletic strategy." Named after the Great Procrastinator, this pattern of resistance is one in which the very preparations for action are transmuted into devices for postponing action. Nor is this always a matter of *unconscious* resistance. As

Burke reminds us, "we may note how legislatures regularly adopt the 'Hamletic' strategy as a way to avoid embarrassing decisions. For if you would forestall a final vote on a measure, and would do so in the best 'scientific' spirit, you need but appoint a committee empowered to find more facts on the subject."[2]

In attempting to account for the resistance to social science findings and the failure to utilize them fully for practical purposes, some emphasis has recently been placed on the status of the social scientist, which is often lower than his client's. The point has been well made that "other things being equal, the amount of utilization is likely to increase with esteem for a science and its practitioners."[23] While this is undoubtedly correct, nonetheless it must be understood that the social scientist has a complex social role which involves much more than hierarchical qualities such as prestige, power, or class. This role consists of a culturally standardized complex of expectations and definitions of function, which leads the social scientist to develop his relationships with clients in specific ways. To understand properly the failure to use social science findings, it would seem useful to examine not only the social scientist's prestige but the other aspects of his role as well, his role conceptions, and the resultant patterns of interaction with his client. It may be useful, therefore, to examine some of the differences between the clinical and engineering models, in terms of the varying role definitions which they entail.

## The Engineering Model

Up to the present, the dominant role definitions of researcher and policy-maker, adopted by most sociologists, have been cast in the classic utilitarian mold. That is, the policy maker defines his difficulties as deriving from inadequate knowledge. He formally operates on the assumption that, if he only had greater knowledge, his problems would capitulate. It is with this in mind, presumably, that he calls upon the applied sociologist. The policy-maker also tends to assume that the inadequacy of his knowledge is somehow accidental or a matter of neglect. He rarely entertains the dismaying thought that his very ignorance may be functional to him.

The applied sociologist who accepts such a definition of his client's role is more likely to conform to the engineering model and to define himself, in turn, as the bearer of facts and figures. He assumes that the client really wants to solve the problems of which he complains. The engineering sociologist recognizes, of course, that he has a job of "communication" to do.

But the engineering sociologist is prone to regard this communication as well done if he reduces his report to fourteen-word sentences and mimeographs it neatly on multi-colored paper. As Wilbur Schramm puts it, "Utilization is sometimes thought of as a process of 'telling people'—writing better pamphlets, drawing better charts, making more and better teaching films, cranking up the transmitters of the mass media. This is clearly an inadequate picture."[23] Inadequate though it is, this is very much the way in which the engineers among the applied social scientists approach the problem of the utilization of social science. It is a fascinating anomaly that, while utilitarianism has been expunged from the *theories* of most sociologists, utilitarian assumptions such as those above still remain deeply embedded in their own role relations with clients. Their heads protrude into the twentieth century, but they shall remain among the half-born so long as their feet are still rooted in the nineteenth century.

The role conceptions of applied social scientists are, of course, still very much in flux and are taking new shapes as they are subjected to new client pressures and temptations. Unaware that the utilization process is, as Schramm calls it, a two-way hook-up, the engineers are particularly vulnerable to an unwitting redefinition of their roles in ways which obliterate their professional distinctiveness and identity.

Thus one finds the "policy scientists" taking over whole the military language of their clients, or would-be clients, and talking, for example, about the need for "intelligence" rather than for information or data.[14] The general tone of their writing has the atmosphere of a military staff issuing urgent directives, mobilizing resources, and preparing for battle. Their rediscovery that ours is "one world" takes on the flavor of geopolitics; their insistence upon "time factors" is devoid of the humanism of the historian and has, instead, the perspective of the tactician. Their new self-images apparently emphasize tough-mindedness, worldliness, and realism, which are well oriented to the military crisis of our time and well adapted for interaction with a military elite. It is another and more doubtful matter, however, whether these new self-images of the engineering sociologists are equally valuable for the development of an independent and self-conscious social science, pure or applied.


## The Clinical Model

A point has now been reached where some of the characteristics of the clinical model can be brought into sharper focus. There are a great variety of such characteristics which need to be clarified; here, however, the clinical model will only be considered as a social system, particularly as it is expressed in its distinctive role relations with clients.[12, 27]

From an engineering standpoint the problems as formulated by the client are usually taken at face value; the engineer tends to assume that his client is willing to reveal the problems which actually beset him. The clinical sociologist, however, makes his own independent diagnosis of the client's problems. He assumes that the problems as formulated by the client may often have a defensive significance and may obscure, rather than reveal, the client's tensions. Not only does the clinician assume that the client may have some difficulty in formulating his own problems but he assumes, further, that such an inability may in some sense be motivated, and that the client is not entirely willing to have these problems explored or remedied. The clinician, therefore, does not take his client's formulations at their face value, any more than he does comments made by an ordinary interviewee; but he does use them as points of departure in locating the client's latent problems. As Emile Durkheim (who more than any other classical sociologist used a clinical model) remarked: ". . . a sick man faultily interprets the feelings that he experiences and most often attributes them to a cause which is not the true one. But these feelings, such as they are, have their interest, and the clinician notes them with great care and takes them seriously. They are an element in the diagnosis, and an important one . . . he is not indifferent as to where they are felt, when they began."[4]

The engineer focuses largely on his relations with those from whom he secures the information necessary to fill his order. He is concerned, for example, about problems of sampling, questionnaire design, or interviewing technology largely as these affect his data collection from respondents. In contrast, the clinical sociologist takes his relationship with his *client* as seriously as he does his relations with interviewees. The clinician does not allow his relationship with his client to be governed by the all-too-common "come back and see me when you've done something" approach. He attempts to arrange his relationship with a client so as to secure the latter's consent to examine the underlying problems of his group.

The engineering sociologist expects his findings to be accepted by his client, and particularly so if they have been acquired in conformity with the best canons of scientific research. The clinical sociologist, however, expects his clients to resist his findings, perhaps because "he that increaseth knowledge increaseth sorrow." The engineering sociologist assumes that his relationship with his client is regulated by the postulate that ignorance is evil, and knowledge power, and that men unequivocally prefer enlightenment to ignorance. Writing in what may be regarded as an engineering vein, E. A. Shils comments, "Truth is always useful to those who exercise power, regardless of whether they wish to share that truth with those over whom their power is exercised. . . ."[24] This is very dubious. Men in power are not merely technicians, concerned solely about the use of effective means to their ends; they are also politicians, committed to morally tinged precepts and symbols, and striving like all other men to maintain a decent self-image.[18] Truths which are inconsistent with their own self-images are demoralizing and thus, in this very real sense, by no means "useful" to them. By assuming that his client wishes to learn the truth, the engineering sociologist has confused an ethical imperative with a description of the learning process. When the applied sociologist recognizes that he has the problem of helping his client *learn* something, and when he recognizes that learning is not accomplished by fact-finding or "communication" techniques alone, then he is on his way to becoming a clinician. Unlike the engineer, the clinician seeks to identify the specific sources of the client's resistance to his findings and he attempts to develop and learn new skills enabling him to cope with his resistance.

It needs to be underscored that these are only a few of the differences between an engineering and clinical sociology. It should also be remembered that there has been a focus on their differences, and a resultant neglect of the similarities which they both share as applied sociologies. What has been attempted were approximate models of the clinical and engineering approaches; any given piece of applied sociology may therefore possess some characteristics of both models. Furthermore, despite this writer's interest in the clinical model, it should not be supposed that he sees no value in the engineering model and no difficulties in the clinical. If the engineer lacks a sophisticated conception of the client relation and an adequate appreciation of the depth and meaning of client resistance, the clinician typically lacks a sophisticated conception of research design and technology. Moreover, one may well be concerned about the practical possibilities of securing client acceptance of the clinical model in relations with groups—as distinct from individuals—and particularly with large scale organizations. Undoubtedly there are important difficulties here, but as the work proceeding at the Tavistock Institute suggests, not insurmountable ones.

An applied sociology has much to learn from the clinical discplines. It should not be assumed, however, as is so often done these days, that the only clinical discipline which can usefully serve as a concrete model is psychoanalysis. There is much to be learned from it, particularly if it is constantly borne in mind that psychoanalysis is an applied *psychology*. As sociologists we are interested only in borrowing elements which are properly applicable to the analysis of *groups,* or for the development of change-inducing relations with them.

Physical medicine itself, or bacteriology, to name only two other clinical disciplines, may be just as valuable as psychoanalysis for the development of a clinical sociology. What we happen to know best is not necessarily what we can best use. Nor should it be supposed that a clinical sociology is characterized primarily by the use of one or another therapeutic device, such as "consultative" or "nondirective" methods. Such devices are probably better suited to a clinical than an engineering sociology. The clinicians' basic commitment, however, is not to a particular therapeutic technique, but, rather, to a distinctive role definition. In short, a clinical discipline is not as such a psychological discipline, nor is it distinguished by a cultish commitment to any specific change-agent.

In fine, then, it has been proposed that applied sociology can profit by deliberately modeling itself, particularly its strategy of client relations, on the *several* clinical disciplines and by adapting them to its own needs. To do so effectively, however, it will have to examine reflectively and to codify systematically the elements of clinical activity in the variety of disciplines where they are presently employed. In this way, we may yet fashion a new branch of applied sociology, a clinical sociology, which can aid in mending the rift between the policy maker and the social scientist and in helping groups in their time of trouble.

## NOTES

1. A. R. Radcliffe-Brown, *The Nature of a Theoretical Natural Science,* Seminar at Chicago University, 1937, p. 8 of an unpublished stenographic record prepared by Sylva Beyer.

2. Kenneth Burke, *Grammar of Rhetoric,* New York: Prentice-Hall, 1952, p. 247.

3. Eliot D. Chapple, "Applied Anthropology in Industry," A. L. Kroeber *et al., Anthropology Today,* Chicago: University of Chicago Press, 1953, p. 819.

4. Translated by the author from the French of Emile Durkheim, *Le Socialism,* Paris: Librairie Felix Alcan, 1928, Ch. 1 (page reference not available at time of writing).

5. Raymond Firth, *Human Types,* London: Thomas Nelson and Sons, Ltd., 1950.

6. Darryl Forde, "Applied Anthropology in Government: British Africa," in A. L. Kroeber *et al., Anthropology Today,* Chicago: University of Chicago Press, 1953, p. 841.

7. George M. Foster, "Relationship Between Theoretical and Applied Anthropology," *Human Organization,* 11 (Fall 1952), 5–16.

8. For a recent psychoanalytic discussion of the concept of resistance, see Anna Freud, *The Ego and the Mechanisms of Defense,* New York: International Universities Press, 1946.

9. William J. Goode and Paul K. Hatt, *Methods in Social Research*, New York: McGraw-Hill Book Company, 1952, p. 30.

10. Alan R. Holmberg, "Participant Observation in the Field," unpublished dittoed paper, May 5th, 1955, p. 6. May be obtained by writing Alan R. Holmberg, Cornell University.

11. For a recent discussion of the concept of resistance by a social psychologist, see Herbert E. Krugman, "The Role of Resistance in Propaganda," *International Journal of Opinion and Attitude Research*, 1949.

12. For another perspective on the clinical model cf. Alfred McClung Lee, "The Clinical Study of Society," *American Sociological Review*, 20 (December, 1955), 648–753.

13. Cf. Alexander H. Leighton, *Human Relations in a Changing World: Observations on the Use of The Social Sciences*, New York: E. P. Dutton and Co., 1949, esp. pp. 138, 153, 176.

14. E.g., Daniel Lerner and Harold D. Lasswell, *The Policy Sciences*, Stanford: Stanford University Press, 1951, esp. Ch. 1.

15. Cf. the full discussion by Robert K. Merton, *Social Theory and Social Structure*, New York: Free Press, 1949, pp. 85–7, for the notion of "general orientations."

16. See Robert K. Merton, "The Role of Applied Social Science in the Formation of Policy," *Philosophy of Science*, 16 (1949), 161–81. There is a full discussion of the whole problem in this article, which accents factors somewhat different from those we discuss here.

17. Cf. Barrington Moore, "Sociological Theory and Contemporary Politics," *American Journal of Sociology*, 61 (September, 1955), 107–15.

18. For a generalized discussion of this problem see Wilbert E. Moore and Melvin M. Tumin, "Some Social Functions of Ignorance," *American Sociological Review*, 14. (December, 1949), 787–95.

19. Russell W. Newman, "Applied Anthropometry," in A. L. Kroeber *et al.*, *Anthropology Today*, Chicago: University of Chicago Press, 1953, p. 741.

20. Talcott Parsons, *Essays in Sociological Theory Pure and Applied*, New York: Free Press, 1949, Ch. 14.

21. Talcott Parsons, *The Social System*, New York: Free Press, 1951, esp. Ch. XI.

22. F. J. Roethlisberger and William J. Dickson, with the assistance of H. A. Wright, *Management and the Worker*, Cambridge: Harvard University Press, 1946, p. 525.

23. Wilbur Schramm, *Utilization of the Behavioral Sciences*, Report of a Planning Review for the Behavioral Sciences Division, Ford Foundation, mimeographed, Sept. 1, 1954.

24. E. A. Shils, "Social Science and Social Policy," *Philosophy of Sciences*, 16 (1949), 222–3.

25. Cf. Sol Tax, "Anthropology and Administration," *America Indigena*, 5 (1945), 21–33.

26. Herbert A. Thelen, *Dynamics of Groups at Work*, Chicago: University of Chicago Press, 1954, p. 1.

27. For another perspective on the clinical model cf. David N. Ulrich, "A Clinical Method in Applied Social Science," *Philosophy of Science*, 16 (1949), esp. 246–7.

28. Cf. Robin M. Williams, *The Reduction of Intergroup Tensions*, New York: Social Science Research Council, 1947, esp. p. 5.

# 2. Survey Research:
## A Tool for Problem Diagnosis
## and Improvement in Organizations

FRANK W. NEFF

Social scientists who use survey methods in their research on complex organizations do not think of themselves as having much in common with clinicians. Most would, in fact, react with feeling to implications of any similarities between them. They would differentiate vigorously their quantitative, statistical, content-specific approach from the qualitative, nonstatistical, more encompassing approach of the clinician.

In this chapter, I should like to suggest the value of survey research in an approach analogous to that of the clinician in the study and improvement of organizations. To clarify this point of view, I wish to discuss briefly the most salient aspects of this approach in terms of values, goals, and methods.

As researchers, our major value is the development and acquisition of knowledge. We are interested in understanding what factors are related to organizational functioning and individual member behavior. We are interested in individual and organizational variables, how they relate to one another, and how these relationships change over time. Whether the organization prospers or fails is irrelevant so long as neither development impedes the study.

However, many of us also hold growth, health, and effectiveness for the organization and its members as core values. To the extent that these values are equal in strength to the generation of knowledge, the social scientist may take on, occasionally, the behavior patterns of the clinician. When he works actively toward goals consistent with these values, he is in the province of the clinician, although he may be simultaneously working at the production of knowledge. As a fence straddler, I am, therefore, interested in the knowledge referred to above; I am also interested in the application of that knowledge in the pursuit of other values.

The goal of the researcher is information with maximum clarity, validity, and generalizability about a more or less precisely delimited aspect of reality—how things really are *in a specific content area*. He is not concerned with problems of applying that knowledge for improvement. The clinician, on the other hand, is centrally concerned with improvement. This goal encourages the clinician to collect and use *all* available data relevant to the object of study or to ways of bringing about changes that will result in better functioning.

The clinician can be distinguished from the researcher in his methods of working. He conducts his study of the object in a normal on-going situation, not in a carefully devised and controlled laboratory setting. Typically, he explores a single case at a time, in depth and breadth, rather than multiple cases in limited content scope. Usually, the object of his investigation and action is not in the state or condition desired by the people asking for his help. And, finally, he continues to work with the client over an extended period of time, using the data collected to facilitate change. Researchers do some of these, but only the clinician engages in all of them.

The title of this volume, *Applied Sociology,* reinforces the notion of going beyond the accumulation and expansion of knowledge into the use of that knowledge to solve social problems. For my purposes, applied also means experimentation with, *and study of,* ways of utilizing research and theory to bring about change. Survey research methodology has become widely known as a tool for obtaining information in a variety of areas about existing problems: the impact of Allied bombing of Germany in World War II, consumer plans for purchase of new autos, attitudes toward Russia, or the ignorance of many voters. Its value in providing data for the description of existing conditions and the diagnosis of problems is fairly well established.

The application of the knowledge gained through a survey to improve the organization is not usually well understood and is even less often attempted. One reason for this is that most social scientists assign a low value to data-utilization activities. A number of researchers in the Organizational Change Program of the Survey Research Center have found, however, that such activities can provide the student of organizations with important opportunities to learn. First, the questions, comments, and interpretations of organization members working on survey data provide many ideas about relationships that might not occur to one "back in the office." Second, the astute observer learns much about the functioning of the organization by watching its members determine actions and implement their decisions. And third, he can study the variables which affect organizational change—the factors which facilitate or hinder efficient, satisfying change.

To make more explicit the ways of using survey research as a diagnostic and improvement tool, the rest of this chapter will report on the observations and insights accumulated by members of the Survey Research Center, particularly by Floyd C. Mann. Frequent reference will be made to a recent project conducted by our staff. The object of study was a production department of an industrial firm, which included six plants and a central office. We did the study while this organization continued to function normally. We were concerned with, and obtained measures of, a broad range of variables. In addition, there was a clear expectation that the information provided by the survey would be used in attempts to improve the functioning of this organization.

As might be anticipated, it is not easy to draw a sharp line between those activities which have diagnostic value and those which effect change. This seems particularly true in research done in close cooperation with members of the organization being studied. Steps taken to obtain an accurate diagnosis often seem to facilitate improvement. When efforts are underway to improve the organization, additional or revised diagnoses are sometimes indicated. For purposes of explanation, however, we shall discuss the processes separately.

## Diagnosis

Diagnosis is used here to mean the process of examining various characteristics of an organization and its members to provide an accurate description of how things stand or are proceeding. It is conducted in the spirit of inquiry, requiring the collection of valid information, examination and evaluation of that information, and assignment of priorities to courses of action which might be taken to improve the state of the organization. A diagnosis made by any approach and in any field is conditioned by the purpose, method, and sophistication of those making it. These will be considered in turn and examples will be drawn from the study referred to earlier.

## PURPOSE

The purposes of any activity are determined in varying degree by the interests of all people participating in it. Persons holding greater power, whatever its source, usually determine more of the purposes.

In the Production Department project, most power relative to the study was possessed by the department head, Survey Research Center (SRC) personnel, plant superintendents, and central office personnel. These persons determined the central purposes. However, through exploratory interviews conducted by SRC personnel and through written suggestions, everyone in the department had some opportunity to influence the purposes. The objectives of the study were reviewed with union officials, both at the company level and within each plant.

Because of previous experience with SRC research, company personnel were interested in having a survey of the attitudes and opinions of all people in the department toward a wide variety of job-related subjects. The purpose was to measure satisfaction and to help identify problems needing solution.

Survey Research Center personnel wished to study further such organizational variables as influence and control, communication, coordination, and effectiveness. We also wished to continue investigating individual variables such as satisfaction and risk-taking propensity. We were eager to explore the impact of increasing technological obsolescence on organizations and the people in them; the present site provided such conditions. We were also interested in working with members of the organization to learn more about using the process and products of research to increase such values as effectiveness and satisfaction. In other words, we wanted to study an organization as it changes.

The differences between the purposes of members of the organization to be studied and those of social scientists as researchers require some resolution or adaptation. In this project, company personnel were sufficiently familiar with the value of the longer-range research objectives and raised few questions about the content of particular interest to SRC personnel. When this is not the case, a major barrier to obtaining an adequate diagnosis may develop in the biases and limitations introduced by inappropriate or restrictive purposes. When the objectives of one party delimit or expand the scope of the study to an extent which is objectionable to the other, a successful project is unlikely.

## METHODS

In discussing the methods used for diagnosis on this research project, it is convenient to divide them according to the phase of the over-all project in which they are utilized: initial exploration, data collection, and data reporting.

*Phase 1: Initial exploration*—We have found in our work with organizations that the data collected through survey procedures are likely to be valuable to the organization if key people in the organization are as heavily involved as the effective research procedures permit. In the present project they were brought into the diagnostic activities immediately. As has been done in many of our projects, a research committee composed of SRC and company personnel was established. This group developed a list of topics which they felt included the areas of central concern to the organization. In a lengthy series of exploratory interviews with people in all levels and job categories in the department, SRC personnel sought other areas to be considered in the diagnosis. Discussions were held with union officials at all levels.

To continue probing the nature of organizational and individual characteristics in our research projects, SRC personnel translate the ideas, suggestions, and requests of company personnel into social-psychological concepts. On the basis of current research information and theories, we determine ways in which the developing project can advance knowledge about organizational and individual behavior. We try to exploit the research potential of the study site as fully as possible for the benefit of our research interests, as well as for the long- and short-range interests of the sponsoring organization.

*Phase 2: Data collection*—With the wealth of material obtained from meetings, interviews, and observations, SRC personnel developed the questionnaires and interview schedules. Frequently, personnel from the organization are not included in this activity. However, in this project, all questions were reviewed with the department head and other members of the Research Committee. They developed a fuller appreciation of the skills necessary for questionnaire construction as the conceptual and measurement requirements of research became clear. This appreciation can be an important factor later in the diagnostic and improvement procedures, for it results in lowered resistance to the research findings. In the project being described, questions were, of course, discussed with union officials.

In this project, as is normally the case, questionnaires were administered and interviews were taken by Survey Research Center personnel.

This was done to insure skilled collection procedures and to reassure company personnel of the confidentiality of their individual responses. Both of these are vital in obtaining valid responses which will be the basic source of objective, quantitative data about the state of the human organization.

*Phase 3: Reporting the data*—Having obtained these basic data, the final phase of the diagnostic activity begins. Normally, the first information available to the organization is straight-run data that provide the percentage distribution of responses to the various questions. Diagnosis continues when these are ready. As time passes, more refined analyses are developed and are made available.

A general procedure for working with data for improvement has grown out of SRC experience with various organizations. We do not have a great deal of quantitative evidence that this method brings more change or has more impact on the organization than other conceivable approaches. We do have enough evidence to convince us that further experimentation and development of the procedure are well merited.

This procedure, which has been called "feedback," was originally developed by Floyd C. Mann. It starts with the assumption that the line organization is hierarchically structured. This structure can be thought of as a pyramid of "organizational families." Each family is composed of a supervisor and the people who report to him, starting with the president and going down through the "link-pins" (member of one family, head of the next lower) to the first line supervisor and his subordinates. The information about the study unit (company, department, etc.) goes first to the head of that unit and then to his "family." Then the "family members" take the data to the subordinate family of which they are "heads." Through a series of conferences at each level, data are presented and discussed, down through this hierarchy of "families."

It is our conviction that the diagnosis must be made by the line personnel of the organization. This does not mean, however, that the researcher is not expected to aid in the process or to provide ideas of his own. In feedback, line personnel participate actively in the discussions, determining which data will be discussed and the sequence of topics. They propose interpretations and specify problems. This involvement of the line is crucial if survey results are to be applied in an organization. Therefore, it is desirable to have the "head" of the family lead the discussion and present the material. He should help in the goal–setting, standard–creating, and decision–making which take place in the discussions. He can serve as a model for his family members when they take the data to the next level in the hierarchy. His demeanor and effectiveness greatly influence what occurs at lower levels in this part of the organization. We have learned that this process usually loses much of its effectiveness when carried out by staff personnel.

Since line leadership is so important, SRC personnel try to establish, as a regular procedure in feedback, discussions with the head of the organizational family before a meeting, his attendance at each meeting, and a "post-mortem" with him, following it. In the premeeting session, we try to help the supervisor understand the data to be presented, clarify the goals of the meeting, plan the sequence of events, and anticipate various reactions. During the meeting we are available to help with any problems about the data and to furnish other research results that might be relevant. In the "post-mortem" with the supervisor we review progress made toward the goals, the various factors affecting that process, changes in procedure that might be helpful, and data preparation needed for the next meeting.

As one might anticipate from the description above, activities in feedback may have diagnostic value one moment, improvement value the next, and then both simultaneously. Here we will try to focus on diagnosis.

In the course of these discussions, questioning and interpretation of the data can help to diagnose more precisely the specific conditions or problems which exist for the total organization, for a division, or even for one "family." What starts out as dissatisfaction with the administrative skill of supervisors may be found to be, in part, a lack of a clear delegation of authority to supervisors for a specific work procedure. Alternatively, comparison of a series of responses from supervisors and nonsupervisors may lead to the conclusion that the training of foremen ought to be examined in depth; or a general dissatisfaction with working conditions may be discussed until the oppressive heat in a control room or the difficulty and hazards of changing nearly inaccessible valves become the specific problems needing solution.

The role of the social scientist in this feedback setting is complex, particularly because changes resulting from the use of survey data have also begun in this final phase. Here I will comment only about those things he does which are relevant for diagnosis.

The typical member of a company has never had quantitative data about the state of the human organization. He is not accustomed to studying questions in this form nor to reading statistical reports of human responses. He is not trained in exploring ways in which the questions raised by responses to one item in the questionnaire can be answered in responses to other items. Sometimes he comes to the data expecting to find a completed staff project with all the information in a brief report of problems and recommendations. Therefore, members of the organization must be taught what is and what is not in the information. The social scientist must help them learn what the numbers represent, how they can be considered and compared, and what manipulations can be performed to expand or concentrate their scope—briefly, how to approach interpretation. One of the first requests from organizational members is for standards of judgment for the data from their organization. It is difficult to help them understand the variety of standards which can be used, the different implications of each, and the idea that they themselves must choose which one or ones to apply.

The social scientist recognizes that diagnosis is essentially those steps in problem-solving which culminate in the selection of one course of action. He therefore tries to assist members of the organization in that process in any way that the data, previous research, or his experience in similar settings make possible. The importance of certain supervisory activities, as demonstrated in other studies, may be mentioned to stimulate a fuller consideration of information from the survey. The puzzling apparent contradiction between responses to two questions might be highlighted to emphasize the need for discussion of these questions throughout the hierarchy of families, or for the collection of other data not initially obtained. The presentation of a series of possible interpretations of a given datum, or the suggestion of other data which might amplify the implications of that datum, may serve the cause of exploring alternative ways of defining or clarifying a problem. Too, when action suggestions are made, based on discussion of certain data, it is sometimes possible to evaluate their consequences from other data at hand.

It is also desirable for the social scientist to have some skill in problem-solving to help individuals or groups with their problem-solving practices. This is probably more needed for groups than for individuals. The readiness with which one interpretation of data is sometimes accepted suggests that more attention should be given to the problem-solving process. The willingness to conclude that so many interpretations are possible and that nothing can be done, also has this implication.

A powerful diagnostic aspect of survey research becomes available as correlational analyses proceed, *if* the company and the social scientists are able to develop acceptable measures of effectiveness in various subunits. Measures of productivity, waste, cost, absence, turnover, satisfaction, organizational strain, and the like have frequently been related to various

SRC measures of the human organization. When such correlations are available, they provide information and motivation for organizational personnel. They demonstrate which variables seem most important for organizational improvement, and thus point to practices which should be instituted or eliminated.

SOPHISTICATION

The skill and understanding which members of the organization being studied and of the Organizational Change Program bring to the diagnostic process vary from project to project. With experience and experimentation, survey methodology continues to increase in precision and power.

SRC personnel try to keep abreast of developments in sociology, anthropology, psychology, statistics, and other disciplines which provide understanding of organizational behavior. These developments (e.g., risk–taking, role ambiguity, game theory) require exploration and experimentation before they can become really useful for applied social scientists and organization members. Sometimes experimentation in a number of projects is required to obtain a high degree of confidence in measuring a social-psychological variable.

Naturally, members of the organization have limited skill in questionnaire design and construction. But their understanding of their organization in the Production Department project sharpened the final data collection instrument. Their understanding of SRC skills promoted acceptance of the inclusion of content which the members did not perceive to be of immediate and direct relevance to them. This latter condition is of great importance in the development of tools for increasingly valuable diagnostic information. Skills of company personnel become more salient as the data are examined and as problem-solving proceeds. If the diagnosis is to be adequate, they must have, or develop, the ability to read data and hypothesize about possible determining or conditioning factors. Our experience suggests that they must also learn how to have thoughtful and open discussions of the data with persons at various levels and in all kinds of work groups. We have found that when this occurs, there is greater likelihood of accurate diagnosis.

What follows is a summary of the ways in which survey research can be a tool in a clinical approach to diagnosis: (1) attention is focused on a single given organization; (2) information with as much breadth and depth as possible is collected about those aspects of the human organization which seem relevant to the researcher and to members of the organization; and (3) joint discussion of the data by organization and SRC personnel

*3 1*

leads to problem identification and clarification, to alternative action suggestions, and to selection of a given action.

## Organizational Improvement

The techniques and results of social science are usually applied in on-going organizational settings for either or both of two purposes. The most frequent, and usually determining, reason is the improvement of the organization or organizational change. (Organizational leaders are not likely to permit changes for other reasons.) The second reason, which is more important to the social scientist although it often receives less attention, is to study the application of research results to accomplish organizational change. Here we will discuss the former.

Efforts to bring about organizational improvement have been made in many different ways. Formal organizational structure, working procedures, interpersonal relations, member skills, and subunit goals are among the areas in which changes are attempted. The volume of management literature and the number of management consultants attest to the energy being invested in changing organizations. All such attempts to change are designed to take advantage of previous experience, training, and general understanding of people and organizations. Some build on the growing body of research which appears in publications devoted to management and administration. It is a rare organization, however, that builds a plan for change on the quantitative description and diagnosis about itself provided by survey methods.

In the remainder of this section of the chapter, the focus will be on the use of survey data in organizational change. Three steps or phases in this activity will be discussed; then some of the beneficial effects will be considered.

THREE PHASES IN ORGANIZATIONAL IMPROVEMENT UTILIZING SURVEY DATA

*1. Accepting the data as valid*—As in any learning situation, the core problems are usually not amenable to direct action because they are emotional in character. Initially, members of organizations are often defensive on a number of counts. They are expected to work with unfamiliar data. Outsiders have learned a great deal about their organizations (and perhaps about themselves), and they do not know whether these data have presented them in a favorable or unfavorable way. They are skeptical that outsiders can have learned much about so many aspects of their organization in such a short time. In many organizations, including the production department of our study, some members doubted that human organizations and the people working in them can be measured.

In that project, the involvement of company personnel in the research process paid large dividends in the early acceptance of the relevance of topics covered. In addition, key personnel had developed much respect for the collection procedures during discussions of questionnaire items before final construction of the questionnaire forms.

Usually a variety of events helps to reduce the doubts and skepticism. Much of the information is in accord with their own observations of key individuals and/or those of respected associates. Sometimes they can check pieces of the data against other sources previously tested. Further exploration of some responses proves the data are accurate. Equally important, the data often are not apparently damning, and much of the need for self-protection is dispelled. We also encourage the development of a non-punitive approach to data by the "family head" and other persons in the meetings.

As the discussions progress, there are fewer challenges of the data, and more attention is paid to their meaning and to the further steps to be taken. In a sense, a new picture of reality evolves and consideration of its action implications becomes the order of business.

2. *Accepting responsibility*—Not infrequently, members of an organization will believe that data reflect beliefs and attitudes accurately, but will contend that the results are misleading or do not apply to their part of the organization: too many groups are included in a given datum; the groups included are markedly different; the people asked were not well informed or were biased; the topic in question is controlled by policy made at higher levels; the demands of competition or of technology were overriding; and so on. In many cases these objections sound legitimate, and often are. As data are reported in smaller subgroups or with certain conditioning factors controlled, it becomes more and more obvious that the data are relevant to the behavior of the persons discussing them. Many times, without additional data, the discussions lead an individual to recognize that he has helped create the conditions reflected in the responses of organizational personnel.

As discussed in the description of feedback, the behavior of the heads of the organizational families in meetings is of great importance. Having them lead discussions and strive to be good "models" for their subordinates reinforces line responsibility and can help keep discussions "goal-centered." That is, line managers tend to keep the objective of organizational improvement present in data discussions. They also tend to think of themselves and their subordinates as responsible for what happens in the organization. As changes in organizational structures or processes come to be seen as desirable, these people are in a better position to bring them about than any staff group.

3. *Solving problems*—When members of the organization accept the data as valid and see themselves as responsible, they can then focus their energies on determining the implications of the data for their organization. Starting from the base of objective data, they can proceed to delineate problem areas, define and clarify more specific problems, and determine alternative approaches to their solution. Usually problems require more information before action decisions can be made, especially in discussions in families high in the hierarchy. In these cases, the solution to the immediate problem, the need for additional information, often encourages discussion of the problem at lower levels in the organization. As indicated in Phase 3 of the section on diagnosis, discussion of the problem at the lower levels in the organization may result in a redefinition of the problem. Or the conclusion may be reached that a different kind of analysis or even study is required to solve the problem. It also happens that the discussions lead directly to changes in supervisory activities or in work procedures or conditions.

Although not specifically stated above, this problem-solving occurs typically in a group setting. It has not necessarily been group problem-solving in the sense of achieving consensus or majority vote. But the better solutions, and the greater changes, have resulted in situations in which the discussion was open and vigorous; the final decisions, however, took cognizance of the ideas and feelings communicated.

Many organizations do not have this kind of meeting as part of their regular processes. Supervisors at all levels may not be skilled in leading such discussions. In the Production Department project, some supervisors and their "families" had quite open discussions of current problems in their meetings. Others had little experience of this sort. In this paper we cannot discuss fully the skills necessary for line personnel to conduct meetings for optimal value from survey data. Members of the Organizational Change Program are cognizant of the importance of both the "work" and the "emotional" aspects of groups attempting to solve problems. To the extent that we perceive individuals and groups able to attend to the way they work, we draw attention to both the cognitive and the emotional requirements of effective group problem-solving. One of the benefits which can accrue to the organization is the increased ability of supervisors to lead productive, satisfying discussions with their subordinates.

# Survey Research: A Tool for Problem Diagnosis

The skills required of the social scientist in this part of the project are many. He must be sensitive to the situation of the members of the organization so that he can anticipate and react constructively to their behavior. Since they are sometimes threatened, as discussed above, it is normal that they occasionally reject him and/or are hostile. Ability to work effectively in such circumstances greatly enhances the likelihood that the data will be accepted and used—and that, as a researcher, he will be able to continue to study that organization.

When one considers the proliferation of meetings and planning and reviewing activities which are required as the data move down the hierarchy, it is clear that a single social scientist cannot handle the load. The problem is ameliorated somewhat by the voluntary nature of our relationship to this activity—line members do not have to involve us. Therefore, the help requested is seldom the maximum potential. But to provide as much help as possible and to train for future needs of the organization, we believe it is desirable to locate and/or train staff members of the organization to perform many of the functions involved.

To summarize what occurs in the phases of feedback for organizational improvement, data collected in the survey are reported back to the organization in a series of meetings organized by "families." As diminishing resistance to the data is accompanied by increasing acceptance of its validity, and as personal responsibility grows, attention is centered on the present situation of the organization, possible sources of present difficulty, and directions for improvement. Alternative actions can be considered, and decisions can be made about steps which will move the organization toward a more valued state. As these developments proceed, they are paralleled by the growing skills of members in interpreting data and in seeking solutions which consider individual as well as organizational needs.

## EFFECTS OF FEEDBACK

Discussions generated around survey data often raise problems for the "family head." He must consider whether his own approach to problems or his way of working with others is most effective in achieving his, his people's, and the organization's goals. It is the premeeting sessions and the post-mortems which are often most valuable in helping line members examine the effectiveness of their own performance. In these sessions, considerable learning occurs about relations between one's own behavior and measures of organizational conditions. The change in individuals which leads to change in the organization often takes place in this setting.

The simple fact of having meetings to discuss the data results in an increase in communications in many organizations. Since the content of these discussions is the organization itself, conditions often not reviewed for some time come to the center of attention, and ideas and opinions are exchanged. The chain of meetings down and up the organizational hierarchy stimulates the flow of information and feeling which provides the basis for change decisions. In the more successful projects, communication within groups and between groups moves to new areas and to new levels. There is an increase in the openness of interaction among members, and this promotes more adequate solutions to problems.

This increase in the amount, scope, and depth of communication brings about greater clarity for individual members in such things as group and individual goals, authority, work, and role structures, and production procedures and systems. It fosters a broader sharing of mutual expectations among role incumbents. This improves the individual's ability to predict what others will do and what is expected of him, thus enabling him to behave more appropriately. Also, knowing how others perceive a variety of conditions within the organization helps the individual determine which actions are more likely to be effective; it helps groups, as well as individuals, plan procedures and/or programs likely to be successful.

As in other kinds of important change, there are modifications in the importance of certain values or a shift in the values held. Supervisors come to feel that concern for the nonjob problems of their subordinates *is* important. Involving members of affected groups in planning for the introduction of new equipment or methods *can* be of great value.

Building on the new knowledge from the survey and from the discussions, company personnel set new goals, devise new systems, modify existing policies, change role relations, etc. In one company, some supervisors decided to learn considerably more about each of their subordinates, at the rate of one per week. In a hospital, a series of meetings between the nursing department and various other groups was established and made a routine procedure for exploring mutual problems and planning experimentation with new ways of coordinating. Although the effects described are not exhaustive, they do reflect some of the kinds of changes which occur in organizations using feedback for organizational improvement.

## *Toward the Development of a New Role for Social Scientists*

The practical, philosophical argument continues in social science between those who contend that the scientist must approach his object of study with no values, save objectivity and certainty, and those who maintain that social scientists must make their results useful in the cause of other values, such as growth and satisfaction. Among academic social scientists, the latter are clearly in the minority. A foreign visitor to SRC recently noted that in his country academic researchers were supposed to take their data back to their offices and ponder it there, unsullied by further contact with people at the research site. The image thus drawn is not inappropriate to conditions in some parts of the United States. Researchers who do just that often provide penetrating insights and comprehensive formulations. The problem remains of getting those insights and formulations into the mushrooming body of knowledge and skill that decision makers need.

The process of survey research and reporting, as described above, is one approach to the problem. The social scientist engaging in it is working in several relatively well differentiated fields. He is more likely to be successful if he has knowledge and skill in each. A good base in the methods of social research, especially survey research, is important. He needs to have as much understanding of organizations and how they work as the field offers. Knowledge of learning research and theory and some background in the dynamics of problem-solving groups are also invaluable. Understanding of personality and individual behavior are useful—especially if the social scientist has developed sensitivity to the reactions and progress of organizational personnel. All these enable him to perform more competently. Moreover, this competence accredits him in the eyes of the organizational members.

As has been observed earlier, the social scientist taking this kind of clinical approach must think it desirable. He wants to help members of the sponsoring or host organization use the information and develop new skills. He wants others as well as himself to use the methods of the scientist in the solution of immediate and mundane problems. Simultaneously, he seeks to achieve the broader social research goal of knowledge. He strives to make the research venture cooperative because this promotes a situation in which data are more likely to be used by the organization. Also, it stimulates training of organizational personnel and provides information and insights not normally attainable otherwise.

In addition, he must be able to accept—if not embrace—the "in betweenness" or marginality of his role. Members of the organization view him as an outsider, sometimes as an egghead from an ivory tower. He is seen by some of the people in his own organization as working in inconsequential areas, as being unscientific, occasionally incompetent, and beyond the pale of "respectability." He does not have a clear and accepted role in either group. Moreover, during the period of working with organizational members, his role shifts, for it depends on the demands of the situation and the changing skills of those members.

Throughout most of this chapter, I have focused on the value of the researcher's skills and products in solving problems of that important social invention, organizations. I should like to close by noting again the circularity of benefits. The social scientist who works with an organization in feedback has the unusual opportunity to study management efforts to bring about change. From further observation and contact with members he can formulate new hypotheses, test his own data-leads on those members for confirmation or refutation, and develop more systematic conceptualizations to explain seeming peculiarities in the information obtained through straight survey techniques. He is also likely to have cultivated a relationship which permits subsequent research. In fact—and this has happened at SRC—an organization can become a real laboratory in which research on organizational variables can be pursued for a considerable period of time and from various approaches. The potential is great that such situations can promote our understanding of the functioning and changing of organizations.

## NOTES

Mann, F. C., "Changing Superior-Subordinate Relations," *Journal of Social Issues*, 7:3, (1951), 56–63.

Mann, F. C., *Human Relations Training Through a Company-wide Study*. Ann Arbor, Mich.: Institute for Social Research, dittoed, 1954.

Mann, F. C., "Studying and Creating Change: A Means to Understanding Social Organizations." In C. M. Arensberg *et al*, (Eds.), *Research in Industrial Human Relations: A Critical Appraisal*, New York: Harper Bros., 1957.

Mann, F. C., & Baumgartel, H., *The Survey Feedback Experiment: An Evaluation of a Program for the Utilization of Survey Findings*, Ann Arbor: Institute for Social Research, dittoed, 1954.

Mann, F. C., & Likert, R., "The Need for Research on the Communication of Research Results, *Human Organization*, 2:4 (1952), 15–19.

# .3.   The Impact of Organization

# and Research Value Structures

# on Researcher Behavior

DELBERT C. MILLER

THERE HAS BEEN A WIDE GAP BETWEEN THE SOCIAL research methods discussed in textbooks and their social application to laboratory and field research. The informal sociology of research methods is slowly being written as researchers are increasingly describing their own social experiences in conducting research. These unwritten materials were commonly defined as extraneous to research reporting; often they were viewed as unique to a given research project because of idiosyncracies of research team members or client personnel.

It took almost ten years for anyone to put the label, "the Hawthorne effect," upon the influences resulting from the presence of researchers or observers in the midst of a social experiment. This signified a belated recognition that the patterned behavior of research subjects could be altered markedly and that controlled experiments might easily (perhaps inevitably) be contaminated by researcher or client behavior. There is no more dramatic instance of this fact than Robert K. Bain's study in the XYZ Laundry Plant.[1]

As a graduate student, Bain planned a sociometric inventory of the interpersonal choices among the workers as part of a larger study. He set out seven steps to guide his behavior after gaining permission from the superintendent. He had firmly decided to play a neutral role, as he thought a good scientist should. After a satisfactory entry in which he was treated with cooperative and friendly acceptance, he began to complete the initial parts of his study. He spent considerable time with the records in the front office and consulted frequently with the superintendent and plant manager. A month went by and workers were beginning to wonder what he was doing. In retrospect, Bain reports that one of his biggest mistakes was assuming that the workers knew what "research for a Master's thesis" meant. Their failure to understand this led to the suspicion that he was a management stooge or spy and not the independent, unbiased university researcher he claimed to be. Unaware of this, the sociometric inventory was made ready. The original plan was to present each worker with a list of all others in the plant of the same race and ask him or her to indicate for each name whether he or she liked, disliked, or felt indifferent toward the person in question, and to rank the "likes" and "dislikes" in order. Bain reports:

This procedure was first tried with members of one work group with poor results. Cooperation was difficult to obtain, and many respondents merely said that they liked everyone on the list. I was forced, therefore, to change the method somewhat and ask each worker, instead, merely to choose from the list the ten persons he or she liked best. I further thought that if I could interview the workers in the privacy of their homes I could secure better cooperation. Therefore, I went to the members of other work groups, requesting permission to interview them at home for the purpose of securing information of a more confidential nature than I had previously gathered. I did not tell them just what this information was, because at the time it seemed that to do so would defeat the very purpose of home interviewing—which was to be able carefully to explain just what information I wanted and why. This was the most stupid mistake that I made during the entire research, and it should not require a social scientist to predict what happened. Here I was, being so mysterious concerning some information that I wanted, and here were the workers wondering what it was all about.[2]

Two days later the rumor started that "Mr. Bain is going to try to find out who likes and dislikes each other here." The rumor was literally true but the interpretation was potentially damaging. However, Bain was able to nullify these hazards by explaining frankly why he wanted the information, and for a while all was well. Home interviewing was abandoned and the workers were interviewed in the plant. Then came the sternest challenge. About halfway through the study, plant officials began to lay off workers here and there because business had slackened. At the time, Bain was engaged in the final phase of his study. With stopwatch and a battery of hand counters he was timing the interactions of a sample of workers. Hostility and suspicion on the part of certain workers became open and obvious. The researcher himself became emotionally upset "to have persons who had apparently formerly liked and trusted me exhibit rather suddenly suspicious and hostile behavior."[3] Bain decided not to try to explain but to carry on as usual and act as if he were not guilty. Although a few remained suspicious, the situation improved enough for the research to be completed.

This incident illustrates the theme of this paper, which is an inquiry into the interaction and possible conflict between the value structure of the research workers and that of the officials and members of the organization in which research is proceeding. Research behavior is often profoundly influenced, as Bain's research experiences indicate. To paraphrase Robert Merton, it follows that planned research activity produces, to a substantial extent, unwilled, largely indirect, and often unanticipated consequences. To foresee and prevent such consequences is made possible by accumulated, transmitted researcher experience. Clinical psychologists have long been aware of their influence in their relationship with a client, no matter how objective their professional behavior might be. Freud's description of patient "transference" is a powerful observation. Argyris' statement that he was asked as a researcher to report a worker's grievance to his boss indicates how a similar phenomenon may occur in field research. The systematic compilation of the researcher's social experiences has been pushed forward by the recent publication, *Human Organization Research,* edited by Richard N. Adams and Jack J. Preiss.[4] Chris Argyris has recently discussed at length the researcher's role in his *Understanding Organizational Behavior.*[5] William F. Whyte has described the pitfalls in the application of research findings to organization.[6] These books will challenge others to report similar experiences, and perhaps all researchers will soon make this data an integral part of their research papers. It should be a requirement for graduate theses.

In this paper I have been challenged to look at four of my own research experiences. I have tried to describe the relationship of my own research oriented values to those of the members of the organization I was researching. I have focused largely on the points of conflict. My purpose is to show the accommodations as well as the conflicts which influence researcher behavior.

## The Navy Yard Fiasco

A most devastating impact of researcher and organizational values occurred when two of my graduate students undertook a study of civilian morale and absenteeism in a United States Navy Yard in the late nineteen forties. The study was planned with the direct cooperation of the Civilian Personnel Officer. A questionnaire was drawn up and plans were made to distribute it in each of the departments. It was to be filled out in the employee's off-duty time and to be returned to a box in the department near the Master's desk. The Masters are civil service employees with tenure, who have responsibilities similar to a general foreman. As the faculty thesis sponsor of the graduate students I objected to this plan of administration because I felt that the questionnaire should be filled out on company time and under supervision to insure both objectivity and a guaranteed return. I also wanted to prevent the contamination that would result from discussions among workers, or by workers with family and community members. Finally I capitulated, for the Admiral refused to assemble the men on company time, and all the thesis-planning effort of the two graduate students was threatened with failure. It was agreed that the Admiral and the Masters would explain the purpose of the questionnaire as an inquiry into employee attitudes. Both the Yard newspaper and the public address system would be used. Then some 16,000 questionnaires would be distributed by the Masters as each shift left the Navy Yard on an announced day. Workers would be instructed to return them the next day to a box near their work stations.

If this distribution plan was fraught with dangers, it was a less threatening situation than the one which exploded after the following decision. To plan a study which might advance research knowledge, we decided we must be able to utilize the personnel records available for each employee. With such records we could, for example, explore the absence histories of each man and could relate them to work groups. We asked ourselves how an anonymous questionnaire could be related to this personal history data. Obviously, this would be impossible, and some method of questionnaire identification was explored. I suggested placing on each questionnaire an identification number in invisible ink. This questionnaire would be placed in an envelope with the name of the worker on it and distributed to him. When he destroyed the envelope it would appear that the questionnaire was anonymous. I feel a flush of shame now, but I convinced myself that this act of deceit was justified in the interest of science. After all, our motives were honorable. We had a firm commitment with the Admiral that all questionnaires would go to the University and that no individual or group identity would ever be revealed to the management of the Yard. This explanation of individual and group protection was to be put in a letter attached to each questionnaire. Guarantee of anonymity, I argued, justified the invisible ink number which was so vital to research. With it, the research promised to provide a definitive test of a basic sociological hypothesis; without it, the research promised to be little more than a conventional survey.

The Personnel Director flatly refused to go along with this scheme. He had many objections. He asked how we would explain how a number appeared on the questionnaire if a questionnaire were accidently left on a steam radiator or other hot surface. He refused to take the responsibility. Instead he proposed placing a black-inked number on the back of the last page. "Why," he said, "the men are used to numbers on everything in the Yard. They won't think anything about it." I had doubts and I searched the literature for some other way. The two graduate students wanted to go on with the research. Reluctantly, I agreed when I could offer no alternative.

The Admiral approved all plans but reported that the Masters were antagonistic. They regarded the survey as a threat to their authority and their practices. The Admiral said he was prepared to overrule them. This was done and the survey distributed. Within ten minutes an urgent request was made for a visitation of the Masters to the Admiral. It was charged that the number found on the back of the questionnaire made it possible to identify the man responding and that the promised anonymity was fictitious. The Admiral was forced to agree and the Masters passed the word to dump the questionnaire. Sixteen thousand questionnaires had already been distributed and for weeks these could be found flying in the wind about the community. The Admiral called in the research group and the Personnel Director. He explained that he had no choice but to make the decision he had made. I took the full blame to shield the Personnel Director from any injury to his career.

Like Bain, I find it easy to define the mistakes in retrospect. The researcher must refuse when expediency is proposed to justify the negation of sound canons of research method. I should have rejected the distribution plan. I should never have promised an anonymity that was fictitious no matter how honorable the research motives. I should have redesigned the research so that group data could be gathered. This could have been done by departments if we had been willing to forego individual records. Research-oriented values trapped me into concessions, first to expediency, and then to slavish devotion to high basic research aspirations. When the damage was done, it was total. How do you assemble 16,000 persons who are spurred to suspicion by their supervisors and explain to them the logic of the ink number? My answer was to let the project die and to take my

*43*

lesson in experience. In this paper I am communicating it so that others may profit by it. In addition, this incident should highlight the interaction between research and organizational value structures.

## Air Force Triumph

In 1951, I was named principal investigator under a research contract made between the United States Air Force and the University of Washington. Its purpose was to explore human relations problems of Air Force personnel manning isolated Air Defense radar stations, "with reference to job requirements, morale factors, and leadership under stressful noncombat conditions and to develop methods for improving effectiveness."[7]

A research team was assembled and initial plans were made for a problem survey of one division. One of the first questions we asked was "What role should we play?" It was suggested by the Air Force personnel that we should be placed in a United States Air Force uniform with a temporary assignment and a noncommissioned rank. It was felt that we could get closer to the men by living in the airmen's dormitory and could learn about the human relations problems by participating in the daily life of the men. Members of the research team objected. What would happen to our research if the men discovered that we were research professors of sociology from a well-known university? From my experience in the Navy Yard, I had learned a lesson about deceit and so declared my determination to be only what I was. The research team concurred and we made our first entry by convincing the Air Force Commander that we could do our research successfully only if we were known as university research sociologists, independent of the Air Force. We further told each assembled site group that all facts and opinions given to us would be held in confidence, and that no individual person nor any air site would be identified in reports or talks with Air Force officials.

This promise was not easy to keep. The Air Force Division Commander welcomed our first briefing session with him. We showed him the problems we had identified and explained their frequency as reported for markedly isolated, relatively isolated, and nonisolated sites. Actual names of the sites were not shown. The Commander expressed his interest and satisfaction and then asked, "What do you think of my site commander at Able Air Defense Command?" I said, "General, I can tell you what qualities of leadership we have found associated with the best and the poorest leaders in markedly isolated, relatively isolated, or nonisolated sites, but I cannot make an evaluation of a specific man. I cannot do this because we must have an absolutely neutral position in order to assemble freely given opinions from your personnel. If any word or rumor of a personal feedback reached a site, the success of our work would be threatened."

I found I had to make this speech twice again in the next few months to the General. After that, the rules were established and accepted.

This preliminary conflict of values was succeeded by an internal unrest among members of the research team and the practical demands of the Air Force. The members of the research team looked upon their research experience as an exciting opportunity to advance sociological research and their own professional careers. This meant they sought to secure material for publication in scientific journals. Surveys of practical problems and manuals describing proposed leadership practices do not win publication in the "status" journals. They are not apt to win anything but the gratitude of some agent in the military establishment and a mimeo distribution to busy and harassed Air Force commanders. Yet the demands for more practical manuals mounted. Finding a balance between basic and practical research was a continuing problem because scholarly values were in opposition to the Air Force's demands for immediately useful tools.

These value conflicts were heightened by an increasing application of classification, ranging from restricted to secret, as each document was examined by a classification inspector. As the Korean War deepened, restrictions were tightened. There were unannounced inspections of our university quarters to see that we were following security regulations for classified data. These regulations were especially onerous because they were unanticipated. When the contract was signed it was for an unclassified project. Later morale matters became subject to security classifications.

One happy interaction between the researcher and the client organization was reported to our home division in the national study on the status of morale, efficiency, and leadership. It revealed that the division in which we were based, and in which we worked most intensively, demonstrated the highest morale and efficiency. This division was led by an outstanding man who had hand-picked his site commanders, and there were good esprit and efficiency. We had worked intimately in this division, living in the sites for months on end, and everyone knew we were feeding problem information back to the Division Commander under the guarantees of individual and site anonymity. The Commander would come to the sites and talk to the men about the problems. He would explain, make changes, and promise future improvements. The site commanders began to follow the same pattern. In all of these relationships between researchers, commanders, and airmen, a new morale program was emerging beside the morale study. This was the Hawthorne effect compounded. Our final research results showed the home division in a very favorable light, not only because it was well led, but also because it had fallen heir to a morale program as an unanticipated consequence of research study. The Commander was delighted with the showing his division had made and congratulated us warmly for our excellent research efforts.

## Cross-Cultural Community Research Problems

The researcher who goes to another country must take into consideration national values. These will intrude in the most unexpected ways and will startle the researcher and threaten his project. In 1954, I began research in an English city of 500,000 population. My research project called for a comparative investigation of the community power structure of this city with an American city of similar size and economy. I had completed much of the research on the American city and was to investigate similarities and differences with the English city.[8]

At the university in the English city I was given my first advice on the differences in the cultural values of social research. I was told that questionnaires were not acceptable and would not be answered. I never put this dictum to the test. Instead, I sought background material on community leaders in the newspaper morgue. Even here, cultural values plagued me. I found that the most important leaders eschewed publicity and that only certain lesser figures were given many press notices. In fact, the editor of the paper, a fairly important figure, used his power so effectively that there was only one small notice about him in his own paper in a 20-year period. It told of his attendance at his daughter's wedding!

As I prepared for my interviews with leading community leaders, I was warned about British reticence. I was told to send a letter on official university stationery stating my purpose, position, and title, being sure to sign Ph. D. after my name. I was to learn the high importance of this advice during my interviewing. The interviews were granted and I was warmly received. But, from the first I encountered opposition to a simple request for educational background. I learned later that this was a most obvious label for the status position of the respondent in British society and that he was reacting to an invasion of his privacy. If he were ashamed of his educational background he reacted negatively; if he were proud of it, it was brash to have it so revealed. I was taught slowly but surely that the British believe one should wait for men to take your measure and that no one but a boor would "sell himself." My techniques for extracting information could never ignore this basic value. The British penchant for understatement is both a personal and public value and no researcher must underestimate this.

I learned that reticence can express itself in many ways. It shows in the careful appraisal of the researcher. It is exhibited in a desire to maintain privacy of person. For my interviews I developed a standard interview schedule. I placed a copy in the hands of my respondents and asked them to check those community leaders they knew and worked with, and to list those they considered most influential. From the beginning, I noticed a curious resistance to make the marks I requested. I was beginning to despair of securing a complete interview when one of my respondents handed the schedule back to me and said, "You tick it off and I'll give you the answers." This was the key to the success of my subsequent interviewing. If I avoided educational background and "ticked" off the answers myself, the interview was as complete as I desired. Ability to recognize cross-cultural values is a sociological necessity, for research feasibility is a function of these values.

Recent experiences in Latin America have taught me that respect for and participation in certain social rituals may make the difference in whether the research may be successfully achieved. The reception and farewell ceremonies are especially important in the research relationship.

## Consulting in a Labor–Management Conflict

In 1957, I was engaged as a consultant to an industrial relations director of a large flour-milling company to help solve a pressing labor–management problem. An established bargaining system was disrupted when differences arose between the American Federation of Labor Council and Local No. 68 of the plant mill workers. Since then, a feud had been going on between them and getting ever more bitter. The precipitating factors were these; Local 68 had withdrawn from the A.F.L. Council and was asking the company to bargain independently with it; the A.F.L. Council refused to recognize this right of secession and demanded that Local 68 return immediately so that a new labor contract might be negotiated; the Council had notified the company that it must bargain with the Council in negotiating for a new contract for Local 68.

The General Plant Manager told the Industrial Relations Director to get a contract signed. His words were, "Tell 68 they are going back into the A.F.L. Council. We are going to sign a contract with the Council and 68 can take it or lump it. We must act this week." The Industrial Relations Director had said, "You'll have a strike on your hands!" It was then that the Consultant was asked, "What should the company do?"

Up to this point the Consultant had secured the patterned bargaining relationship of the parties and had a factual picture of the factors precipitating the problem. He took the view that an understanding of the interlocking character of the labor–management social system was of critical importance since a resolution of the problem might result in replacing traditional bargaining with an alternate social system.

The Consultant report, with a full analysis of this problem, has been published.[9] The purpose of this paper is to show how the Consultant, Industrial Relations Manager, and General Plant Manager played their roles in the resolution of the problem. The Consultant, working with the Industrial Relations Director, analyzed each action pattern for possible repercussions upon the values of each participant, pattern of control, and social costs incurred. Part of the Appraisal Sheet for the reconstruction of the established bargaining pattern is presented below.


## APPRAISAL WORK SHEET

*Alternate Action Patterns*

1. *Reconstruct Established Bargaining Pattern.* Company will refuse to bargain outside the Trade Association and insist that Local 68 go back into the AFL Council.

   A. Values of each participant

   Local 68 is humiliated by being forced to return to the Council. Company is satisfied to establish tried and successful area of bargaining; fear of competitive disadvantage in future strikes is dispelled and the power of Local 3 is diminished. Association is satisfied to maintain area bargaining.

   B. Pattern of Control

   Require Local 68 to return to Council by NLRB decision. Company will work with Council and Association to get Local 68 to go back to Council. Association puts pressure on Council to achieve reestablishment of traditional pattern.

   C. Social Costs

   Local plant relations which have been very good may be seriously weakened as Local 68 is coerced to return to the Council. A strike may result.

Two other alternate action patterns were similarly analyzed and carefully weighted.

At the termination of consultation, the Industrial Relations Director reached a preliminary recommendation. The Consultant made no recommendations because he took the view that a responsible official could do this best within the context of the situation. He knew that the Industrial Relations Director would have to persuade the General Plant Manager on the wisdom of any course of action. It was the Industrial Relations Director who feared that Local 68 could not be forced back into the A.F.L. Council, and that if attempted, would bring a strike action.

The Industrial Relations Director reported his recommendations to the General Manager. The manager maintained that everything must be done to restore the traditional bargaining pattern and get Local 68 back into the Council. Strategy was carefully discussed, and the two managers agreed to put the *pressure on the A.F.L. Council rather than on Local 68*. The General Manager called the International Vice-President of the A.F.L., located in a regional city center, and told him that the local Council would have to "come off its high horse and get 68 back into the Council" or the A.F.L. was going to lose one of its strongest unions. The International Vice-President made a hurried trip to the big city. The Vice-President convinced the A.F.L. Council leaders that they must effect a reconciliation. The Vice-President and the A.F.L. Council President were quietly admitted by management upon the company grounds, and for some days they browsed about talking with Local 68 leaders and members. Finally, Local 68 voted to stay in—the Council had "eaten crow," and members of Local 68 were satisfied. (Local 68 leaders said, "the big boys admitted their mistakes and practically got down on their knees and asked us to come back.")

A contract was later negotiated with high satisfaction to all parties. The result was a re-establishment of the traditional pattern.

The role relationships emerge in this case as the significant indicators of the different value orientations. The Industrial Relations Director can be seen as a buffer and a mediator between the union leaders and the General Manager. He is the person who must relate what Roethlisberger calls the "logic of worker sentiments" with the "logic of managerial cost and efficiency." This was especially borne out when the parity agreement was drawn between Company X and Local 3 of the ILWU (Local 3 was an organization of warehouse workers in the mill). Health and welfare provisions had been included for the first time in a contract with Local 68. The General Manager tried to cut down these provisions in the bargaining with Local 3 members (and, perhaps, respecting their aggressive leaders), insisted upon a parity package for Local 3 and convinced the General Manager of its importance.

The General Manager, in his dealings with the International Vice-President of the Union, provides practical knowledge for expediting action. His more immediate responsibility for economic results may have prompted him to pursue his goal of restoring the established bargaining pattern. Bringing the International Vice-President into the situation was the catalyst which restored the equilibrium.

The Consultant may be seen as a man with special ability in defining the alternate actions and their possible repercussions, and, perhaps, in giving the Industrial Relations Director more influence to resist direct coercion of the local union. If true, the social diagnosis proved useful because a wrong decision could easily have caused a large loss to the company and the workers. In addition, labor relations may have been worsened for an indefinite period.

## Conclusion

These four examples of research and consulting experience illustrate the convergence of organization and research value structures on the researcher. In each case, researcher behavior is challenged or reinforced by the value structures which impinge upon him. The traditional advice to the researcher is to establish himself in a "neutral," "pure," and "detached" role. Argyris claims that if a researcher does this, both he and "his subjects" may feel alienated by his "objective" techniques. He believes that the researcher may miss the complexity of the organizational behavior he is studying unless he can observe the subjects when they are acting naturally as "whole" human beings. He advises the researcher to become as fully aware as possible of his subjectivity, and to "measure" its impact upon the situation he is studying.[10] He points out that the subject's "set" toward the researcher influences the data he will provide and that the researcher's needs influence the research relationships he desires to create. All of us in the Air Site research understood this from the first days when airmen would greet us with the salutation, "Hello, Doc. When are you going to put us on your couch and find out about our morale?" Each sociological researcher felt he must destroy this image and build a more realistic one. He realized, as Argyris points out, that it was important for him to feel free to express himself as fully as possible so that, by his behavior, he could communicate to the subject the feeling that he, too (the subject), might find it helpful to express himself unambiguously.[11]

Researcher behavior is a product of organizational and research values. As far as possible, the researcher role should be foreseen so that it can become an important part of the research design. Since, to a large extent, much of planned research activity produces unwilled, largely indirect, and often unanticipated consequences, the researcher must be ever sensitive and vigilant. He must be able to improvise and compromise between the two value worlds in which he seeks to live and work.

## NOTES

1. Robert K. Bain, "The Researcher's Role: A Case Study," *Human Organization*, 9 (1950), pp. 23-8.

2. Robert K. Bain in R. N. Adams and J. J. Preiss, eds., *Human Organization Research*, Homewood, Illinois: The Dorsey Press, 1960, pp. 147-8.

3. *Ibid.*, p. 149.

4. *Op. cit.*

5. Chris Argyris, *Understanding Organizational Behavior*, Homewood, Illinois: The Dorsey Press, 1960, pp. 33-7.

6. William F. Whyte, *Man and Organization*, Homewood, Illinois: Richard D. Irwin, Inc., pp. 71-103.

7. Selected publications include the following: F. James Davis, "Conceptions of Official Leader Roles in the Air Force," *Social Forces*, 32:3 (March, 1954), 253-258; F. J. Davis and Robert Hagedorn, "Testing the Reliability of Systematic Field Observations," *American Sociological Review*, 19:3 (June, 1954), 345-8; E. Gross, "Some Functional Consequences of Primary Controls in Formal Work Organizations," *American Sociological Review*, 18:1 (August, 1953), 361-71; E. Gross, "Primary Functions of the Small Group," *American Journal of Sociology*, 60:1 (July, 1954), 23-9; Glenn C. McCann, *Morale and Human Relations Problems in AC and W Sites*, Air Force Personnel and Training Research Center Technical Memorandum CRL-TM-56-5, April, 1956; C. D. McGlamery, "Developing an Index of Work Group Communications," *Research Studies, State College of Washington*, 21 (1953), 225-30; N. Z. Medalia, "Unit Size and Leadership Perceptions," *Sociometry*, 17:1 (February, 1954), 64-7; N. Z. Medalia, "Authoritarianism, Leader Acceptance, and Group Cohesion," *Journal of Abnormal and Social Psychology*, 51:2 (September, 1955), 207-13; Nahum Z. Medalia and Delbert C. Miller, "Human Relations Leadership and the Association of Morale and the Effectiveness of Work Groups," *Social Forces*, 33 (May, 1955), 348-352; Delbert C. Miller and N. Z. Medalia, "Efficiency, Leadership, and Morale in Small Military Organizations," *The Sociological Review*, 3:1 (July, 1955), 93-107; D. C. Miller, "The Shaping of Research Design in Large Scale Group Research," *Social Forces*, 33 (May, 1955), 383-90; Edward Gross and D. C. Miller, "The Impact of Isolation on Worker, Adjustment in Military Installations of the United States and Japan," *Estudios de Sociologia*, 1:1 (Fall, 1961), 70-86; Nahum Z. Medalia, Glen C. McCann, and Delbert C. Miller, "Morale and Human Relations Leadership as Factors in Organizational Effectiveness," *Studies in Organizational Effectiveness*, Raymond V. Bowers (ed.), Washington,

# Delbert C. Miller

D.C.: United States Air Force Office of Scientific Research, 1962, pp. 85–114.

8. Major publications include Delbert C. Miller, "Industry and Community Power Structure: A Comparative Study of an American and an English City," *American Sociological Review*, 23 (February, 1958), 9–15 and Delbert C. Miller, "Decision Making Cliques in Community Power Structures," *American Journal of Sociology*, 64 (November, 1958), 299–310.

9. Delbert C. Miller, "The Application of Social System Analysis to a Labor-Management Conflict: A Consultant's Case Study," *Conflict Resolution*, 3 (June, 1959), 146–52.

10. Chris Argyris, *Understanding Organizational Behavior*, Homewood, Illinois: Dorsey Press, 1960, p. 33. Cf. Elliot Jaques, *The Changing Culture of a Factory*, New York; Dryden Press, 1952.

11. Argyris, *op. cit.*, p. 34.

# Part II

# PRACTITIONERS

# AND CLIENTS

# 4.  Experiences with the Criminal Community[1]

## LEWIS YABLONSKY

IN RESEARCH AND PRACTICE WITH THE "CRIMINAL community," problems arise which rarely confront the social scientist working in other categories of human behavior. The first section of this paper will discuss several of the traditional issues which have affected the interaction between the social science practitioner and the client in the criminological area. The latter part of the paper will deal with a new social construct known as Synanon, which provides some different insights into these issues.

### Traditional Issues

#### THE DUAL ROLE: RESEARCH AND PRACTICE

The social scientist working in the criminal community has the dual role of practitioner-researcher. Although the primary focus of the social scientist may be research, the criminal client often perceives in the process some implication for "help." He may even experience some useful personal insight. The social scientist is generally aware of this impact and its effect on the nature of his interaction with the criminal client.

The practitioner whose role is "treatment-oriented" (e.g., group psychotherapist, prison administrator, parole or probation officer), may—often inadvertently—systematize his observations and findings on a continuum from highly structured to unstructured research analysis. He may develop a specific research project as a subsidiary to his treatment approach (e.g., evaluation study) ; or at a less structured level, record observations which later enter into theoretical considerations. This duality of function tends to affect the nature of all interactions and impacts the social scientist has with the criminal community.

In a therapeutic–focused setting, the collection of "research data" leading to vital theoretical considerations has many precedents. The work of such pioneers of treatment as Aichorn, Moreno, and Shaw has stimulated research useful to the development of criminological theory. Recent sociologist–directed group therapy has also demonstrated its value in this area. Group therapy with offenders does not necessarily produce cogent research data, but often in an unanticipated way, it suggests worthwhile clues for further investigation.

### LEGAL IMPACTS

By definition, the "criminal community" consists of individuals involved with legal issues. They are either about to be adjudicated, are already convicted, or are in fear of criminal status.[2] The social scientist often has great difficulty convincing his client that information obtained from him (either for research or therapeutic goals) will not have punitive consequences. It is difficult to assure him that his "freedom," his parole, or his probation status will not be affected by his interaction with the social scientist.

The status of the practitioner is also often confused by the offender community because of the legal issue. In my work with gangs in New York I found that some gang boys who met with me almost daily—some over several years—never fully believed that I was not "really a cop." Many prisoners in group therapy settings were also convinced that I was seeking "inside information" for the court and parole board. It was not always easy to assess the effect of their suspicions on their "group therapy" responses.

Another issue, the legal responsibility of the practitioner to report known criminal acts, remains a complex problem. Can the client be completely open and responsive to someone who is obligated as a citizen to report information about illegal behavior to the authorities? What does a street gang worker do legally when he learns that *his* assigned gang plans to commit a robbery or a homicide? The policy in our New York gang project was to make it clear to our clients that we worked in close cooperation with the police. When we "informed" we could not be accused of "letting the gang boy down." (Because of our police policy, boys would often leak information to us so they would have a good reason for not "turning on" a gang war.) [3]

Another difficult factor of legal impact on the practitioner–prison community relationship is the element of "legally enforced" cooperation. As a subject in the research or treatment program, the parolee or the prisoner may "cooperate" with strong negative feelings. He is uneasy about the invisible threat of the practitioner's control over his freedom,[4] his legal status, or, if behind walls, his privileges. Although seldom discussed, the implied threat of reprisal is bound to affect the interactions between the social scientist and his often involuntary client.

## STATUS DIFFERENTIALS

Although all social scientists are confronted with special status problems related to their client's position and their own within the social system, the "criminal community" presents some particular difficulties. With the rare exception of the "white collar" criminal, the general criminal (research) population comes from a lower-class background. This fact, combined with the special characteristics of criminal subcultures (e.g., drug addicts, gang members, "crime syndicates," professional thieves, etc.) interferes with communication. Such factors as language meanings, criminal motivational systems, levels of aspiration, and subculture norms tend to differ from those in the inclusive social system. The social scientist entering the criminal community must be aware of these factors and of their effect on interaction.

## THE LOCATION OF INTERACTION WITH THE CRIMINAL COMMUNITY

There are different sets of problems operating in the criminal community inside of and outside of custodial walls. Inside, the emotional tone of the environment, the depressed position of the offender, the inmate norms (formal and informal), all tend to affect the nature of the interaction and produce extraneous elements for research or treatment. (One argument is that custody produces a set of personal problems for the offender which, in an ideal institution, are "treated" when he is in custody. When released from this "ideal situation" he reverts to the set of personal problems he had before he was placed in custody.)

In the "outside–the–walls" criminal community, the social scientist may be placed "off-balance." Certain "dives" and "hangouts" which are the natural habitat of many offenders are off-limits for the "square" social scientist who obviously does not belong.

The problems and advantages of studying criminals "in the open" are cogently described by Sutherland and Cressey:

Another method of studying crime is by association with criminals "in the open." It is asserted by those who have had intimate contacts with criminals "in the open" that criminals are not "natural" in police stations, courts, and prisons and, that they must be studied in their everyday life outside of institutions if they are to be understood. By this is meant that the investigator must associate with them as one of them, seeing their lives and conditions as the criminals themselves see them. In this way, he can make observations on attitudes, traits, and processes which can hardly be made in any other way. Also, his observations are of unapprehended criminals, not the criminals selected by the processes of arrest and imprisonment.

There is no doubt of the desirability of securing information in this way, but it is clearly limited by considerations of practicability. Few individuals could acquire the technique to pass as criminals; it would be necessary to engage in crime with the others if they retained a position once secured. One individual could not build upon the work of another to a very great extent, for precise, controlled, techniques of observation could scarcely be employed. It would be extremely difficult to secure information regarding the origin of most of the attitudes of the criminals, for few of them would permit interrogations regarding the processes by which they became criminals. Nevertheless the more information we can secure in this way, the less likely we are to be led astray by the other methods.[5]

(Some of the problems indicated by Sutherland and Cressey are not pertinent now since the development of Synanon.)

In addition to the issues described by Sutherland and Cressey, other conflicting alternatives and differential conditions exist which complicate one's work with the criminal in the "open community." For example, in my research with violent gang members, there was often a real dilemma about specific interviewing location. On the street corner the gang boy is generally a "wise-guy" showing off for his "buddies." In the researcher's office, particularly when alone, he is apt to be uncomfortable, suspicious, and "careful." The research location thus poses different sets of factors which have impact on the interaction and tend to produce different kinds of data.

In interaction with the gang, its momentary size, its role composition, and its current emotional state greatly affect the interview response. There are other issues, such as whether or not the group at hand is comprised of fellow gang members, their relative status and power in the gang, the imminence of a gang war, or whether they are on their own "turf" (territory). All of these factors may affect the interaction pattern and responses.

# Experiences with the Criminal Community

Research or practice within custodial walls poses additional problems. The practitioner must understand both the formal and informal social structure of the "prison community." Thomas Osborne was a pioneer in this field. He entered the prison community in 1913 to study and experience the nature of incarceration. This initiated a flow of social investigation into prisons that has produced perhaps the most significant findings of criminology.[6] Since that original effort, the participant-observation of Hans Reimer, Norman Hayner, Ellis Ash, Richard Korn, and a recent collection of research essays edited by Donald Cressey have established a body of basic knowledge about prison social structure vital to the strategy of any social scientist entering the "prison community."[7] The nature of inmate leadership, institution norms, "prisonization," inmate discipline patterns are all significant factors which are bound to affect the impacts and interaction patterns of the social scientist and his client "inside the walls."

The social scientist dealing with clients other than the criminal does not usually have serious problems about "location." He meets his client in a standard office or other conventional place. In addition, he is confronted with a somewhat different set of problems than that posed by the gang boy "on the corner," the criminal in the "prison community," or, in the extreme case, a drug addict in his "pad."

## Synanon: A New Frontier for Criminological Research

A new setting for criminological research called Synanon has emerged. In this section I will discuss some new, albeit raw, insights I have developed after two years of research and work in this unique setting for criminal rehabilitation. My recent Synanon experience modified many of my earlier perceptions about "traditional" social scientist–client interaction.

Briefly, Synanon is an anti–criminal society inhabited and managed by ex–addicts and criminals. The organization, founded and developed by a layman, Charles E. Dederich, has been successful with almost 400 criminal-addicts, most with long criminal and addiction backgrounds.[8] The organization is currently operated in four localities: Santa Monica, California; San Diego, California; Westport, Connecticut; and Reno, Nevada, with a fifth Synanon House scheduled for San Francisco.[9]

The "open" nature of the organization, the candor of the people who reside there, and the development of their ability to conceptualize their criminal and addictive experiences provide a new frontier for criminological research. At Synanon, the social science researcher has fewer problems.

# Lewis Yablonsky

Since Synanon is free from governmental control, it provides a research person with the largest collection of ex-criminals and addicts available in one place anywhere in the open community. Moreover, the philosophy of "truth seeking" engendered at Synanon, in a unique form of group therapy, opens new avenues for understanding criminal behavior. The Synanon member is encouraged to discuss his past and present behavior with his associates and these interactions are open to social science investigation. The procedure is considered to be part of the Synanon "therapeutic process": *Important to his self-understanding is a close understanding of the Synanon social system and its treatment process.*

An illustration of the Synanon member's learned ability to "conceptualize" about his location in the Synanon social system is revealed by Zev, a former addict, currently clean (i.e., "off drugs") at Synanon for over two years. Zev is an unusual Synanon member because of his college background. However, the following example of an articulate description of some of his Synanon experiences (after being there 13 months) has been duplicated by less–educated Synanon members.

### ZEV "GROWS UP" IN SYNANON: A CASE IN POINT

The processes, characteristics and phases of "growing up" in the Synanon social system are here described by Zev Putterman, in a lecture to my graduate U.C.L.A. social work seminar. (The talk by Zev was tape recorded.) Zev was asked to contrast his past role as a "patient" in other treatment settings with his role in Synanon.

Zev was 34 when he arrived at Synanon. In addition to his roles of addict and patient, he had completed his college education and achieved some success as a theatrical producer and director. Zev's ability and unique background as a teacher, student, producer-director, drug addict, and patient are revealed in his description of his "encounter with Synanon." His articulate statement documents some of the phases of "growing up" in Synanon.

*Zev's story*—"I will try to give you the benefit of my contact with various institutional approaches to my disorder, which has been labelled by psychoanalysts as constitutional psychopath, complicated by drug addiction. I guess in your frame of reference, sociopath would be more applicable. At any rate, this diagnosis was made 14 years ago, by Dr. Abram Kardiner, a pretty reputable Freudian psychiatrist, after eight months with the man.

Over a period of 13 years, I wound in and out of private, public, State, County, and Federal institutions for drug addicts; also private hospitals for people with the whole spectrum of emotional and psychological disorders. What I think is relevant to examine here today, in the light of my experience, is what happened to me in the 13 months that I've been at Synanon that has made it possible for me not to behave as I did previously.

There is no evidence, as yet, as to whether I have been changed on a deep and meaningful level; but there is plenty of face evidence that my behavior has manifested a change which is so drastic from what it was 13 months ago that, to me, and people who knew me before coming to Synanon, it's almost unbelievable.

What I wanted to point out to you, in brief, is that what happened at Synanon did not happen at the Menninger Clinic in Topeka; the Institute of Living in Hartford; three times at Lexington, Kentucky; New York's Metropolitan Hospital; Manhattan General; the Holbrook Sanitorium; or the Westport Sanitorium. . . .

When you think of an addiction history of 14 years, people have the image of 14 years of constant drug use. The thing that makes a person a drug addict, to me, is the equation that he learns after his first detoxification. A drug addict becomes a drug addict, not when he just becomes addicted to drugs; but when he learns this equation. They kick their habit physiologically; they have decided consciously to change their behavior; they are going to manipulate themselves in every way that they know in order not to repeat what they've been doing; and BINGO, they repeat exactly those processes which got them to the point that they didn't want to get to. This, to me, is when a drug addict becomes a drug addict. The drug addict, to me, is the person who has taken his first cure, and then gone back to dope. *The institution he goes to is part of his addiction process* [emphasis added].

Now, let's discuss institutional settings and their differences. I think the very first difference between Synanon and other set-ups is that the addict on the outside has heard something about this thing called SYNANON. He knows it has something to do with drug addicts, and that there are no psychiatrists there. He hears that they're all drug addicts and that they're not using drugs. If they are a group of drug addicts, they're using drugs, and if they are not using drugs, of course, they're *not* the kind of drug addict that *I* am. Because if they were the kind of drug addict that I am, why they would be using drugs. So this is the first impact that Synanon has. In other words, you're convinced that this sounds very nice; but it's not true.

Certain circumstances force people to come to Synanon. The AA (Alcoholics Anonymous) always uses the phrase "You reach your own bottom." So, let's assume that I had reached a "bottom"; and I had tried everything else in the western world—I think just about everything else; you know, chemical cures, as well, which I didn't bother to mention.

Anyway, I came to Synanon. At first—something very strange happened to me. I came into this place early in the morning. I had just gotten off the plane; I'd flown 3,000 miles. The usual reception at a place where a person has volunteered for a cure, is "Welcome aboard!" This was not the case. I was told to sit down and shut up, in just about those words; you know, literally, "Sit down; shut up."

I figured I was talking to a disturbed person who didn't understand who he was talking to. In the first moment of contact, instead of being told "Welcome aboard" you're told to shut up and sit down. Whereupon, being loaded on a variety of opiates, I explained that I had just arrived in California; that I flew in from New York; and that I had talked to a Board Member; whereupon the magic words, "shut up and sit down" were readministered. I began to realize that reason has nothing to do with the behavior of these people; these are not reasonable people, obviously; because I was being perfectly reasonable. So I shut up and sat down, because I had no alternative. If I'd had an alternative, I would have said I'll come back another time. But I was 3,000 miles away from my connection. I didn't have that resource.

I sat down for a number of hours, and then I was called by some people into a room. Oh, first of all, my luggage was taken away from me. And one of my pieces of luggage contained a variety of drugs, nonnarcotic in nature, that were prescribed for me by my psychiatrist. When I left New York, I said "I'll be gone for six months," and he wrote five prescriptions for six months worth of five different kinds of medication . . . you know, to ease withdrawal . . . nonnarcotic: psychic energizers, tranquillizers, sleeping medication—a whole satchel full of it.

In the intake interview—I've been subjected to many intake interviews, by social workers, psychiatrists, psychologists and charge nurses, you know. And I was usually asked a variety of questions, and I had my pat answers. You know, am I white or black—I'm white. In this instance I wasn't asked anything. They didn't even want to know my name. I mean literally, they did not say to me, "Who are you?" They proceeded to tell me who I was. Their only contact with me had been a phone call from Westport, which lasted maybe a minute, and then my contact with the guy at the desk, who didn't listen to what I was saying. So they were telling me who I was.

They told me things like, I would never make it, I was a mama's boy,

# Experiences with the Criminal Community

I was spoiled, I was a compulsive talker, I was unable to learn anything, I was probably incurable; that if I didn't shut up they would throw me out; that they were not interested in learning anything from me because I had nothing to teach them—which of course, to me, was absolutely absurd—because, you know, I had come there to enlighten the West Coast. This is a shocking experience. I'm making it humorous, but it shook me up; it shook me down to my feet.

After being screamed at by Reid Kimball, who has tapped his sources of rage better than anyone I've ever met, and being thoroughly humiliated by six dope fiends staring at me, he would use devices like this: He said, "There's an accumulative 37 years of sobriety in this room, and 82 years of dope addiction in this room; so therefore your 14 years of addiction and 3 seconds of sobriety doesn't count." Now, that was reasonable to me. So you see, I was being hit on a reasonable and a nonreasonable level, as I saw at the time.

So, they were talking about me as if I wasn't there. After this thing happened, you know, "Let's take him downstairs, let's do this to him. . . ." I wasn't being consulted, and the first thing I thought, when I heard about Synanon was there won't be any "we" and "they" alienations, because these are folks like me, and they know how sick I am.

I was then taken outside by a man by the name of James Middleton, a gargantuan character that I would never have an opportunity to communicate with—even shooting dope. It would just be a matter of conning him, or him hitting me over the head. And he proceeded to take my little satchel with medicine in it. You know, to me he looked like Ally Oop . . . and he took this satchel of medicine and led me downstairs to the basement, which was pretty grim, and looked like the 23rd Precinct in New York. He took the satchel and opened the bottles, and proceeded to pour them into the toilet. I said, "Now, wait; you see, you don't understand—my psychiatrist gave me these—you don't understand: these are nonaddicting drugs—none of these drugs are addicting drugs, and they're legitimate. See, my name is on them." And while I'm saying this, he is like grunting and pouring my medicine out.

This is another important aspect of Synanon as different from another institution. The first thing I picked up in this indoctrination, being a manipulative type of guy, was this; when people didn't want me, or didn't seem to want me, I, of course, wanted them. The appeal to me was somewhat like a fraternity appeal on a college: the fraternity which is most difficult to get into is naturally the most desirable.

Well, what had been communicated to me immediately by "sit down and shut up," you know, as if I were rushing the house, was that this club is rather exclusive and they're not particularly impressed with me; so naturally they must be pretty good; because my self-esteem was pretty shitty—although it didn't look that way.

Then, my personal property (and I think a person's property represents to them who they are) you know, your resumes, and for people in my business your 8 x 10 glossies and your theatre programs—you know, this is who you are—plus a few pieces of clothing and an electric shaver—things you picked up that are pawnable. These things were taken away from me brusquely. And I was given "schmatas" is the only word I can think of . . . I was given unseemly clothing.

There was nothing institutional about the clothing. There was a plaid shirt which didn't fit. And I was very specific in asking for cotton, because my skin gets sensitive during withdrawal. I was given a wool plaid shirt, because I asked for cotton; and a pair of khaki pants that didn't fit, and rubber go-aheads, or flip-flops, or suicide–scuffs, which were very uncomfortable. And then I was taken upstairs.

There I was. My luggage was gone, my resumes, my identity, my drugs . . . my pride. I also got a haircut; just because I protested too much. I had my hair cut off rather short, and by a guy who didn't particularly care for the cosmetic value of a haircut. I didn't need a haircut. The day before I had been to Vincent of the Plaza and had a haircut.

I went up into the living room, and was introduced to a few people. I recognized a couple. I recognized a couple as drug addicts. Like, I saw scar tissue on their arms. I saw that they were—like maybe they really were drug addicts.

Kicking my habit at Synanon had a big effect on me. It was a process which, again, was very different from the institutions. The institutions I had been to all had detoxification procedures of one kind or another. Every detoxification procedure that I've ever been involved in, although they may be medically necessary for people with a heart condition, or people who are over 93, really were *not* necessary, I discovered at Synanon. In all of the settings I had been in, the bit was to exaggerate your symptoms so that you can get medication. Because if you get medication, you feel better. Which is very simple: If you get medication you feel better; if you don't, you feel badly. I don't think there is anything pathological in this kind of behavior. So the thing to do, of course, is to get medication.

Well, at Synanon, of course, I was told, with the flushing down the drain of the medications I had brought that I was not getting any medication. And I said, you know, "I'm going to get quite sick—I'm not feeling very good." "You will not get any medication."

I said, "You don't understand. You see, I'm going to be *really sick*. You see, I'm from New York, and they've got *good* dope in New York; and I'm strung out, and I'm going to really get sick."

They again repeated, "You will not get medication. If you want medication, you can *leave* and get medication. But here, you won't get medication."

This immediately stopped a whole process which would have gone on for two or three weeks if medication were given. This is another important thing: I had my biggest manipulative device taken away from me because there was nothing to manipulate for, except maybe a glass of water. That's about it. You know, and how much of a con game would I have to run down to get a glass of water.

Then Candy Latson (at that time a coordinator at Synanon) started his therapy. The second day I was there I started to get sick. The drugs held me for, oh 24 or 30 hours. He came up to me and said, "Little brother"—he referred to me as "Little brother" which offended me to the quick. "When are you going to get sick?" I WAS sick, and he KNEW I was sick. So he comes over and he says, "Little brother, when are you going to get sick?" Now this is significant. Do you know what this did to me? I wouldn't give him the satisfaction of knowing that I was sick. Because his attitude was ridiculous, as far as I was concerned. So I said, "Oh, I'm all right."

Now what he had done by this simple, little, intuitive thing, "When are you going to get sick?" is he let me know that he knew that I knew that he knew. He immediately stopped the possibility of—you know, he didn't give me sympathy; he didn't give me any kind of "understanding"— and yet, he gave me understanding on a very deep level. Like it became a challenge to me to see how *un*sick I could be in withdrawal during the next four or five days. And I noticed another thing: There would be some people in the house who would come over, and kind of be concerned about me. I'd get a back rub; if I wasn't vomiting, I'd get a milk shake . . . and sometimes I would drink the milk shake so that I could vomit, and show them how sick I was. There were still these things that were going on that weren't getting me anywhere. This is very important in understanding why Synanon seems to work.

And then Candy did something to me that was very important: they made me think they had a secret. They made me think that they knew something that I didn't know. I snapped to this: that it was quite true.

65

They *did* know something I didn't know—as they *still* know many things I don't know. It wasn't just a mystique. They really had information I didn't have. And they weren't willing to share it with me, particularly; which, you know, got my nose open. I became quite curious about what *is* it? Candy would drop a concept on me—you know, an incompleted statement, like a Zen cat and run off in the other direction. He would say something like, "Just stay." You know, like a Zen master will clap me on the head, and I'll have *enlightenment*.

Well, this is what was going on during the period of detoxification, Synanon-style, which is a cold-turkey withdrawal; because, it's bad and it's wretched; *but* it's not all that wretched, and not that bad. And no one is terribly impressed with it—no one is very impressed with it. You're hit with ridicule; you're hit with shots like Candy used to do every morning. Every morning he would come over, and say "Hey, little brother, when're you going to get sick?" With a little grin, you know. And I wouldn't cop to being sick. I just wouldn't.

Now, what happened when I wouldn't cop to being sick, was that I wasn't as sick as I usually had been. In other words, my nonpurposive symptoms went right along; but my purposive symptoms were destroyed by the Synanon context . . . the purposive symptoms being the symptoms that a person unconsciously manifests in order to get dope, approval, sympathy, understanding—a fix. But, you know, the other things: the nausea, the diarrhea, that goes on for the best part of this thing continued.

I was up off the couch in four days. Now, I had been kicking habits; I was a specialist in observing myself kicking habits. You know, reading Cocteau, as another frame of reference in kicking habits—how he kicked his habit; and all of my evidence crumbled. You see, all of my evidence was destroyed by the experience that I was sleeping by the seventh day—I hadn't slept without medication, in or out of a place, in seven years. I had not been able to sleep. I was sleeping within seven days.

On the fifth day I was rewarded for kicking my habit by receiving a mop! I thought the least I deserved—you know the *least* I deserved was a week at a country club—you know the *least*—for what I'd been subjected to. Instead, I was rewarded not at all. Because there really was not any reason for a reward. I heard things like, "Not shooting dope is not worthy of a reward. . . ." "People don't shoot dope! Therefore, *not* shooting dope doesn't earn any reward." It's like saying, "Congratulations for not beating your wife," or "Thank you for not murdering my sister." You know, one doesn't do this, so naturally you're not going to get a big hand.

# Experiences with the Criminal Community

No one at Synanon is going to applaud you because you're not shooting dope and because you're mopping the floors. Somebody's got to mop the floors; and you're constantly told you don't know how to do anything else. You begin to think maybe they're right; because at this point you're pretty broken, psychically and physically, so you find yourself mopping a floor.

And then, the other magic thing begins to go to work: this thing about the secret. I think this is what motivates you to mop the floor *well*. You begin to see that if you mop the floor well, you won't feel as guilty as if you mop the floor badly.

In most institutional settings, and in most psychoanalytical, or socially oriented, or tradition-directed treatment centers for dope fiends, your guilt is usually ameliorated: You're a sick fellow; you can't help yourself; you have an acting out disorder; together we'll work this thing out, re-socialize you, and everything will be "crazy." So, of course, what people like myself do, is, they take all this ammunition, they fuel themselves with the fact that they're an acting out disorder. What can they do? They have all the data, so they go and act out.

You see, in Synanon, they lay guilt upon guilt upon guilt. In other words, every time the energy flags a little bit—like mopping the floor, the corners aren't done. Instead of being told, well, you know, he's still sick; he hasn't really kicked yet; he's new and he hasn't done much floor—mopping in his time, you are made to feel that *that* dirty corner represents a dirty corner in your psyche; your gut. You think that you really are ridiculously bad at mopping floors, and you get guilty, you see, and your guilt is fueled.

Now, whenever you are in an institutional setting, your guilt is explained away—it's lightened. The burden of guilt is lightened. In Synanon, whenever things begin to get buoyant, and you permit your insanity to return as self-compensation for your low self-esteem you're told you're *not* unique in nature, and get smashed on the head with a velvet mallet. It doesn't crush the tissue, but you feel the impact of it, which is an important thing.

Now, by this state in Synanon, you are beginning to learn something. You are beginning to find out that everybody there from the members of the Board of Directors, down to yourself—has had a history akin to your own. Somewhat akin. In other words, most of them came in and they kicked their habits. Most of them came in and anticipated something completely else. You know, *no* drug addict anticipates being humiliated because he has decided to kick a habit. He does not conceive of this. I conceived maybe that because these are other drug addicts, maybe they'll be

6 7

kind of tough. But I did not expect to be laughed at for doing the right thing, like kicking a habit.

Now, much of what I'm saying is exaggerated because I'm that type of person. There are people who come to Synanon *without* the resumes and the 8 x 10 glossies, who are not smashed quite as hard as I was. They came in with a bird cage on one foot, a boxing glove on the other, and, like, they're in bad shape. You can see that they don't have any of the totems of success, or any illusions; so there's no reason for them to be ridiculed the way I was ridiculed. But they still will not be able to get rewarded for bad behavior.

For instance: I think this is significant in looking at the total Synanon picture. A friend of mine arrived from New York about three months after I got here. My friend, Herb, was addicted to barbiturates, as well as heroin. And he got pretty damn sick, and began to act pretty crazy. This is interesting. Reid Kimball, who is one of the directors, came down and told Herb that if he acts like a nut, we'll have to throw him out, because we can't handle nuts. In other words, Herb, you'll have to go to Camarillo, or some place where they handle crazy people. We don't handle crazy people; *so you're not allowed to be crazy here.* Now, I've been in three hospitals with Herb, and I know how crazy he is. Now, literally, this happened to work. *Don't Be a Nut!* And you know, he wasn't. He just couldn't act crazy if he wanted to stay at Synanon and he didn't!

Herb was a pretty sick guy, physically. But he was able to curb his emotional symptoms, because of the Synanon approach to him. Candy could obviously not go over to Herb and say things like, "When are you going to get sick, little brother?" But, you know, he also didn't go over to him and say things like, "Aw, poor boobie-baby-boy," so that Herb would act crazy to get some more "poor boobie-baby-boy" which is symptom reinforcement. Instead, he got what he could get. There were three or four other guys over there who had themselves convulsed when they came in, who said, "Well, man, you go into one of these wing-dings every 8 or 10 hours; and, you know, we're all here, and you'll be cool, and don't worry, and stay away from the furniture you won't fall off."

And this is another significant thing in terms of an institution and in terms of understanding the Synanon thing. Well, about this time—about three to four weeks after my arrival—I began to notice that the place was full of me. The place was full of me. In other words, in every other institution I had ever been at, I had had a very schizie feeling. There were the doctors, and I was kind of like them because I was kind of like them, because by some fluke, they became doctors, and I was a dope fiend. And I'd look at them, you know, and I felt like I kind of had a foot in their camp. And then I was with the dope fiends and there, you know, I'm a dope fiend . . . And there was kind of this "we-them" thing, and I kind of felt that I was straddling them both. But I really knew that my soul was with the dope fiends, because the doctors did not know where it was at— they really didn't!

At Synanon, in contrast, I saw a million manifestations of *me*—in everyone—even in the guy I called Alley Oop, Jimmy Middleton, who's extremely different. Candy's different. He's colored. Yet Candy can spot things in me so quickly, that are exactly me. He knows when I'm gaining; he knows when I'm conning; when I'm lying to myself. I can't do this when he's around because he sees himself in me too.

The contract that had been set up all my life: the "we-they"; my father and me; my psychiatrist and me; the warden and me; the teacher and me; you know—this contract was smashed at Synanon. I became aware that the place was run by 100 Zevs—different aspects of me. Different aspects of me were all there. So, when I hated somebody's behavior, I hated me; when I approved of somebody's behavior, I approved of me. My sense of alienation with the "we-they" equation—the hip and the square; the culture and the subculture; the in-group and the out-group; the Jews and the gentiles; the white and the black—all of the "we-they" equations that we had learned—primarily for me they had been a square— they had been destroyed. It was just destroyed by the reality—it wasn't conceptual—there it was.

I began to see that, if I mopped a corner right, first of all I wouldn't be so guilty—even if nobody saw the corner. You see, I felt funny. And secondly, I didn't have to be afraid of being busted by people like me if I did the corner right. And thirdly, I'd probably be able to stop mopping soon. I wouldn't have to mop for the rest of my life. Because, it seems eternal, absolutely eternal. You know, they'll tell you you'll be mopping for "X" period of time; but let me tell you: you're mopping for three months, brother and it seems like a *long* period of time. A long time. Since then I have moved up into other more important jobs in Synanon.

I begin to see what Lew (Yablonsky) articulates as "social mobility" at Synanon. We don't have a caste system. We have a kind of a class system, based on clean seniority, productivity, "mental health," talent, etc. I've just begun to climb this status ladder and I'm beginning to understand now that I'm hooked into the organization and want to move up—the side effect may be getting well and growing up from being a baby to my 34 chronological years of age."

# Lewis Yablonsky

Zev is an unusual client, and this in part accounts for his articulate assessment; however, there are other ingredients emanating from Synanon which have produced his conceptual ability. One of these is the Synanon emphasis on the client's self-appraisal, and his understanding of Synanon. (For example, it is mandatory that each read my *Federal Probation* article on Synanon.) Another is that I, as a social scientist, can relate to him in a way that could not possibly occur in any other institutional setting. Perhaps, most important, Chuck Dederich has encouraged and facilitated an ethos of "truth-seeking" that pervades the organization.

### THE "HIP" SOCIOLOGIST: A CASE STUDY

The sociologists of the early "Chicago School" developed the groundwork for much of our current theory about social problems.[10] Since their stimulating *empirical* work, most of the theorists have been of the "long-distance" variety—so removed from the "people" they describe that the validity of their work is questionable.

As a counterbalance to this ivory-tower, "let's all quote each other," type of sociological analysis, many sociologists (myself included) have moved into the center of our "research fields."

Close-up "applied sociology" is as fraught with problems as ivory-tower sterility. To illustrate this I will here report on my Synanon experience.

### THE PROBLEM OF OVERINVOLVEMENT

In my pre–Synanon research, working with violent gang youths, prisoners, and drug addicts both in lock-ups and in the open community, I had always felt that the best way to (in social work jargon) "establish rapport" with my clients, was to talk their language.

My own "hipsterism" in this regard, when I first arrived at Synanon, clarified a "professional disease" which later became known there as the "Yablonsky-effect." I began to do this in my early Synanon research days. In particular I began to "hang-out" with two residents, Frankie Lago and Jimmy Middleton. (Both had been "boss" drug addict-criminals with about twenty years of combined prison time behind them before "cleaning-up" at Synanon.) We were "buddies" and in fact the association (in addition to being personally gratifying) produced for me some important knowledge about Synanon, crime, and drug addiction.

After about six months in my association with Synanon, in the so-called "big-shot synanons" (intensive group therapy sessions which included the Synanon Executives) I was severely criticized by Chuck Dederich for my "appalling, atrocious behavior." It was pointed out to me *very forcefully* by Chuck and other Synanon executives (all ex-addicts themselves) that my "buddy approach" with the "patients" was reinforcing their symptoms. Chuck and the others gave me a vicious "haircut" (a verbal dressing-down) and it hurt. But I began to see something. True, I was gathering useful information about Synanon from Frank and Jim, but my emphasis on their "gory" criminal background was in some measure approving and reinforcing this component of their personalities; the dimension of their personality that Synanon was trying to change.

I was asked, or told in a synanon, "Why don't you talk to them sometimes about sociology or academia or world politics?" "Why not indeed," I began to think.

This personal (and somewhat painful) experience caused me to review the general professional attitude toward criminological research and treatment. In fact, it now seems to me that many professionals may do much harm with their research. Many criminologists have an intense (and perhaps vicarious) personal interest in the criminal exploits of their subjects. Many are intrigued *voyeurs* of the criminal world.

In the drug addiction field, my cursory review of current professional conferences and papers reveals a tremendous preoccupation with the symptom—the patterns of destructive drug use, how they evolve and the hallucinatory effects of the drugs. In comparison, fewer publications are concerned with the causes and treatment of the problem. My professional self-assessment in this area continues, but I am more sensitive and more aware of the pronouncements of my colleagues on drug use.

Among professionals there is almost admiration for the "cute, interesting, exciting world of crime and addiction." In my past work I found this to be true among professional "gang workers" in New York City. They would almost brag about "their tough gangs." In response to a question I asked about his gangs' criminal-addict patterns, one of these workers replied, "Oh man, this is a real down [sharp] group of kitties. *We* have all kinds of weapons and they'll use them at a moment's notice." Then, laughingly, he commented in response to a question on drug use: "Oh yeah, all the kids fool with some drugs—not much *H*,—but you know, smoking pot and pills. The other day they wanted me to get high with them. Naturally I wouldn't—but I think I lost status because I acted square!"[11]

### FUTURE PROBLEMS

Based on my own work with gangs and more recently with ex-criminal-addicts in Synanon, I am convinced of the "research profits" which accrue to the field of sociology from the work of applied sociologists who dare to enter the "criminal world" intensely. Yet this more daring "sociological role" must be acted out with caution and restraint. Ned Polsky, writing in Howard Becker's *Outsiders*, tends to suggest that we go all the way. He states:

> If one is effectively to study law-breaking deviants as they engage in their deviance in its natural setting, i.e., outside the jail, he must make the moral decision that in some ways he will break the law himself. He need not be a "participant observer" and commit the deviant acts under study, yet he has to witness such acts or be taken into confidence about them *and* not blow the whistle. That is, the investigator has to decide that when necessary he will "obstruct justice" or be an "accessory" before or after the fact, in the full legal sense of those terms. He will not be enabled to discern some vital aspects of criminally deviant behavior and the structure of law-breaking subcultures unless he makes such a moral decision, makes the deviants believe him, and moreover convinces them of his ability to act in accord with his decision. The last-mentioned point can perhaps be neglected with juvenile delinquents, for they know that a professional studying them is almost always exempt from police pressure to inform; but adult criminals have no such assurance, and hence are concerned not merely with the investigator's intentions, but with his sheer ability to remain a "stand-up guy" under police questioning.[12]

Although I have gone to this extreme in my research, I cannot wholly agree with Polsky's suggestions. Becoming a "stand-up guy" dips too deeply into criminal behavior for any nonlawbreaker, even if he is a bona-fide "applied sociologist." Overinvolvement of this kind in language and behavior has the dangerous tendency of reinforcing the criminal's symptom.

In my judgment, the "applied sociologist" working in the criminal community must proceed with caution. He should avoid: (1) being considered a "foolish buff," a crime fan, or a voyeur intrigued by "cute" crime patterns; (2) becoming a tool in any illegal activity; and (3) reinforcing the criminal motivations of his clients by his neutrality about their behavior.

Synanon has the beginnings of an important criminal research center which will enable the applied sociologist to avoid some of these pitfalls. Further "live" explorations of this kind should provide more insights into the role of the applied sociologist in the "criminal community."

## NOTES

1. For the purposes of this paper, the term "criminal community" refers to illegal deviants in all age groups, both inside and outside of custodial walls.

2. This issue is different in the Synanon situation, discussed in the latter part of the paper.

3. See Lewis Yablonsky, *The Violent Gang*, New York: The Macmillan Company, 1962.

4. Currently, according to California State Law, probationees who are "drug addicts" receive a Nalline test. This involves shooting a drug into the addict to see if he is "off" drugs.

5. Edwin H. Sutherland and Donald R. Cressey, *Principles of Criminology*, Chicago: J. B. Lippincott Company, 1960, pp. 69–70.

6. Thomas Mott Osborne, *Within Prison Walls*, New York: Appleton, 1914.

7. See especially Donald Clemmer, *The Prison Community*, New York: Rinehart & Col, 1958; Richard Korn and Lloyd McCorkle, *Criminology and Penology*, New York: Holt-Dryden, 1956; and Donald Cressey, ed., *The Prison*, New York: Holt-Rinehart Winston, 1961.

8. The organization is described in detail in my book, *Synanon: The Anticriminal Society*, Macmillan Company, 1964. An earlier article with the same name appeared in *Federal Probation*, September, 1962. Chuck Dederich is widely read and self-educated in the social sciences. His insights and theoretical contributions have been of enormous help in developing this section. His important theoretical and research contributions are extensively documented in my book on *Synanon*.

9. If the present rate of expansion continues, this information will be out of date by the time it is published.

10. It is important to note that the live and significant data collected first-hand by the "Chicago School" researchers in the 1920–1930 period were mainly relevant for that time and place. Many recent theorists on social problems have overdrawn on this old sociological bank account. The time is long overdue for a resurgence of field-study and case history methodology to replenish our sociological storehouse with live and meaningful data. We need such data as a case for valid theorizing about the changing social problems of the post-war era. (See Lewis Yablonsky, "The New Criminal," *Saturday Review*, Feb. 2, 1963.) Such contemporary data would aid the long-distance sociological theorists and statisticians to build their speculative theories about social problems on a firmer base of actual human behavior.

11. The *gang worker's* viewpoint is increasingly important since some recent sociological researchers use this person as a basic or exclusive source for their research data. For example, according to Short, Tennyson and Howard, ". . . the availability of detached workers as intimate observers of the boys, particularly in the gang setting, offered a rare opportunity to gain more complete and objective insights into the behavior of these boys than could be provided by any other method." James F. Short, Jr., Ray A. Tennyson and Kenneth I. Howard, "Behavior Dimensions of Gang Delinquency," *American Sociological Review*, 28:3 (June 1963), 419. What's wrong with direct research interaction with gangs?

12. Howard Becker, *The Outsiders*, New York: The Free Press, 1963, p. 171.

# 5.   Experiences with the Military

NEHEMIAH JORDAN

*The Setting*

IN A LARGE PROJECT FOR TRAINING OPERATIONAL crews as units at military bases, we introduced a novel technique for training selected military personnel. The new technique consisted of running simulated exercises for the crews, feeding back to them objective accounts of their performance, and then generating crew discussions based on group dynamic principles. The aim of the discussions was to evoke self-criticism and encourage self-improvement.

The program as such was the administrative responsibility of the military, but the success of the program was the functional responsibility of a corporation especially created for the purpose. The corporation prepared the material for the exercises and maintained a research and development staff to evaluate and improve the program. It also maintained a staff of field representatives to act as a liaison between the corporation and the military as well as to guide and assist the military in administering the program. The personnel of the research and development group and of the field representatives consisted almost exclusively of social scientists.

Although the introduction of this special training technique involved the interaction of individual social science practitioners and individual clients, it is also fair to say that the social science practitioner was a differentiated social entity—the corporation—and the client was another differentiated social entity—the military command. For the present discussion it is sufficient to distinguish the research and development group and the field representatives within the corporation from the division headquarters and the bases within the military.

# Experiences with the Military

## The Training Problem

On the whole the crews numbered between ten to fifteen men. One member of each crew had a unique and important job. Not only was this job left out of the discussion, but these key crew members received little if any benefit from the over-all training program. Although there was an individual training program available for these crew members, the consensus was almost unanimous that it was poor. There were rumblings.

The crew training program was of paramount importance. Until this worked reasonably well, no attention could be paid to the problems of individuals. As this was being achieved, the rumblings grew louder. Finally, the top command echelons in the military urged the top management of the corporation to find some way of using the highly developed and available techniques for neglected key crew members. Management thought it was a good idea and handed the job to the research and development group. And with this our case begins.

## A Possible Simple Solution to the Training Problem

The people in the research and development group had enough experience with the program to be able to apply the crew training program to these individuals without ever leaving their offices. To train the key member of the crew, they extended the technique of simulation to the other members of the crew. All that was needed was to describe clearly how to accomplish this. Top management and the military command would then send this description to the individuals involved with an order to implement it as a new program. But as every practitioner knows, nothing would have guaranteed failure better than such a direct approach. Even if the research and analysis people had been able to take this step, field representatives and military personnel would have looked upon the order as an increase in their already heavy load of duties, and as an imposition from the outside. They would have implemented it perfunctorily, if at all.

But the research and development people would not consider such a step. They interpreted it as using "expertise," as relying on experience leavened by common sense. Their whole academic training was predicated upon the proposition that common sense is untrustworthy, that the only thing worthy of the name "knowledge" is that which has been rigorously tested in a laboratory or experimental setting. In the present case the experimental study had to be conducted in the field and previous sad experience with such attempts pointed to many difficulties.

An important lesson was learned the hard way. It is almost impossible to conduct a successful experiment in the field unless all the individuals involved are intrinsically interested in its success. With the exception of the professional investigators, nobody can be expected to become interested in the research on the basis of elegance of experimental design, the beauty of rigorous controls, or the profundity of the hypotheses being tested. This occurs only when those involved feel that their effort and activity in the experimental setting *may* lead to solving problems that are real for them.

## INTRODUCING THE NEW TRAINING PROGRAM

Although the research and development team responsible for introducing this new training program was armed with authorizations signed by vice presidents and by generals, they decided not to use these directly if at all possible. Nevertheless, they did use them implicitly and the authorizations were a necessary prerequisite for the success of the effort. The press upon individuals in our modern mammoth organizations is so great that they will not permit themselves to become involved in anything unless they are assured that their superiors look upon it favorably. We have here the paradox of the organization man: it is difficult to involve him either with orders or without orders. Throughout the effort, the practitioners trod a *chary* path between telling people what to do, and arousing their spontaneous desire to do what had to be done.

The practitioners' guiding principle was that all those whose effort was needed for the success of the project should see in it a means of achieving personal goals. This required more time than the actual testing of the new program, but it was this spadework that assured the success of the program.

The initial strategy with the individuals whose involvement was sought was the same for all. First a short, objective account of the history of the problem was given (it was in this context that the interest of higher levels of management or of the higher echelons of command was indirectly and nonthreateningly communicated). Then the individual was asked whether he himself was confronted with the problem and if so how. This permitted the person to unburden his troubles and enabled the practitioner to be honest in his role of the able specialist eager to help. The practitioner would then outline what he intended to do and how it might help the person. At the same time he would solicit his advice to improve the project. Finally a plan for future action, based upon this discussion, was summarized and approved by the research development team. A letter containing this summary was then sent to the person interviewed for his final approval.

This technique was applied first to the field representatives. The one indicating greatest enthusiasm for the project was chosen. It was then applied to the military personnel in that representative's division, starting with the highest echelon. Every person contacted gave approval. As an added result of these discussions, the practitioners obtained a good picture of the problems confronting these individuals as well as the nature of the social environment for the experimental program. It was only after all discussions were concluded that the final details of the program were set and the actual implementation was begun.

The difficulties expected in field experimentation emerged. Many of these could have destroyed the project had the psychological responsibility for its success rested mainly upon the shoulders of the small research and development group. Because all involved were also psychologically involved, they did not wait for the harassed practitioner to cope with the dilemmas. But even more; despite the lengthy preparation, the practitioners' definition of the military situation and its unique problems was faulty. The suggestions by the field representatives and the military during the initial spadework and the actual testing of the program did much to refine the program and make it more adequate.

## The Immediate Outcome

From an objective experimental standpoint the outcome was a failure. Because of attrition of men in the military environment, the number of subjects and controls at the end of the trial was too small for statistically significant results. Only possible trends could be demonstrated quantitatively. From a qualitative standpoint the picture was different. To a man, the military personnel directly involved in the program, as trainers and as students, liked it. They sent formal letters to division headquarters recommending adoption of the technique throughout the division.

The research and development group issued two reports: a quantitative survey with little that was tangible, and a description of the technique used with a summary of the testimonials.

### EPILOGUE 1

The recommendations from the base were disregarded by the division training officer and the training technique was not implemented. The practitioners had made a serious error in their strategy. They had contacted the division training officer at the outset of the program and achieved his involvement. But they failed to maintain and systematically reinforce it. The recommendations reached his desk more than six months after the initial contact and by that time all involvement was gone. The division officer viewed these recommendations as additional work and worry to an already crowded workload, and as suggestions from an outside group. They were defeated by a pocket veto.

## EPILOGUE 2

Military transfer policies being what they were, the training officer was transferred to another post within a year. To replace him, division headquarters chose the officer who was directly involved in testing the new training technique. Within several months after his appointment, a new over-all training program was introduced into the division. As part of that program, without being identified as such, the training techniques developed experimentally the year earlier were incorporated without any significant change.

Question: Was the training officer who ran the experimental training program appointed to the position of division training officer by chance?

# 6. The Consultant to Business—

# His Role and His Problems

BURLEIGH B. GARDNER

OVER THE PAST TWENTY YEARS I HAVE BEEN engaged in consultation and research for business organizations. In this work I have been applying my knowledge and research skills as a social scientist to business problems. Thus my concern is for the problems of human behavior, those of interpersonal relations, of individual or group motivation, of individuals functioning within a system. And, to a large extent, my work has been concerned with problems of communication both within organizations and to the public.

After years in research on communities and on organization, I became actively involved in the applied social sciences, first in a personnel research position at the Hawthorne Plant of Western Electric Company, next as head of the Committee on Human Relations in Industry at the University of Chicago, and, since 1946, as head of Social Research, Inc., a research firm composed of social scientists.

As an organization, we were first largely involved in helping companies with internal problems of human behavior. We worked on problems of low morale, problems of Union-Management conflict, problems on organization, problems of individual adjustment. In the course of this we developed a variety of tools to help in the analysis and diagnosis of problems.

In the late 1940's, when companies became concerned with consumer behavior, we were increasingly involved in consumer and market studies. This rapidly evolved into the field popularly known as "motivation research." Since then there has been a vast growth in the application of social sciences in the field of marketing and advertising research.

In all this work there are certain basic conditions in our relation to clients. (1) We are outsiders. We are not part of the organization and can be aloof and objective in our evaluation of it or its actions. (2) We have a special body of knowledge and skills. We do not think like the other executives for we have special points of view and ways of examining the problem and coming to conclusions. (3) We have no responsibility for decisions or for their execution. We can only present conclusions or make recommendations. Others must decide whether or not to accept and act on them. Each of these conditions presents certain problems, responsibilities and opportunities.

*We are outsiders.* Theoretically, as outsiders, we are not caught up in the internal problems of interpersonal relations, of management politics, etc. Nevertheless, we are brought in by an individual or group, and, unless careful, we will become too closely identified with certain people or points of view. It is important to gain the confidence of a broad group, especially when working on internal problems. For example, when working on problems of union-management friction it is essential that the union accept the consultant, or he may become the source of additional conflict.

*We have a special body of knowledge.* As specialists in the social sciences we have knowledge and skills not familiar to the average executive. When we interview or observe, we are aware of things which he might not notice or would interpret differently. To maintain a good working relationship with the executive we must reassure him that in spite of our special knowledge we are basically sensible and we understand his position.

At the same time we must seek constantly to reorient the men we deal with so that they can grasp our point of view and begin to think about the problems along different lines. In fact, much of our work can be thought of as educational—we bring to our clients a body of knowledge and an orientation, and try to help them to assimilate it.

*We have no responsibility for decisions.* As consultants we are not part of the action patterns of the organization. We may influence decisions and give direction to the actions, but someone else must take the burden of responsibility. But this forces on us a special type of responsibility. In the first place, we must struggle to give the right advice. When we recommend a change in organization or in personnel, or a fresh approach to marketing or advertising, we must try to be as certain as possible that our advice is sound. Of course, in many situations we are asked to draw conclusions on problems where research is inadequate or where the present state of knowledge is not adequate. In such cases we may refuse to advise or else point out the limitations of our advice. In this we are often in the position of a doctor when dealing with obscure ailments; he does the best he can but does not claim omniscience.

We have a further responsibility not to make recommendations which cannot be carried out. If a course of action is impossible to execute, we cannot stop there. We are trying to help executives solve real problems in a real world, and we must help them find possible courses of action, even if these possible ones are less than perfect. I now want to illustrate some of the above points.

## The Case of the Hospital Administrator

A hospital administrator asked for our help in setting up a training program for his department heads. There was constant friction in the group, employee turnover was excessive, and there were many other problems which he thought would be solved by a good supervisory training program.

After a long discussion with him, we felt that a training program was ill advised and recommended that we study the situation first. We also suggested that part of the problem lay in his own behavior. As a result of this, he agreed to the following course of action: (1) We gave him a personality test to give us and him a better understanding of his needs and response to the situation. (2) We interviewed all his department heads. (3) We sat in his office and observed how he worked and especially how he dealt with people. During all of this we were working with him closely, interviewing him, discussing problems, and suggesting possible courses of action.

As he gained better insight into the situation, he improved his handling of problems and also developed ways of fostering cooperation in the group. While he made use of regular problem-solving conferences with the department heads, he never returned to his original idea of a formal training program. It wasn't needed.

We were actively involved in this situation for about eighteen months, but at the end made only an occasional visit every few weeks. In fact, after the first period of fairly intense activity, as the administrator began to work out the problems, we deliberately reduced the time spent in the organization.

The success in this case was dependent upon several factors. The first was that we gained his confidence so that he accepted the personality tests and in subsequent interviews talked freely about himself and the situation. Secondly, the consultant working with him was able to establish a very warm, friendly, relationship and was accepted as a friend and not just an expert. Finally, we were able to gain the confidence of the department heads and employees so that they could talk freely without concern that we would report them to the administrator.

From my experience, the consultant dealing with the human problems of an organization should have the following abilities and qualities:

1. He should be primarily concerned with helping the organization solve its problems. He is not there for his personal education or interests. What he gets from the experience must be subordinated to serving the needs of the organization. If he is only serving himself, the client becomes either a guinea pig to be observed or experimented with, or a source of income to be exploited.

2. He must be extremely knowledgeable about the dynamics of organization and the behavior and motivations of people in work situations. He is dealing with complex problems, and often any action or change leads to widespread and unanticipated reactions. Lack of understanding of these possibilities can lead to recommendations which will do more harm than good.

3. He must be able to gain the confidence of the people with whom he works, and establish and maintain good personal relations with them. Without these, his ideas or recommendations will be rejected. In some cases, strong negative reactions on the part of people in the organization make it impossible for him to get the information he needs. Furthermore, in many situations, giving advice is only the first step. The next is the problem of changing behavior. For example, it is one thing to recommend delegation of authority, but it often requires careful and intensive work with an individual executive before he can habitually follow through. Often, the consultant must practice a form of counseling to help the individual change his behavior as well as his thinking.

4. He must not force his ideas and recommendations on the organization. Sometimes the consultant becomes so determined to have his recommendations carried out that he forgets his role. If he forces actions on reluctant people the execution is bound to be poor and may lead to failure. In such cases the people in the organization must accept the blame, not the consultant.

5. He must make a continuous effort to help the people in the organiza-

tion understand his thinking. One of the important things the social scientist brings to his consulting role is a body of knowledge and concepts. He must constantly be the educator, trying to pass on his knowledge to the people he deals with. Often, the growth of understanding within the organization is his most valuable contribution.

When dealing with problems of consumer behavior or market research the role of the consultant shifts somewhat. In the first place, the executive in advertising or marketing is not personally involved with the consumer. This means he does not have to change his habitual patterns of dealing with people, only his ways of thinking about the "customer." As a result, there is less need for the consultant to establish and maintain a close personal relationship with the client.

It is still important that the consultant be respected for his knowledge. He must represent knowledge which is beyond that of ordinary experience. He must also show that he can use his special understanding in a common-sense, practical way.

Again, it is important that he be skilled in communicating his knowledge and ideas. He must be able to explain special and abstract ideas in understandable language. He must be an educator who tries to give his clients new and better ways of thinking about people as consumers.

This activity of the social scientists as researchers and consultants applying their skills to problems of business is growing rapidly. More and more Ph.D.'s are finding careers with business firms and research and consulting organizations. More and more faculty members are spending part of their time serving business and industry. Our small organization is served by five faculty members from four universities, on a regular consulting basis and, from time to time, we employ the service of others.

What does all this mean for the individual social scientists and for the social sciences? Will this lead to greater understanding of our society and of people? Does it lead to a reduction of basic research or to the development of the fields? From my experience, I believe it does something of both—it contributes to the advancement of knowledge and it retards development. On the whole, however, I believe its contribution is much greater than its retardation.

First, let us consider the drawbacks. The social scientist working within an organization tends to be restricted in what problems he can work on and to the questions he may pursue. He is also severely limited in what information he can publish. Inevitably, cases damaging to the organization or to individuals in it must be kept confidential. Findings which offer competitive advantages, such as special marketing knowledge, cannot be revealed.

Furthermore, few organizations have reached the level of sophistication where they will encourage or support serious social science research. Largely they rely on their employed social scientists to apply the existing knowledge of their fields to the immediate problems. Thus, they rarely make it possible for the social scientist to work seriously at extending the boundaries of knowledge.

The social scientist, working for a research organization serving business, is caught in the same trap. He cannot pursue problems which interest him unless they happen to be problems to the clients. And, because of the confidential nature of the client relationship, rarely can he publish more than bits and pieces of his work.

Also clients of research organizations rarely sponsor basic research. All their interest centers on immediate problem-solving which does not necessarily contribute to the advancement of knowledge.

These are problems with which we have struggled from the inception of Social Research, Inc. We all had strong academic and research inclinations, yet enjoyed the task of applying our knowledge to the on-going problems of business. This meant that we did not want to relinquish completely the basic pursuit of knowledge, despite the need to deal with immediate problems. As a result we have worked out a compromise.

*1.* We seek out clients who are interested in special research and who are willing to support some measure of it. Sometimes these can be considered basic studies even though of modest size. Often they involve the development of new techniques or the application of known techniques to new problems.

*2.* We do not overspecialize to the extent of being trapped in one type of problem. Since we deal with a wide variety of studies of consumer behavior, mass media, employee morale, personality studies, etc., we are able to bring to each study experience and the concepts developed from diverse studies. This cross-fertilization contributes greatly to expanding our knowledge and to increasing our problem-solving ability.

*3.* We seek opportunities to publish. From the start we have watched for opportunities to report research findings or theories in articles, monographs and books.

*4.* We spend our own money on research to the limits of our budget and manpower. Sometimes we will do a modest study on some topic of interest to us. Or we may experiment with some techniques in conjunction with a study for a client. By all these means we try constantly to advance the field of knowledge and to maintain our own lively interest in basic as well as applied research.

Let me turn now to the contributions of the work of the social scientist in the business field. First, it puts the social scientist face to face with reality. His theories and advice must meet its test. In my experience the effort of trying to fit theory to the complex realities, of trying to diagnose problems and plan remedial actions is stimulating and leads to better understanding. In general, I believe that the social scientist who has this experience not only increases his own knowledge but improves the quality of his other work, whether it be teaching, research or theorizing.

Furthermore, there is the influence of the social scientist upon the executive. As the executive works with the social scientist he develops greater understanding of human behavior and of social systems. He will understand the human needs and values that must be served by any effective organization.

Finally, as executive understanding develops, it generates the desire for more knowledge. Out of this desire will come more support for research and development in the social sciences.

# 7.    Experiences with Labor Unions

JAMES W. CARPER

THE MOST ACTIVE AND FRUITFUL PERIOD OF THE
American labor movement took place during the depression of the 1930's.
The development of the labor movement during this period was attended
by feverish enthusiasm, mass demonstrations, pitched battles, murder,
arson, and treachery. Men made total commitments; they were willing to
take risks that endangered their lives. Other voluntary organizations (such
as lodges or cooperatives) have also had as their aim the protection and
betterment of a dues–paying membership. But the formation of an Elks'
lodge or a cooperative grocery arouses almost no opposition because such
organizations do not seriously attack the existing social and economic
structures of society.

During the revolutionary period of any movement, technical advice is
not important and analytic comments are seen as attempts to kill the revolutionary spirit. The sort of people who were doing the organizational
spadework in the union movement during this developmental period—the
great body of largely unknown men who were "pulling shops" and leading picket lines—were extremely pragmatic men. On the firing line, immediate decision-making counted for a great deal—theory and analysis for
almost nothing. The battle was fought and partially won in the 30's by
desperate men who vaguely felt the changing industrial system impinging
on what they believed were their inherited rights: individualism, self-
determination, the tradition of frontier society. In the clutches of these
changes, and quite realistically, a propelling desperation was unleashed in
men who needed bread to eat and a roof over their heads. No group of
intellectuals told these men how to get their rights or the bread and the
roof.

There were leaders who might be called intellectuals or who had a
philosophical–political heritage. But even when leaders were themselves
committed to theoretical points of view (*e.g.*, Dubinsky of the International

Ladies Garment Workers Union or Hillman of the Amalgamated Clothing Workers Union), the organizational structures reflected the practical,
immediate contingencies rather than the long-range theoretical view. (An
exception may be the structure developed by the Dunne Brothers and Far-
rell Dobbs, Trotskyist Teamsters of Minneapolis. Whether or not this
structure originated from their definite philosophical views, time has
proved it to be extremely practical. It is the basic structure on which Hoffa
has built his empire within "the labor business," as he, at times, refers to
trade unionism.)

Today the American labor movement is still characterized by a pragmatic bread-and-butter philosophy. But it can no longer be called a revolutionary movement. The leaders of industry and those who tend to shape
social thought made a partial compromise with the firebrand labor leaders
of the 30's by giving unions a superficially acceptable status as institutions.
No longer, as a result of this recognition, can a strike be couched in terms
of class struggle. It must have an apparently logical, even though contrived,
economic rationalization. Consequently, the pragmatic fighters of the 30's,
who by and large are still the leaders of the labor movement of the 60's,
must depend on technical experts to buttress their case.

What does this mean for the professional social scientist actively working in a union, working for men who are accustomed to diagnosing a situation intuitively, and acting directly upon that diagnosis or, when necessary,
asking their "expert" to develop a rationale for a position? It means that
the professional social scientist will probably be working for a labor leader
who, because of the very nature of his job, is a "practical" social scientist.
The labor leader has been with the organization far longer than the social
scientist and can claim, without arrogance, far greater knowledge of the
history and workings of the organizational machinery. Tossed in the arena
with these active and practical men, the professional dare not take refuge
in specialized social science terminology for fear of being distrusted as an
impractical longhair or labeled "professor," and thus be considered as
having limited usefulness.

Above all, the social scientist in this setting has not developed what we
might call "professional magic." Their "magic" relates more to how a
professional is viewed by his union colleagues than to what he can or cannot in fact accomplish. For example, the union lawyer has "magic" in
the eyes of unionists; the social scientist does not. Why? Because the
lawyer has at his fingertips a body of knowledge which is simply not available to the average union leader—extremely intricate legalisms, Latin
terminology, the complicated sophistry of a very old discipline. The law-

*87*

yer, therefore, holds a prestigeful position in the labor movement. The social scientist is expert in a new discipline. He has as his body of professional knowledge a codification of how and why any given organization, group or system functions. This is precisely the body of information the union leader has about his own organization—not analytically, but pragmatically. The lawyer has a *mystique* surrounding him and, in addition, a specific function no one else in the labor movement can perform. Only a lawyer can take a case to court, and lawyers speak to other lawyers in handling legal matters. What the social scientist does is to pass his analyses and recommendations on to the activist to expedite, refashion or discard, depending on political contingencies.

Given this situation, the labor lawyer can range far beyond the field of his own specialized technical competence, as did Arthur Goldberg, an attorney who advised unions on many matters of policy, not always legal in nature. He is credited with having master-minded the expulsion of the Teamsters from the AFL-CIO. The most important decisions in that particular maneuver were not legal, but political and organizational. They involved such questions as what effect breaking up old-time alliances would have on the total labor movement and whether the greater acceptability of labor by the American public (predicted as one result of the Teamsters expulsion) would balance the losses labor would certainly suffer from severing one important segment of the movement from the whole. There was also the question of whether or not the expulsion of the Teamsters would really correct the abuses which caused the expulsion.

A good legal mind can deal with all these problems adequately. Or, at least, there is no reason why a good legal mind cannot deal with such questions adequately. But these are also precisely the kinds of questions to which a good sociologist has devoted his professional career. The sociologist is, in all likelihood, not consulted on this kind of question; the lawyer is. The lawyer is recognized as an advisor, not necessarily because he is trained to give this kind of advice or because he has previously been able to advise in these areas but, rather, because in his own area of professional legal knowledge he has been consulted and has given successful advice.

The social scientist who acts as an outside consultant for labor unions is quite rare; a lawyer working as an outside consultant is common. Normally, the social scientist holds a staff position, and his effectiveness will depend upon how he is accepted in his specific role of "giver" of advice.

Within the bureaucratic–political structure of a union, the "receiver" (union official) views himself as buying pieces of advice only from an outside expert. Disregarding the nature or quality of the advice, the reasons are obvious. In a staff position, the expert, whether social scientist or attorney, falls within the organizational chart which defines who gives and who responds to orders. Advice given by an expert, when in the position of "responding" to orders may be construed as impertinent, presumptuous, disloyal and even as threatening to the authority of the "boss." This is especially true if the advice moves into the area of interpretation of policy, the hallowed preserve of the elected leader. Because of organizational constraints, the union official feels much freer to discuss organizational problems and to follow the advice of an expert on retainer than with his more knowledgeable house attorney, research or educational director.

The dividing line between policy and operations is thin and blurred. At one point, in setting up a course in handling grievances, I was ordered not to give the shop stewards copies of their contracts. Not having experience in dealing with such situations, I moved into a head–on collision on the esoteric (at least to my boss) problem of professional rights and administrative policy. If I had understood more clearly, I could have sidestepped the issue by making up a manual using all the clauses in the contracts from the various shops represented, a technique which would have been pedagogically more sound, and which would have allayed the political fears of my superior. As it was, he felt it important to reconfirm his position as boss, invoking his right to determine policy. I was viewed, among other things, as being impertinent and untrustworthy. I might add that during this period he was discussing his personal organizational problems with a "professor" from a university who was teaching some of the courses I was setting up.

The social scientist, especially the one trained in sociology and political science, has as his specialization the knowledge of organization; how policy is made; how it is translated into operations; and what changes should, or can be made if operations should break down. Such analyses, because of the role of staff experts, are particularly sensitive. If the social scientist is used at all (he may be limited to "chores") he will develop relationships with elected officials lower on the organizational chart than his superior, with line functionaries, and rank-and-file members. Since his relationship as advisor to a higher official gives him prestige, and since he is not held responsible for operational failures (a firing of an employee or a collective bargaining settlement that is viewed as unsatisfactory by the rank-and-file), he may develop a popularity and trust with those below him. As a result he will be able to collect "intelligence" not available to his superior. Transmitting this information is quite ticklish unless the social scientist has the complete trust of his superior because, coupled with the popularity he may be accumulating, transmitting points of view that are critical of the administration may raise suspicions as to his loyalty. Most staff experts have heard, at one time or another, the half-joking statement from a superior, "This guy wants my job."

Most unions are one-party political organizations, and disagreement with an established policy or questions about the efficacy of policy may be viewed as insurgent or disloyal. If the social scientist lacks political know-how, he may start saying what he thinks too boldly. If he is not dismissed as disloyal and untrustworthy, his opinions (even if correct) may be discounted by the reaction: "We knew that all the time." Beside being one-party political systems, unions exhibit an interesting and unique symbiosis between the political and bureaucratic. Key positions on all levels are elective. The elected official is responsible for policy and program, as well as for execution of program. Therefore, every bureaucratic action has political implications. For example, a particular union may be working toward a goal of a 35-hour week for industrial workers. If, however, the winning of the 35-hour week means giving up weekly salary increases, following the formal policy may prove politically catastrophic for the bureaucrat responsible. Racial integration in unions is now stated as top policy, but the problems of translating policy into action may be suicidal for those officials faced with implementing the policy.

I have defined the *limits* of the situation for the sociologist—what he cannot do as a staff member of a labor organization and the political taboos he had better not transgress. One thing is certain: he will not be in the easily defined situation of an expert working in a corporation. The job of the corporation sociologist is clear-cut—he produces studies, makes reports, and his recommendations affect directly *only* operational aspects of the organization. The situation is more complex for the union sociologist. He finds himself in turgid political waters, faced with continuous ambiguity and a professional role which has to be redefined on a day-to-day basis.

What *can* a social scientist do when faced with this situation? Wilensky[1] sees the expert as "supplying intelligence" of different varieties. The "facts and figures" man gives technical, economic or legal intelligence: that is, he builds a case. The "contact" man supplies the labor leader with the political and ideological intelligence he needs to function in our highly complex modern society. And, finally, the "internal communications specialist" supplies the same political and ideological intelligence, but for purposes of internal analysis and control.

Can the social scientist contribute more to the labor movement now than he could in the past? In assessing the current needs, the answer is clearly "yes." With the shift in the requirements of the work force will come a shift in the approach of unions. Technological changes have meant fewer and fewer semiskilled and skilled industrial workers (the population which responded to the "modern" unionism evolved in the 30's). Technological changes require more and more white collar employees, technical employees, and service employees. Furthermore, a segment of the work force, the Negro, by and large deprived educationally, is demanding entrance into the work force and calling on unions to be responsible for achieving it. (Undereducated and undertrained, they are unable to move into the expanding market for technical jobs and resent being placed in the low-level jobs referred to as "dead end" jobs.) Certainly the social scientist can be useful in advising on necessary changes in union approach and structure needed to cope with these important social changes.

Is the social scientist being called on to advise? Probably not as much as necessary. Paul Jacobs[2] points out that unions have not changed. He believes this to be their current weakness. Furthermore, during this period, which should be a transitional period, unions have not sought the help of social scientists. Jacobs emphasizes that social scientists are leaving the labor movement and that each year it is more difficult to recruit them. Russell Allen,[3] a committed trade unionist and an experienced staff expert, who left the labor movement for a position in a university, states:

The work of union staff professionals is bound to have its frustrations, but it also has solid rewards. The trend is in the direction of a more settled role as the unions become more like the sociologist's model of a bureaucracy. This development can, in turn, bring its own set of frustrations—narrower specialization, centralized adoption of policy and program, and so forth. To some professionals (I among them) the tighter centralized control will be a source of more discontent than the narrowing functions—all of this will depend on the individual's own values, his weighting of ends, and means, his assessment of the inter-relationships of functions and process in the whole scheme of unionism in American society.

But just as I am convinced that unions cannot live in easy comfort with the professional and intellectual staff in their ranks, I am equally convinced that the unions cannot grow and develop without them and without the ideas and contributions they make. Furthermore, the intellectual-professional must not make adjustment to his environment so important that he abdicate the only really important function which he has; namely, to differentiate his contributions from that of others and to make it as affirmative and as constructive as he can. The phenomenon of the anti–intellectual among professionals in the labor movement is fairly common—the fellow who derogates his own college

## James W. Carper

training, who tries so hard to be "one of the boys" that he sells out, literally, the one asset he has above all. If the intellectual does not believe in himself, who *will* believe in him?

The question raised by the professions is: Given the opportunity, are there individuals qualified to enter the labor movement and operate successfully? The other question is: Will social changes, as in the 1920's and the 1930's, cause the unions to revise drastically their approach and their structure? If the answer to both is yes, the social scientist will have an expanded role in the labor movement.

## NOTES

1. Wilensky, Harold L., *Intellectuals in Labor Unions,* New York: The Free Press, 1956.

2. Jacobs, Paul, *The State of the Unions,* New York: Atheneum, 1963.

3. Allen, Russell, "The Professional in Unions and His Educational Preparation," *Industrial and Labor Relations Review,* 16:1 (October, 1962), 28.

# 8. Organizational Strains in the Researcher-Practitioner Relationship

HYMAN RODMAN AND RALPH L. KOLODNY

SOCIAL SCIENCE RESEARCHERS, TO AN INCREASING extent, have been moving into clinical settings, such as mental hospitals, general hospitals, child guidance clinics, and social work agencies, and into other professional settings, such as schools and courts. It is well known that problems often arise when a social science researcher enters a clinical agency or similar professional setting. What we are interested in exploring is whether there are similarities in the problems faced by researchers and practitioners in these professional agencies, and whether certain of these problems stem from the organizational structure of the professional agency. We shall deal primarily with the relationships between researchers and practitioners in health and welfare agencies under those conditions when only one or a few researchers are part of a larger agency.[1] We feel, however, that our work may have implications for research endeavors in any professional agency.

Most of the writings on researcher-practitioner relationships are based upon the personal experiences of their authors, as is true of our report. But, in addition to this, we have made an attempt to highlight some of the major themes that emerge in the writings on researcher-practitioner relationships. For an overlapping bibliography on these relationships, and more generally for references to other forms of interdisciplinary team research, the reader is referred to the excellent bibliography to be found in Luszki's book.[2]

In their less charitable moments, researchers complain that practitioners "can't see the forest for the trees" while practitioners, in turn, wonder whether researchers "can see the human beings behind the statistics."[3] This kind of problem, as well as others, frequently plagues the relationship between researchers and practitioners. In attempting to locate the difficulties that arise in the course of this relationship, reference is often made to personality differences or to personality problems. Blenkner talks about "traits of temperament of a lasting character" that divide researchers and practitioners.[4] In their discussion of anxieties associated with research in clinical settings, Mitchell and Mudd suggest the existence of a "deeply instilled bias for the 'intuitive' on the part of the clinician against the bias for the 'logical' of the researcher."[5] They also suggest that many clinicians, in their first anxiety reactions toward research processes with their clients, "are reacting to inexperience, the unknown" and that "if their anxiety persists as evidenced in their continued inability to discuss or accept the fact that clients are not harmed by research procedures it can but be labeled as 'neurotic anxiety.' "[6] It is true, of course, that one cannot understand practitioner-researcher difficulties unless attention is paid to personality variables as they apply to the behavior of individuals or groups of individuals in particular professions. At the same time, it seems to us, that an understanding of these difficulties is likely to be incomplete if we do not also take a close look at those factors, other than personality variables, that may influence the actions and feelings of practitioners and researchers toward one another.[7]

In this chapter, we shall be focusing on one such factor, the formal organization of the clinical agency, and we will attempt to spell out some of the ways in which the strains that may be found between researchers and practitioners are built into the formal organization of the agency. Our purpose in so doing is not to discourage the undertaking of research in a clinical agency but to show the ways in which agency structure, of necessity, conditions the response of researchers and practitioners to each other, so that the strains which arise between them may be better understood and managed. Since our aim is to illuminate problem areas, our attention will be devoted to "stresses" and "difficulties" rather than to an examination of the more benign aspects of researcher-practitioner interaction. It should be noted, therefore, in the interest of keeping a balanced view, that despite these stresses, satisfying and productive working relationships have been developed in a good many agencies among administrators, researchers, and practitioners.[8]

# The Researcher-Practitioner Relationship

## The Researcher as Evaluator

There is general agreement on the need for research activity in clinical agencies. The literature is replete with suggestions and even demands that practice be subjected to systematic investigation. Many reasons are advanced for undertaking research, such as benefits to the staff from increased morale and sharpened perceptions of the possible consequences of their techniques. The ultimate purpose of research, however, is to evaluate the effectiveness of practice (although it is recognized that "research cannot produce here and now the 'ultimate' evaluation of efforts to bring about psychosocial changes in individuals.") [9] This orientation is reflected in the following statement:

As more time, energy, manpower and funds have been devoted to mental health, as more scientifically trained professional workers have become involved in the problem and as competition among community programs of all types for manpower and public funds has increased, the need for methods of evaluating mental health activities is obvious. It becomes mandatory that more scientific evidence be furnished if and where this is possible, or otherwise lack of knowledge concerning the results of enormous human effort can lead to wastage, furtherance of untested beliefs and possible counter trends which may obstruct the onward march of hard-won progress.[10]

One aspect, then, of the relationship between researcher and practitioner is that the former may be evaluating the work of the latter. At the outset, therefore, practitioners may feel threatened by the researcher and ambivalent about undertaking the research, since the researcher, whether he likes it or not, is in the position of possibly "criticizing" the work of the practitioner. Inherent in the role of the researcher is the concept of a "corrective agent" who, through his "findings," will help practitioners improve their practice. Researchers in social work write of their "focus on developing more 'knowledgeable' ways of proceeding towards social work goals."[11] The implication is that before research, the agency practice was characterized by "less knowledgeable" ways of proceeding towards social work goals. Although the researcher may want to see himself as an "enabler" in his relationship with the practitioner rather than as an "evaluator," the corrective and evaluative aspects of his position, as he takes his place in the structure of the agency, are sensed and reacted to by the practitioners. As Wilensky and Lebeaux point out, objectivity has a critical tone to it, and "what the social scientist thinks of as 'objective investigation' the practitioner often takes as 'hostile attack.' "[12] Subsequent resistance on the part of the practitioners cannot be dismissed as merely irrational, for these, in part, are reactions to be expected to the researchers' role in the organization.

For the practitioner, the painful aspects of the evaluation process cannot be glossed over. "A public relations man who usually operates on the basis of shrewd guesswork is likely to feel his 'status' is in danger when an outsider threatens to question his guesswork by scientific method."[13] The practitioner's convictions (and occasional doubts) that his efforts are helpful often lead to an ambivalent attitude toward research, for it purports to test the efficacy of his efforts. This attitude is neatly reflected by Wirth in a review of Albert Rose's book, *Regent Park: A Study in Slum Clearance*. Wirth writes:

It is good for those of us who are interested in low-cost housing programs to have all of these convictions written down; yet it must be recognized that these conclusions are by no means satisfactorily documented and validated. Much more study remains to be done before we have evidence on hand definitely to assay the costs and benefits of public housing. Most social workers, however, are prepared to take the benefits for granted even without adequate proof in the firm conviction that the benefits will show up in time.[14]

The questioning attitude of the researcher is likely to be irritating to the practitioner. This is not because the practitioner is naïve or blind to inadequacies in practice. Often it is because the probing of the researcher, at least initially, is an extra burden to the already overworked practitioner. With a host of patients or clients to be seen, he may view the researcher's persistent request for "evidence" rather than "impressions" as carping and quibbling. As Naegele phrased it, researchers kept therapists on their toes by asking, "How do you know?" and therapists kept researchers on their toes by asking, "So what?"[15]

Assaying this situation, Pollak, in his comments on research in social work, has noted that, to date, researchers and social workers have collaborated under circumstances most likely to cause friction because they meet each other at the point of evaluation. This places the researchers in the position of critical analysts and induces defensiveness in the social workers. Pollak suggests, as a remedy for this situation, that researchers begin not with evaluative studies in agencies but begin, rather, by working with the social workers on projects in such a way that the workers are able to perceive the researchers as helpful colleagues, rather than as critics.[16] Such preevaluative, collaborative work may have the advantage of teaching researchers more about the complexity of the problems that confront practitioners. Researchers are then more apt to try to develop better research instruments to reflect the complexities of practice. This may be a chastening experience for a researcher, but it may not only reduce practitioner defensiveness and but also increase mutual respect.

Even under these conditions, threatening features of the research process remain. Built into the researcher's function is the role of innovator. This is parallel to the situation in an industrial organization where the goals of the research and production departments may be at odds because the former has a vested interest in discovering inefficiency and in altering the production process, while the latter has a vested interest in resisting changes that would upset the department and possibly disclose its inefficiency. In the same vein, in the relationship between researchers and teachers of psychotherapy in mental hospitals, the teachers may look upon research as an effort "to undermine established authority and to destroy what the teachers are building within the limits of the administrative Procrustes."[17]

It is not only the evaluative aspect of the researcher's job which leads to organizational strains between researcher and practitioner. Actually, the very ways in which the activities of researchers and practitioners are organized and the monetary and prestige values attached to these different sets of activities have a definite bearing on the strains. The basic function of a clinical agency is to help or treat the clients or patients it serves. A number of these agencies, however, are also engaged in research work. The important question, therefore, is what place research activities hold within the agency and the consequences of the differences between research and treatment.

Our analogy can be developed further. In an industrial organization,[18] the workers on the line are engaged directly in the manufacture of a product while the staff members serve in an advisory capacity. In a similar way, the practitioners in an agency are engaged directly with therapeutic goals, while researchers serve in an advisory capacity or, at any rate, their findings may be potentially advisory.

Like the staff workers in an industrial organization, the research workers in a clinical agency have an inconsistent status. For example, the research workers are often younger than the practitioners and have had less, if any, clinical training or experience. On the other hand, researchers have usually had more formal academic training; they are "evaluators" of the practitioners; and they are closer to the administrator. This makes for status inconsistency, and, as some studies have shown, various forms of dissatisfaction or desire for change tend to develop in such a situation.[19]

## Work and Time Organization

An additional factor that transforms the hyphen between researcher and practitioner into a thorn is the extreme difference between the research job and the therapeutic job.[20] The use of time by the researcher and by the practitioner is one difference. The practitioner is engaged in a continuous job of seeing clients or patients. His time schedule is organized by sessions with clients or patients in the office, or, occasionally, in the homes, and his appointment calendar shows few empty spaces. The researcher, however, is working on a project; his time is not organized on an hour-to-hour basis and there are often large blanks in his appointment calendar. Of course, the researcher's time may be as tightly organized as the practitioner's if he is conducting a series of research interviews, but after the interviews are completed they must be recorded, examined and analyzed, and written up into a final report, article, or monograph. It is clear, therefore, that the researcher's activities and his organization of time differ markedly from the practitioner's. That these differences are not always appreciated is illustrated by a brief phone conversation between one of the writers and a social worker.

> Social worker: I wonder when you would have time to get together with me?
> Researcher: Well, I am free on Tuesday afternoon, or anytime Wednesday or Thursday would be O.K.
> Social worker: Boy, that's quite a schedule; you're really living the life of a lotus-eater!

The comments of Ekstein and Wallerstein on this point are interesting. They note that teachers of psychotherapy in mental hospitals sometimes see researchers in these settings as "living a parasitical life, free from schedules and responsibilities."[21]

One aspect of the differences in time organization between practitioners and researchers is the fact that the practitioner focuses upon a series of individual cases, while the researcher focuses upon a general problem. Occasionally this gives rise to the attitude that the researcher is not interested in individuals and the practitioner is not interested in general problems. Practitioners, for example, may complain bitterly that their own or other agencies accept clients or patients only if their problems fit the research interest of people at the agency. In addition, they frequently object to changes in their service routine that are required by a research project and may, as a final expression of protest, undermine it.[22]

## The Researcher-Practitioner Relationship

Researchers, on the other hand, may complain that practitioners are so involved with their patients or clients that they object to the use of follow-up studies or control groups. Florence Hollis has written on this point:

> This study would have been strengthened immeasurably had it been possible to follow up the cases, at say a year after closing. There is considerable resistance to such follow-up in the casework field. In the writer's opinion there is very little rational basis for this resistance. There will always be certain individual cases which it is impossible or inadvisable to follow but these would be the exception rather than the rule.[23]

In addition, Martin Wolins, in referring to the use of control groups in social work has commented that, "in suggesting control groups I am advocating denial of service, strongly opposed by every social work practitioner to whom I have mentioned it."[24] Making use of control groups is especially difficult in public agencies.[25]

The problems are compounded if the researcher requires the practitioner to change his procedures. For example, he may be asked to record more fully and more frequently. This is extremely important for the researcher, for he cannot hope to carry out his task without all the data he needs. For the practitioner, recording is less important. Even in social work, the practitioner is less diligent about recording than agency administrators would prefer. This is true despite the prominent place of recording in the literature and the belief commonly held by those from related disciplines that social workers "over-ritualize" their work through voluminous recording and thus "do too much of the work that psychologists and psychiatrists seem to do too little of."[26] Recording is, in fact, not often attended to with anywhere near the diligence agency administrators hope for. This is attested to, for example, by the notices one sees posted from time to time advising workers that vacations cannot be taken until recording is brought up to date, and by the workers who spend many days, prior to leaving an agency permanently, catching up on their recording. The practitioner may feel that he can remember the essential points he is concerned with, and by saving time from recording, can devote himself to what he considers his basic job—clinical work. In addition, because of the strong democratic ethic among social workers, items like race, religion, and national background may not be recorded, especially on a client's fact sheet, and this may lead to difficulties for the researcher.[27] Research work and clinical work differ; each has a different attitude toward recording. It is easy to see that these dissimilar viewpoints will affect the researcher-practitioner relationship.[28]

## Credit and Anonymity

Another problem may arise from the different roles played by researcher and practitioner: the credit assigned for the publication of research reports. To the researcher, publication represents the culmination of his work and he expects to get primary, if not sole, credit for publication. The practitioner who has cooperated with the researcher, however, typically feels that he has contributed a great deal to the research report and expects to get substantial, if not equal, credit for its publication. The researcher who has had to overcome the resistance of the practitioner may tend to minimize the practitioner's work, whereas the practitioner who has had to sacrifice important time may overemphasize his part in the research.[29] If, in addition, the research report is largely exploratory and descriptive and makes use of case material that has been supplied by the practitioner, the latter has all the more reason to feel that he should get a considerable amount of credit for the final published report. Thus, due to the roles they play, the researcher and the practitioner have differing perceptions of the size of the latter's contribution. This is compounded by the fact that the researcher ordinarily writes the final report[30] and decides upon the credit to be given to other participants on the project. He not only sees things differently from the practitioner, but also has a limited number of possibilities for assigning credit. Perhaps the television industry has an easier time with this problem because the credit to be assigned is part of a contract, and because there is more scope for indicating greater and lesser "stardom." The researcher publishing an article often faces the choice between coauthorship and footnote mention—and there is a wide gap between the two. In addition, certain journals, due to space limitations, are reluctant to accept articles with more than two or three authors, and may want to omit footnotes that acknowledge a long list of participants in a research project. This, of course, adds to the strains in the relationship between researcher and practitioner.

There are fewer space limitations when a book is to be published. Therefore, a more just distribution of credit is possible. Between magnanimous coauthorship and mere footnote mention, are the possibilities of secondary authorship ("with the assistance of" or "with the collaboration of") and of more or less protracted mention in the Preface or Acknowledgments. However, the problem is not simply one of space limitations or "just" distribution of credit, but also of the different role-players' interpretations of what is "just."

Publication credit is therefore a sensitive issue, and is usually not discussed until the research report has been written, and sometimes not even then.[31] This is another area in which the researcher has power, and through which he can broadcast credit (or blame) to a large audience. Because of this, the researcher can exert pressure upon the practitioner to gain his cooperation. That it may not even occur to the researcher to discuss publication with the practitioner does not lessen this pressure. It may also be significant that social science researchers are often very responsive to the canon of confidentiality that protects the people from whom or through whom they gather their data. So much so, in fact, that they may all too readily grant anonymity to those who would prefer a share of the credit.

## The Patterns of Communication

We have indicated, so far, how the role of the researcher and the nature of the organization can create strains between practitioners and researchers. Another source of strain can be found in the communication patterns of the researcher.

When research first begins in a clinical agency, it is almost always a creation of the agency's administration. The administration may feel that research work offers the only hope for new findings and techniques that can reduce the increasing demands for service or help to meet these demands more effectively. The publication of research results is also an effective way of gaining prestige for the agency. Thus, research work is usually established because of needs expressed by the administration rather than the practitioners. In addition, according to some writers, it is the administrator who is expected "to work through the resistance [to research] of inexperienced board members and staff."[32] This puts the researcher in a clinical agency in a unique position. His work has been created by the administration and, at least initially, he has his main contacts with it. This special position of the researcher will usually mean that he is not attached to any service department of the agency. It might also involve the creation of a special research group which, by name, often becomes a patrician institute among plebeian departments. In those instances where the researcher is a part of a service department—perhaps because he is working both as a practitioner and as a researcher—he may have certain responsibilities to the head of the service department and also to the administrator of the agency. This may lead to strain because the administrator, researcher, and especially the department head, may all wonder, at times, where the researcher belongs.

There is perhaps another factor that binds the researcher and administrator together. This is the "loneliness" that Schmidt sees in the administrative position.[33] The administrator may therefore welcome a researcher as someone to talk with in a way that he cannot talk with the regular members of his staff.

## The Problem of Marginality

The special tie that the researcher has with the administrator cannot be overemphasized. The formal organization of his job, at least in the beginning, isolates him from the rest of the agency and at the same time binds him closely to the administrator. Not only are the researcher's activities different, but also he is usually not part of a regular agency department. For these reasons he has a marginal position within the agency.[34] Even his research findings are marginal to the agency in the sense that they are usually published for a wider audience. Compared to the research department in an industrial organization, the research department in a direct service agency suggests fewer changes for the worker in clinical practice. This is due to the complexity of the service task. It is indeed a reflection of the weakness of the researcher's position that the purpose of most of the changes he requests is to enable him to carry out his research task, not to improve service. It is, therefore, not surprising that difficulties develop when the researcher must work closely with the practitioner to carry out his task. The researcher's marginal position in the structure of the agency itself and in the profession of the workers in the agency deserve close study. Practitioners may think he is playing a "luxury role," perhaps useful but certainly not essential to carrying out the agency's task and commitment to the public. He is not part of the "line" organization of the professional agency. His formal training is "academic" rather than "clinical," and can lead to conflict with the practitioners about understanding human behavior. Actually, the orientation of the researcher to personal and social problems may not differ greatly from that of the clinical practitioner, but his marginal position and his inconsistent status[35] may lead him, at times, to feel isolated, without support, and unessential to the agency. In some cases it may make him a useful target for negative feelings displaced from authority figures in the supervisory chain and structure.

# The Researcher-Practitioner Relationship

The practitioners within an agency share a professional culture which they act out in their daily experiences. This is so whether they do or do not identify with one specific agency. The lone researcher or the few researchers within a clinical agency are "strangers" who may be vitally interested in the professional culture of the society in which they reside, but who nevertheless maintain their own distinctive customs and beliefs. They do not commit themselves to the mores of this new society to the extent that its members do, and their acceptance by the society, therefore, is always conditional and tentative.[36] Like the traditional marginal man, the researcher and what he does are somewhat mysterious. As a social worker laughingly remarked to one of the writers, "Nobody knows what you're doing but you." This attitude may be reinforced if the researcher begins his task with only general ideas about the problems he hopes to tackle and the ways he will approach them. Since he cannot immediately explain his research problem to the practitioners and may take time to explore what is researchable in the agency, misconceptions can arise about his role, usually reflecting the anxieties of the practitioners about their own performance.

In one instance, one of the writers entered a social work agency to explore what was researchable. After several months, he presented a questionnaire to the social workers. One of the things they were asked was to give their impressions of what the research worker was doing in the agency. At an early staff meeting the administrator had explained that *exploration* was the research worker's function, and this was repeated by the researcher to each practitioner who asked him about his work. Despite this emphasis upon *exploration*, eight of the twenty-five social workers who answered the questionnaire mentioned that *evaluation* was a function of the researcher's job. This was done in terms such as "assessment," "evaluation," and observation in relation to the "adequacy of service" and the "achievement of agency goals." Two examples of such responses were: "Mainly he seemed to be observing, asking questions on an informal level, and I thought that he was reading records and evaluating the work of the agency"; and "Gathering statistical information and studying what an agency such as ours does, what its good and bad points are."

Because of his distinctive role of "evaluator" the researcher is placed in a marginal position by the practitioner. His sense of marginality may also stem from his feelings about the means and ends of science and social action. Both may hold some attraction for him but both may also appear to be in opposition. As Tax has said, "Our action anthropology thus gets a moral and even missionary tinge that is perhaps more important for some

*103*

of us than for others."[37] Or as Towle suggests in her discussion of the relations between social scientists and social workers (whom she refers to as "scientific missionaries"), "Today, it looks as if the social scientists, in studying the missionary, risks becoming one."[38] One may or may not agree with Towle's further comment that it may be necessary for the researcher to become a "missionary" in some measure "if he is to be an understanding and hence a useful collaborator."[39] However it is not difficult to understand the researcher's internal struggle when he faces the possibility of becoming part of what he is studying, and thereby runs the risk of losing the "objectivity" he has been taught to value so highly.

## Denial and Displacement

Up to this point we have concentrated upon the ways in which the formal organization of a clinical agency leads to strains in the relationship between researchers and practitioners. We now want to focus upon some reactions to the formally induced strains. The first reaction we will discuss is denial and displacement, in which the researcher is not merely isolated by the practitioner, but "annihilated." Obviously, such a response does not lead to a better working relationship.

By denial and displacement we refer to the practitioner's refusal to take the researcher or his findings seriously. The researcher who suggests that a particular clinical practice is defective may be told that he is "merely projecting," and that it is his own personality that is defective.[40] In this way, the practitioner may ignore the researcher, or, at the very least, he may ignore some of the researcher's remarks. The practitioner, therefore, attempts to eliminate the tensions in the relationship by creating a situation that permits him, in a sense, to deny the role of the researcher.

It is perhaps to be expected that certain professional groups, such as psychiatrists and social workers, should resort to this type of denial and displacement. They have, after all, been especially trained to observe personality functioning, and are not nearly so well trained to observe the functioning of a social organization.

We suspect that this type of response is rare. This is fortunate, for although it may protect the practitioner from the threatening researcher, it also inhibits the researcher's contribution to the clinical agency.

Apart from the professional self-restraint and general good sense of most practitioners, this kind of response does not occur frequently because of the administrator-researcher tie: any outright attempt to annihilate the role of the researcher becomes an attack upon the administration.

When denial and displacement do occur, however, they need not inhibit the researcher permanently. If he tries to understand the sources of these defenses and does not merely react to them as though they were personal attacks he may, in the long run, enhance his relationship with the practitioner. There are, after all, many matters of common interest to researchers and practitioners, and these may override defensiveness.

## One–Way Humor

One of the most noticeable reactions to the strains between practitioners and researchers is the informal humor that may develop between them. As we have observed it, the humor is not symmetrical—most of the humorous remarks are made by the practitioner and directed toward the researcher. It is our belief that this humor reflects the ambivalence of the practitioner toward the researcher, and that its one-sidedness reflects the researcher's marginal position in the clinical agency.

Humor manifests itself in the somewhat sarcastic, but kindly manner of addressing the researcher. In a social work agency he may be called "Doctor" and "Professor."[41] The latter term may be related to the stereotype of the researcher as an intellectual far removed from the problems of the everyday world. Other humorous remarks of a similar nature refer to the "Ivory Tower" that the researcher occupies; to the fact that he "has his head in the clouds"; or to his "high-falutin' gobbledygook."[42] These all serve to emphasize the idea that the researcher is different, and occupies a marginal position within the agency.

Humor directed toward the researcher is a reflection of the different jobs that are done by the practitioner and the researcher. The following three joking comments, for example, all devaluate the writing and publishing that the researcher does: "I've got an idea—why don't we all stop working and just write"; "What are you doing with your time? Just writing?"; and, after a practitioner made an especially perceptive comment, a researcher said, "Gee, that's an interesting remark!" The practitioner replied, "Why don't you write another article on that?"

Another type of humorous remark reflects the practitioner's ambivalence toward the researcher's recording. In the lunchroom one day a social worker called out loudly and jokingly to one of the writers sitting alone at a table, "Hey, what are you doing there? Are you taking notes on group process?" At another time, during a conversation, a social worker in the group turned to one of the writers and said, "Now I hope you're not going to go along [to the administrator] and tell him what we said." The writer replied, "That's just what I was going to do," and everyone laughed loudly.

These jokes seem to indicate a fear on the part of the practitioners that their activities will be reported, and a desire to gain recognition through having their work reported. A not uncommon remark that is jokingly interjected into an informal conversation with a researcher—"Are you taking all this down?"—reflects this ambivalence very well.

Perhaps the humorous remarks that have the greatest significance, however, are those expressed by the practitioners as part of their working relationship with the researchers. Releasing some of their hostility in this acceptable manner enables the practitioners to cooperate with the researchers. For example, one of the writers received a birthday card from some practitioners who were collaborating with him. It was signed "From your resistant researchers." Practitioners have also opened a research meeting with, "Well, what magnificent ideas are we going to come up with today?", and have said in the course of a meeting with the researcher, "Boy, this is one of my resistant mornings." In these ways the practitioners can jokingly express a degree of hostility toward the researcher or his work without actually upsetting the relationship.

Radcliffe-Brown has pointed to the way in which joking develops between individuals who have an ambiguous relationship with each other,[43] and Rose L. Coser has added that in a hierarchical structure humor tends to be directed downward.[44] What we are saying is that there is a tendency for the humor to be directed not only "downward" but also "sideways" from those who play a more central role in an organization toward those whose role is peripheral. This humor, although it is not reciprocal, serves a social, as well as a psychological function.[45] And we suspect that, as the "peripheral" researchers come to play a more central role in a clinical agency, there will be greater reciprocity of humor.[46]

## Formal Responses to Strain

The formal structure of an organization is not absolutely fixed, and various kinds of formal changes can and have been made to minimize the strains we have discussed. For example, the use of research consultants provides "external structural supports"[47] for the researcher who occupies a marginal position within a clinical agency. In this way the researcher spends part of his time interacting with someone who shares his viewpoint, and he can gain the encouragement he needs to persevere in his research tasks. This kind of formal provision is especially valuable and necessary for the lone researcher in a clinical agency.[48]

Another formal response to the potential stresses we have discussed is the appointment of a professionally trained practitioner to the researcher's role.[49] In this way there may be less mistrust and more understanding between researcher and practitioner, but such an appointment does not necessarily eliminate all problems.

Another type of formal response is the use of "research-practitioners" who know the research focus of their job before they start to work.[50] This is a typical practice where a grant has been provided for a specific research or demonstration project. If the practitioners are made aware of the research aspect of their job and the job draws practitioners with an interest in research, some of the difficulties we have discussed can be eliminated. The practitioner, indeed, may be the one who originates the research and who hires the social scientists. Under such circumstances there is a better likelihood of minimizing the tensions inherent in researcher-practitioner relationships.

A final type of response, which, however, takes us away from this paper's major focus upon researcher-practitioner relations within a clinical agency, is the creation of a research unit within an academic, rather than a clinical, setting. Under such an arrangement, the practitioners may become the marginal men. But such an arrangement does serve to provide organizational support for abandoning one's traditional clinical role, so that, for example, psychiatrists will "modify their methods of inquiry to the special requirements of social research."[51]

It should be clear, however, that the formal strains that arise in the relationship between practitioner and researcher in a clinical agency are not dissipated by the appointment of practitioner–trained researchers or research-oriented practitioners. This is because the goals of the researcher and the practitioner differ. Regardless of who plays the roles, a certain amount of stress must be expected of their relationships.

The validity of our argument becomes clear when we examine situations in which the same person plays both roles. If what we have said about the tensions that arise between researcher and practitioner is correct, then one would expect to discover strains within the person who plays a dual researcher-practitioner role. In other words, one would expect to find a role–conflict situation, and this has been reported in the literature.

Perry and Wynne, for example, discuss the role of the clinical researcher in a research hospital. They point out that the clinical researcher faces "conflict between his role as therapist and his role as researcher." The role conflict is "built into his job."[52] Barnett discusses the difficulties of being both an anthropologist-researcher and an administrator with policy-making functions.[53] Holmberg, who was both the *patrón* of a Peruvian *hacienda* and a researcher, describes the difficulties of "playing the dual role of God and anthropologist."[54]

The most complete account of the strains inherent in the dual researcher-practitioner role is superbly portrayed by Fox, in her study of a group of clinical investigators and their patients.[55] The clinical investigators or research physicians had the dual responsibility of caring for patients with little-understood diseases and of conducting research upon them. Fox deals with the stresses that come from this kind of dual responsibility and with the ways in which the clinical investigators tried to cope with these stresses. It quickly becomes clear that the major factor underlying the stresses faced by the clinical investigators is the organization of their job—the fact that they have two roles to play, and that these roles are often at variance. As one of the clinical investigators said, "We're caught in an eternal conflict between being physician and medical researcher."[56]

## Summary and Conclusion

The relationship between researcher and practitioner may be plagued by a variety of problems, and personality factors are often cited as the core of these problems. On the one hand we hear of the "neurotic anxiety" of the practitioner when he is faced with research, and on the other hand we hear of the defective personality of the researcher who projects his own problems upon the clinical agency he is studying. Personality factors are not irrelevant, but they may often mask the nature of the role relationships between researcher and practitioner. It is the nature of this role relationship within a professional agency, and the strains that stem from this role relationship, that have been the primary focus of this paper.

The organizationally–structured stresses in the relationship between researcher and practitioner are too frequently overlooked. For example, there has been practically no discussion of the related questions of credit for publication and anonymity in the relationship between researcher and practitioner.[57] It is of little wonder, therefore, that the question is only rarely discussed by researcher and practitioner before and during their research collaboration, and that this often becomes one of the chronic and insidious problems in the relationship.

Other aspects of the formal role relationship of researcher and practitioner that we have discussed are the evaluating nature of the researcher's role, and his special tie to the administrator. Because of this, the practitioner feels that his work is being assessed by someone with a vested interest in discerning errors who is also in a position to report these errors to the administrator. In addition, the researcher's primary job is tangential to the practitioner's primary job, and they organize their time very differently—thus making it all the more difficult for them to understand each other and to collaborate effectively. As a member of the "staff" organization of the agency, the researcher finds himself in a marginal position, and this may intensify his ties to the administrator, and therefore add to the strain in his relationship with the practitioner.

Certain reactions to the strains between researcher and practitioner— denial and displacement on the part of the practitioner, the development of a one-way humor relationship, and various changes in the formal organization—have also been discussed. From this it becomes clear that, although some strain is inevitable in the relationship between researcher and practitioner, it is also possible to move toward alleviating this strain through a direct recognition of its most important source—the social organization of the clinical agency.

## NOTES

1. Many different variables are involved in the relationship between researcher and practitioner. Some of them are: the specific organizational setting; the composition of the researcher-practitioner group (e.g., the disciplines represented and the number from each discipline); the relative status of the discipline and the representatives of these disciplines; the source of support for the research and for the agency's clinical program; basic or applied research; length of time of the research project and the security of employment of the project members; the nature of the research being done; differences in value and in personality organization of the researchers and practitioners. We do not know any-

one who has systematically pursued the association of any of these variables to differences in the nature of the researcher-practitioner relationship. Although the following references focus more upon interdisciplinary research within the social sciences than upon researcher-practitioner relations, they do take note of some of the variables involved in collaborative efforts: Gordon W. Blackwell, "Multidisciplinary Team Research," *Social Forces*, 33 (May, 1955), 367–74; R. Richard Wohl, "Some Observations on the Social Organization of Interdisciplinary Social Science Research," *Social Forces*, 33 (May, 1955), 374–83; Margaret Barron Luszki, "Team Research in Social Science: Major Consequences of a

Growing Trend," *Human Organization,* 16 (Spring, 1957), 21–4.

2. Margaret Barron Luszki, *Interdisciplinary Team Research: Methods and Problems,* Washington, D.C.: National Training Laboratories, N.E.A., 1958.

3. Cf. Ozzie G. Simmons and James A. Davis, "Interdisciplinary Collaboration in Mental Illness Research," *American Journal of Sociology,* 63 (November, 1957), 297–303. Simmons and Davis point to the difference in methodological approach as the major barrier to collaboration. Some workers had a "clinical" point of view and some a "quantitative."

4. Margaret Blenkner, "Obstacles to Evaluative Research in Casework: Part I," *Social Casework,* 31 (February, 1950), 56.

5. Howard E. Mitchell and Emily H. Mudd, "Anxieties Associated With The Conduct of Research In A Clinical Setting," *American Journal of Orthopsychiatry,* 27 (April, 1957), 314.

6. *Ibid.,* p. 320. According to Young, researchers attribute problems in their relationships with practitioners to arrogance, narrow-mindedness, and authoritarianism in the practitioners' personalities. See Donald Young, "Sociology and the Practicing Professions," *American Sociological Review,* 20 (December, 1955), 647.

7. Urie Bronfenbrenner and Edward C. Devereux, "Interdisciplinary Planning for Team Research on Constructive Community Behavior," *Human Relations,* 5 (1952), 187–203: A major interdisciplinary problem was that the team members were initially person-centered rather than task-centered.

8. Since 1950 the Russell Sage Foundation has spurred the development of effective researcher-practitioner relations across many fields of social science and professional practice. For a general report of the problems and successes of this program, see *Annual Report 1958–1959* and *Annual Report 1959–1960,* New York: Russell Sage Foundation; see also Ralph L. Kolodny, "Research Planning and Group Work Practice," *Mental Hygiene,* 42 (January, 1958), 121–32; Hope Leichter and Judith Lieb, "Implications of a Research Experience with Caseworkers and Clients," *Journal of Jewish Communal Service,* 36 (Spring, 1960), 313–21.

9. Elizabeth Herzog, *Some Guide Lines For Evaluative Research,* Children's Bureau Publication, 375 (1959), 79.

10. *Evaluation and Mental Health,* Public Health Service Publication No. 413, Washington, D.C.: U.S. Department of Health, Education, and Welfare, 1955, p. 6.

11. "The Function and Practice of Research in Social Work," *Social Work Research Group* (May, 1955), 28.

12. Harold L. Wilensky and Charles N. Lebeaux, *Industrial Society and Social Welfare,* New York: Russell Sage Foundation, 1958, p. 20.

13. Stephen E. Fitzgerald, "Public Relations Learns to Use Research," *Public Opinion Quarterly,* 21 (Spring, 1957), 141–46.

14. Mary Wirth, *Social Service Review,* 33 (March, 1959), 102. Cf. Robert C. Angell, "A Research Basis for Welfare Practice," *Social Work Journal,* 35 (October, 1954), 145–8, 169–71.

15. Kaspar D. Naegele, "A Mental Health Project in a Boston Suburb," in Benjamin D. Paul and Walter B. Miller (eds.), *Health, Culture and Community,* New York: Russell Sage Foundation, 1955, 317.

16. Otto Pollak, "Comments," *Social Service Review,* 30 (September, 1956), 298.

17. Rudolf Ekstein and Robert S. Wallerstein, *The Teaching and Learning of Psychotherapy,* New York, Basic Books, 1958, p. 7.

18. Melville Dalton, "Conflicts Between Staff and Line Managerial Officers," *American Sociological Review*, 15 (June, 1950), 342 51.

19. Stuart Adams, "Status Congruency as a Variable in Small Group Performance," *Social Forces*, 32 (October, 1953), 16–22; George C. Homans, "Status Among Clerical Workers," *Human Organization*, 12 (Spring, 1953), 5–10; Gerhard Lenski, "Social Participation and Status Crystallization," *American Sociological Review*, 21 (August, 1956), 458–64; Gerd H. Fenchel, Jack H. Monderer, and Eugene L. Hartley, "Subjective Status and the Equilibration Hypothesis," *Journal of Abnormal and Social Psychology*, 46 (October, 1951), 476–9; Irwin W. Goffman, "Status Consistency and Preference for Change in Power Distribution," *American Sociological Review*, 22 (June, 1957), 275–281; Roland J. Pellegrino and Frederick L. Bates, "Congruity and Incongruity of Status Attributes within Occupation and Work Positions," *Social Forces*, 38 (October, 1959), 23–28.

20. Cf. Joseph W. Eaton and Robert J. Weil, "Psychotherapeutic Principles in Social Research," *Psychiatry*, 14 (November, 1951), 440–1.

21. Ekstein and Wallerstein, *op. cit.*, p. 6.

22. In one case we know of, the researchers' only recourse was to shift their interest from a comparison between experimental and control patients to a study of the resistance of the practitioners to the research project.

23. Florence Hollis, *Women in Marital Conflict*, New York: Family Service Association of America, 1949, 220–21. See also Margaret Blenkner, "Obstacles to Evaluative Research in Casework: Part II," *Social Casework*, 31 (March, 1950), 99.

24. Martin Wolins, "Comments," *Social Service Review*, 30 (September, 1956), 345; see also Margaret Blenkner, "Part II," *op. cit.*, p. 98.

25. F. Stuart Chapin, *Experimental Designs in Sociological Research*, New York: Harper, 1947, 168–69.

26. Ekstein and Wallerstein, *op. cit.*, p. 74–5.

27. Eleanor Gay, "Collecting Data by Case Recording," *Social Work*, 3 (January, 1958), 77.

28. Some discussions which refer to differences in attitudes or values of researchers and practitioners in particular, or which discuss researcher-practitioner relations in general are: Donald Young, "Sociology and the Practicing Professions," *American Sociological Review*, 20 (December, 1955), 641–8; Robert C. Angell, *op. cit.*; R. Richard Wohl, *op. cit.*; Lawrence K. Frank, "Research for What?", *Journal of Social Issues*, Supplement Series, No. 10 (1957); Mary E. W. Goss and George G. Reader, "Collaboration Between Sociologist and Physician," *Social Problems*, 4 (July, 1956), 82–9; Jurgen Ruesch, "Creation of a Multidisciplinary Team: Introducing the Social Scientist to Psychiatric Research," *Psychosomatic Medicine*, 18 (March–April, 1956), 105–12; Erika Chance, *Families in Treatment*, New York: Basic Books, 1959; Yngvar Løchen, "Some Experiences in Participant Observation from a Norwegian Mental Hospital Study," paper presented at Eastern Sociological Society meetings, New York, April, 1960. See also Frank L. Sweetser, "Sociology and Urban Renewal," *Alpha Kappa Deltan*, 28 (Winter, 1958), 42–7; W. L. Slocum, "Sociological Research for Action Agencies: Some Guides and Hazards," *Rural Sociology*, 21 (June, 1956), 196–9; Robert W. Lamson, "The Present Strains Between Science and Government," *Social Forces*, 33 (May, 1955), 360–67.

29. This is not altogether unlike the way in which men seem to underestimate

and women to overestimate the frequency of marital coitus. See Alfred C. Kinsey *et al., Sexual Behavior in the Human Female,* Philadelphia: W. B. Saunders, 1953, 349.

30. Researchers and practitioners can have a very different notion of the importance of writing the final report. As we point out further on, practitioners occasionally belittle the writing job, as in the phrase, "just writing."

31. Another problem of publication is the issue of censorship. Do any of the practitioners or administrators within the agency have the right to censor the researchers' publications? This issue is related to other variables, such as the type of agency involved and the source of research support. See Daniel J. Levinson, "The Mental Hospital as a Research Setting: A Critical Appraisal," in Milton Greenblatt, Daniel J. Levinson, and Richard H. Williams, (eds.), *The Patient and the Mental Hospital,* New York: Free Press, 1957, p. 641.

32. Mitchell and Mudd, *op. cit.,* p. 312. Cf. Paul C. Agnew and Francis L. K. Hsu, "Introducing Change in a Mental Hospital," *Human Organization,* 19 (Winter, 1960–61), 195–9.

33. William D. Schmidt, *The Executive and the Board in Social Welfare,* Cleveland: Howard Allen, Inc., 1959, 35–6.

34. See Daniel J. Levinson, *op. cit.,* pp. 633–49. Writing more generally about the position of the social sciences in medicine, Jaco points out the marginality of that position by indicating that most social scientists in medical schools are situated in low-status departments such as psychiatry, preventive medicine and public health, and nursing schools. E. Gartly Jaco, "Problems and Prospects of the Social Sciences in Medical Education," *Health and Human Behavior,* 1 (Spring, 1960), 29–34.

35. Lenski, in his discussion of status inconsistency (the lack of status crystallization), relates it to marginality. Gerhard E. Lenski, "Status Crystallization: A Nonvertical Dimension of Social Status," *American Sociological Review,* 19 (August, 1954), 412.

36. Cf. Donald Young, *op. cit.*

37. Sol Tax, "The Fox Project," *Human Organization,* 17 (Spring, 1958), 18.

38. Charlotte Towle, "Implications of Contemporary Human and Social Values for Selection of Social Work Students," *Social Service Review,* 33 (September, 1959), 262.

39. *Ibid.* Unlike Towle, Gordon feels such a development is unfortunate. Noting that circumstances have favored "the moving into social work research of (researchers) who were already well identified with the aims, objectives and values of social work and most informed about it," and have discouraged "those from entering this field whose identification with social work was neutral or possibly negative" he warns that, "researchers may have become so much like social workers in general that their capacity to contribute to the profession has been impaired." William E. Gordon, "The Future of Social Work Research," *Social Work,* 3 (October, 1958), 99–106.

40. As we have already discussed, this is similar to the researcher who attributes the difficulties in his relationships with the practitioner to the practitioner's personality. The reader interested in material related to this tendency to explain problems of social organization by focusing upon psychological factors should consult: C. Wright Mills, *The Sociological Imagination,* New York, Oxford University Press, 1959, pp. 8–11, 186–188, *et passim;* Robert N. Rapoport, "Notes on the Disparagement of 'Sociologizing' in Collaborative Research," *Human Organization,* 16 (Spring, 1957), 14–15; Alfred H. Stanton and Morris S. Schwartz, *The*

*Mental Hospital,* New York: Basic Books, 1954, p. 39; Peter M. Blau, *The Dynamics of Bureaucracy,* Chicago: University of Chicago Press, 1955, pp. 54–5. Personalities, of course, may be defective, and we do not mean to imply otherwise. Luszki, for example, points out that "often problems resulting from the individual personality are erroneously attributed to the discipline." Margaret Barron Luszki, *Interdisciplinary Team Research: Methods and Problems, op. cit.,* p. 50.

41. The marginality implied here becomes apparent when one considers that the researcher is placed in the highly ambiguous position of being a doctor without patients or a professor without a class.

42. Chris Argyris, "Creating Effective Research Relationships in Organizations," *Human Organization,* 17 (Spring, 1958), 35.

43. A. R. Radcliffe-Brown, *Structure and Function in Primitive Society,* New York: Free Press, 1952, pp. 90–104.

44. Rose Laub Coser, "Laughter Among Colleagues," *Psychiatry,* 23 (February, 1960), 81–95.

45. See Rose Laub Coser, "Some Social Functions of Laughter," *Human Relations,* 12 (1959), 171–82.

46. A beautiful illustration of joking within a group of research physicians is given by Fox. In at least some of the illustrations, the "researcher" seems to be joking about the physician's role; in most other instances, the "physician" seems to be joking about the researcher's role. And even where it is not possible to specify the direction of the humor of these research physicians, much of the humor is seen to reflect, and tends to overcome, the role conflict. Renéc C. Fox, *Experiment Perilous,* New York: Free Press, 1959, pp. 63–4, 76–82.

47. Robert N. Rapoport, *op. cit.,* p. 15. Cf. Jurgen Ruesch, *op. cit.,* p. 110.

48. See *Annual Report 1958–1959* and *Annual Report 1959–1960,* New York: Russell Sage Foundation.

49. "The Function and Practice of Research in Social Work," *Social Work Research Group* (May, 1955); Margaret Blenkner, "Part I," *op. cit.,* p. 59.

50. Emily H. Mudd, "Knowns and Unknowns in Marriage Counseling Research," *Marriage and Family Living,* 19 (February, 1957), 78.

51. Joseph W. Eaton and Robert J. Weil, *op. cit.,* p. 452.

52. Stewart E. Perry and Lyman C. Wynne, "Role Conflict, Role Redefinition, and Social Change in a Clinical Research Organization," *Social Forces,* 38 (October, 1959), 62–5.

53. H. G. Barnett, "Anthropology as an Applied Science," *Human Organization,* 17 (Spring, 1958), 9–11.

54. Allan R. Holmberg, "The Research and Development Approach to the Study of Change," *Human Organization,* 17 (Spring, 1958), 12–16.

55. Renée C. Fox, *op. cit.*

56. *Ibid.,* p. 62.

57. In Luszki's summarizing report of five conferences on the problems of interdisciplinary team research, involving one hundred and seven research workers, only four lines are devoted to the question of research publication, and even these are not specific to the researcher-practitioner relationship. Margaret Barron Luszki, *Interdisciplinary Team Research: Methods and Problems, op. cit.,* p. 215.

# 9.    Social Research and the

# Pan-American Health Organization

NICHOLAS J. DEMERATH

THIS IS THE REPORT OF A CONSULTANCY AND A survey which has certain implications for social research in Latin America. In recent years, individual anthropologists have been employed for brief periods by the Pan-American Health Organization executive arm, the Pan-American Sanitary Bureau. The Bureau is also the World Health Organization's regional office for the Americas. Typically, the administrator of one of the regional offices identified a need for anthropological help and added a U.S. anthropologist to his staff. The anthropologist would complete one or more ethnographic surveys, offer certain advice, and depart— not always in agreement with the policy decisions and actions of Bureau personnel. There had been differences between anthropologists and administrators over matters of appropriate responsibility, recognition and prestige, freedom of publication, usefulness of reports, and advice.

## The Problem

After one rather hectic separation, the Director General, concerned about the utilization of social science in the agency, decided to retain a consultant. As first stated to me, the consultant, "the problem" was to account for the Bureau's experiences with anthropology and anthropologists. My preliminary reconnaisance led to a reformulation: What were the Bureau's social research needs and how should the agency provide administratively for tackling them? My guiding hunch was fourfold. (1) Past interpersonal, interprofessional difficulties were attributable chiefly to structural factors. (2) Administrative planning and action might better be put primarily in a context of structural rather than personal manipulation. (3) Anthropologists were no more likely than other social scientists or nonhealth personnel to encounter difficulties under existing conditions. (4) Finally, an identification of applied social research and administrative needs broadly conceived, and to be developed by Bureau personnel guided by the consultant, was the way into the problem as reformulated.

## Method

Interviews, both group and private, were conducted from time to time with 220 of the Bureau's personnel and about 30 outsiders between November 1956 and October 1958. The objectives were to tap experiences and thinking on social research needs, utilization, and previous experience with social scientists—chiefly anthropologists. The procedure was semi-structured and informal. Interviewees were selected to reflect (1) operating programs, (2) health specialties, (3) organizational levels, (4) regional differences, and (5) ancillary institutions in Latin America. Interviews were conducted in Spanish as far as possible, recorded promptly and in detail. My data analysis was grossly qualitative, the idea being to locate uniformities in and patterns of course. Familiarity with operating programs and organizational character was gained by direct observation, reading, and a great deal of travel.

In November and December, 1957, my wife and I visited the zone (regional) offices, certain projects, and counterpart activities in Guatemala and Mexico. My wife served as an observer of maternal and child clinics, certain household practices and the way of life, when her experience as mother and wife and nursery educator led her to see and ask about many things I would have missed. My spoken Spanish, long unused, became passable toward the end of the first eight weeks' journey. Then, during the period from June to August of 1958, I visited zone offices and health projects in Colombia, Peru, Bolivia, Chile, Argentina, Paraguay, Brazil, Venezuela, and Puerto Rico. On returning from both trips, numerous discussions were held with the Washington staff. The Latin American visits took me into schools of public health, the national ministries, projects of integrated health services, health centers and clinics, hospitals, and all of the zone offices.

## Nicholas J. Demerath

I had the benefit of an *ad hoc* committee of anthropologists composed of Professors Benjamin Paul, Ozzie G. Simmons, and Edward Wellin of the Harvard School of Public Health, Professor George Foster of the University of California at Berkeley, Professor Richard N. Adams of Michigan State University, and Professor John P. Gillin of the University of North Carolina. All are specialists in Latin American culture and all have had experience with intercultural health programs in some of the countries. We corresponded and held one meeting in Chicago in December, 1957, during the annual meeting of the American Anthropological Society.

## Results

The findings included two types of needs for applied research: (1) operating programs, (2) internal administration. Another product was an administrative plan for a regularized research facility in the Pan-American Sanitary Bureau.

#### A. SOCIAL RESEARCH IN SUPPORT OF HEALTH PROGRAMS

In connection with the various health programs and services visited, there were numerous statements of social research needs. To enumerate and illustrate all of them here would, in itself, require a paper much longer than this one. Suffice it to say that most of the suggestions pertained to a great variety of *barriers to more effective work* in maternal and child health, nutrition, nurses' training, medical and public health schools, malaria eradication, hospital administration, dentistry, etc. The barriers involved nonscientific ideas of illness and medicine, the position of "popular medicine," value conflicts, communicational failures, incorrect perceptions, inadequate motivations, and tactical failures by health personnel. A few brief illustrations are in order.

Let us consider *malaria eradication* where, as one man said, it might seem that people are rather "automatically converted to the benefits of the program." Actually, eight critical cultural impingements were noted in a conference with four malariologists.

1. There are the difficulties of blood sampling; beliefs that each drop of blood lost is absolutely irreplaceable; that the loss of blood reduces one's powers irrevocably, that blood taken in the parasite surveys will go to someone else; and the beliefs about male virility, "strong blood" versus "weak blood".

2. There are the difficulties of access to the house. Doors have been

*116*

slammed in the faces of malaria teams in various regions. In the special surveys, barriers to access are the more critical because the teams must go back into the house every couple of weeks to check.

3. There are the barriers to scientific explanation of the causal sequence: the beliefs that malaria is caused by eating cane or by eating mangoes and the like, rather than the belief that it is caused by mosquitoes.

4. There is the problem of marking houses that have been sprayed. Various beliefs about colors and numbers posed difficulties because survey markings must be both clear and permanent. For example, in Haiti the colors red and blue are taboo, being associated with witchcraft. Furthermore, certain numbers—the number 13 in Haiti and 41 in Mexico—must be avoided. There was one case in Haiti where the individual simply moved his house when it was given number 13 by the eradication team.

Still other sociocultural barriers to malaria control operations—cleaning, moving, spraying—may also apply to other health programs as well. For example,

5. There are beliefs involving matters of familial authority. In some cultures, the wife alone cannot give consent to having the house sprayed; only the man of the house may do this. Yet, in order for him to discuss the matter with the eradication team, he must often lose a day's work and pay.

6. There are beliefs and practices related to sacred places and things in the house—the altar, the fireplace. In certain parts of Mexico, for instance, the placing of the umbilical cord in the fireplace is believed to determine the size of the infant's genitalia.

7. The loss of scarce animals, especially chickens and goats, is feared in some places. Some of these animals are also used in voodoo rituals so they have a value beyond their simple economic worth.

8. Violation of community power structures pose difficulties. For example, in Mexico it may be unwise to ask the mayor to give his support to the eradication program because he is generally the man chosen by the dominant national party and may not, necessarily, represent or even tie into the actual leadership of the community.

Malaria people reported that in one country where eradication was planned some time ago, there was a three week course on movie projectors —their operation and maintenance—but almost nothing on the human aspects of the program. A million dollars a year was spent for malaria eradication, but the public information job, it was said, was unsatisfactory because of inadequate awareness of human relations. And some routines violated good sense. For example, in one program it was decided to make the key people in various communities "honorary, voluntary health educators." They were given certificates signed by the Minister of Health, recognizing "devoted service in behalf of the malaria campaign." But these certificates were sometimes given *before* the people had actually done anything for the malaria program!

There were numerous illustrations of cultural barriers and misunderstandings in the *maternal and child health and nutrition programs*. In Colombia, for example, it was reported that food given by C.A.R.E. had been rather amusingly misused. The dry milk was used to powder the lines for football or soccer fields by the local citizenry; and the cheese, because it was soft and sweet, rather than the salty hard variety the people were used to, was fed to the chickens.

Less frequently cited than the program obstacles noted above, but no less significant, are needs for technical *aid in using and developing human organizations for accomplishing public health objectives*. Here we refer to those groups of people, and structures of leadership, influence and prestige that either facilitate or frustrate the accomplishment of health objectives. The fact is that every human population is organized no matter how impoverished, illiterate, or "primitive" it may appear by urban-western standards. There are social strata and "natural" groupings even without formal or administered groups. And some individuals or families always have more power, more prestige, and more influence than others. Although they recognize this in theory, quite a few health workers deal with their client populations as though they were undifferentiated masses without social organization. The behavioral scientist can make a real contribution, at this point, in simply getting across the fact that there *are* organizations, and helping to identify them. The methods of identifying these community structures may be systematic, or they may be quite informal but nonetheless effective.

For example, in Colombia, near Cali, a professor of medicine described a systematic leadership study of a community of 18,000 people that has proved invaluable in a variety of ways. When a health team wanted proctoscopies and rectosigmoldescopies, they simply went to the informal or natural leaders that had been identified in the study, and the leaders went and got them without difficulty.

In some places, to be sure, the social organization is so minimal that no program—health or any other kind—can be very effectively or efficiently conducted. This is the case with the recently immigrated and rapidly growing masses in large Latin American cities. Here the problem is one of community development, as well as of identification of the minimal organizations which have grown up naturally. In the past thirty years in the United States, the deliberate development of community organizations has become the specialty of numerous applied social scientists, social workers, and health specialists. With the coming of technical assistance programs, these community development people have adapted their technique to problems such as village aid in Pakistan and India with considerable practical effect.

A well-known problem of health organization is *the position of the professional or technician* in many Latin American countries. Often, in governmental affairs, politicians and administrators disregard or do not seek professional or technical advice. But in Latin America, there is some reason to believe that the empirically minded professional gets fewer hearings than his colleagues in the United States and Europe. In one country, physicians told us that there was no need for more hospital buildings. There were already hospitals and health centers, amply equipped, that could not be opened for want of qualified personnel. However, the politicians wanted more buildings to impress their constituencies, and proceeded to commit several millions more to what has been called "facadismo." Though the Pan-American Health Organization (PAHO) has already given much attention to improving the professional's position, it will be a long-term effort, necessarily, and one to which social scientists may well contribute.

Briefly, we would comment on the PAHO's *health education programs.* The needs of organization for health and health programs suggest more work with community groups, the careful utilization of existing community structures and the development of new ones where necessary. This does not mean less reliance on publication and mass media, but requires, in addition, more concentration on person–to–person contact, for there is considerable evidence that attitudes and habits may be changed more effectively through group situations.

*Experimentation with different procedures or program alternatives* is needed. Advice based on descriptive knowledge can be helpful, but where controlled comparisons are possible, they should be made. It is hardly surprising that medical scientists should ask for such inquiries. For example, in the field of nutrition at the Institute for Nutrition, Central America and Panama (INCAP) at Guatemala City, the director discussed the possibilities of experimenting with various techniques of communication and persuasion under controlled conditions. The problem was to discover the most effective means for gaining acceptance of an all-purpose food and, correspondingly, aiding its commercial production. Even in the field of malaria eradication, it was suggested that experimentation with different training methods and contents would ·tell us something about eradication approaches as well as the efficacy of some social science instruction. In general, such experimentation is the surest method for testing new policies and procedures in any kind of organized effort. The "dry run," also, is the best basis for informed review and planning.

Certain needs and opportunities exist in the *educational programs of several schools of medicine and public health* with PAHO ties. In Mexico City, the school of public health has employed local anthropologists on a part-time basis to lecture to their students. These anthropologists also aid the field experiences of the public health students and faculty. To date, the contributions seem limited mainly to descriptive ethnographic survey materials dealing with rural areas and with Indian peoples. Yet, there is a faculty opinion that far more attention should go to the conditions and ways of life of urban populations, beginning with Mexico City itself. Here, and elsewhere, there is the hope that behavioral scientists might be able to advise on the health problems of a country, a region, or a class of people, or communities, rather than a single small society or tribe. In other words, generalizations are needed. This in turn requires more powerful theory and abstraction of a sort rather recently developed, as well as studies of urban life in the burgeoning cities of Latin America.

At the medical school in Cali, Colombia, the department of preventive medicine has utilized social science aid in community analysis and development work, a central element of their health effort. On Rockefeller funds, a full-time social anthropologist from the United States was appointed in 1958. He was to work with nutrition surveys and also impart, through certain courses required of all medical students there, anthropological viewpoints and concepts. Personnel exchanges with other universities and schools, both in Latin America and in the United States, are encouraged here. A United States anthropologist resident in Lima on a USPHS research grant, lectured for six weeks at the new medical school in Arequipa, Peru, as a consequence of a friendship with a faculty member. There are other instances of informal arrangements between public health personnel and several competent social scientists, most of whom have been associated with Cornell in its Vicos project. For example, the director of a health center 40 miles from Lima enjoys the friendly advice of an anthropologist he has known for several years, but sees rarely, since he is now located at Cuzco, a good distance from the health center. The man who has recently lectured at Arequipa has also given a course at the University of San Marcos which, it was reported, attracted medical students there.

In Chile, the School of Public Health at the University of Santiago sought the appointment of a full-time social scientist to augment a part-time arrangement with staff of the Institute of Sociology at the University of Chile. The Ministry of Health, in its health education program, employed a folklorist whose knowledge of varied ways of life, ranging from remote Indian communities to Santiago, is impressive. In the School of Medicine at the University of Chile, the professor of physiology planned a teaching program in "medical anthropology." The Institute of Sociology, financed by the University and by UNESCO, represents one of the few real concentrations of social research talent to be found in all of Latin America. In 1958, there were four full-time sociologists with expertness in survey and related research techniques. These may have completed a number of competent and significant field inquiries. With planning and financial support, their inquiries might cover health problems from time to time.

In Rio de Janeiro, there is a Center for Social Science Research, supported by the Brazilian government and by UNESCO, which engages in cooperative work with the Institute of Sociology in Santiago. The potential for health research here resembled that of Santiago, though the staff is more heterogeneous, including economists and political scientists, as well as sociologists and anthropologists.

### B. INTERNAL MANAGEMENT AND ORGANIZATION

A second type of applied research and development was needed, said our informants, on the Bureau's *internal management and organization.* As with any agency so far-flung, operationally complex, and culturally heterogeneous as this one—and notwithstanding its distinguished history as the oldest international health agency—there was room for more effective methods of (1) personnel selection, training, assignment, (2) communications, (3) motivation and morale maintenance, and (4) review and planning. In connection with the latter two, the services of public policy economists and health economists were indicated for the following matters: What should be the relationships between health programs and the societies and economies in which they are conducted? How can these be seen and stated more clearly? In planning a health effort, what about the economy of the country? Can it afford this health program? Can the economy support a larger, healthier population? What are the connections between advancing health levels, overpopulation, economic growth and development? Still other policy questions were suggested for health and behavioral scientists and economists. Will a health program endanger traditional values presently beneficial for the people in question? Will a given program contribute to further "de-Latinization" and thus exacerbate problems of life adjustment for masses of people? How can long-range, extensive programs be broken down and translated into components useful and meaningful to individuals and work groups, month by month and year by year?

## Administrative Plan and Recommendations

A strategy by which the Bureau could establish a continuous research service was developed on the basis of the survey and of planning with several top Bureau administrators. Acting as a secretary and stimulator, I sought, through the survey and review of field findings, to conduct a kind of review and planning effort in which a variety of health specialists, administrators and social scientists all participated. Involvement of those who would execute the plan was a principal objective, of course. Predictable scarcities of qualified manpower and financing were kept in mind. It was thought that the way to begin was with one or two visibly and measurably successful applications to carefully delimited problems that would demonstrate the practical values of social research. There were four elements to the plan.

1. The place of social research in Bureau operations should be spelled out both philosophically and administratively. Primarily, social scientists would be employed to serve health programs as research specialists and not as health administrators or health specialists. The social scientist, within broad dictates of program impingement and resources, would enjoy autonomy in research planning and execution, but recognize the necessity to use and relate the health expertness of his colleagues. The health specialists, in turn, should not expect magical accomplishments. Easy contact and collaboration between social scientists and health professionals inside and outside the Bureau is to be desired. Notions of social scientists as exotic personages, as strangers, as sources of threat, and the like should be dissipated as quickly as possible. In addition, Bureau research should commonly, if not always, create new knowledge capital for the advancement of theoretical social science. Thus, scholarly publications and contacts should be supported if they are consistent with the primary purpose—applied research.

2. Two kinds of social science positions were recommended; headquarter and field positions, where personnel would be attached to the regional staffs and assigned for research to specific operating projects and programs, respectively. Appointees would rotate between the two fre-

quently enough to learn the duties, skills, and resources of both sets of positions, but not so often as to impair continuity or quality of performance. The two kinds of jobs would be reinforcing and complementary, and at least two appointments—one in each type position—should be made to initiate the activity. One social scientist alone in a large health organization is likely to be submerged to the point of losing his professional identity and, hence, his real professional potential to the organization.

3. By working with foundations, national governments, graduate schools, schools of medicine and public health throughout the Americas, and especially in Latin America, to improve social science education and the education of social scientists, the Bureau might well help to alter certain general conditions of science and society which now have a negative effect on the performance of its mission. We refer to the shortage of full-time social scientists who are versed in modern research methods and who recognize the interdependence of systematic theoretical and applied work—a shortage especially critical now in Latin America. And we refer also to the dearth of full-time positions at competitive salaries and prestige levels for such people there.

4. Finally, the director general of the Bureau should have an outside social science advisory committee to guide and support the matters noted above. This committee should be composed of distinguished social scientists from Latin America and elsewhere, and a minority of distinguished health professionals with social-medicine orientations.

## Subsequent Developments

Soon after the work from 1956 to 1959 was completed and the recommendations made, certain officials of the Bureau became apprehensive about the pay-off of research, still fearing there might be "too much theory." The Director General, who requested my help, was succeeded by a new man. Then, two top administrators who were committed to the plan left, one to Geneva and one to a United States university. The new Director General for perfectly good reasons, was occupied with health and economy questions for some time. But, I regarded this situation as one of "unfinished business;" kept in touch with old acquaintances in the Bureau, and made new ones. I was curious about the fate of the earlier findings and the resulting plan. Also, I felt a responsibility to my informants in the Bureau and in the countries, and to my *ad hoc* advisory group, to keep an eye on the possibilities.

In 1960, my colleagues and I at Washington University had established our Medical Care Research Center with multidisciplinary attention to the administrative sciences, health and medical care. Then, early in 1961, conversations with Bureau officials indicated certain needs for practical studies and consultation to which some resources of our Center might be appropriately adapted. Now, however, we speak of operational analysis, practical studies, planning, review,—not "research." We have begun to work together, but where the new path may lead is unknown. Of only one thing are we sure: we are parties to a process, not to an open-and-shut job.

# Part III

# CASE STUDIES

# IN APPLIED

# SOCIAL SCIENCE

## 10. The Emergence of Pluralistic Public Opinion in a Community Crisis

WARREN BREED

THIS CASE STUDY OF A BIG CITY IN TRANSITION WILL be presented in five parts: (*1*) a brief theoretical introduction presenting the notions of "public opinion process" and "pluralistic structure"; (*2*) the setting—relevant facts about the city; (*3*) the distribution of individual opinions about the issue; (*4*) the body of the report, dealing with groups: the early unsuccessful groups, the new single-purpose moderation groups, existing groups supporting moderation, the power elite, and prosegregation groups resisting change; and (*5*) an analysis of the process of conflict and development of an opposition faction.

The case of New Orleans is perhaps quite similar to others in the South, and in various "underdeveloped areas," in which a previously underprivileged and disenfranchised group finally achieves representation in the arena of pluralistic opinion-making. The question of greatest interest to social science is the *process* of change and although this report must fail in the attempt to describe the process completely, it is hoped that further study will be encouraged by what is told here.

*Theoretical Background of Community Decision-Making*

How does a big city resolve a crisis involving all of its citizens? What causes a community to abandon century-old patterns of social relationships? What are the factors which affect the actions of various segments of the system during conflict? These are basic questions about social structure, social process and social change. The New Orleans school desegregation crisis of 1960 presented us with an opportunity to examine such a problem first-hand.

For the two central concepts of structure and process we take our theoretical basis from two existing notions. For "structure," the work of MacIver, Truman, Kornhouser and others maintains that societies can take various forms—folk, totalitarian, mass, pluralistic, etc.—and that pluralism is the western ideal.[1] A pluralistic structure contains many groups representing a large proportion of the members of society, each group expressing itself on public issues and thereby mediating changes in the relationships among the groups.

The second area of concern, "process," is formed more specifically by the theory of public opinion, especially the theory of the formation of public opinion.[2] A significant contribution was made by MacIver when he broadened the notion of public opinion to include these three elements: ground of consensus, structure of communication, and opinion alignment. The first includes the traditional "culture" of a group, its values and institutionalized patterns. The third refers to the distribution of individual opinions, as seen in opinion polls. We will refer to both of these elements of public opinion, but will emphasize the second element: the structure of communication within and among groups operating in the community to work out a solution to an issue. Whether or not structural change occurs will depend upon the outcome of the process.

According to the existing theory of public opinion formation, when two or more sides are formed on an issue in a community, much intercommunication will flow through and across groups—both primary and secondary groups. Arguments and dealings on both sides will be based upon existing institutions ("ground of consensus") and new interests and developments. Finally, after much discussion at many levels of the system, a solution is reached. If both sides are strong, compromises can be effected, but the debate cannot last forever and the solution sets policy at least temporarily.[3]

## New Orleans 1960

*The Setting.* The central fact about New Orleans in early 1960, according to the structure just described, was that it was not pluralistic on the race issue. Fuller demonstration of this condition is given later in this report. Certain other salient characteristics of the city will be presented here.

The population of New Orleans in 1960 was 627,525. The public schools enrolled some 92,000 children, the Roman Catholic schools about 49,000. Private schools—many having sprung up in response to threatened desegregation—taught several thousand more. The Negro proportion of the community was 37 per cent (a higher ratio than is found in other cities which had experienced desegregation problems). The proportion of Negro children in the public school system was about 57 per cent. Unlike most southern cities, New Orleans is ethnically heterogeneous, with large French, Italian, German, Irish and other nationality backgrounds. But these elements had become considerably assimilated by 1960, thus were not potential "pluralistic" groups. Roman Catholics constituted almost two-thirds of the white population.

A NAACP suit to desegregate the public schools had been filed in 1952. NAACP lawyers had not rushed the matter, but had accommodated to a long, gradual, legal process, which reached the lower federal courts and the United States Supreme Court 37 times. Few Orleanians knew much about the suit during the 1950's, as shown by surveys. Thus when Federal Judge J. Skelly Wright, himself an Orleanian, finally decreed desegregation in May 1960, the shock was considerable, even though only the first grade in a few schools would be affected. The remainder of this report describes what followed. We will confine our attention entirely to the white community.[4]

### THE DISTRIBUTION OF INDIVIDUAL OPINIONS ON THE ISSUE

Several sets of data show the existence of a strong prosegregationist sentiment in the city, although opinions were found to shift over time. A city cross-sectional survey done at Newcomb College in 1958, using a probability sample, showed the following distribution of answers to a question as to what the respondent thought the school system should do.

|  | Per cent |
|---|---|
| Should never desegregate, regardless of legal orders | 44 |
| Should desegregate only when the court specifies it and all delaying measures are exhausted | 27 |
| Should be considering the pros and cons of desegregation | 10 |
| Should start planning now for eventual desegregation | 15 |
| Should plan to desegregate some grades within the next 1–5 years | 5 |

On May 4, 1960, the school board announced the results of a postal card ballot they had sent to parents of public school children.

|  | White | Negro |
|---|---|---|
| Prefer to keep schools open though desegregated | 2,707 | 11,407 |
| Close schools before desegregated | 12,299 | 679 |
| Per cent of ballots returned | 61.37 | 47.03 |

Thus, as the time of decision neared, "popular" opinion—as represented by the parents of white children—had swung even further (82 per cent) toward a segregation-at-any-cost position.

A final index of opinion is found in the November 8, 1960, election for the school board. Mr. Sutherland, incumbent member, who had supported the board's decision of the summer to accept the court order and admit token desegregation, won re-election. He received 55,491 votes, against his three segregationist opponents, who tallied 31,176, 10,041, and 2,818 votes respectively. (It is important to note that while the Citizens' Councils fought Sutherland, he was backed by prominent business and professional men and by an intense telephone campaign, conducted by many of the women who had worked for open schools earlier in the year.)

From these data we can conclude that most Orleanians were for segregation, and that few were for integration. At least 44 per cent (in the poll) were bitter-enders, and as many as 82 per cent of the parents (in the postal ballot) preferred no schools to some desegregation. That segregation was strongly legitimized and institutionalized in the community is seen in this extensiveness of opinions and in the declarations of most community leaders.

What we cannot know from these data is the intensity and depth of individual opinions. From other observations, however, we know that at least some Orleanians felt the issue very deeply. The women who kicked and spat at parents taking their children to the two desegregated schools; the persons who made obscene and threatening telephone calls; the men and women who responded with aggressive emotions to speakers at Citizens' Council rallies; the persons who worked many hours to defeat desegregation; the thousands of parents who spent several hundreds of dollars to send a child to a private school rather than keep him in the public schools; the several who went to their clergyman for troubled conferences about their feelings; those who chose the strongest of the five alternatives on the poll question and added their own volunteered epithets to the interviewer —these Orleanians felt the issue and the threat of change very deeply.

After these, there was the large majority of segregationists by cultural transmission—they were raised in the South; those who held no particular feelings but went along with the majority through something like "pluralistic ignorance"; some who said little; and finally those willing to desegregate.

Thus individual opinions were crystallized well before 1960. The large majority of citizens favored segregation, and a relative handful, integration.

### SHIFTING THE EMPHASIS TO THE GROUP

Having suggested the range of popular opinion, can we now assume that the schools would close, short of military force? To do so would mean, of course, the neglect of certain other crucial elements in community decision-making. Principally, we refer here to the phenomenon variously thought of as leadership, authority, or power. It is true that such power may simply reflect majority opinion. But it also may rest more heavily on the activities of smaller segments of the community—groups and leaders— who are able to wield crucial effective power at key moments. The discussion will now turn away from "popular opinion" to the activities of these other elements, especially as they are seen to vault the barrier of an old tradition of silent acquiescence into the forum of discussion. At all times, the reader should remember that strong resistance to change will pervade the community.

### THE FAILURE OF ANTISEGREGATION GROUPS BEFORE 1960

In early 1960, not a single white moderate group supported even token desegregation publicly. This in itself is a remarkable fact in an old, large, and heterogeneous population. Not that people had not tried.

A year or two after the 1954 court decision, three separate groups formed for the purpose of exploring problems expected to arise with the shift to desegregation. All of the groups failed. An organization backed by the Catholic hierarchy published pamphlets and presented a series of excellent speakers, but attendance was negligible and nothing further was tried. A state affiliate of the Southern Regional Council also foundered. The Citizens Forum on Integration, a biracial group composed predominantly of social workers, professors and other "southern liberals" offered nationally-known speakers from successfully desegregated areas. This group was jolted by the charge that one of its leaders was linked with Communist fronts, and here again attendance declined to the point of discouragement and eventual dissolution.

Meanwhile, the Roman Catholic archbishop had announced impending desegregation of the parochial schools. The reaction from parishoners was swift and powerful, taking the form of decreasing or discontinuing contributions to the church and failing to honor pledges for capital projects. Parochial school desegregation was postponed—until 1962.

The major organized group behind this resistance to change was the (white) Citizens' Council. This group will be discussed after our treatment of the rise of moderation.

These failures epitomize the situation. Orleanians were not ready to change. In the period between 1957 and 1960, New Orleans harbored no organized activity which even considered the problems related to desegregation. Scattered actions by the state chapter of the American Civil Liberties Union, by an occasional group of clergy, and by a few individuals constituted the total antisegregation force publicly expressed by the white population. For all practical purposes the "monopoly of propaganda" and of organization was complete.[5]

**Table 1—The Emergence of Moderate Groups: Number of Column-Inches Devoted to Groups and Interests from February to December 1,[a] for Moderation (Open Schools) and for Segregation.**

| ACTION BY: | FEB. Seg. | FEB. Mod. | MAY 1-15 Seg. | MAY 1-15 Mod. | MAY 16-31 Seg. | MAY 16-31 Mod. | JUNE Seg. | JUNE Mod. | JULY Seg. | JULY Mod. | AUG. Seg. | AUG. Mod. |
|---|---|---|---|---|---|---|---|---|---|---|---|---|
| Pressure Groups[c] | 0 | 0 | 8 | 0 | 66 | 22 | 110 | 122 | 210 | 90 | 285 | 320 |
| Churchmen | 0 | 0 | 0 | 0 | 0 | 0 | 0 | 92 | 0 | 116 | 0 | 85 |
| Educators | 0 | 0 | 0 | 0 | 0 | 0 | 0 | 0 | 0 | 26 | 39 | 58 |
| Business | 0 | 0 | 0 | 0 | 0 | 0 | 0 | 0 | 0 | 0 | 12 | 7 |
| Labor | 0 | 0 | 0 | 0 | 0 | 0 | 0 | 0 | 0 | 0 | 0 | 21 |
| School Board[d] | 0 | 0 | 18 | 2 | 26 | 0 | 88 | 18 | 112 | 26 | 68 | 51 |
| State Politicians | 0 | 0 | 0 | 0 | 186 | 0 | 52 | 0 | 170 | 12 | 347 | 0 |
| Orleans Politicians | 0 | 0 | 0 | 0 | 0 | 0 | 0 | 0 | 0 | 0 | 2 | 0 |
| Courts[e] | 0 | 0 | 0 | 18 | 0 | 4 | 36 | 14 | 134 | 38 | 0 | 202 |
| Other | 0 | 0 | 14 | 0 | 18 | 0 | 10 | 44 | 0 | 12 | 75 | 126 |
| TOTAL | 0 | 0 | 40 | 20 | 296 | 26 | 296 | 290 | 626 | 320 | 828 | 870 |

a All data taken from the *New Orleans Times-Picayune*. The months of August and November were read every day; for the other time periods, papers were read every other day, from a random start, and weighted. All pages were read. The paper did an objective job covering both sides.
b November is divided because a new phase started on Nov. 16, the day of street rioting by segregationists protesting the original desegregation of two schools on Nov. 14. May is divided, as explained in the text, because Judge Wright's decision came on May 16.

# The Emergence of Pluralistic Public Opinion

## The Influence of an Event: The Court Decision

Judge Wright's federal court decision was the bugle call heralding the showdown. By the end of May the issue was clear to those who confronted the facts: permit token desegregation or close the schools. In the terms of public opinion theory, Judge Wright's ruling was the "event" that produced the necessity for community action. We shall examine what happened from the standpoint of the emergence and dynamics of groups seeking to maintain another structural element common to all cities in the nation, the public school system.

Table 1 presents the direction and rate of change and the elements producing the change. To suggest the precipitous climb of public activity unloosed by Judge Wright's decision, the month of February and the first 15 days in May are given; they show a level of zero activity in February and not very much more during the first half of May. This relative quiet can represent the "before" part of the natural "experiment."

**Table 1 (Continued)—The Emergence of Moderate Groups: Number of Column-Inches Devoted to Groups and Interests from February to December 1,[a] for Moderation (Open Schools) and for Segregation.**

| SEPT. | | OCT. | | NOV. 1–15 | | NOV. 16–30[b] | | DEC. 1–15 | | TOTAL | |
|---|---|---|---|---|---|---|---|---|---|---|---|
| Seg. | Mod. | Seg. | Mod. | Seg. | Mod. | Seg. | Mod. | Seg. | Mod. | Seg. | Mod. |
| 76 | 20 | 42 | 0 | 58 | 198 | 157 | 89 | 160 | 36 | 1172 | 897 |
| 0 | 0 | 0 | 0 | 0 | 42 | 0 | 26 | 0 | 12 | 0 | 373 |
| 0 | 0 | 0 | 40 | 0 | 20 | 29 | 129 | 28 | 38 | 96 | 311 |
| 0 | 0 | 0 | 0 | 0 | 16 | 0 | 12 | 0 | 8 | 12 | 43 |
| 0 | 0 | 0 | 4 | 0 | 8 | 0 | 8 | 0 | 0 | 0 | 41 |
| 8 | 26 | 28 | 60 | 13 | 136 | 70 | 101 | 16 | 206 | 447 | 626 |
| 26 | 4 | 28 | 0 | 1268 | 411 | 757 | 106 | 964 | 82 | 3798 | 615 |
| 0 | 2 | 0 | 0 | 0 | 132 | 2 | 187 | 0 | 122 | 4 | 443 |
| 10 | 0 | 0 | 56 | 22 | 124 | 18 | 19 | 14 | 562 | 234 | 1037 |
| 20 | 10 | 0 | 1 | 152 | 196 | 511 | 99 | 166 | 280 | 1060 | 771 |
| 140 | 62 | 192 | 164 | 1513 | 1283 | 1544 | 776 | 1348 | 1346 | 6823 | 5157 |

c The segregationist pressure group was always the Citizens' Council; the moderate pressure groups were CPE and SOS.

d The school board (and also Orleans politicians) can be seen as a kind of dependent variable, shifting toward the moderate side as other groups announce for moderation.

e Segregationist court actions were always taken by state courts, and moderate actions always by federal courts with the single exception of the 10 inches for September, a federal action.

*133*

### THE EMERGENCE OF MODERATE GROUPS

Moderate groups opposing the status quo—and school-closing—can be divided into two types. The first are the already-existing organizations, and the second are the newly-formed *ad hoc* groups. We have already seen that all existing groups—the kinds of organizations to be found in any American community—were silent on the race question until the summer of 1960. They had learned—especially by the failure of the three attempts above described—that to step "out of line" meant danger. Hence, the "deafening silence" on this issue in an otherwise noisy and heterogeneous city.

For this reason we will describe the "new" groups before returning to the existing community organizations. They are two in number, SOS (Save Our Schools) and CPE (Committee for Public Education).

*The two "new" groups*—SOS emerged first and was immediately defined by the community as radical, mostly because its membership represented "the southern liberals." It had organized in 1959, but emerged publicly only at the time of the school board's postalcard poll (late April, 1960). Operationally, it waged an extensive campaign, publishing pamphlets to the community, a newsletter to insiders, letters to the editor, and communications to officials; leaders appeared on television. SOS organized a car pool to drive the few remaining white children to the Frantz school (which had been desegregated), and members attempted to persuade parents to return their children to the school. Who were the members? For the most part, they were social workers, Tulane professors and faculty wives, together with several lawyers and business people, none of whom could be considered members of the power elite. These latter were somewhat marginal in terms of attitudes, size of income and ethnicity, and all had participated in earlier "liberal" movements (including the three earlier failures) as well as civic and cultural programs. These "southern liberals" had at last been presented with a situation within which they could openly voice their principles and attack segregation—but this time in conformity with a specific federal court order. Yet their strategy was not to demand integration, but to call for open schools.

Community reaction was, predictably, strong. SOS was quickly defined as suspect, "too radical." This evaluation was not surprising coming from the Citizens' Councils (who asked the state's two U.S. Senators to investigate the group as possibly subversive), but it spread to most other parts of the community too—even, almost unbelievably, to personal friends of SOS leaders.

While SOS was openly accepted and applauded by a few, and stigmatized by most—although community influentials probably studied the SOS arguments—another group appeared. This was the CPE (Committee for Public Education). While it advocated exactly the SOS goal—open schools despite token desegregation—it was not stigmatized. Perhaps SOS had drawn and absorbed the enemy fire. More likely, it was the composition of CPE that prevented denunciation. None of its leaders had established a "southern liberal" reputation; that is, they had not previously become known as opponents of segregation. They were engineers, doctors, lawyers, employees of national oil companies, and several Tulane professors—not known as activists—and their wives. Women did much of the work, as with SOS.

Now for the first time, there was a group urging open schools that could not be stigmatized as "liberal." To the city's leaders, especially to the school board and to "the power structure," CPE could be interpreted as "truly representative" of that theretofore silent but respectable and responsible segment of parents of the city's school children—and a group from whom they could anticipate support. (SOS leaders were parents too, but discountable by individual reputation on the issue.) One could make the argument (see Table 1) that the "respectable" support by CPE and several professional groups had a major effect on the school board's apparent decision by the end of June to back open schools.

The two new groups did not work together. CPE leaders discussed joining SOS but decided against it—some of them shared the general suspicion of SOS. SOS did more, but the mere existence of the uncontaminated CPE presented community leaders with a group whose image could stand for gradual change with a measure of safety. CPE never became really "controversial." Thus a new sense of legitimacy was conferred on eventual token desegregation.

### CERTAIN EXISTING GROUPS ANNOUNCE FOR MODERATION

Only one white organization, SOS, had announced for gradual desegregation before Judge Wright's order. It is conceivable that no other groups would join SOS and CPE, that the entire community would simply follow the Citizens' Councils and let their schools be closed. But because public schools are dear to Americans, and because the community was not completely sold on the Citizens' Council ideology, opposition did form. June and July were the crucial months; by July the school board and powerful downtown leaders had clear evidence that strategic portions of the city were willing to fight alongside SOS and CPE to keep the schools open.

Which portions? Clearly, church groups, mostly clergy, were among the first to declare, as seen in Table 1. These were followed by professional groups and labor organizations. The business community—usually considered the focus of "power"—was silent until November, with one exception. The Young Men's Business Club rejected an open-schools recommendation of its own study committee on the problem. But the Junior Chamber of Commerce voted to support open schools on August 10. These two groups are an interesting contrast; the Junior Chamber is small and draws from upper and upper-middle class men, while the YMBC, with 3200 members, is less exclusive.

Because we are working in the dimension of time-process, the groups which announced for open schools are listed here. The list is not exhaustive, but contains virtually all the groups to announce, and the date of first coming out for open schools.

April 27. SOS.

June 1, N.O. Council of PTA. (But one week later a second meeting voided this "open schools" resolution, although some delegates remained afterward and voiced their belief in open schools.)

June 6. Gregory School PTA.

June 22. CPE.
Episcopal clergy of N.O.
United Church of Christ clergy.
Presbytery of N.O. area (86 pastors and elders from each of the 43 Methodist churches in the district).

June 25. Tulane University Senate.
Presbyterian clergy.

July 5. Family Service society.

July 14. 30 Methodist clergy.

July 15. 94 clergy of city.

July 25. A.C.L.U chapter.

Aug. 3. Independent Women's Organization.

Aug. 7. Teamsters' Union.

Aug. 16. 4 integrated locals of United Packinghouse Workers Union.

Aug. 18. Jr. Chamber of Commerce.

Aug. 19. Central Labor Council.

Aug. 21. Archbishop Rummel (Roman Catholic) deplores school-closing possibility.

Aug. 24. Student Alliance for Education.

Aug. 29. College Young Christian Students of N.O.

During the summer, then, New Orleans transformed itself on the age-old issue of segregation. From a city with a single public ideology—the ideology of segregation—it became pluralistic. Numerous voices—the voices we call "public opinion"—were now being heard. No group or individual challenged the old without strain; plentiful discussion and dissension preceded each group's decision. No group escaped unhurt; members resigned or dropped out, friend suspected friend, and recriminations and sanctions were visited against the open-schools forces. The community was intense that summer. Yet with every new group to announce for open schools, the potential punitive reaction diminished, the larger number of defectors diffusing the segregationist hostility.

*136*

# The Emergence of Pluralistic Public Opinion

The last part of the community that we will examine for its part in the crisis is difficult to label, but broadly it can be called "the upper class" or "the power elite." We do not have the precise data to call it either one or the other—we did not attempt to locate "the" elite. Most New Orleans observers, however, if required to select the local elite, would cite most of the group we will discuss. Its members belong to old families, to the leading men's club or clubs, to large corporate organizations, and generally they resemble such circles found in other American communities.

Two things stand out in the elite's relation to the crisis: it joined the public debate very late (November), and it showed a distinct split within its ranks. The second fact may explain the first one. Our conclusions are based on the contents of three large newspaper advertisements, all signed by members of the elite.

Two of these statements took a broadly "moderate" direction. One backed the incumbent Mr. Sutherland for re-election to the school board, the other followed the street riots of November 16, calling for law and order. The third advertisement heralded states' rights and praised segregationist state officials. There was little if any overlap between the names attached to the third statement and the other two, although many men signed the latter. A comparison of the two groups is given in Table 2. It appears that while the two moderate groups displayed higher scores on a series of criteria of prestige and economic position, both groups contained many prominent men.

**Table 2—Comparison of Business and Professional Men—Moderate and Prosegregation—on Six Criteria of Community Prestige and Leadership**

| | MODERATE | | PROSEGREGATION |
| --- | --- | --- | --- |
| | Back re-election of Sutherland | Bus. and Prof. Men for Law and Order | Tenth Amendment |
| In Social Register | 54 | 62 | 34 |
| Member Boston Club [a] | 4 | 45 | 4 |
| Physicians | 3 | 9 | 8 |
| Lawyers | 17 | 13 | 14 |
| Tulane Univ. Board of Administrators | 6 | 2 | 0 |
| Economic Leaders Scale[b] | 23 | 12 | 6 |
| TOTAL | 98 | 105 | 107 |

[a] Long considered the most important men's club in the city.
[b] Developed by Thomas Ktsanes.

We can safely assume that many of these leaders were privately, although not publicly, seeking to lead their community during the summer months. The seeming split prevented their doing so, or postponed their assuming public leadership roles until much damage had been done. The appointment of a mayor's biracial committee, for example, might have formed a crucial leadership style during the summer; the split, we are speculating, could have been one factor forestalling this move.

It is significant to note that when the public schools opened, desegregated, in September of 1961, 12 months later, the "moderate" group from the elite took the mantle of leadership and guided the community to peaceful change.

### COMMUNICATION NETWORKS

Once having announced for moderation, what did these groups *do?* This is a question oriented to the notion of process.

The very fact that a group considered announcing implies a condition of interpersonal interaction among the membership. The fact that some groups postponed their announcement for some weeks implies internal debate on the issue, and probably also implies a fear of possible consequences for the group and individual members. We can imagine that arguments were presented and answered, that consequences were considered, that allies were sought, tactics planned, and so on.

Once a group published its statement in the mass media, further actions and reactions bubbled, echoed, and resounded within the community. The group's action was only the beginning; it was broadcast, published and commented upon in the media, whereupon it became part of the agenda for personal communication among individuals.[6] The "two-step flow of communication" was in operation, both to and from the media. Oral discussion would be followed by letters to the editor, in speeches and meetings, in further planning and in more conversations among people.

At the highest level of influence, this grass-roots activity cannot have gone unnoticed. Power elite members must have been interested spectators, watching to see if sufficient respectability and urgency characterized the demands for moderation. Members of the school board, sitting atop the powderkeg, doubtless followed the communication process keenly; as the crucial decision-making group, we have already suggested that the appearance of the new moderates in June must have galvanized their decision to stay in the game of open schools.

Seen more generally, New Orleans was a veritable beehive of buzzing on the issue in the summer of 1960. There seemed to be no end of meeting, telephoning, planning, commenting and circulating petitions. Talk was frequent, intense, and centered on the one issue. Most discussions would eventually turn to "the question"; at parties someone would say, "Let's not talk about integration tonight," but they always did.

Almost everybody was involved: parents and children, teachers and administrators, newcomers and natives, Catholics and Protestants, businessmen interested in luring new industry and their employees—and all the rest who sensed a dramatic shift in the most basic status system of the community. It was a period of intense "collective behavior."

### ACTIONS BY INDIVIDUALS

Any sociological frame of reference may result in the neglect of particular individuals in favor of groups, strata, traditions, and so on. This report would be false did it not specify that several individual persons "made a difference" in the crisis. A few of them were: the United States attorney, M. Hepburn Many, who nullified many of the state moves by rapid countermoves in the form of injunctions—the contrast with his counterpart in Little Rock is striking; one member of the school board, who prevented the collapse of the board during the difficult period between May and June, and kept them from resigning; Mrs. Mary Sand, president of SOS, for maintaining her ideals and acting in accordance with them in the face of bitter public scorn and considerable threat of personal danger; Leander Perez, leader of the segregation forces, who breathed fire into the Citizens' Councils and apparently master-minded their actions; and several others who appeared on the scene for shorter intervals, such as one Methodist minister and one mother, who sent their children to the mixed schools through picket lines of female "cheer leaders."

Aside from these particular individuals, there is another sense in which a "group" framework can obscure reality. Within any group, all members are not equally concerned and equally active on an issue. Rather, one or more persons do most of the work. Like the "power" situation in a community in which a few activists account for most of the influence on public decisions, a small number of activists can dominate any organization. Individuals as well as groups, strata, tradition and events, affect the decision-making process. They are especially important as "opinion leaders" and "activists."[7]

### RESISTANCE TO CHANGE

The (white) Citizens' Councils were most active in preserving segregation—and therefore inviting school-closing. The Councils had organized in 1955 and 1956, and had been instrumental in the destruction of the three attempted moderate organizations of the late 1950's.

Composition of the group is not known, but their mass meetings were for the most part attended by older persons from the upper-lower class. Some persons from higher strata contributed financially, but were disinclined to identify themselves publicly with the Councils. Very few prominent persons were leaders in the group—perhaps just enough to reflect legitimacy. (Generally, a fair hypothesis is that the more "Deep South" a community, the more "respectable" it is to join the Citizens Councils.)

During critical periods and with prominent segregationist speakers— governors and attorney-generals from neighboring states—mass meetings attracted up to 8,000 persons. The speeches were of the kind long familiar to Deep South oratory, and audience response was enthusiastic and somewhat revivalistic in tone.

Until Judge Wright's decision, the Councils enjoyed a "monopoly of propaganda" on the race issue. Their aim was to perpetuate segregation, and to this end they employed the classic propaganda strategy of appealing to values already held by the audience—those of sectional virtue and autonomy and white supremacy. Using the devices of name-calling and endless repetition, they succeeded in rallying popular support through the years.

With the challenge from moderate groups, however, the Councils did not cease firing. They were too committed to stop. What they did is not known. However, two things are perhaps related to the Councils. One was the further entry of state officials into the problems of Orleans Parish, speaking on the side of the Councils. The other was the harassment of the moderate activists. Who baited, set and sprung the trap of harassment is difficult to say. When reprisals were organized on a large-scale basis, however, it became conventional in the community to place the blame on the organized prosegregation group. Activists were besieged with telephone calls and letters characterized by obscenity and threats against them and their children; unwanted taxis were sent to their homes at all hours and packaged dinners delivered to their doors, C.O.D. Although they did not result in deaths or serious injuries, such tactics are illegitimate in a fair fight. They were carried out only by the most extreme segregationists; how many moderates they kept from activity is difficult to say, but surely it was some.

The harassment exemplified the larger conflict. When an activist received an accusatory telephone call, the caller would deliver a monologue and hang up; there was no give-and-take. Similarly in the wider community, each side was engaged in the double purpose of talking to others inside the group, thereby reaffirming beliefs in self and partisans while, at the same time, directing their appeals to powerful decision-makers. The two sides were talking past each other. It is our impression that among the 400,000 whites in the city that summer, few debates occurred in which a segregationist and a moderate would face each other and argue the issue. Emotions and ego-involvements had reached such a pitch that rational argument was not only difficult but also painful. A person's position was so deeply anchored in the values forming the core of his self-identity that rational consideration of an opponent's views was so threatening to the self as to recommend flight rather than conversation.

The Councils led the forces of resistance, and a great variety of tactics were used. Not only did they praise the existing system and prophesy doom as the consequence of change, but they also took legal measures. Because of the extent of these measures, the state legislature held no less than five special sessions during the winter following desegregation, with segregation as the major issue.

## Analysis

Having sketched the setting, the issue, and the development of a public opinion situation as seen in the emergence of moderate groups, three topics will now be analyzed. These will deal with the question of "power," with the kinds of groups which emerged, and with the type of issue.

*Who exercised influence?*—Our evidence suggests that "the power elite" was not as crucial in this crisis as would have been expected from such communities as Middletown or Hunter's Regional City. Rather, because the elite was split, actions were taken by a series of activists who lead groups and opinion leaders who aroused and rallied sentiment in portions of the community already favorable to change. The power elite remained as a latent force; the following year (1961) it grasped the reins and led the community to peaceful desegregation.

*Analysis of the emerging groups*—Why did these particular groups emerge to oppose tradition? Why did they do it at a certain time—early or late? Why did other groups refrain from action? We will continue to utilize the concepts of (1) groups and their values and interests, and (2) the community context, seen in terms of the political public opinion situation.

The "easy way" would have been to do nothing, and to let state and federal forces dictate action. Conversely, any group that advocated change knew it would be subject to reprisals from the dominant majority.

To ask why certain groups risked sanctions is to ask four questions: Who were the members? How did they come together as a group? What were their values and inter sts? And how did they weigh the consequences of opposing the status qu ?

Some of these questions can be answered more readily than others. Many members of SOS, CPE, the clergy, Tulane educators and social workers were born ar raised outside of the South and therefore had not internalized rac views during childhood. Further, many of the "native" dissenters had been educated outside the region, or had traveled widely and lost the ethnocentrism retained by their neighbors.

The question about surviving reprisals can be answered partly in terms of the other questions, the geographical origin of members and the group values. In addition, as more and more groups joined the opposition, the likelihood of reprisal decreased. The addition of new moderate groups diffused the target zone. One thinks of the subjects in Asch's experiment striving to preserve rational choice in the face of 16 "stooges" giving a wrong answer; when one other subject began giving correct answers, the situation was much "improved."[8] Still, in the New Orleans situation, the risk was greater for some than for others and at no time could a group publicly oppose segregation and escape censure. Professors in a private university are least exposed; retail merchants and moderate clergymen with an indigenous congregation will anticipate the noose from many quarters. Boycotts and the case of the harried moderate ministers of Little Rock are clear examples. Several New Orleans churches lost membership support after clergy action, but because the clergy pronouncements were moderate and based on scripture, rather than political ideology, the retaliation was slight.

When several groups began to speak for moderation, this very fact transformed sociocultural structure. This, in turn, made it less difficult for other groups to speak out on their own.

The fact that most of the community did not join the moderates, then, indicates that either their values and interests lay with segregation, or that they calculated that endorsing segregation would bring pain. Seen broadly, the opposition could easily be viewed by the average townsman as traitors. Irrespective of the correctness of this view, it was widely recognized during the crisis by all the white residents, and remained (and still remains) a brake to rapid change.

The next question asks: How did the moderate groups get organized? Even the existing groups had to initiate informal discussion before coming to a formal decision, and there are bits of evidence that these groups engaged in considerable background talk before coming to a formal public resolution of their stand. The clergy and the business elite, of course, are the kinds of collectivities that meet one another through the daily criss-crossing and overlapping civic, social and professional activities. Thus channels for discussion of an issue are already provided. SOS, too, drew together men and women who had worked for earlier "liberal" causes, and a few telephone calls alerted a sizeable band for preparatory meetings.

Probably the only group whose successful organization was problematic was CPE. A nucleus of about 20 persons met privately at first; these invited about 30 more persons, and newspaper publicity after the first public meeting resulted in the attendance of about 400 persons a few weeks later. The original handful, linked by a series of friendship chains, were able to draw from the community-wide population many others interested in maintaining the public school system via the mass media.

The final question deals with the values and interests. All the opposition groups can be subsumed, albeit broadly, within two categories. Waller, 30 years ago, referred to them as the humanitarian and the organizational values.[9] All of the groups probably possessed some of both. SOS and the clergy could be thought of as leaning toward the pole of humanitarian values, and the business elite as leaning toward the pole of organizational values—interest in maintaining property values, a national image of a community qualifying for new industry and favorable school bond rates, and so on. It is significant in terms of action that the propaganda of the "humanitarian" SOS, however, was beamed directly at the business elite and stressed the financial loss suffered by Little Rock when that city's schools closed. Of all the groups, CPE probably can be distinguished for actually doing most accurately what it purported to be doing: working to keep the schools open and running. It is also interesting that the groups which leapt earliest into the fray were the most ideologically humanitarian—SOS and the clergy. The business elite, feeling exposed to possible business loss and also being aware of a sharp internal schism, was unable to act until late in the year.

*Type of issue*—How relevant to other community decision-crises is the one described here? This is a question about the type of issue involved. It is difficult to imagine an issue facing a big city that involved more of its people more deeply than this one. The salience was extreme. An age-old pattern dictating a basic dimension of the status-and-reward system of the community was threatened. For this reason it is possible that the patterns developed in this study will be pertinent only to crises in other communities where the issue is equally basic.[10]

## Warren Breed

*Summary*

An event—Judge Wright's decision of May 16—signalled the new situation: desegregation or closed schools. This event forced the community to focus—at long last—on the race issue.

Before that time, an almost complete absence of organized opposition to school segregation had prevailed. Groups which had tried to challenge the system had failed.

Individual opinions overwhelmingly favored segregation, and many individuals held these opinions deeply.

The eventful decision was brought about by forces outside the *dominant* white community—by Negro leaders and the federal government. Within the community there existed no force powerful enough to demand consideration of the change.

The first groups to emerge and stand for moderation were the southern liberals and the professional groups from the clergy, college faculties and social workers, who at last were presented an opportunity to protest segregation with a court order on their side. Somewhat later came a few other "progressive" organizations and some labor unions. Business groups, with one exception, remained silent for many months.

These groups strengthened one another by diffusing the harassment from segregationists, and all were strengthened by the threat to a basic community institution, the public school system.

The body holding the final decision—the school board—was influenced by the show of moderation, and made its stand for open schools on this basis.

The business "power elite" entered the scene late, possibly because of a split within its ranks.

In the absence of a clear position by the power elite, leadership was assumed by a plurality of individuals and groups, from the heads of associations to opinion leaders within smaller portions of the community. No monolithic "power structure" dominated the scene, although it might have had the split not occurred.

Resistance to change was spearheaded by one group, the Citizens' Councils. This group was presumably associated with the harassment of moderates before and during the crisis.

Communication processes took many forms, with the mass media reflecting actions and thus suggesting other actions to a variety of individuals and groups. A kind of "double two-step flow" could be observed.

An individual would meet another, discuss the issue and meet with other peers; their communication would result in the group's formal announcement in the media; this information would then enter other quarters of the community and "bounce" among them, initiating still further actions, and so on.

The process of stigmatization was at work. One individual with a questionable (e.g., possibly "communist") background would brand a group, and a group (CPE) working for aims identical with those of another group (SOS) would decide not to work with it. Many groups probably decided to remain silent out of fear that criticizing segregation would result in disrepute for the group and its members.

On the issue of segregation, perhaps the basic process was the shift in the structure of the community from a nonpluralistic to a pluralistic one. As a consequence, public discussion became more rational, although much irrationality remained.

## NOTES

Acknowledgments are due Forrest E. LaViolette for criticism and suggestions, and to Charles Chandler, who gave valuable assistance at all stages of the study. He was working with a grant from the Public Affairs Research Council of Louisiana.

1. William Kornhouser, *The Politics of Mass Society*, New York: The Free Press, 1959; R. M. MacIver, *The Web of Government*, New York: Macmillan, 1947, Chaps. 2 and 3; David B. Truman, *The Governmental Process*, New York: Knopf, 1959.

2. W. Phillips Davison, "The Public Opinion Process," *Public Opinion Quarterly*, 22 (Summer 1958), 91–102; Herbert Blumer, "Collective Behavior," in A. M. Lee (ed.), *New Outline of the Principles of Sociology*, New York: Barnes and Noble, 1946, pp. 189–196; R. M. MacIver, *Academic Freedom in the United States*, Columbia University Press, 1051, V. O. Key, *Public Opinion and American Democracy*, New York: Knopf, 1961, Chaps. 1, 3, 8, 10, 16, and 21.

3. For a discussion of several approaches to community decision-making, see Peter H. Rossi, "Community Decision Making," *Administrative Science Quarterly*, 1 (March 1957), 415–43. For illustrations of two widely differing approaches, see Floyd Hunter, *Community Power Structure*, Chapel Hill: University of North Carolina Press, 1953; and Elihu Katz and Paul F. Lazarsfeld, *Personal Influence*, New York: The Free Press, 1955. A classic community decision study is Richard L. Schanck, "Test-Tube for Public Opinion: A Rural Community," *Public Opinion Quarterly*, 2 (January 1938), 90–5. Also relevant are the more recent studies of community conflict over fluoridation of the water supply.

4. For a detailed treatment of the structure of the Negro Community of New Orleans, see Daniel C. Thompson, *The Negro Leadership Class*, Englewood Cliffs: Prentice-Hall, 1963. Considerable divergence of interpretation may be found between Thompson's report and this one. For further information on the events of 1960, see Louisiana State Advisory Com-

mittee of the U.S. Commission on Civil Rights, "The New Orleans School Crisis," Washington, D.C., 1961.

5. The one possible exception is the Southern Conference Education Fund, with an office in New Orleans staffed by paid personnel. The SCEF director was the member of the Citizens Forum who was accused of Communist affiliations (which he denied under oath). The SCEF did little in the city's school situation of 1960; one possible reason is that several integrationists asked SCEF not to intervene, on the grounds that the stigmatized organization would stigmatize the entire desegregation movement.

Evidence exists, from several sources, that prominent Jewish leaders deliberately chose not to back desegregation publicly, although they privately approved, on the grounds that their espousal might boomerang against the change.

6. The role of the two daily newspapers was to mirror activities; they did not provide leadership during this period. Television stations also provided information, and gave some leadership as well.

7. "Opinion leaders" are described in Katz and Lazarsfeld, *op. cit.* "Activists" are a key element in the public opinion scheme of Key, *op. cit.*

8. Solomon E. Asch, *Social Psychology*, New York: Prentice-Hall, 1952, Chap. 16.

9. Willard Waller, "Social Problems and the Mores," *American Sociological Review*, 1 (December 1936), 922–33.

10. See Ernest A. T. Barth and Stuart D. Johnson, "Community Power and a Typology of Social Issues," *Social Forces*, 38 (October 1959), 29–32.

11. Blumer, *op. cit.*

# 11.    Local Voluntarism in Race Relations Strategy: The Illinois Experience with Community Human Relations Groups

## RICHARD ROBBINS

### Introduction

THE RANGE OF AN APPLIED SOCIOLOGY MUST OF necessity be very wide. The term suggests the most minute and detailed policy recommendations requested by an administrative organization. At the same time it suggests a set of broad sociological propositions, applied or "practical" in character only because verifiable knowledge is made available; the contribtuion to the intellectual forum is "there"—to be accepted, rejected, revised, ignored. It is the same with intergroup relations. For example, a military command may ask a social scientist for a precise report on the consequences of desegregating units at the platoon level rather than at the regimental level. Or a sociologist, from a lifetime's experience in studying the ways of prejudice and discrimination, may choose to present his wisdom in a few rough-hewn generalizations, such as: "Wherever the direct attack is feasible, that is, the attack on discrimination itself, it is more promising than the indirect attack, that is the attack on prejudice as such. It is more effective to challenge conditions than to challenge attitudes and feelings."[1] It does not follow, however, that the myriad studies are without a common theme to be submitted, unrelated and *seriatim* to

This report is adapted from a larger study written for the Institute of Government and Public Affairs, University of Illinois. I am indebted to the Institute's director, Gilbert Y. Steiner, for advice and counsel.

the forum. On the contrary. Both highly-circumscribed report and broad generalization are addressed to the fundamental question of *an effective strategy of change*. What, then, is the present climate of change in American race relations and how does that change bear on applied research?

We are approaching, however circuitously, national consensus on the need to proceed more rapidly in the pursuit of equality of opportunity. American Negroes, especially, display impatience with counsels of "gradualism" and "tokenism" in such vital matters as the denial of the ballot and of employment because of racial identity. And the more "progress" they make, the more militant they must become. For, as de Tocqueville saw long ago, groups press forward from hope, as much as from despair.

Consensus scarcely means unanimity, still less the disappearance of regional pockets of intransigence, North and South. Nevertheless, if we are to retain the theoretical framework developed by Gunnar Myrdal two decades ago—the existence of "an American dilemma" called out by the basic contradiction between a democracy's ethical postulates (the American creed) and its actual record of racial discrimination—we must recognize that the emphasis on articulating the contradiction in values has been giving way to a stress on implementing more forcefully the values embodied in the Creed.[2] This is the meaning of the Negro nonviolent revolution which reached its climax in 1963 in mass demonstrations in the streets. Without this stimulus there would have been no civil rights legislation to debate in 1964. When Myrdal wrote, whites acted and Negroes reacted; by 1964 Negroes acted, whites reacted.

The watershed of this change was, of course, the historic Supreme Court decision of 1954 declaring racial segregation in public schools unconstitutional. Today it is not surprising that the Court's subsequent strategic guideline, enunciated in 1955, to advance "with all deliberate speed" toward desegregation, preoccupies us more than the great symbolic decision reversing *Plessy* v. *Ferguson*. Indeed, recent events have underscored the search for newer techniques to complement and supplement a legal strategy of change. Southern Negro leaders are adapting more widely the Gandhian approach of direct, nonviolent action to test segregation—sit-ins, freedom rides, economic boycotts. Everywhere they insist on *"less* deliberate speed."

If this reading of the national trend is correct, then it follows that an applied sociology of intergroup relations will be directed increasingly at analyzing the effectiveness of strategies of change, even if at some cost to traditional research on "causes" of prejudices and manifestations of discrimination. The setting will be that of social conflict, as integral to progress in race relations as cooperation, but conflict turning on means rather than ends. For enlarged consensus of the injustice of segregation and discrimination must lead to greater divergence over pragmatic questions of how and when to reduce these racial barriers to equality of opportunity. This is the decade of the timetable. Negroes know very well that in the decade since the Supreme Court decision only one per cent of the biracial school districts in the Deep South have been desegregated. And in the desegregated districts there are only a handful of Negro children.

TWO STRATEGIES

Initially, in action research on racial problems, we should distinguish between appropriate *consensus strategy* and a defensive *counter strategy*. The first aims at a closer fit—although never in this life a perfect fit—of means to ends, of deed to Creed. The second aims at effectively delaying—although with no prospect of reversing—those inexorable changes in the direction of fulfilling the Creed.

Strictly speaking, sociologists do not treat the two sets moralistically as "higher" and "lower"; in the South, for example, resistance to, and readiness for, school desegregation require the same degree of meticulous analysis. A broader humanistic sociology, however, while remaining wholly committed to objective research in the actual technical work, is informed by a moral recognition of the injustices as well as the social consequences in institutionalizing racist doctrine. Consequently it is committed in its choice of research problems to exploring more effective ways to advance consensus strategy and to contain defensive strategy in American race relations.

Indeed, there is nothing in principle to prevent sociologists, as both professionals and citizens, from making an even more emphatic commitment. At its annual meeting in 1963, for example, the Society for the Study of Social Problems, representing almost a thousand sociologists, sent a resolution to the President and to Congressional leaders on pending civil rights legislation. It touches first on the professional issue citing "the overwhelming evidence . . . that segregation and other forms of discrimination are psychologically, economically, and socially detrimental to those who are deprived." But the resolution's concluding note carries the sociologists, as citizens, from the classroom to the front lines "Immediate action is required to strike down discriminatory barriers on all fronts—local, state and national—by voluntary as well as legal means. Dramatic steps are called for. The present legislation before Congress proposed by the Administration is such a step."

This attraction to consensus strategy is not so much a matter of the social scientist's "liberal bias" as it is a product of his awareness of history

*149*

and his concern for the moral problem of the endless tension between social systems and human freedom.[3] Historically the "winds of change" have
been crumbling the fortress of white supremacy, whatever the future may
hold for a racial counter-chauvinism, with white and black roles reversed.
Morally—not moralistically—when we have rightly recorded the ambiguities beclouding any moral issues and when we have properly noted
the tendency of reformers to slip into dogmatism, when we have discounted
Edmund Burke's wise counsel to preserve as one improves, and when we
have become impatient with what William Graham Sumner called the
crescive character of institutions, we will see that at bottom the proponents
of consensus strategy have justice, as well as history, on their side.

## THE STRATEGY OF CONSENSUS

Considering consensus strategy alone, then, we still confront the question of what are effective modes of action. In American society, with its
complex web of group interests and its three-tiered federal political structure, we can speak of no single history, only multiple strategies. A paradigm, based on the American Creed, illustrates the complexity of the
strategic problem in the pluralistic society.

It starts with *value premises,* and here the burden of our argument has
been that even in the Deep South a new consensus is emergent. Conflict
over strategy is in the process of replacing conflict over ideology. As we
turn from ends to means, we take the next step and focus on strategic *levels
of action*—national, regional, state and local—and on methods of parceling
out policy responsibility.

At each level there are *two separate but connected spheres,* that of
public law and government and that of private initiative and interest
groups. On all levels and in both spheres there are found the appropriate
*catalytic agents*—organizations combatting prejudice and discrimination.
These may be general institutional groups—armies, unions—pressing consensus strategy as one of many goals, or they may be highly specialized
intergroup relations organizations devoted exclusively to this end. Again,
a professional agency might be required for one task and a voluntary association for another.

Finally, it is necessary to consider the key question of *intensity of thrust,*
the degree of conflict risked by the catalytic agents and the speed with which
they intend to advance. The terms "militancy" and "gradualism" would
be relevant here were they not so often employed as verbal shields and as
means of abdication on the critical substantive issue: militant or gradualist *toward what?* Used honestly, however, they bracket the range of

thrust. Reverend Martin Luther King's program of direct, nonviolent resistance touches the NAACP's reliance on court test and legislative pressure. From there we are moved far over to former President Eisenhower's appeal for "a change in the minds and hearts of men" through education, broadly defined.

The new conflict over strategies of change suggests as many problematic issues as the old conflict over antithetical values. It is as if the present civil rights situation were a great map where the terrain seems well marked and the distant city appears finally attainable but where the travelers now fall out over alternate routes and dangerous roadblocks.

## The Illinois Experience

In this section, I report on the research that deals with only a segment of the total paradigm. It concerns intergroup relations consensus strategy in the state of Illinois. The level of action is the local community, in both public and private spheres. The catalytic agents consisted in 1960 of fifteen municipal human relations commissions established by ordinance, and twenty privately organized community human relations councils.

The commissions cluster in the metropolitan centers and in medium to large cities, the councils in the vast Chicago suburban belt and in smaller cities downstate. Each group is a voluntary association save for the professionally-staffed Chicago Commission. All are affiliated with the Illinois Commission on Human Relations located in Chicago.

The Illinois Commission was established during World War II by the state legislature to combat rising racial tension and to promote equality of opportunity. It was particularly directed toward encouraging the kind of grass-roots local community strategy congenial to the conservative political ethos in downstate Illinois with its emphasis on "letting the local people solve their own problems." All the commissions and councils share in common the desire to effect a reduction in discrimination in employment, housing, public accommodations, and the social services. Their intensity of thrust, in both public and private spheres, is modest and non-militant. The limitations on thrust are specific and rather atypical for a leading urban-industrial state.

Illinois contained a million Negroes in a population of ten million in 1960, and in the city of Chicago there are now more than 800,000 Negroes, twenty-three per cent of the total city population. Throughout the state, and in metropolitan Chicago in particular, serious and pressing racial problems occur principally in employment and *de facto* segregation in housing and the public schools.[4] Yet in 1960 at the state level there was neither a fair employment practices commission nor a general antidiscrimination commission with enforcement powers that could have been invoked as a "last resort" when conciliation and persuasion proved inadequate. (In 1961 the Illinois General Assembly did pass an FEPC law, but it is very limited in scope and its impact on local situations still remains to be seen.)

## AGENCIES AND APPROACHES

The Illinois Commission is confined to a program of persuasion, education, research, and the stimulation of local voluntarism. It cannot directly intervene to strengthen the role of community groups when local consensus strategy appears insufficient as happened in two well-known cases, the one concerning school desegregation in Cairo in southern Illinois, and the other in a proposed integrated housing development in Deerfield, a middle-class suburb north of Chicago.[5]

The ordinances creating the local commissions restrict them as well as persuasion and conciliation; their chief advantage over similar private groups does not lie in "law over education" but in the enhancement of commission status due to the official label. Not even the Chicago Commission has enforcement powers; it is not a "little FEPC." (In 1963, however, the city government of Chicago did pass, over considerable opposition, a fair housing ordinance of this type, that is, something "with teeth.") Granted that at both state and local level the power of public bodies to hold hearings on complaints and, if necessary, to seek redress in the courts, is mostly held in abeyance while conciliation does its work. It remains true, however, that the effectiveness of a strategy of state and local law depends in part on the power to enforce sanctions. For even if the power is used very infrequently its sheer "presence" adds weight and authority to the mandate assumed by public commissions.

As a demonstration of consensus strategy in the urban-industrial North, therefore, the Illinois experience constitutes a special and somewhat "old-fashioned" case study. The strategic response derives from the older tradition of local voluntarism: grass-roots action of a moderate cast, emphasizing persuasion and conciliation, developed without professional staff organization and instituted without that close reinforcement of community voluntarism by "FEP type" of state and local laws now familiar in New York or Pennsylvania.

Yet the approach may be instructive to sociologists precisely because of the defects of its virtues. Small voluntary associations attempt to grapple with "big issues" such as race relations or delinquency control at the level of small community or city neighborhood. This receives skeptical treatment in the literature in the light of trends toward complex organization, mass society, and more decisive intervention of national government in local problems. However, some students of American society argue that, exactly because of these trends, it is more important than ever to strive for a "restoration of community." They would make voluntary groups in town and neighborhood the essential links between the individual and the amorphous social order. If the commissions and councils in Illinois are effective within their modest mandates, then localism and voluntarism deserve at least a footnote status in a literature now inclined to assign such ideas to history, to a de Tocquevillean nineteenth century.[6]

## Organizational Effectiveness of the Local Commissions and Councils

In 1960, at the request of the Institute of Government and Public Affairs, University of Illinois, I conducted a short study of the network of action groups. We asked: How effective are the local commissions and councils in devising strategy to advance equality of opportunity?

Although social scientists have written abundantly on general strategy to curb prejudice and discrimination, they have not examined as closely the effectiveness claimed by the intergroup relations organizations devoted exclusively to combating intolerance.[7] The tendency to limit discussions of the organizations to a straightforward description of their programs and to the encouragement of their activities may be explained in various ways. One obvious factor is that effectiveness in so nebulous an area as "promoting brotherhood" is too vague for precise measure. Another is the obvious hesitation on the part of the social scientist to engage in tough-minded analysis of a group which is, after all, "doing some good." In any event, methodological material on organizational effectiveness in intergroup relations activity has not yet been adequately developed.

### METHODOLOGY

The method employed in the study consisted in following out the paradigm described above. But two special challenges arose immediately: how to compare the effectiveness of groups in communities varying so much in socioeconomic structure and racial composition; and how to construct an index of group effectiveness in any single community, not necessarily valid for intergroup relations organizations in general but at least appropriate to the Illinois system.

The first difficulty was met through *comparative community analysis.* Its point of departure is the familiar community case study of the *Middletown* genre. However, in place of treating several problems in one city, the observer sacrifices depth to scope and studies only one problem— commission-council strategy—in several cities within a region. Arranging the Illinois groups in terms of metropolis, suburb, and hinterland city facilitates comparisons useful not only for race relations strategy but also for a broader urban sociology. For example, one byproduct of the study was the development of a sociological typology of different suburbias, somewhat at variance with the prevailing psychological portrait of a middle-class "suburban way of life."[8]

In the chain of community comparisons, Chicago proper, with its immensely complex racial problems and its staffed rather than voluntary commission, had to be considered *sui generis* and beyond the capacity of a study limited in time and resources and conducted as a one-man enterprise. (What is required is a national metropolitan comparison with the Chicago Commission compared to the one in Pittsburgh rather than to those in Peoria and Rockford.) Moreover, of the many neighborhood councils in Chicago concerned with racial stability and neighborhood conservation—the great city counterparts of the commissions and councils elsewhere in Illinois—only one was affiliated with the Illinois Commission, and its roster of groups defined the study universe.

Some of the earlier relevant literature was reviewed, including Clifford Shaw's conception of the role of the neighborhood in delinquency control and Saul Alinsky's program for neighborhood revitalization, the "Back of the Yards" movement. In the end it was feasible to make tentative assessments of two present-day experiments in urban grass-roots—or better "block committee"—race relations strategy, both premised, like the Shaw and Alinsky plans, on a cooperative effort by a professional staff and volunteers. Both the well-known Hyde Park-Kenwood program and the Organization for the Southwest Community aim at arresting blight and conserving neighborhoods. An important corollary is the acceptance of racial open occupancy so as to avert the exodus of whites from newly integrated areas and the creation of new all-Negro ghettos.

The two cases do indeed provide some evidence that block committee voluntaristic strategy works effectively against real estate "panic selling," "block busting," and other demoralizing practices. It would be hazardous, however, to frame conclusions from just two experiments in Chicago, much less to see in these programs and a few comparable ones in New York and Philadelphia the beginning of a "restoration of community" in big city zones of transition.[9]

The second methodological challenge, the problem of what constitutes effectiveness in intergroup relations work, presents a multitude of difficulties to specialists in this field.[10] Effectiveness is especially hard to gauge when a group cannot cite quantitative evidence such as the number of complaints successfuly processed or the cases won in the courts. In this respect, the Illinois commissions and councils are not unlike a National Conference of Christians and Jews; the NCCJ branches and the local commissions have similar mandates to "promote understanding" and "further opportunity" but how effectively they do so is another question. The members of the Illinois group invariably described specific successes, although the color line terminated in this public facility or that employment channel. They defined effectiveness, just as frequently, in terms of "changing the climate of opinion" or "really making the people here aware of discrimination."

Without pretending to resolve the question of effectiveness, the Illinois study does seek to circumscribe it more concretely. It proposes two sets of dimensions of effectiveness.

*Internal dimensions.* An organization's structural strength and leadership; the establishment of a realistic goal-strategy relationship; the intensity of thrust; and the "statistics" of individual achievements.

*External dimensions.* An organization's expectation of a favorable climate of opinion; its access to local power structure; support from ethnic and racial minority subcommunities; support from important sources not in the power structure (*e.g.*, ministers' associations) ; and the appropriateness of program response to type and intensity of local human relations problems.

These indices were weighted numerically and then the internal and external sets were combined to produce an over-all assessment of each group on a continuum as *inactive-ineffective, minimally effective, moderately effective, or effective.*

While the evaluations were made by the writer on the above basis, they stem directly from field work in the communities over a four-month period. Open-ended questionnaires were used in oral interviews of a sample of the active members of councils and commissions. Additional interviews were conducted with other strategic persons in the communities, principally in local government. A total of 134 respondents comprised the sample. Directors of state commissions outside Illinois returned mailed questionnaires that permitted comparisons of the state-local division of labor elsewhere.

Parenthetically, a number of qualifications should be stated. The scale employed as a measure of effectiveness was an exceedingly rough instrument, limited to supplementing the observer's judgment and not intended to replace it. Further, considering the restricted mandate of the local voluntaristic approach in Illinois, expectations of group effectiveness had to be couched with restraint. We anticipated that the councils and commissions would at best reduce, not eliminate, racial discrimination in their respective communities.

Finally, it was clear that even if the local official commissions were to obtain enforcement powers, and even if the local private groups were to take on a far greater militancy than they evidenced in the course of the study, the effectiveness of local voluntarism would still be of an auxiliary or liaison character. For the critics of grass-roots strategy and of "restoration of community" programs can show, at the least, that local levels, in both public and private spheres, are increasingly interdependent with state, national, and (in a symbolic sense) international levels. Federal and state agencies "reach into" local defense plants and community public housing to assure nondiscriminatory employment and occupancy. Federal district courts are often the pivot of *local* conflict over desegregation in the South. (News of Little Rock and Birmingham travels swiftly to Africa.) Under such circumstances, no commission or council can be an island unto itself.

## Summary and Conclusions

With all these reservations acknowledged, the data support the general conclusion that the community voluntary associations in Illinois make a modest but meaningful contribution to the reduction of racial problems in the state.

1. The effectiveness of the great majority of groups was found to be minimal to moderate. A small number of moribund or near-moribund groups was balanced by a small number of vigorously active organizations, unquestionably effective within the necessary limits of the persuasion-education mandate. But again, in the great majority of groups, effectiveness turned out to be more of a cyclical matter than a permanent condition of

a council or commission. One of the most important precipitates of a group's rising curve of effectiveness appeared to be the emergence of a crisis. In a concrete situation demanding clear and specific responses from leaders and members, a group would coalesce, deal effectively with a racial situation, then recede once more to a latent state.

2. In a broad sense, the commission form proved more effective than the council type, although there were a number of striking exceptions. In any case, posing the question of "commission versus council," of public versus private sphere, in so general a way is largely an academic exercise. The more precise generalization is that the form chosen hinges explicitly on the model of the community.

A biracial city or suburb, with diverse interest groups and a wide span in class structure, suggests the need for an ordinance commission as a municipal mediating agency among multiple interests variously concerned with manifest problems of racial discrimination.

A middle-class "bedroom" suburb, ethnically diverse but racially homogeneous, perhaps anticipating but not yet confronting Negro immigration, would be expected to establish a private stand-by council whose effectiveness would derive from a role as an informal educational agency. Such a private group might seek to develop a more informed community opinion on questions of race and property values, and similar issues.

In short, the issue of commission *versus* council underlines, as do so many others in the study, the greater value in comparing the strategy of local voluntarism in differing community contexts instead of attempting to assess the Illinois network as a whole as either effective or ineffective.

3. The effectiveness of local human relations groups is related not only to community type but to different subregions within a state. The easy national distinction between just two categories, North and South, on an index of racial practices, suffers from oversimplification. Without in any way accepting the ingenuous Southern argument that the North is "just the same" as the South because racial tension can break out in Chicago as well as in New Orleans, we need to acknowledge a subregional transition to "Southernism" in northern states adjacent to the Middle South, such as Illinois, Indiana, Missouri. (Even New Jersey had a completely segregated subregion, adjacent to Delaware, until little more than a decade ago.) In Illinois there is a pattern of increasing social segregation of Negroes as one moves southward from Springfield toward the confluence of the Ohio and Mississippi Rivers at the gateway to the Border South.

This subregional context does much to explain the ineffectiveness of the East St. Louis Commission when leading Negroes either cooperated with the white political machine or found themselves in political wilderness; the resistance to an official commission in Carbondale where the University was integrated but the community was segregated; and the resistance to any human relations organization whatever in Cairo (thirty-eight per cent nonwhite and described by one respondent "as racially more southern than the South"). These three cities are all Southern cities in racial as well as in geographical terms. By the same token, the moderate effectiveness of the Alton Commission must be counted as a special achievement in view of the system of prevailing Southern mores within which it has operated. In these subregional terms, the study recommends the establishment of a staffed field office for southern Illinois, to be maintained by either the Illinois Human Relations Commission or the new FEPC.

4. At the state level, the study suggested that the auxiliary effectiveness of local groups can best be strengthened by the creation of a state FEPC or general antidiscrimination commission with enforcement powers in housing and employment. A step of this kind, consistent with that taken by other northern urban-industrial states, would undoubtedly supplement voluntary localism without necessarily pre-empting it.

Evidence from other states indicates that a comprehensive state agency with regional-local branches does tend to overshadow the *official* local commissions, the special pride of the Illinois system. But experience also shows that the activity of *unofficial* human relations councils and fair-housing committees is likely to be expanded *pari-passu* with the growth of a more forceful state commission. This is especially the case in states undergoing rapid suburbanization of principal cities, with the increased prospect of rising Negro in-migration into previously homogeneous, middle-class suburbs. We have seen this situation to be ideal for private human relations groups (point 2).

The value of a working relationship between a strong state agency representing the power of the law, held in reserve but brought to bear when local persuasion and conciliation break down, and a network of local private groups, representing the power of persuasion at the grass-roots primary group level, is now being demonstrated in the suburban areas of greater Boston and the New York-Northeastern New Jersey area. The suburban belt of metropolitan Chicago displays similar migratory trends and potential racial strains and the majority of private groups in Illinois are located there. Open occupancy in housing is the basic challenge, not only in the suburbs but in certain sections of the inner city, adjacent to the Negro ghettos, where white bigotry remains pervasive.

5. Irrespective of changes at the state level, local ordinance commissions of the persuasion-education type can be maintained in their present

form. However, the largest metropolitan industrial areas, with high proportions of nonwhite minorities, would seem to require staffed enforcement commissions—"little FEPC's"—in place of the present reliance on local voluntarism. In Illinois there are only two cities which constitute all or part of the "metropolitan model," Chicago and East St. Louis, and in neither city do the commissions have this necessary enforcement power.

6. As noted above, the data point to a correlation of the commission form with the biracial, diversified cities and suburbs; and the council form with the more homogeneous suburbs and independent towns. The material requires, however, a further subdivision of the "suburban way of life" within the metropolitan framework.

Council-commission effectiveness in northeastern metropolitan Illinois—where eighteen of the thirty-five groups in the universe are concentrated—turns on at least four differing suburban race relations contexts. Here it is possible only to illustrate from a detailed intersuburban comparison of councils in Deerfield and Evanston and a commission in Park Forest. The analysis shows how Evanston's present resistance to merit employment in some sectors of the economy could be dealt with more realistically were an official commission—"called for" in the biracial suburban model—established to supplement an already effective private council. (Such a commission was indeed formed shortly after the study was completed.) It demonstrates that Deerfield's rejection of a racially integrated housing project involves too many special factors to serve as proof of either the general viability or futility of the private human relations council in suburbia. And it concludes that Park Forest's acceptance of its first Negro family, achieved principally through effective liaison between commission and local government in advance of the actual crisis, could serve, in contrast to the Deerfield experience, as a model for other suburban communities facing similar tensions over race and housing.

7. In central Illinois, case studies were employed primarily to assess the effectiveness of human relations strategy when two groups play complementary roles in pursuit of the same goal by different means. As everyone knows, in many cities there is a great deal of overlapping of function and considerable confusion as to proper jurisdiction among a large number of groups dedicated to promoting equality of opportunity. The Illinois material throws some light on this vexing organizational problem, the question of whether the local human relations field is "overchurched."

The analysis of Champaign-Urbana, for example, indicates the utility of maintaining a private council, at least temporarily even after the establishment of an official commission. There is a functional division of labor. The commission has the major role of investigating and recommending,

159

and the council is thereby freed to intensify its "gadfly" role. Or in the words of a respondent: "Someone has to act judicial and someone has to shove." On the other hand, in a number of communities the expectation that the local NAACP's militancy of thrust would compensate for the limited effectiveness and gradualism of a community human relations group did not work out. The fact is that in the smaller cities of the North the type of local voluntarism practiced by NAACP branches is often far weaker than the image of a militant, even "radical," organization would suggest.

8. A final question concerns the "exportability" of the Illinois strategy of local voluntarism. It appears to have definite utility for sections of the Middle South where segregation is diminishing and the public climate is now more receptive to local human relations activity, but still hostile to the idea of enforcement commissions at the state level. It has far less relevance for the Deep South—save for the larger cosmopolitan cities such as Atlanta or Dallas. Here, in general, segregation remains entrenched and, in particular, consensus strategy for the Negro community lies in direct, nonviolent conflict between separate white and Negro interest groups, characterized by a kind of racial "collective bargaining," in which purely local strategy is inseparable from the "presence" of the federal executive branch and federal district courts. The Illinois commission-council approach, with its emphasis on racially mixed groups working out problems by conciliation and persuasion, does not really fit the deep Southern pattern of institutionalized legal and social conflict in the context of a national public opinion.[11] Only direct confrontation at the polls and in the streets will move the white community in Mississippi.

In the last analysis, the moderate effectiveness of the network of groups in Illinois does not establish in any definite sense the superiority of the local way over the state-national way. What the study conveys is the limited but measurable effectiveness of one strategy among many in one corner of a pluralistic society. Local voluntarism in the North, in public and private spheres, succeeds in "doing something about discrimination here at home" in an Alton or a Peoria—for all the dominant trend to a mass society and a welfare state.

## NOTES

1. Robert M. MacIver, *The More Perfect Union*, New York: Macmillan, 1948, p. 247.

2. Gunnar Myrdal, with Richard Sterner and Arnold Rose, *An American Dilemma, The Negro Problem and Modern Democracy*, New York: Harper, 1945, Ch. 1. In 1963 in comments mark-

ing the twentieth anniversary edition of this classic work, Myrdal notes further progress toward equality of opportunity, but now finds both Negroes *and* whites caught up in the common problem of a sluggish economy marked by poverty as well as affluence. The Negro unemployment rate is twice that of whites (due in part to persisting discrimination), but whites form the majority of a depressed "underclass" composed of the poor, the aged, the underskilled, the marginal. For Myrdal the great challenge of the sixties is to confront this general problem, of which racial discrimination is an integral part.

3. C. Wright Mills' work, for all its polemics and intemperate criticism of other sociologies, is a persuasive argument for a return to the humanistic tradition in sociology. See his *The Sociological Imagination,* New York: Oxford University Press, 1959.

4. A brief survey of the extent of discrimination in employment, housing, and public accommodations in Illinois appears in the larger study deposited with the Institute of Government. At the time (1960) I was criticized for allegedly exaggerating the extent of racial discrimination in Chicago, in such suburbs as Evanston and in the "other Illinois," the state's deep south. But subsequent events have shown that, on the contrary, I scarcely did justice to the bitterness and sense of frustration of my Negro respondents as they described the pattern of discrimination in "the land of Lincoln." *De facto* school segregation in Chicago is perhaps the prime example.

5. For details, see Bonita Valien and Willis A. Sutton, Jr., "Community in Chaos: Cairo, Illinois," in Robin W. Williams, Jr. and Margaret W. Ryan (eds.), *Schools in Transition,* Chapel Hill: University of North Carolina Press, 1954, and Wilma Dykeman and James Stokeley, "The 'South' in the North

(Deerfield)," *The New York Times Magazine,* April 17, 1960. New material on both communities appears in the larger study.

6. This issue has provoked extensive controversy. For criticism of "restoration of community" at the urban neighborhood level, see Richard Dewey, "The Neighborhood Urban Ecology and City Planners," *American Sociological Review,* Aug., 1950. On the disparity between rhetoric and reality in the small community ethos, see Arthur J. Vidich and Joseph Bensman, *Small Town in Mass Society,* New York: Doubleday, Anchor Ed., 1960, and C. Wright Mills, *The Power Elite,* New York: Oxford University Press, 1956, Ch. 2. On the other side, defining democracy itself in terms of meaningful local voluntarism, are Baker Brownell, Arthur E. Morgan, Saul Alinsky, Richard Poston, Paul Goodman, Jane Jacobs, and many others. The Brownell-Poston thesis, emphasizing cooperative community planning along regional lines, is now being applied in the Community Development Program, Southern Illinois University. I am indebted to the staff for background and interviews.

7. This is not to deny the great value of the *general* strategic propositions in the literature. See for example Robin M. Williams, Jr., *The Reduction of Intergroup Tensions,* New York: Social Science Research Council, 1947; R. M. MacIver, *The More Perfect Union,* New York: Macmillan, 1948; and George E. Simpson and J. Milton Yinger, *Racial and Cultural Minorities,* New York: Harper, 1958, Chs. 22, 23. One of the most insightful attempts to relate the American Creed to strategies of change is Robert K. Merton's "Discrimination and the American Creed," in R. M. MacIver (ed.), *Discrimination and the National Welfare,* New York: Harper, 1949.

8. The idea of "suburbia" as a middle-class state of mind, a psychic terri-

tory bounded by *angst* and conformity, has considerable validity as a criticism of middle–class life—whether lived inside the city or in a suburb. But it cannot be used with confidence in more specialized studies such as ours where "suburbia" runs the gamut from patrician exclusive communities still closed to Jews, to an all-Negro working-class suburban ghetto. Interestingly, the Negro ghetto was only a short distance from Park Forest, home of "the organization man," where, after some resistance, the first Negro family was finally permitted to purchase a home in 1960. See William H. Whyte, Jr., *The Organization Man,* New York: Simon & Schuster, 1956. See Bennett Berger, *Working Class Suburb,* Berkeley: University of California Press, 1960, for a very different kind of suburb.

9. Among the Hyde Park-Kenwood studies, see Peter Rossi and Robert Dentler, *The Politics of Urban Renewal,* New York: Free Press, 1961, and Julia H. Abrahamson, *A Neighborhood Finds Itself,* New York: Harper, 1959. Charles E. Silberman, *Crisis in Black and White,* New York: Random House, 1964, argues persuasively that this approach to neighborhood action is of great importance; Negroes become directly and personally involved in their fate. In this area, the strategic voluntary groups and the staffed Southeast Chicago Commission (SECC), which wields effective legal and political power, work at different facets of the same problem. My estimate of the tough-minded strategy employed by OSC to contain panic selling and other kinds of racial exploitation is based on interviews with its staff and on participant observation.

10. I am indebted to Professor Robert B. Johnson for mimeographed summaries of his pioneer research on evaluating organizational effectiveness of such groups as the American Friends Service Committee.

11. The agreement reached by white and Negro leaders in Birmingham, Alabama, following a bloody race riot in the spring of 1963, is a classic illustration of this point. The two groups in no way worked together in a joint council or commission. Indeed, the white committee failed even to initiate steps toward desegregation which it had promised to carry out after agreeing to this kind of "armed truce" in intergroup relations. Breathing space achieved and tension temporarily eased, the white leadership simply let matters drift, inviting the resort to violence and bombing (including the murder of Negro children) by those intransigent whites who moved into the vacuum left by the *ad hoc* white committee. There was the appearance, but never the reality, of the Illinois approach. The citizens' committee was nothing more than a pious fraud.

# CRIMINOLOGY AND DELINQUENCY

## 12. The Effect of Accommodations in Justice Administration on Criminal Statistics

DONALD J. NEWMAN

*Criticisms of Criminal Statistics*

PROBABLY NO ASPECT OF CRIMINOLOGY IS EASIER TO criticize, and consequently has received more criticism, than statistical descriptions of the crime problem.[1] Whether statistics are used to indicate the extent of crime or the representativeness of criminal samples, or are quoted in any context, denunciations of the statistical base quickly follow. With minor exceptions, statistics about crime and criminals are taken from some point in the process of administrating of justice: crime reports made by the police, arrest tabulations, or numbers of persons charged, convicted or sentenced. In general, criticisms are directed to the following points· (1) Because of the lack of uniformity of laws in all places, and of methods of reporting and tabulation from one jurisdiction, or one police station to another, the comparative value of data is lost; (2) Only certain types of crimes, the "conventional" offenses, are reported, while significant criminal activity, such as racketeering and white collar crime, is omitted; (3) Because many, if not most, crimes are undetected, unreported and unsolved the parameter of criminal conduct is not visible, and per-

# Donald J. Newman

haps forever unobtainable. These criticisms envisage the "true" incidence of crime to be broader than administrative practices, including all conduct proscribed by statutes, proceeded against or not. Such criticisms also lead to an evaluation of enforcing agencies as inefficient, or worse, for not enforcing legislation more effectively.

No attempt will be made here to review the work of those who advocate better and uniform crime reporting,[2] nor will there be particular emphasis on documentation of spectacular breakdowns in law enforcement by corruption, bribery and the like, as was the fashion in earlier crime surveys.[3] Instead, as the basis for crime statistics, we shall analyze both the popular conception and the actual operation of the system of criminal justice, and shall interpret the data gathered from this system.

## Purposes of Operational Analysis[4]

The administrative process by which suspects become defendants and defendants are convicted is, of course, the formal means of labeling and treating certain persons as criminals. Statistics taken from some point in this conviction process become "data" (statistics about crimes not solved or criminals uncaught are usually "estimates") and, from them, all sorts of conclusions are drawn about the nature of crime and of criminals. Both the actual value of such data and an understanding of the typical conclusions drawn from such statistics depend upon an accurate assessment of the basis of this labeling process and its operational characteristics.

The problem of commenting on any source of criminal statistics is complicated because the meanings attributed to them, no matter how carefully gathered, and the conclusions drawn from them depend basically upon conceptions of how the justice system works, or more likely, should work. For example, it can be argued that the real universe of crime is all conduct which violates criminal statutes, whether such conduct is of concern to enforcing agencies or not. On the other hand, it can be argued that criminal conduct is not merely defined by statute, but only by statutes that are invoked by administrative practice. Thus, although laws may proscribe fornication, social gambling, or working on the Sabbath, it would be artificial to include all such conduct within the crime universe because these laws are typically not enforced, nor in many cases were they ever intended to be fully enforced. When they are used, the purpose is not to convict on the basis of the conduct, but, for example, to "get" a person whose conduct is known to be more criminal but when evidence of the higher crime

*164*

is lacking. The meaning of crime and the purposes and consequences of the justice system differ markedly in each of these conceptions. They illustrate the long recognized discrepancy between "law on the books" and the "law in action."

It is the purpose here to view the law in action and to raise some issues about the meaning and value of data taken from the system in operation. Two major approaches will be taken. A brief operational conception of the justice system will be presented and an analysis will be made of accommodations at the adjudication stage. The first purpose of this presentation is to criticize the critics of crime data. To do this we will present an operational image of criminal justice which challenges both the basic conception and the premises of typical criticisms and evaluations. Our second goal is to give warning about the use of conviction records as indices of the extent of crime or of the types of criminals.

## The System of Criminal Justice Administration

Probably the most common image of the criminal justice process approximates what Arnold has called the "Ideal of Law Enforcement" that "repudiates the idea of compromise as immoral" and commands the state to "enforce the Law" uniformly, automatically.[5] This image relates both to the definition of criminal conduct and to the ways of proceeding against it. Crime is defined by the words of the statutes, with little allowance for administrative interpretation and none for discretion. The *nullum crimen* principle sets not only the outer limits of criminal conduct but also the minimum limits. If it is on the books, it is a crime; and if it is violated, the violator is a criminal. Statutes not only define crime, but become mandates for enforcing agencies. It becomes the duty of police, prosecutors and courts to search out all proscribed conduct and fully invoke the process against those who engage in such conduct. The purpose of criminal procedure is to separate the guilty from the innocent, and to give the guilty their full due, both by convicting them of the maximum crime supported by the evidence and by meting out the appropriate punishment. Although the police cannot possibly detect all crimes, if for no other reasons than limited resources and inefficiency, the assumption remains that, once invoked, the conviction process, based on legally relevant evidence, should culminate in the adversary technique of trial to convict the guilty and to free those against whom there is insufficient evidence. The statutes define what conduct is criminal, the police act as intake agents, the prosecutors, more skilled in law, screen evidence, and the juries or the judges make the ultimate determination. The process is complex only as law is complex, but the administration is routine and mandatory, with little room for discretion and none for compromise. The oil which runs the machine is evidence, and the machine is Law.

How widely such an image is held is debatable. Yet common criticisms of the system and the typical use of data gathered from it are based on it. There is the allegation of "real" crime outside administrative concern, and the use of labels from the system to define the extent of "known" crime. These rely equally on the assumptions that crime is determined by statute, not practices, and that labels assigned to convicted defendants are the statutory equivalents of their actual conduct. To think of the administrative process in these terms is to oversimplify it, and to interpret data from the system without an awareness of its operational complexity is to do the system and statistics a disservice.

The administration of criminal justice is an involved and complicated process of decisions and discretionary choices of the persons who administer it. As with all systems in which men must decide the fate of other men, it must necessarily accommodate itself to fit rules to cases, to determine its own goals, to maintain its equilibrium and to perform its functions effectively and uniformly. It is by no means automatic, nor does it, in theory or in practice, fit the image of full enforcement, maximum implementation, and trial-by-combat discussed above. At least three distinctions from this image must be made to define the basis of the justice system and its operational character.

### THE DETERMINATION OF CRIMINAL CONDUCT

Although legislatures have the formal duty of defining criminal conduct, the list of penal statutes does not necessarily set a minimum mandate for administering agencies. Statutes define the outer limits of criminal conduct beyond which the police, courts and other agencies cannot go, but it does not necessarily follow that all statutes must be fully enforced to these limits. Statutes may be enacted as expressions of desirable morality but with no intention of full and relentless enforcement[6] (adultery). They may be retained due to legislative oversight or a conscious hope of strengthening the "arsenal" of the prosecutor, but without expectation of general enforcement (blue laws). They may prove useful although they are vague and not clearly limited, either inadvertently, deliberately, or as a necessary limitation of all attempts to write generalizable word formulas (gambling).[7] Furthermore, due to the lag between the volume of criminal statutes and the resources and budget allowances for their enforcement, the enforcement agencies must make allocation decisions of which laws are to receive primary enforcement attention. The question of mandate, then, is itself a complex one, and a more realistic definition of criminal conduct is one of practice within the outer limits fixed by legislation rather than of reliance on the words of the statutes themselves.

### DISCRETION WITHIN THE SYSTEM

The administrative process does not turn solely upon the basis of admissible evidence. There are points in the process when discretion is formally allowed and when decisions to invoke or not invoke may hinge upon bases other than evidential. The prosecutor, for example, has wide discretionary powers in deciding when and what to charge and even whether to charge at all, despite sufficient evidence. Not all persons validly arrested must be charged; the prosecutor has the power of *nolle prosequi* which may be based upon extra-evidential criteria. He is a buffer between the legal requirements for arrest and the finality of conviction. He may consider individual differences not recognized in statute, the "welfare of the community," the "ends of justice," or just about any other factor within the discretion conferred upon him.[8] In addition to prosecutor's discretion, formally recognized discretionary powers are conferred upon the judge in sentencing, and upon post-conviction authorities. This discretion is not limited to legally relevant evidence but may be used to consider many cultural and psychological variables as distinguishing criteria. At least at the points of charging, sentence and corrections, then, the system makes discretionary allowances. There are some checks, formal and otherwise, on the exercise of this discretion, but their analysis is beyond the scope of this paper. Nevertheless, at these points, discretion is recognized and expected. Among other things, it makes allegations of "disparity" in charging or sentencing a less clear criticism of the system than if the "full enforcement ideal" were really the case.

In addition to points of recognized discretion, it is clear that discretion must be assumed at points when it is not formally permitted. The police, for example, cannot physically enforce all laws equally even if they should wish to do so.[9] And, in the task of fitting laws to persons, courts must choose among consequences of labels and sentences if they wish to individualize justice. Discretion, then, whether granted or assumed, is a part of the system and forms the basis of the accommodations discussed below.

### THE GUILTY PLEA

The conviction process relies primarily on the guilty plea, not on the trial. Adversary it may be, but adversary in pleadings, not in combat.

Although there are fluctuations among jurisdictions, between 80 and 90 per cent of all persons charged plead guilty.[10] The trial, and particularly the jury trial, is comparatively rare, considering the arrest and charging base. The guilty plea is by far the most common form of adjudication in felonies, misdemeanors and ordinance violations, and it occurs in rural and urban courts at about the same rate of frequency. Not only does the guilty plea predominate adjudication but the entire conviction system also operates upon an expectation of a continually high proportion of such pleas. The rather unrealistic cry is often heard that if all arrested in a single day exercised their prerogative to plead not guilty, the system would be swamped for months or years. It is, of course, unlikely that all cohort defendants will plead not guilty. Yet the system is so finely balanced in some congested urban court systems that even a small increment in not guilty pleas would seriously strain trial resources. The guilty plea has obvious advantages for the system; it not only clears the dockets and frees the prosecutor from trial efforts, but at small cost assures conviction of the guilty, thus protecting the community (after all, even the best prepared trial may result in acquittal of guilty and dangerous persons) and has the further psychological advantage of recording confessions of guilt. To imprison or otherwise incapacitate a person who, although convicted, steadfastly maintains his innocence is somehow disturbing, whereas the guilty plea precludes this doubt, unreasonable as it may be. The criminal justice system is not only characterized by guilty pleas but relies on, and benefits from, a continuing high rate of such pleas. This presents a different administrative process than a system based on trial.

The conviction process, then, is unlike the quasi-automatic full enforcement image. For statutes provide merely the outer limits of permissible official action; they are not necessarily mandates to administrators. The process must rely upon discretion, given or assumed, by those who operate within it, and the chief means of conviction is by plea rather than trial. With these in mind, we can analyze accommodations, both routine and individualistic, which are necessary for efficient, effective administration of the process.

## Accommodations in the Conviction Process

The term "accommodations" will be used here to refer to decisions, for the most part routine and systematic, to proceed to less than full implementation of the conviction process in spite of sufficient legal evidence to do so.[11] The effects of such accommodations are either (1) non-invocation against persons clearly guilty of criminal conduct, or (2) less than full implementation warranted by the criminal conduct of defendants and the evidence against them. Both of these affect any statistics derived from the system. The first excludes from tabulation those known to be guilty but nevertheless not processed, and the second affixes criminal labels and sentences inconsistent with and less serious than the actual criminal conduct could warrant.

Accommodations occur at each of the major stages of the administrative process, investigation of crimes, arrest, charging, adjudication, sentencing and post-sentencing treatment. Limited space prohibits thorough analysis of each. Instead, one stage, adjudication, will be used for illustration. Two reasons make this a particularly crucial point at which to demonstrate such accommodations: (1) conviction is the formal labeling stage, and the crime for which the defendant is convicted fixes the outer limits of his sentence; and (2) adjudication is, in theory, a nondiscretionary phase of the process. While prosecutors have discretion in charging, and the judge in sentencing, theoretically the only basis of acquittal or conviction is sufficient evidence. Acquittal of guilty defendants is within the *power* of the judge and cannot be attacked, but is not recognized as a *discretionary* choice.[12] Conviction without sufficient evidence is of course not allowed, although the guilty plea presents particular problems here because, ordinarily, the evidence is not fully presented so that the judge can weigh it accurately.[13] But selecting the crime on which to convict the defendant and the relationship of this selection to his actual conduct is another matter. A defendant can be convicted of a less serious crime than the one of which he actually is guilty.[14]

Accommodations at adjudication fall into two major categories: (1) acquittal of guilty defendants in spite of evidence sufficient to convict them; and (2) charge reduction in exchange for a plea of guilty.[15] While both have some characteristics in common, they are sufficiently distinct to be viewed separately. A major difference is that the acquittal accommodation is a decision not to convict, and thereby to release the defendant from official control. In contrast, the reduction decision retains control but modifies the label and consequent sentence.

#### ACQUITTAL OF GUILTY DEFENDANTS

It could be argued that determination of guilt is never certain until after trial, and that judicial acquittal of the "guilty" is not really an accommodation at all, but a finding based upon insufficient evidence to

*169*

convict. While this might be the case if inability to conivct is held to be the same as "innocent,"[16] in most routine dismissals of this nature the evidence is clearly sufficient to convict. There is little doubt, certainly no reasonable doubt, that defendants engaged in the conduct for which they were arrested and charged. Very often defendants admit the offense voluntarily, and occasionally offer guilty pleas which are refused.

The acquittal of the guilty decision can be dichotomized as to general purposes of the judge who acquits: (1) interpretation and review of, and possibly attempt to control, earlier investigation, arrest and charging decisions; and (2) attempt to individualize justice. The first category can be further refined to include (a) acquittal as a reflection of the judge's belief that the conduct is not really criminal because it does not fall within the legislative proscription, or the legislative intent of enforcement of the law; and (b) acquittal as a protest against methods used by the police in investigation or arrest. Judges were observed to acquit in petty gambling and adult sexual relation cases on the general grounds that the law was not intended to cover such instances. And acting in review of prior procedures, judges used acquittal when police methods were felt to be unfair, although this unfairness was technically short of entrapment, illegal search, or unnecessary force. In Detroit, for example, one judge routinely acquitted both prostitutes and homosexuals when in his opinion the vice squad had "enticed" them into the criminal conduct.[17] In addition, acquittal was sometimes used as a reward for informants.

In attempting to individualize justice, judges used acquittal under several circumstances.

1. When postconviction resources were felt to be inadequate to deal effectively with the conduct involved, particularly when alternatives short of conviction were available, acquittal was used. In cases of drunks, domestic disputes, bad check cases and some sex offenses acquittal was used when such alternatives as the Salvation Army or Alcoholics Anonymous agreed to take the drunks, when reconciliation occurred in the domestic fights, when restitution was made in the check cases, when the boy agreed to marry the girl in statutory rape cases, or when the peeping Tom agreed to seek psychiatric help.

2. Acquittal was used because of the excessive cost of conviction to the defendant and the low risk of his reviolation. This occurred particularly where defendants were young, had no previous record, and/or when defendants were otherwise "respectable" persons and the judge felt that the prior processes of arrest and charging were enough to "teach them a lesson" but that a conviction record would work some hardship beyond

the formal sentence, such as loss of employment or inability to enter the armed services.

3. Acquittal was used because of mitigating circumstances in the case. This occurred most frequently where victim or complainant had contributed to the criminal conduct as in assault charges growing out of barroom fights, larceny by prostitutes from their clients, and the like.

4. Acquittal was used in a variety of situations or unusual circumstances ranging from the low intelligence or emotional instability of certain defendants to the judicial belief that such conduct as contained in the charge is really "normal" behavior within certain racial or class subcultures.

In general, summary acquittal of the guilty does not account for a high proportion of the cases charged, although it was used in all courts studied. Cases reaching the adjudication level have already passed through police and prosecutor screens with the bulk of the decisions not to invoke the process made here. In this sense, acquittal by the court can be viewed as a review of prosecutor discretion and it is likely that the values expressed here, short of personal antagonism, are rather quickly translated into police and prosecutor practices.[18] If the judge regularly refuses to convict in routine adultery cases, for example, continued and relentless police activity to discover adulterous relationships and to press for trial would be fruitless. Consequently, much conduct likely to result in acquittal never gets to the judge: when it does, acquittal quickly follows.

CHARGE REDUCTION FOR REASONS OTHER THAN SUFFICIENCY OF EVIDENCE

Whereas acquittal is outright forgiveness on the part of the court and whereas it is relatively infrequent because of prior screening, charge reduction is compromise, bargaining with the guilty, and a very common, almost routine practice in those jurisdictions where it is necessary to avoid mandatory sentencing provisions.

Charge reduction is a major part of a broader "negotiated plea" process[19] and as such it affects defendants in two ways: (1) by reducing the criminal record, the "label," which attaches upon conviction, to one less than the defendant's actual conduct would objectively warrant, and (2) by achieving the ordinarily less severe sentencing consequences of conviction on a lesser charge. For the most part these are related, but a case can be made so that the criminal record may occasionally have independent significance from the sentencing provisions. Where the reduction is from felony to misdemeanor, for example, the defendant may not only markedly reduce the possible sentence but also avoid both the stigma and consequences of felony conviction in the process. In other cases, however, where a felony is reduced to a lesser felony, for example, the labeling advantage is minimal, particularly where post-conviction authorities, aware of bargaining, tend to treat the defendant as if he had been convicted of the original charges. In either case, to generalize about conduct distribution from the statistics of conviction records, without considering the effect of the discrepancies between conduct and official label is devastating.

The primary purpose of most charge reductions is to avoid the sentencing consequences of conviction on higher charges. Charge reductions occur most commonly in those jurisdictions and in those cases where there are legislative controls on judicial sentencing discretion.[20] Charge reduction is a necessary adjustment for individual differences where the full use of sentencing discretion is blocked by statutory rigidity. In effect, it moves the sentencing decision back to the adjudication and charging stages. This is most clearly illustrated where statutes fix both the minimum and maximum sentences in a given offense. In Michigan, for example, sale of narcotics carries a mandatory minimum sentence of twenty years imprisonment, the maximum being life, without the possibility of probation. The difficulty presented by this to prosecutors and judges is that it removes the possibility of distinguishing cases once the charge has been brought and the conviction recorded. Both the youthful first offender whose criminal conduct consists of selling a single marijuana cigarette to a buddy, and the chronic, professional pusher face twenty years minimum incarceration if convicted of sale.

Consequently, the practice is to reduce the charge in the first instance, the case of the young defendant, and convicting "on the nose" only where there is judicial and prosecutor desire to incapacitate the organized criminal. However rationalized, whether as interpretation of the way the legislature intended the law to be used, or merely as perception of differences in circumstances and defendants not accounted for in statute, charge reduction here is an attempt at equity in consequences, where such equity is denied by statutory limitations on sentencing discretion.

It might be asked why the exercise of this discretion is not moved back in the process to the prosecutor's original charging decision where discretion is expressly given, or why the police, as aware of differences in cases as the court, do not modify the bases of their arrest. The answer is that similar discretion is exercised by both prosecutor and police in many cases (and even types of cases) and variations between states and court jurisdictions occur. It happens in Michigan that arrest, charging and bargaining are fairly distinct and that judges play a more visible and active role in charge reduction here than in some other jurisdictions—Kansas, for example. The explanation of jurisdictional differences is a complex one involving factors relating to the development of customs in one place, a sort of historical accident, as contrasted to another, although both methods have similar consequences.

Variations in the history of customs is inadequate as a total explanation. The reduction of charges at, or just prior to, the adjudication stage serves certain specific purposes that would not be possible if all such discretion were left to the police at arrest, or the prosecutor in bringing the original charge. Charge reduction is based upon a prior decision to convict the defendant rather than to acquit him. Noninvocation of the process may be easily accomplished by the police in failing to arrest or by the *nolle prosequi* powers of the prosecutor. Once the decision is to convict, however, the process must be started; the arrest made and the charge brought. Here the other purposes of bargaining come into play. In the illustration given of two cases of the sale of narcotics, the motive for reduction was an equitable balance of consequences based on the different criminality of the two defendants.

Equity, the individualization of justice, is only a part of the motivation for the negotiated plea. As a matter of fact, charges are routinely reduced, and while the balancing of consequences by differences in defendant characteristics or mitigating circumstances in cases may be expressed by court or prosecutor, a primary purpose of reduction is to induce defendants to plead guilty. The entire system of criminal justice administration rests upon a predictably high rate of guilty pleas and in view of limited trial resources and persistently high crime rates, a conviction accommodation device is necessary to maintain efficiency and speed at this stage. Since every accused defendant has a right to trial, there must be a differential advantage given to that high proportion who waive this right and thus relieve trial congestion. Because of the Michigan and Kansas mandatory sentencing structures, the best inducement for a guilty plea is charge reduction to modify statutory sentencing requirements.

Furthermore, because certain offenses are nonprobationable, and the prisons crowded, charge reduction lessens strains on the post-conviction resources as well as those of the trial. Thus, while equity in consequences may be achieved by reducing charges in one case and not another, or by reducing further in one case, the practice has become so routine and systematic that individual differences are only occasionally offered as rationalization.

*173*

Charge reduction at the adjudication level also means that the court has a more active role in the expression of the values involved. The judge can either initiate or directly condone bargaining, can take it into account in his sentencing decision, and, in general, can implement policies or desires about certain types of offenders or certain laws. If bargaining were solely the province of other agencies, its visibility would be reduced and the directness of judicial check on this process lost. Since bargaining in great part is concerned with the manipulation of sentencing alternatives, negotiations at the adjudication level act to contain the sentencing decision within the province of the court. Were there no statutory restrictions on judicial sentencing powers, the need for charge reduction as a bargaining device would be unnecessary except, of course, where the conviction label is of some particular significance. In jurisdictions with statutory sentences, however, charge reduction is the alternative when judges find their sentencing discretion controlled, and when defendants become reluctant to plead guilty to offenses with high maximum or minimum mandatory sentences or to crimes which exclude them from probation. If defendants are to be induced to plead guilty, and if the court wishes sentencing choices beyond those listed as mandatory, then charge reduction is the major way of accomplishing these ends, while retaining the sentencing decision within the province of the court.

Because any crime can be downgraded, and examples of reductions of virtually all types of felonies and misdemeanors are noted, the range of downgrading (i.e., how far the original offense is reduced) is of particular interest and the question of limits, if any, on manipulation of the original charge, is of particular significance. Generally, reductions can be classified as either to lesser included offenses, or to "illogical" lesser offenses. Some common reductions noted were: murder to manslaughter or negligent homicide; armed robbery to robbery unarmed, attempted robbery, larceny or assault; sale of narcotics to possession or addiction; burglary to larceny or illegal entry; rape to assault; carnal knowledge to indecent liberties; drunken driving to reckless driving; and the like. Some reductions bring substantial sentencing benefits, reducing the maximum punishment as much as tenfold, and, of course, reductions from felonies to misdemeanors reduce both sentence and record.

The only limitation on the range of reductions appears to be an inarticulated but common practice of reduction to a count which bears some categoric similarity to the original charge. Homicides, for eaxmple, involve reductions from murder to manslaughter or negligent homicide or assault or attempt. But offenses that are grossly inconsistent, such as

174

larceny or possession of narcotics, are never arbitrarily added in place of murder, unless these offenses are part of the actual conduct involved in the major crime. The "illogical" lesser offense, then, is never categorically different from the original charge; it is "illogical" ("inconsistent" would be a more accurate term) only in the sense that the added offense contains some element of proof not required in the original charge, or omits evidence of some element necessary to the major charge, and is therefore somewhat inconsistent with the fact situation.

Although the general, overriding consideration in charge reduction is the maintenance of a steady flow of guilty pleas, specific attempts to individualize justice may underly the reduction decision in about the same fashion as the motives for acquittal of the guilty. Thus judges may concur with the prosecutor's move for reduction because (1) the conduct does not warrant the conviction record or the mandatory sentence of the greater charge, (2) the effects of conviction on the lesser count are equal or better than conviction on the higher charge, (3) the lesser charge is more suitable because the defendant, although guilty of the greater charge, deserves a break because he is young, respectable or otherwise deserving, (4) the lesser charge is justified by circumstances in the case which mitigate higher liability, (5) the lesser charge permits probation and thereby allows restitution, or enables the defendant to support his family, (6) the lesser charge is a suitable reward for informants or states' witnesses.

Charge reduction is common, almost routine. About the same types of bargains are offered to all who wish to avail themselves of them; there was no evidence of arbitrary use nor discriminatory denial of negotiation. All in post-conviction authority are aware of this process so that a member of the Michigan Parole Board could comment: "This one is from Wayne County and it says robbery unarmed. Let's see what kind of a gun he used." Another parole official remarked: "It's almost impossible to tell what a man actually did by the formal charge under which he was sentenced." Unfortunately, the fact of charge reduction does not usually appear in judicial statistics.

THE EFFECT OF ACCOMMODATIONS ON CRIMINAL STATISTICS

The effects of the two accommodations, acquittal and reduction, on statistics gathered from the conviction process are apparent. The acquittal decision effectively removes some guilty from the tabulation at conviction and sentencing stages. These are not undetected or unknown criminals. Their conduct and identity have been discovered but nevertheless they are released. The reduction process, on the other hand, retains control, but modifies both the label and the sentence of the persons convicted. To conclude that a particular criminal is a certain behavioral type from his conviction record is obviously a dubious technique. To generalize about the crime problem of a given community by the types of convictions recorded there, is likewise of little value. To assume that only good risk, minor offenders are placed on probation, as their records might indicate, leads to the disillusionment of many new probation officers unaware of the extent and range of bargaining. Legislators who fix severe punishments to certain crimes, such as sale of narcotics, may conclude that this punishment is effective when conviction rates decline. But they fail to take into account the accommodations that are available within the system for avoiding legislative mandate.

In short, statistics taken from the surface of the system are more likely to be inaccurate than reliable indicators of the distribution of criminal conduct. Failing to recognize criminal procedures as a complex pattern of decision-making, of discretionary choices by administrators and paying little attention to the flexibility of the system in accommodating laws to cases, is an error in any conclusions based upon conviction records or tabulations taken from any point in the conviction process. A careful analysis of how the system operates and how it records its business is a prerequisite for the use of data gathered from it.

Furthermore, to criticize statistics taken from the system because they do not include all "real" crimes, or to allege inefficiency or corruption because some persons are released from the process and others are not labeled as severely as their conduct could warrant, is to attribute to the system characteristics it does not have, nor necessarily should have. The "law" is no more clearly statute than practice. The desirable consequence of procedures is no more a clearly accurate labeling than an equitable balancing of record and punishment among differing cases and defendants. A slot-machine model of administration is neither as realistic nor more just than a system devoted to speedy disposition of cases with ample attention to due process and civil rights, but with discretion to accommodate cases to law and law to persons.

## NOTES

1. See, for example, Ronald Beattie, "Criminal Statistics in the United States —1950," 51 J. Crim. L. Crim. & Pol. Sci. (May–June 1950), 49; and also by Beattie, "Problems of Criminal Statistics in the United States," 46 J. Crim. L. Crim. & Pol. Sci., (July–Aug. 1955), 178. See also Thorsten Sellin, Research Memorandum on Crime in the Depression, New York: Social Science Research Coun-

# Accommodation in Justice Administration

cil, 1937, and C. C. Van Vechten, "Differential Criminal Case Mortality In Selected Jurisdictions," *American Sociological Review,* 7, (1942), 833 and Donald Cressey, "The State of Criminal Statistics," *3 Nat. Prob. and Parole Assoc. J.* (1957), 230.

2. See Thorsten Sellin, "The Uniform Criminal Statistics Act," *40 J. Crim. L. & Crim.* 879 (March–April 1950). Also by Sellin, "The Basis of a Crime Index," *22 J. Crim. L. & Crim.* (1931), 335 and United States Federal Bureau of Investigation, *Uniform Crime Reports,* Washington, D.C. annually.

3. For a list of these surveys, see Virgil Peterson, *Crime Commissions in the United States,* Chicago: Chicago Crime Commission, 1945. See also National Commission on Law Observance and Enforcement, *Report on Lawlessness in Law Enforcement,* Washington, D.C., Gov. Print. Office, 1931; Roscoe Pound and Felix Frankfurter, *Criminal Justice in Cleveland,* Cleveland Foundation, 1922; Missouri Association for Criminal Justice Survey Association, *The Missouri Crime Survey,* New York: Macmillan, 1926; Illinois Association for Criminal Justice, *Illinois Crime Survey,* 1929, and Ernest J. Hopkins, *Our Lawless Police,* New York: Viking, 1931.

4. For the past several years the American Bar Foundation, on the basis of a Ford Foundation grant, has been conducting a three-state study on the administration of criminal justice. The three states under analysis are Michigan, Kansas, and Wisconsin, and the study is due for publication within a year. Frank J. Remington, Professor of Law at the University of Wisconsin, is director of both the field and analysis phases of the project, which is devoted precisely to this point of analyzing routine practices in justice administration. The author is associated with this project, and from it has gathered the data for this paper.

5. Thurman W. Arnold, *The Symbols of Government,* Yale University Press, 1935, p. 162.

6. Arnold comments: "Most unenforced criminal laws survive in order to satisfy moral objections to established modes of conduct. They are unenforced because we want to continue our conduct, and unrepealed because we want to preserve our morals." *Ibid.,* p. 160.

7. For an excellent analysis of ambiguity in defining criminal conduct, see Frank J. Remington and Victor G. Rosenblum, "The Criminal Law and the Legislative Process," *Law Forum* (1960), 481.

8. See, for example, Williams, "Discretion in Prosecuting," *Crim. L. R.* (April 1956), 222; Klein, "Discretion Not to Prosecute," *32 L.A.B. Bul.* (1957), 323; Comment: "Discretionary Power of Attorney General to Enter Nolle Prosequi on a Criminal Indictment" [*People ex rel Elliot v. Coveill* (Ill.) NE 2d 156] 42 *Ill. B.J.* (Nov. 1953), 189; Baker and Delong, "The Prosecuting Attorney and his Office," 25 *Crim. L. & Crim.* (1935), 695.

9. See Joseph Goldstein, "Police Discretion Not to Invoke the Criminal Process: Low-Visibility Decisions in the Administration of Justice," 69 *Yale Law Journal* (1960), 543 and Frank J. Remington, "Police Detention and Arrest Privileges," 52 *Jour. Crim. L., Crimin. & Pol. Sci.* (1960), 386. See also Charles Breitel, "Controls in Criminal Law Enforcement," 27 *University of Chicago Law Review,* (1960), 427.

10. See American Law Institute *A Study of the Business of the Federal Courts,* 1934; Institute of Judicial Administration, *Law Enforcement Statistics Study,* New Jersey, 1955; Leon Marshall, *Comparative Judicial Criminal Statistics,* 1931; and Mark S. Boerner, *Administrative Justice,* unpublished, 1959.

11. Actually, accommodations can be

*177*

# Donald J. Newman

in either direction. One type is illustrated by a decision not to invoke the process in spite of sufficient evidence to do so, yet another can be illustrated by a decision to invoke in a type of case where non-invocation is the norm. For example, the decision to convict a particular defendant of fornication when the ordinary practice is not to convict anyone of fornication regardless of evidence is an illustration of this reverse type of accommodation. For a discussion of just such a case see Remington and Rosenblum, *op. cit.*, pp. 493–4.

12. *State v. Evjue*, 254 Wis. 581, 37 N.W.2d 50 (1949).

13. Some courts use a Post–Plea–of–Guilty Hearing to substantiate their own acceptance of the plea. Thompson, "Judges Responsibility on a Plea of Guilty," 62 *W. Va. L. Rev.* (1960), 213. It was noted in Michigan that the chief focus of pre-sentence reports by the Probation Department was on the matter of guilt or innocence rather than on etiological factors more traditional in such reports.

14. A person charged with a crime can be convicted of that crime or any lesser included crimes, but the general rule seems to be, and the Model Penal Code proposes, that judges charge the jury about included offenses only when the evidence makes it appropriate. [See Amer. L. Institute, Model Penal Code, Tent. Draft No. 5, Sec. 1.08, p. 30, comment pp. 42–3 (1956)]. In the routine charge reduction situation there is little doubt that the evidence supports the greater charge, but reduction is accomplished anyway. Thus the plea situation is quite different from trial. The question is unsettled whether judges have discretion to accept lesser charges where evidence supports a higher offense, particularly when the lesser count is somewhat inconsistent with the fact situation or ignores significant facts (armed robbery

reduced to unarmed robbery although defendant used a gun). There is no doubt this is a common practice but the issue is rarely raised on appeal because the defendant, obviously guilty of a higher crime, has received a "break" in both label and sentence and has no desire to overturn this. In a parallel situation, the inducement of a plea by sentence promise and dismissal of charges raises the issue of the bargained plea in a recent Federal case. In *Shelton v. U.S.*, 234 F (2d) 132 (1956), 242 F (2d) 101 (1957), 246 F (2d) 571 (1957) and 358 U.S. 26 (1958), the defendant moved to vacate a bargained plea on the grounds it was not voluntary, although the bargain (dismissal of other charges and a sentence promise) was honored by the government. Appellate Court commented: "It is generally known that the great bulk of the criminal cases are disposed of by pleas of guilty made after some discussion between the defendant and/or his counsel and the prosecuting attorney in which the latter frequently makes some commitments as to sentence he will recommend or as to other charges or prosecutions he will drop; if this were not so, or, if this court holds that it may not be so, there will be few inducements for any person to plead guilty. . . . It also appears that the prosecutor in good faith tried to live up to his commitments and to a very large extent was successful in his efforts. Nor can it be said that any of the promises were inherently improper, for the offer to help obtain the dismissal of the federal prosecutions in other districts does not differ fundamentally from the usual practice where the prosecutor agrees to nolle prosequi all except the charges on which plea is to be entered." [Dissent in 242 F (2d) 101, majority opinion in 246 F (2d) 571]. For a more detailed analysis of this case, see NOTE: "Plea of Guilty Induced by a Promise of Leniency," 36 *Tex. L. Rev.*

(1957), 97. For a discussion of lesser induced crimes, see NOTE: "Submission of Lesser Crimes," 56 *Col. L. Rev.* (1956), 888.

15. There are accommodations other than charge reduction in the negotiated plea process, but in general these are variations on the theme of controlling sentence limits. Charge reduction is used in illustration because it is common, and because it contains some issues relevant to the use of criminal statistics not so apparent in the other inducements. These other inducements include (1) sentence promises, (2) dropping of extraneous charges, (3) concurrent prosecution in the case of the multiple offender, and (4) the decision not to invoke the habitual offender law where it could be used. For discussion of various bargains, see Donald J. Newman, "Pleading Guilty for Considerations: A Study of Bargain Justice," 46 *J. Crim. L., C., & P.S.* (1956), 780, and Justin Miller, "The Compromise of Criminal Cases," 1 *So. Cal. L. Rev.* (1927), 1.

16. Juries are not required to rationalize their acquittal decisions in any way. Reasons for acquittal may be based upon factors other than evidential, ranging from community sentiments to all forms of personal bias. Prosecutors and courts have observed that juries typically will not convict, regardless of evidence, in certain types of cases in which defendants face high mandatory minimum sentences (a young defendant facing a mandatory 20 to life term). Consequently, such cases rarely get charged, but when they do, judges typically acquit either in anticipation of, or in sympathy with, jury behavior. In the cases that were observed, there was sufficient objective evidence to convict, yet facing a jury, defendants were nonconvictable. Jury behavior is under analysis in a study conducted by the University of Chicago Law School. See Harry Kalven, Jr., "Report on the Jury Project," in *Aims and Methods of Legal Research,* Ann Arbor: University of Michigan Press, 1955, pp. 155–88.

17. The range of the "enticement" concept of unfairness was illustrated by a judicial acquittal of prostitutes who had accosted and solicited plain clothes vice officers who were in an unmarked Cadillac. The Judge said the use of the Cadillac was unfair since the vice squad typically used unmarked Fords.

18. Arrests and charging may persist in spite of routine acquittals, due, among other things, to basic disagreement between offices on the nature of the problem. For example, the Detroit police typically define their duty to be the control of prostitution, whereas the courts read the law literally to be control of accosting and soliciting for purposes of prostitution. The first interpretation rests on the illegality of the conduct, the second on its visibility and nuisance aspects. Obviously, following the first leads to types of investigation and enforcement incompatible with the second. The difference persists so that police arrest "prostitutes" but the court acquits if they did not "accost or solicit."

19. See note 15.

20. For an analysis of the influence of sentencing structure on administration, see Lloyd Ohlin and Frank J. Remington, "Sentencing Structure: Its Effect on the Administration of Justice," 23 *Law and Contemporary Problems* (1953), 495.

# 13. Uniform Crime Reporting: Suggested Improvements

DAVID J. PITTMAN and WILLIAM F. HANDY

*Historical Development of the FBI Uniform Crime Reporting System*

IN 1927, AFTER YEARS OF DISCUSSION, THE INTER-national Association of Chiefs of Police (IACP) formed a committee with instructions to research the field of criminal statistics and the reporting of crime, and, after this preliminary step, to establish a uniform crime reporting system and agency for all law enforcement agencies in the United States.[1] This committee met in 1928 and established a crime classification and collecting system, which became effective in June, 1929, with the IACP acting as the national clearing house for the criminal statistics of 400 cooperating agencies.[2]

The IACP Committee devised a crime classification system based chiefly on legal commonalities among offenses. All crimes were divided into two categories. The first, Class I (or Part I), included murder, rape, robbery, aggravated assault, larceny, burglary, and automobile theft. All other crimes were designated as Class II (or Part II) crimes. These included 20 subcategories ranging from sex offenses to parking violations. Class I crimes were those the committee felt would most likely be reported

This article was first published in *Sociology and Social Research* 46, (1962) 135–43. This research was supported by the St. Louis Metropolitan Police Department and in part by a USPHS Research Training Grant (MH 7081) and a USPHS Graduate Training Grant (MH 5804) from the National Institute of Mental Health, United States Public Health Service. The editorial assistance of Marilyn Harrington, Social Science Institute, Washington University, is appreciated.

to the police and were accounted for under the term "crimes known to police." Class II crimes were those less likely to become known to the police because of their invisibility and the unwillingness of the victim to report the crime,[3] and were classified under the term "crimes cleared by arrest." Data on these two categories were published twice annually.

On September 1, 1930, by Act of Congress, the system of uniform crime reporting was transferred to the Federal Bureau of Investigation (FBI), where it has remained.[4] The FBI has expanded the system to include other crime-relevant data collected from law enforcement agencies. The data are published in the *Uniform Crime Reports.*

Many aspects of the FBI crime reporting were criticized through the 1930's and 1940's. The culmination of critical appraisals was reached in a 1957 *Life Magazine* article in which Thorsten Sellin, noted American criminologist, was extremely critical of the uniform crime reporting system.[5] Shortly after this article appeared a Consultant Committee—composed of Dr. Peter P. Lejins, a University of Maryland sociologist; Dr. Charlton Chute, Institute of Public Administration, New York; and Stanley R. Schrotel, Cincinnati's Chief of Police under the auspices of the FBI and the IACP—carried out a detailed study of the uniform crime reporting system and made concrete recommendations for its alteration.[6] The Consultant Committee's recommendations parallel in certain respects the criticisms offered by Sellin.[7] Of the suggestions for changes in the *Uniform Crime Reports,* the following were accepted: (1) the system of designating crimes "Class I" or "Class II" was to be abandoned. For "Class I" was substituted "Index Crimes"; for "Class II," "Other Crimes;"[8] (2) negligent manslaughter, larcenies under $50, and statutory rape were to be excluded from the new category of Index Crimes; (3) beginning with 1959, only one report was to be issued annually, with preliminary reports published quarterly showing trends of crime in cities of over 100,000 population.

These changes, significant as they are, do not correct certain deficiencies in the present crime classification system from both an information and a research point of view. (We will discuss this later in this paper.)


## The Uniform Crime Reports

All United States law enforcement agencies receive from the FBI a series of blanks requesting information desired for the *Uniform Crime Reports* (UCR). Cooperating agencies complete these forms and return them to the FBI, which tabulates crime rates and trends for presentation in the quarterly preliminary reports and the annual UCR. Of the requested information, some is released in the reports and some is not. In addition, some composite data are prepared for release.

Let us examine the kinds of data that are requested by the FBI in their *Uniform Crime Reporting Handbook.*[9] For Index Crimes, the FBI requests the number reported to police, the number of reports found to be false, the number of actual offenses, and the number cleared by arrests. Only the last two statistics are reported in the UCR. In the class of murder, information about manslaughter by negligence is called for but is not reported as an Index Crime. Similarly, information is requested but not reported for larcenies under $50. In supplementary reports, stolen property is classified by type and value, and rape is designated as statutory or forcible. Robbery is further classified by place of occurrence, burglary by type of building victimized, larceny by value of amount stolen (under $5, $5 to $50, and over $50), and automobile theft as joy-riding or other. Also reported for Index Crimes are the number not cleared by arrest, the number of persons charged, and whether they were found guilty (and if so, of the charged crime or of a lesser one). Age and race of all persons charged with Index Crimes are reported. Rural and urban distribution of Index Crimes is determined from the department's location.

For "Other Crimes," the cooperating agency reports only the number of offenses cleared by arrest (and not the number known to the police, as is the case with Index Crimes) and the age and race of those charged by the police.

It is relevant to our problem to emphasize the fact that certain data that are obtained from the cooperating agencies by the FBI are not published in the UCR. Much of this data has relevance for criminological studies. These unpublished data concern: (1) larcenies by number known to the police under $5, and $5 to $50; (2) larcenies by type—pocket-picking, purse-snatching, shop-lifting, thefts from auto of auto accessories, of bicycles, and all other; (3) automobiles recovered, by number stolen locally and recovered locally, number stolen locally and recovered by other jurisdictions, and total stolen locally; (4) stolen property by type—currency and notes, jewelry and precious metals, furs, clothing, locally stolen automobiles, and miscellaneous (their value is tabulated); (5) aggravated assault by type of weapon—sharp object, blunt object, gun, personal weapon, poison or acid, explosive, and other; (6) auto theft by joy-riding and other; (7) murder and nonnegligent manslaughter by distinction between willful killing without process of law and the justifiable killing of a felon by police or private citizen.

This classification system and the reservoir of data obtained from the cooperating local law enforcement agencies by the FBI comprise the most systematic and accurate information on the occurrence of crime in the United States. This information is partially reported in the published *Uniform Crime Reports,* which present the crime trends and rates and police-employee data for the entire country with further analysis by geographic region, urban-rural residence, and population divisions through time.

## Limitations of Uniform Crime Reporting

As previously noted, changes were made in the criminal classification scheme used in the *Uniform Crime Reports* as a consequence of the work of the Consultant Committee of 1958. Despite this, there are still major limitations in the classification scheme and in the analysis of the data obtained from the cooperating agencies.

Of course, it is only fair to note that the cooperation of local law enforcement agencies in filing reports with the FBI is not mandatory. Thus, the local agencies' cooperation may reflect the climate of relations between federal and local authorities, and the reporting to the FBI may be irregular, incomplete, and different from year to year.[10] A long-range campaign to obtain the cooperation of all agencies in reporting their crimes is necessary. It is perhaps possible that many states will follow the lead of California and require the compulsory reporting by all local law enforcement agencies of their crimes to the appropriate state division.

The 1958 Consultant Committee made other suggestions for revisions in the *Uniform Crime Reports* which were not accepted or are still under investigation. (1) In establishing the national crime picture, both Index and Other Crimes should be tabulated, excluding only certain minor crimes. (2) Since data on Other Crimes are not collected extensively enough for either rural or urban areas, procedures should be initiated to increase the number of reporting units. (3) The meaning of the designation "Index Crimes" (or the old "Part I" category) is not clear. Unfortunately, for the mass media and the lay public, Index Crimes are synonymous with major crimes. This, of course, is untrue, since Other Crimes include arson, child molestation cases, and narcotics violations. The only distinguishing attribute of Index Crimes is that they are the ones that supposedly are most frequently reported to the police. (4) A category of crimes of special importance to police and their work should be established. This category would include crimes usually well reported and those which give a good indication of crime trends.[11]

The 1958 Consultant Committee was aware that if the current classification and analysis scheme were to be revised too radically, comparison with previous years would be impossible. This objection, however, must be examined more minutely in terms of three crucial elements—namely, crime reporting, crime classification, and crime analysis—involved in uniform crime reporting.

## CRIME REPORTING

A major problem which has plagued crime statistics (as well as those of mental disease, sexual pathologies, and physical disease) is the incomplete reporting of all cases that occur in a population. For example, only the offender may know of the act which is defined by law as a criminal offense, or the victim may be unwilling to report the act to the police. Furthermore, private police—of business establishments and local public housing authorities, for example—may be reluctant to report all crimes to the police. The police themselves can affect crime reporting directly by under-reporting the number of actual offenses, as occurred in Kansas City, Missouri, in 1960; by intensive drives to arrest certain types of offenders such as the public intoxication offender, as in Rochester, New York, in 1955; and by the individual policeman's downgrading of an offense in official report, as occurred in St. Louis in 1961. But these limitations in current crime reporting should not detract too much from the fact that the largest reservoir of crime information currently available is contained in the *Uniform Crime Reports.*

## CRIME CLASSIFICATION

Criminal classification systems typically have been constructed on the basis of either the nature of the criminal offense or the psychosocial attributes of the offender. The FBI system previously discussed has been based on the offense or act, not the offender. However, it should be noted that basic demographic data about offenders, such as sex, race, and age, are collected. Criminologists, fortunately, in the last decade have retreated from their global conception of offenders and criminality—the tendency

*184*

to group all crime and offenders together without reference to type of offense and, to a lesser extent, to the offenders' psychosocial attributes.

As previously noted, the current FBI crime classification scheme is composed of seven Index Crimes and twenty Other Crimes. This classification scheme is still satisfactory for several reasons.

1. Index Crimes are viewed as those most likely to be reported to the police. But as Sellin[19] has noted, there are variations in the accuracy of reporting. According to him, the crime most often reported is bank robbery, followed by assault on an officer, but even these may be misreported. Homicides and suicides may be misclassified because of inadequacies in the coroner's office. Of course, there is always the danger of misclassification by the police themselves.

2. The Index Crimes are disproportionately weighted with crimes against property, particularly burglary. (See, for example, Table 1, which

**Table 1—Distribution of Index Crimes for City of St. Louis and the United States for 1960, by Number and Per Cent**

| CRIME | CITY OF ST. LOUIS[a] | | UNITED STATES[b] | |
|---|---|---|---|---|
| | Number | Per Cent | Number | Per Cent |
| Murder and Nonnegligent Manslaughter | 67 | 0.3 | 9,136 | 0.5 |
| Forcible Rape | 269 | 1.1 | 15,555 | 0.8 |
| Robbery | 2,157 | 9.2 | 88,970 | 4.8 |
| Aggravated Assault | 2,128 | 9.1 | 130,230 | 7.0 |
| Burglary | 10,623 | 45.5 | 821,057 | 44.1 |
| Larceny $50 and Over | 4,146 | 17.8 | 474,911 | 25.5 |
| Auto Theft | 3,959 | 17.0 | 321,402 | 17.3 |
| Total | 23,349 | 100.0 | 1,861,261 | 100.0 |

[a] 1960 Annual Report, St. Louis Metropolitan Police Dept.
[b] Uniform Crime Reports, 1960, Federal Bureau of Investigation.

presents the distribution of Index Crimes for the City of St. Louis and the United States for 1960.) Consequently, Index Crimes have become an index of property-crime violations, not an index of major or serious crimes in a community. Therefore, the term "Index Crimes" should be changed. We would suggest that current Index Crimes be subdivided into two categories. One would be called "Person Crimes" and would consist of murder and nonnegligent manslaughter, forcible rape, robbery, and aggravated assault cases known to the police. The other would be "Property Crimes," consisting of burglary, larceny, and auto theft cases known to the police.

3. Crime classification could be greatly improved with the use of sub-classifications for certain Index Crimes. Because of inflationary pressures the division of larceny at the $50 point is unrealistic. We would suggest $300–$500 as a breaking point for distinguishing between petty and grand larcenies. Data are currently collected for automobile theft by the sub-categories "joy-riding" or "other"; these subtotals should be reported. Data for the subclassifications of robbery (highway, business, and miscellaneous) and burglary (residence day, residence night, other day, and other night), on which the FBI receives information from the local agencies, should be reported in the annual reports.

4. Dr. Arthur Meyers,[13] statistician for the St. Louis Metropolitan Police Department, has made the excellent suggestion that Index Crimes of property violations be classified into attempts and completions, and that the value of the property taken in robberies and burglaries should be tabulated.

5. Robbery should be classified as a person crime, but this is not the current practice of the FBI.[14]

These suggested changes for improvement in the crime classification system would still allow comparisons with crime categories now in use.


## Crime Analysis

One of the major problems involved in the current *Uniform Crime Reports* is the analysis of crime rates through time by specific categories. Although it is useful to know the number of Index Crimes and the number of persons charged with Other Crimes and Index Crimes, scientific interpretation of these statistics is needed. From a scientific point of view, *Uniform Crime Reports* are at their weakest in this area.

To establish crime trends through time and for specific areas, rates must be computed. This involves comprehensive knowledge of the population base on which rates are constructed. Unfortunately, crime rates are constructed on a crude population basis, i.e., the number of cases per 1,000 or 100,000 population. Previous research[15] has established that criminal activity is significantly related to area of city and region of country, to age, sex, race, and economic status. Therefore, it would be advantageous to construct specific rates for the last four qualifications for all crime and for particular types of crimes. This is essential since the demographic characteristics of cities, states, and regions vary considerably in the United States. Furthermore, crime rates should be constructed on standardized populations to allow for variations in state and regional population pyramids.

Since in the United States population growth is extremely high in certain states and stagnant in others, corrections for population changes should be made in the crime rates. Admittedly, this is a complex task because an accurate census is taken only every ten years; population data in the last years of a decade must be based on the best available samples and estimates.

For certain categories of crime, namely, burglary and larceny, rates of crime known to police, based on resident population of certain city areas, are unsatisfactory. For example, the central business district, with a negligible resident population but with a large daytime working population and numerous business and commercial establishments, will generally show the highest crime rate in the city. A burglary rate for this area should be based on opportunities present—the number of business establishments or the amount of square feet of floor space used for business and commercial purposes. Larceny rates for the central business area, if based on population, should reflect the daytime swelling of population.

Criminal statisticians as yet have not become as sophisticated as social epidemiologists or demographers. Indeed, there is an excellent opportunity to apply statistical techniques used in those fields to the problems of crime analysis.

## Summary

This paper has presented a review of the historical development and current status of the FBI system of uniform crime reporting. A statement of the limitations of the current system with suggestions for revisions has been presented in terms of crime reporting, classification, and analysis.

## NOTES

1. International Association of Chiefs of Police, Committee on Uniform Crime Records, *Uniform Crime Reporting*, New York, 1929, p. 10.

2. *Ibid.*, p. 10.

3. Walter C. Reckless, *The Crime Problem*, New York: Appleton-Century-Crofts, Inc., 1955, pp. 8–9.

4. Paul W. Tappan, *Crime, Justice and Correction*, New York: McGraw-Hill, 1960, p. 36.

5. "Crime in the United States," *Life Magazine*, 48 (September 9, 1957).

6. Federal Bureau of Investigation, *Uniform Crime Reports, Special Issue* (1958).

# David J. Pittman and William F. Handy

7. *Life Magazine, op. cit.*

8. Tappan, *op. cit.*, pp. 36–7.

9. Federal Bureau of Investigation, *Handbook on Uniform Crime Reporting* (1955).

10. Federal Bureau of Investigation, *Uniform Crime Reports, Special Issue* (1958), 11–12.

11. *Ibid.*, p. 17.

12. *Life Magazine, op. cit.*, comments by Sellin.

13. Arthur Meyers, Jr., Statistician, St. Louis Metropolitan Police Department, Personal Interview, August, 1961.

14. Federal Bureau of Investigation, *Uniform Crime Reports, 1960*, 4.

15. Reckless, *op. cit.*, pp. 56–75.

# 14.    Delinquency and Opportunity:

## An End and a Beginning of Theory

JEROME HIMELHOCH

THE TITLE WILL, I HOPE, BECOME A SELF-FULFILLED
prophecy. It is meant to convey that I view Cloward and Ohlin's theory
of differential opportunity[1] as the culmination of the sociologistic tradition, represented variously by Durkheim, Merton, Sutherland, Shaw, and
McKay.[2] In brilliant and original fashion, Cloward and Ohlin synthesize
social structure variables culled from the above authors. This is an achievement that has significance not only for delinquency and deviance, but for
sociology in general. By this title I wish also to exhort the toilers in our
vineyard to transcend the sociologistic tradition and to work toward a still
more generous synthesis that will embrace within one conceptual scheme
both social and personality variables.

This will be the major theme of my paper. In it I shall first summarize
the theory, with applause for its cardinal virtues. Then, I shall dwell upon
its venial sins and the means for their absolution through the acceptance
of additional variables, particularly the variables of personality.

What I advocate is the synthesis of the concepts of social structure and
the concept of modal personality. By *modal personality* I refer to the ideal-
typical system of psychological traits which presumably characterizes most
members of a given group. I am also suggesting that we should make
explicit the psychological assumptions which underlie every sociological
analysis. I am definitely *not* making a plea for the psychologistic explanation of social phenomena as the fortuitous resultant of unrelated events
in individual personalities. Moreover, I am not advocating a sterile
eclecticism which seeks correlations without any conceptual framework.

*189*

## Definition of Delinquency

Cloward and Ohlin begin by clearly identifying their dependent variable: adolescent, male, subcultural delinquency in the metropolitan slum. "A delinquent subculture is one in which certain forms of delinquent activity are essential requirements for the performance of the dominant roles supported by the subculture," (p. 7). Delinquent activity is "behavior that violates basic norms of the society, and, when officially known, it evokes a judgment by agents of criminal justice that such norms have been violated," (p. 3).

Because the operational definition of delinquency is a stumbling block for most researchers, the authors have made a most intriguing suggestion. To identify delinquent acts, use the criteria of law enforcement officers in a given community. Discover which illegal acts officers select for official action.

## Three Etiological Concerns

Having defined their dependent variables, the authors ask three distinct etiological questions. What is the origin of pressures toward deviance? How do different subcultural adaptations to these pressures evolve and become selected? What accounts for change and persistence in these subcultures?

### THE ORIGIN OF PRESSURES TOWARD DEVIANCE

The authors explain the pressures in terms of Merton's celebrated theory of anomie.[3] The root cause is status-frustration, the disparity between aspiration and opportunity. Lower-class "adolescents who form delinquent subcultures . . . have internalized an emphasis upon conventional [status] goals. Faced with limitations on legitimate avenus of access to these goals, and unable to revise their aspirations downward, they experience intense frustrations . . ." (p. 86). Sharing this problem, they search for collective nonconformist solutions. Delinquent subcultures solve the problem by giving lower-class boys alternative routes to status.

Developing and clarifying the concepts of earlier writers, the authors vividly delineate three distinct ideal-typical subcultures. ". . . the criminal subculture prescribes disciplined and utilitarian forms of theft; the conflict subculture prescribes the instrumental use of violence; the retreatist subculture prescribes participation in illicit consummatory experiences, such as drug use . . . criminals value stealth, dexterity, wit, 'front,' and the capacity to evade detection; street-warriors value 'heart'; retreatists place a premium on esoteric 'kicks' " (p. 14). This taxonomy is a distinct advance over earlier conceptions of delinquency in general or of the undifferentiated delinquent subculture. Before youths may form or join delinquent subcultures, they must become alienated, i.e., they must withdraw the attribute of legitimacy from conventional norms and transfer it to unconventional norms.

### THE EVOLUTION AND SELECTION OF DELINQUENT SUBCULTURES

How is the genesis of the three subcultures to be explained? What accounts for their selection by different groups of lower-class boys, once the subcultures have become established? Cloward and Ohlin's answer is a brilliant theoretical innovation. They reformulate and synthesize Merton's "push" theory with the Sutherland, Shaw, and McKay "pull" theories.[4] That is, they integrate the theory of anomie with the theories of differential association and cultural-transmission. "The concept of differential opportunity structures permits us to unite the theory of anomie, which recognizes the concept of differentials in access to legitimate means, and the 'Chicago tradition,' in which the concept of differentials in access to illegitimate means is implicit" (p. 151). "Given limited access to success-goals by legitimate means, the nature of the delinquent response that may result will vary according to the availability of various illegitimate means" (p. 152).

*The criminal subculture*—The development of the criminal subculture depends upon opportunities to learn and practice theft. These "illegal opportunity structures," in turn, presuppose the integration of different age levels of offenders and the integration of the "adult carriers of conventional and of deviant values."

*The conflict subculture*—"Those adolescents in disorganized urban areas who are oriented toward achieving higher position but who are cut off from institutionalized channels, criminal as well as legitimate, must rely upon their own resources for solving this problem of adjustment. . . . These adolescents seize upon the manipulation of violence as a route to status not only because it provides a way of expressing pent-up angers and frustrations but also because it does not cut them off from access to violent means by vicissitudes of birth" (p. 175). ". . . the area lacking integration between age-levels of offenders and between carriers of conventional and criminal values cannot generate pressures to contain frustrations

*191*

Jerome Himelhoch

among the young. Violence comes to be ascendent, in short, under conditions of relative detachment from all institutionalized systems of opportunity and social control" (pp. 178–179).

*The retreatist subculture*—"Retreatism [drug use] arises from continued failure to near the goal by legitimate measures and from an inability to use the illegitimate route because of internalized prohibitions or *socially structured barriers,* the process occurring while the supreme value of the success-goal has not yet been renounced" (p. 181). Retreatism arises because of "double-failure" in a neighborhood in which drugs are available. After failing first in legitimate status-striving, the boy then fails again either as a thief or as a street warrior, after which he finally renounces not only the norms, but the success goal as well. Not all who are double failures, however, become drug users. "Some will respond to failure by adopting a law-abiding lower-class style of life—the 'corner boy' adaptation. It may be that those who become retreatists are incapable of revising their aspirations downward to correspond to reality" (p. 184).

SEQUENCES OF ADAPTATION

In their all too brief portrayal of "sequences of adaptation" (pp. 184–86), Cloward and Ohlin give us one of their most useful ideas: the transition to adulthood as a crucial turning point and a new source of failure for the late adolescent delinquent boy. They leave the consequences of this idea implicit and they do not fully exploit what might be called "a theory of life-cycle variation in environmental press."[5] This would include life-cycle variations in legitimate and illegitimate opportunities; in salience of peer group versus school, job, and family; and in community tolerance of deviance. The authors tell us, "Access to success-goals by illegitimate means diminishes as the lower-class adolescent approaches adulthood" (p. 184). Accordingly, the formerly successful juvenile thief or bopper may now experience failure, if in response to community expectations he cannot join the rest of his gang in the transition to a law-abiding lower-class adult role and if he is furthermore unable to graduate to adult professional crime. He becomes a law-abiding "corner man," if he can lower his aspirations, if he has maintained close attachments with conventional adults during adolescence, and can now assume adult kinship and occupational roles.[6]

*Stability and change in delinquent subcultures*—Of the three gang types, the thieving gangs are most resistant to change because they are integrated with the drug-using gangs and also with adult criminals. Through the latter, moreover, the juvenile thieves interact with conventional adults

*192*

as well. Since the conflict gangs are integrated in neither of these ways, they are most susceptible to outside influences for change. For integration and stability, the drug-using gangs occupy an intermediate position.

In the last section of the book, Cloward and Ohlin present a fascinating and, to the best of my knowledge, original historical analysis of ethnic factors in urban delinquency. They introduce the new independent variable of *stage of immigrant assimilation,* which determines type of slum neighborhood organization, which, in turn, causes variation in type of adolescent gang. During the first stage, the status-frustrated, disorganized, and uncontrolled immigrant boys turn to violence as a path to status. In the second stage, the numerically dominant minority group develops illegitimate (and legitimate) opportunity structures through rackets and the political machine. These allied institutions produce integrated neighborhood organization and social controls over the young. As a result, the criminal delinquent subculture flourishes. In the third stage, many minority group members "negotiate passage to a higher socioeconomic position by either legitimate or illegitimate routes" and move away from the slum. This leaves a residual of failures without organization, legitimate or illegitimate opportunities, or social controls. Once again, juvenile violence becomes the major problem of delinquency. As new groups move in, the cycle may be repeated. For example, with Negro racketeers and politicians striving to wrest control from the Italian and Jewish syndicate leaders, New York Negroes may move into stage two. If this happens, delinquent Negro youths in Harlem and Bedford-Stuyvesant may turn from street fighting to organized theft.

Although Negro areas are a possible exception, "we predict that delinquency will become increasingly aggressive and violent in the future as a result of the disintegration of slum organization" (p. 203). The rackets, especially gambling, have become an impersonal corporate bureaucracy with absentee owners. The rackets require highly specialized skills and no longer recruit their employees from the graduates of neighborhood boys' gangs. Another factor which weakens slum neighborhood cohesion is the construction of large impersonal housing projects. A third factor is the decline of the neighborhood-based political machine, for its services to the lower class have in large measure been taken over by the bureaucratic welfare state. On the basis of these trends, the authors predict that fighting and drug-using gangs will wax, while thieving subcultures will wane. It takes courage to make a prediction which will enable readers to test the validity of one's theory.

To prevent delinquency, the authors argue, we must reorganize slum

*193*

communities. "Legitimate but functional substitutes" for the traditional slum social controls and avenues of social ascent "must be developed if we are to stem the trend toward violence and retreatism among adolescents in urban slums" (p. 211).

## Positive Contributions of the Theory

To recapitulate, I consider the following to be the main virtues of the book: (1) a clear definition of the dependent variable, (2) the definition of delinquency in terms of the criteria used by law enforcement officers, (3) the precise distinction among the questions which theory must answer, (4) the concept of illegitimate opportunity structure, (5) the successful crossbreeding of anomie with differential association, (6) professional crime viewed as an agency of delinquency control, (7) clarification of the usually fuzzy concepts of "community integration" and "community disorganization," (8) types of gang viewed as functions of neighborhood opportunity structure, (9) the transition to adulthood as peculiarly stressful for delinquent boys and as important in the etiology of drug use, (10) the stages of immigrant assimilation and their effects upon subcultural adaptation, and (11) the plausible prediction of increased violence and drug use.

## Weaknesses of the Theory

Having dealt with the strengths of the theory, I now turn to what I consider its weaknesses. My major criticism is the over-simplified view of motivation which characterizes not only Cloward and Ohlin, but the sociologistic tradition in general. In criticizing that tradition, I do not deny its enormous contribution to contemporary social science. Nor do I advocate the opposing sin of psychologism, which impoverishes the social environment just as sociologism impoverishes the psyche.

Cloward and Ohlin, like others in the Durkheim-Merton-Sutherland-Shaw-McKay tradition, tend to ignore personality variables. These are taken as given rather than problematical, or constant rather than variable.

One cannot, however, operate without psychological assumptions at all. Just as every physics has its implicit metaphysics, every sociology has its implicit psychology. Cloward and Ohlin, like Merton, endow their human actors with just enough psychological attributes so that their behavior can be predicted from their position in the social structure. People then become like iron filings in a magnetic field or steel balls in a pinball machine.

Only one original human motive is assumed: the tendency to conform or to internalize cultural elements. Given the propensity to internalize, people learn "the culturally prescribed success-goals." Although Merton himself acknowledges that there is more than one cultural goal,[7] it is the goal of status which writers in the Mertonian tradition have used to explain delinquency. This status usually connotes occupational and/or pecuniary prestige which serves as a means to upward mobility in the class system. Accordingly, internalization leads to status hunger, which henceforth functions as a simple and sovereign motive. Status is to many sociologists in this tradition what sex is to Freudian psychology or class interest to Marxian history. Like the Freudians and Marxists, these sociologists ingeniously twist and transmute their sovereign motive so that it can explain many diverse things.

In Cloward and Ohlin's implicit psychology there is one other element in the structure of personality. That is the degree to which people internalize the legitimate or illegitimate norms governing the pursuit of status. People also vary in the degree to which they internalize the status goal. They are, moreover, capable of renouncing either the goal, the norms, or both.

## A Theoretical "Status Dilemma"

One of the achievements of Cloward and Ohlin is to shed some light on the lamentably vague concept of success goals and to point out that these goals are probably quite different in the various social classes. ". . . the criteria people use to rank one another vary depending upon social-class position. That is, there is no uniform agreement throughout the class structure as to the basis for invidious distinctions. The upper-class person tends to rank others primarily in terms of style of life and ancestry; the middle-class person, in terms of money and morality; the lower-class person, in terms of money alone" (p. 93). The authors also suggest that the carriers of middle-class values "devalue the materialistic [i.e., money] success-goals" toward which many lower-class youngsters orient themselves (p. 97).

The authors then assert that *within the lower class* there are many different "success goals" and these provide us with a useful typology (pp. 90–97). The upwardly mobile "college boys" want middle-class status,— some of them with an increased income, some of them with no increase in money. Another group, "are oriented toward a definition of success that stresses a change in economic position, but they do not seek to change their style of life or to affiliate with the carriers of middle-class values (p. 95). These boys who seek higher status, i.e., more money, "within their own cultural milieu," provide most of the recruits for delinquent gangs. Finally, there are the nonaspiring "corner boys," who "do not exhibit serious distress about remaining in their present membership-group position *and* their present economic status" (p. 95).

This repudiation of the notion of *common* success goals strikes me as realistic. It is an advance over the assumptions of Merton[8] and Cohen[9] about universal striving for middle-class status. At the same time it involves Cloward and Ohlin in a dilemma. Without a common goal, the Mertonian thesis of lower-class status discontent is untenable. In fact, Merton explicitly states, "in a society where similar success-goals are held out to a considerable part of the population, low social and economic status will be more highly correlated with crime than in societies where rigidified class structure is more often coupled with differential class symbols of success."[10] It is these differential symbols which Cloward and Ohlin document so convincingly in their section on "Types of Aspiration" (pp. 90–7).

In the rest of the book, however, the authors talk repeatedly of "common" and "conventional" success goals. This they have to do to sustain their thesis about the special pressure for deviance in the lower class. The goals become "common" only if they can all be subsumed under the rubric of status-seeking or mobility-striving. This is what the authors do.

When lower-class persons strive for money, are they necessarily seeking status? Moreover, when they aspire to social acceptance within their group by living up to their class code, are they pursuing status? That is, are they competing for individual, invidious, scarce positions on a prestige ladder? Is it not possible, in fact, that lower-class culture may induce many people to cooperate for shared goals rather than compete for individual rewards? Finally, may not persons in all classes frequently desire goods and services for their intrinsic properties, rather than as symbols of status?

Even if we grant that all status is invidious, does it follow that all types of status represent a "common" or "conventional" goal? Status may come in the following varieties: general American, upper-class, middle-class, lower-class, conformist peer group, and nonconformist peer group. The opportunity structures—the means to the achievement—of these various types of status may have nothing in common.

Merton's theory of deviant motivation is logical if one assumes a common pursuit of status, as defined by middle-class criteria. In this case, differential access to the means, like a college education, for the achievement of middle-class prestige will frustrate lower-class youths. Suppose, however, one posits for lower class and for middle class different status goals, with criteria set by different reference groups—as Cloward and Ohlin do in one section of their book. In this case it does not follow that differential access to the *same* means involves unequal opportunity to achieve *different* goals. To be specific, may not a college education be useless as a means to the achievement of a high income for those who wish to stay within the working class? Are not the means to a relatively high living standard now available to millions of working class youths through semiskilled and skilled jobs in unionized industries? (To be sure, there is a severe problem of unemployment for high school dropouts; but a high school diploma is probably within reach for most lower-class youth.)

It might, incidentally, be helpful for us to demarcate the boundaries between classes, as all too few of us do. It might be useful to adopt Miller and Riessman's distinction between "stable working class" and "lower class."[11] In the lower-class of unskilled and unemployed, and particularly among the racial minorities, there are barriers to success as defined by either the stable working class or the middle class. Cloward and Ohlin's analysis might fit this depressed proletariat, which constitutes part, but not all, of the slum population. Even for these "residual" and ghettoized slum dwellers, however, the analysis works only if one can demonstrate that they are competing with members of a higher class for a common prestige goal.

## Does Instrumental Status Seeking Explain Gang Behavior?

Even if we grant that hunger for the "conventional" goal of socio-economic status drives slum boys to look for unconventional means, do the delinquent gangs satisfy this hunger? Do they provide the boys with the functional equivalent of a middle-class job with a good salary and prestige, or of the education for it? Moreover, is delinquent behavior instrumental rather than expressive? Finally, can instrumental status seeking adequately explain the appeal of delinquent subcultures, with their rich and varied customs, beliefs, and attitudes?

197

# Jerome Himelhoch

## THE THIEVING GANG

The semiprofessional thieving gang, in which boys concentrate exclusively on crime that pays, might provide an alternative route to the kind of status that the middle-class boys win on a legitimate job. That is, the boys might get money and goods, a higher living standard, and deference not only from the peer group but also, conceivably, from neighborhood adults and the general population. (Some might, however, withhold respect if they knew the source of the money.) Accordingly, the theory of instrumental status seeking might fit this type of gang.

Like Cohen, the authors acknowledge, however, that there is an aggressive and expressive component in most delinquent behavior, even in that of the criminal gangs. Unlike Cohen, they minimize its importance. If its appearance is nonutilitarian, its essence, they tell us, is utilitarian, rational, and instrumental (pp. 166–71). "Conspicuous defiance of conventional values" and stealing "just for the hell of it" are *really* motivated by an effort to impress and gain acceptance from adult professional criminals. Instead of being carried out for their own sake, these acts are part of "anticipatory socialization." This might in some cases be the *latent* function of the behavior, although it has a teleological flavor reminiscent of the "Unseen Hand" described by Adam Smith. It is hard to believe, in any event, that it is a *manifest* function, i.e., that the boys recognize and intend this consequence.[12] Accordingly, status seeking fails to explain the *motivation* for the expressive or aggressive behavior.

## THE FIGHTING GANG

Although the authors acknowledge that violence provides "a way of expressing pent up angers and frustration," they view it primarily as "a route to status." The boy who successfully beats up youngsters from other gangs will earn "rep" in his adolescent reference group. Nevertheless, he will not thereby raise his living standard or win prestige among neighborhood adults. Although the latter may fear him, they will not admire him. Accordingly, I do not see how the conflict gang can be an alternative route to the *conventional* status goal.

I would say that street fighters may instrumentally seek *peer-group* status and at the same time expressively work off aggression. Various boys may, in fact, be driven by one or more of a large number of needs or goals: to frighten, maim or kill; to aid and support friends; to revenge injustice; to win attention and admiration; to earn "rep" in the gang; to outrage conventional people; to get themselves hurt as atonement for sin;

to prove their manhood; or even to engage in vigorous "body-contact" athletics.

The authors fail to account for the appeal of violence other than as an opportunity for status competition allegedly open to all. They do not put forward any positive explanation for its emergence. What endows the boys with that anger and destructiveness that are so ready to erupt when social controls are withdrawn? Is it, for example, instinctual aggressiveness, or aggressive parental role models, or a frustration-aggression sequence?

*Can all boys succeed at violence?*—At one point, the authors state that violence is widespread in disorganized neighborhoods because it is an alternative route to success in the status race open to all boys. "In the world of violence, such attributes as race, socioeconomic position, age, and the like are irrelevant; personal worth is judged on the basis of qualities that are available to all who would cultivate them. The acquisition of status is not simply a consequence of skill in the use of violence or of physical strength but depends, rather, on one's willingness to risk injury or death in the search for 'rep.' A physically immature boy may find a place among the warrior elite if, when provoked, he will run such risks, thus demonstrating 'heart' " (p. 175). Can one so easily dismiss such factors as technical skill and body build? Furthermore, do all boys have equal "heart"?

A little later the authors acknowledge the foregoing questions and, in so doing, weaken their earlier argument. Here they state ". . . not all who would acquire success by violence or criminal means are permitted to do so. . . . Those who excel in the manipulation of violence may acquire 'rep' within the group. . . . But prestige is, by definition, scarce— just as scarce among adolescents who seek to acquire it by violence as it is elswhere in the society . . . some persons will become upwardly mobile in conflict groups and others will remain on the periphery" (p. 183). A certain number of failures can, of course, be expected to drop out and, as the authors suggest, these may turn to drug use. At the same time, many boys who are physically or psychologically unable to gain prestige in conflict gangs presumably stay in the groups. May this not mean that motives other than status hunger are impelling them?

### THE DRUG USING GANG

That boys turn to drug use solely because of status frustration also seems unlikely. In view of our scant knowledge, I suggest an alternative hypothesis: in a neighborhood with access to drugs, boys with certain personality needs form or join narcotic groups as a response to severe frustration. They might find themselves blocked in the gratification of a strong wish—status, aggression, love, dependency, to name a few. Because many late-adolescent addicts reportedly are afraid to have sexual relations, to get married, or to take a job, perhaps some are trying to prolong an infantile dependency. For other more extrapunitive personalities, the frustration of any strong wish might result in bopping behavior—assuming that the neighborhood offers opportunities to learn and to wage street warfare.

Cloward and Ohlin assume it to be self-evident that drug users retreat or withdraw from normal relationships and role obligations. This may be true of the younger, minority group addicts of recent years. According to Clausen[13] and Becker,[14] it is not true of addicts in the medical profession. It also does not seem to characterize the upper status drug users in the Ivy League colleges. These persons are not low-aspiring, or low-achieving, or withdrawn from conventional society. By calling drug use "retreat," rather than proving that this is the case, Merton, and Cloward and Ohlin have concealed a conclusion in their choice of terms.

According to the authors, drug users have renounced both the status goal and the legitimate norms. It would follow that they are the one class of delinquents who are free to engage in expressive rather than instrumental behavior. This is confirmed by the statement, "Retreatism may include a variety of expressive, sensual, or consummatory experiences . . ." (p. 25). Nevertheless, we are told a little later that the drug users have not given up the success goal after all, for they are still instrumentally pursuing status. "The cat does not seek to impose this system of values on the world of the squares. Instead he strives for status and deference within the society of cats by cultivating the kick and the hustle. Thus the retreatist subculture provides avenues to success-goals, to the social admiration—which the members feel are otherwise beyond their reach" (p. 27). If this is so, they cannot be *retreatists* in the Mertonian sense of renunciation of *both* the status goal and the norms.

It is true, of course, that in all three types of gangs, the boy who achieves the values of his subculture wins prestige *within the gang*. Is this, however, a functional equivalent of the general American, or the middle-class, or even the lower-class "conventional" status goal? Why should a deprived slum boy join a delinquent gang to acquire pecuniary prestige—unless perhaps it is a semiprofessional gang of thieves? If all he wants is *peer group* prestige, why does he not join a legitimate neighborhood organization, like a PAL unit, church youth group, settlement house group, athletic team, or nondelinquent strcct-corner gang? If boys join delinquent gangs, it must be because the gangs give them *something in addition to the opportunity to compete for status within the group*. The authors fail to account for the appeal of the specific subcultural content of the delinquent gangs. Why are boys attracted by such values as negativism, short-run hedonism, excitement, group autonomy, and masculine toughness? Theories which stress such factors as masculine identity crisis, adolescent status discontent, lower-class culture, and reaction-formation to middle-class values provide at least partial answers to this question.[15]

My criticism of the inadequacy of the status drive as a complete explanation of motivation refers primarily to the authors' description of the *formation* of delinquent gangs. Following the lead of Cohen,[16] they adopt a more sophisticated theory of motivation for the *affiliation* of new members with established groups. In a delinquent gang " 'core' members are persons who experience a marked discrepancy between socially induced aspirations and the possibilities of achievement. But once a subculture has come into being, it then exists as a force in the neighborhood and may attract persons for whom it promises to serve a wide range of needs and motives" (p. 188). I agree that the motives that lead boys to *form* gangs may not be the same as those that induce other boys to *join* established organizations. Nevertheless, I contend that a variety of motives—and not just status seeking—are involved in *both* processes.

## Unverified Assumptions

Cloward and Ohlin build an imposing theoretical edifice upon unverified assumptions. Since each unproven proposition rests upon earlier ones, the validity of the final propositions is seriously imperiled. They do, to be sure, thoroughly and judiciously sift the evidence for each assumption. Yet, in the present state of our knowledge, they might have done better to have stated the alternative interpretations of the facts, and then suggested the theoretical implications of each. If they had done this, they might have ended with a less satisfying structure and iconoclasts might have felt less compulsion to try to demolish it!

I have outlined the assumptions which lack convincing empirical evidence, and which I have not already discussed.

1. The three types of gangs actually occur with significant frequency in relatively pure and unmixed form.

2. Lower-class adolescent boys experience more status deprivation than boys of other classes.

3. Within the lower class, delinquents have higher status aspirations and experience more status deprivation than corner boys. The latter are more capable of lowering their aspirations than the former.

4. Lower-class predelinquents perceive their deprivation as unjust, and, becoming alienated, then become delinquents. An alternative possibility might be that, *after becoming delinquents,* boys experience deprivation that they regard as unjust.

5. Lower-class predelinquents first strive (in reality or imagination) for conventional status by legitimate means, then fail (in reality or imagination) and finally turn to illegitimate means. An alternative proposition would be that they start with illegitimate means in the first place. Is it plausible that preadolescent or early adolescent boys think seriously about adult vocational problems *before they become delinquents?*

6. Lower-class predelinquents first internalize conventional norms, then experience unjust deprivation, then become alienated from conventional norms and, finally impute legitimacy to unconventional norms. An alternative possibility is that, beginning with early childhood, the boys simultaneously learn *both* the delinquent and the moralistic norms—and feel ambivalent toward both. This might be true of Americans generally, with minor class variation in the content of the delinquent and the moralistic norms.

## An Alternative View of Delinquent Motivation

Having concluded my litany of criticisms, I shall now presume to suggest how a basically good theory can be improved. My position is in agreement with that of Cohen and Short in a recent publication. They state: "One kind of question we can ask is this: How do circumstances on the actor or personality side and on the situational side interact to determine delinquent behavior? What do you have to take into account in personality and in the situation, and what are the rules for predicting the outcomes of various combinations of personality components and situational components?"[17] This is also the position taken by Moles, Lippitt, and Withey.[18]

In contrast to this psychosocial approach, Cloward and Ohlin espouse a sociologistic explanation when they assert, "Given limited access to success-goals by legitimate means, the nature of the delinquent response that may result will vary according to the availability of various illegitimate means."

I suggest several ways to reformulate this theory.

1. At any given position in the social structure, such as the urban slum, determine empirically the modal personalities and, within each, the relative strength of each motive. Status drive of some sort would probably be only one of several motives in most modal personalities.

2. Discover empirically the legitimate opportunities for the achievement of each of the strong, shared goals or motives. At the same time this implies determining the socially structured barriers to the achievement of the goals.

3. Enumerate the adjustment problems which this psychosocial situation creates for each modal personality.

4. Determine the availability of illegitimate opportunities for the solution of each adjustment problem.

5. The nature of the delinquent responses in a given neighborhood may then be predictable from the interaction, on one hand, of the several modal personalities with their adjustment problems and, on the other hand, the several illegitimate opportunity structures capable of offering solutions to the problems.

In short, personality variables and social variables are necessary to determine the nature of the collective problems and collective solutions. At each point in a delinquent career we must look at both the social environment and the personality needs. For "sequences of adaptation," personality needs would serve as intervening variables at each transition. Moreover, personality variables include more than just the strength of the status drive and the degree of internalization of legitimate norms. For example, whether a status-frustrated boy joins the "warriors" or the "cats" may depend in part upon the relative strength of his need for release of extrovert aggression versus his need for gratification of introvert fantasy.

On the basis of reports by recent researchers, such as Short, who have attempted to work with the Cloward-Ohlin typology of gangs, I suspect that most gangs are mixed and that most slum neighborhoods offer a variety of illegitimate opportunity structures.[19] These would take the form of organizations, potential membership and reference groups, and role models. If these opportunities are equally available in a neighborhood, the kind of gang different boys organize or join will depend upon the kind of adjustment problem they are trying to solve. Each type of gang might attract a different modal personality type with a different problem. If we look at the situation even more closely, we might find that, not only does each gang attract boys with a common general need, but each role within a gang attracts a boy with a different specific need.

Even if a boy finds only one type of illegitimate opportunity structure in his neighborhood, it does not follow that his personality needs are irrelevant to the nature of his response. If a boy has a strong enough motive, he may seek out a role model or reference group that is not immediately available in the neighborhood. We must consider not only the availability of learning and performance opportunities, but also the nature and strength of the personality needs that they can satisfy.

If we admit the possibility of several adjustment problems, of which status frustration is only one, there may be a place for the theories which Cloward and Ohlin reject. For example, lower-class mother-centered child-rearing, the demands of lower-class culture, and the obstacles to achieving masculine and adult identity, along with class and ethnic barriers to conventional financial or occupational success, might singly or in combination produce the adjustment problems that call for shared delinquent solutions. Other stresses worth mentioning are, for example, conflicting or ambiguous role definitions by family, school, and peer group; the conflicting demands of these roles; and the frustration of the boy's affectional and dependency needs by family members. The response of different modal personalities to different combinations of these variables might account for the different adjustment problems that can find solutions in different kinds of delinquent behavior. The solution would depend both upon the kind of adjustment problem and the kind of illegitimate opportunity available. In other words, the theory of differential opportunity may, and should, be retained, even though we need not limit ourselves to Cloward and Ohlin's theory of the origin of the pressures toward deviance or of the particular problems that delinquent gangs solve.

## Conclusion

Cloward and Ohlin provide a multitude of provocative ideas for research and theory-building. The real value of the book lies in the variables it gives us. Accordingly, although the specific ways in which the authors have combined the variables may be questionable, their book has lasting significance. If further development will admit more variables, both social and psychological, and will acknowledge the plausibility of a number of alternative hypotheses, the theory will, I believe, gain in predictive power. It will also, in my opinion, explain more adequately slum gang delinquency of the male adolescent. But, perhaps more important, it will have much to tell us about the causes of female, suburban, middle-class, and rural delinquency as well. In any event, for some time to come it will be unwise to write about or to study the causes of juvenile law breaking without facing the issues raised in *Delinquency and Opportunity*.

## NOTES

1. Richard A. Cloward and Lloyd E. Ohlin, *Delinquency and Opportunity: A Theory of Delinquent Gangs*, New York: The Free Press, 1960. Page references to this book are given in parentheses in the text.

2. Emile Durkheim, *Suicide: A Study of Sociology*, trans. by J. A. Spaulding and George Simpson, George Simpson, ed. New York: The Free Press, 1951; Robert K. Merton, *Social Theory and Social Structure*, rev., New York: The Free Press, 1957, chs. 4, 5; Edwin H. Sutherland and Donald R. Cressey, *Principles of Criminology*, 5th ed., New York: J. B. Lippincott Co., 1955; Clifford R. Shaw and Henry D. McKay, *Juvenile Delinquency and Urban Areas*, Chicago: The University of Chicago Press, 1942.

3. Merton, *op. cit.*

4. Cf. note 2 above.

5. For the concept of "press," see Henry A. Murray, *Explorations in Personality*, New York: Oxford University Press, 1938.

6. This summary of retreatism is based in part on Cloward and Ohlin's earlier version of their book, *New Perspectives on Juvenile Delinquency*, New York: New York School of Social Work, Columbia University, 1959, mimeographed.

7. Merton, *op. cit.*

8. *Ibid.*

9. Albert K. Cohen, *Delinquent Boys: The Culture of the Gang*, New York: The Free Press, 1955.

10. Robert K. Merton, "Social Conformity, Deviation, and Opportunity-Structures: A Comment on the Contributions of Dubin and Cloward," *American Sociological Review*, 24 (April, 1959), 187.

11. S. M. Miller and Frank Riessman, "The Working Class Subculture: A New View," *Social Problems*, 9 (Summer, 1961), 86–97.

12. For the concepts of "manifest" and "latent" functions, see Robert K. Merton, *op. cit.*

13. John A. Clausen, "Drug Addiction," in Robert K. Merton and Robert A. Nisbet, eds., *Contemporary Social Problems*, New York: Harcourt, Brace and World, Inc., 1961, 207.

14. Howard S. Becker, personal communication to the author.

15. Talcott Parsons, *Essays in Sociological Theory*, Rev. New York: Free Press, 1954, pp. 304–05; Herbert Bloch and Arthur Niederhoffer, *The Gang: A Study in Adolescent Behavior*, New York: Philosophical Library, 1958; W. B. Miller, "Lower Class Culture as a Generating Milieu of Gang Delinquency," *Journal of Social Issues*, 14:3 (1958), 5–19; W. C. Karaceus and W. B. Miller, *Delinquent Behavior: Culture and the Individual*, Washington, D.C.: National Education Association, 1959; Cohen, *op. cit.*

16. Cohen, *op. cit.*, pp. 148–49.

17. Albert K. Cohen and James F. Short, Jr., "Juvenile Delinquency," in Merton and Nisbet, eds., *op. cit.*, pp. 89–90.

# Jerome Himelhoch

18. Oliver Moles, Jr., Ronald Lippitt, and Stephen Withey, *A Selective Review of Research and Theories Concerning the Dynamics of Delinquency,* Ann Arbor, Michigan: The University of Michigan, Institute for Social Research, 1959, mimeographed, ch. 10.

19. James F. Short, Jr., personal communication to the author.

15.　　Community Leadership in the

Voluntary Health and Welfare System

CHARLES V. WILLIE

AFFILIATION WITH ASSOCIATIONS IS ESSENTIAL FOR those who choose to change their society—be the change for good or evil.[1] As stated by Floyd Hunter, "power of the individual must be structured into associational clique or institutional patterns to be effective."[2] Mirra Komarovsky describes voluntary associations as "channels of power"[3] and Robert Merton speaks of "organizational channels to influence."[4] These observations suggest the need for a critical analysis of the composition of formal associations and the characteristics of persons who exercise official decision-making responsibility or who influence decisions through informal means.

The study reported here focuses upon one system of a community—the voluntary financing and planning of health and welfare services. It is limited to an analysis of the composition of its highest decision-making units —the Board of Directors of the Community Chest (the United Fund) and the Board of Directors of the Council of Social Agencies (the Welfare

Acknowledged with appreciation is a grant from the Health Information Foundation which supported this study. This study was initiated in the Department of Preventive Medicine at the State University of New York Upstate Medical Center. Acknowledged with thanks is the aid rendered by my research assistant, Mrs. Annette Greenberg.

Council). Essentially, this is an analysis of formal community leadership in the voluntary system.

The study setting is Syracuse, New York, a middle-sized city with a population of nearly a quarter of a million, and the central city for the Onondaga County metropolitan area, with approximately one-half million persons in 1960. Syracuse was founded in 1825. It is an industrial city with more than 500 manufacturing industries within or near the city limits and it has one major private university, a state medical school, a Catholic college, and a public junior college. The governmental structures for county and city have evolved through several forms. Presently, the city and the county have full-time executive officers and part-time representatives in legislative assemblies, all elected by popular vote. For the county, a full-time executive elected by popular vote is a recent mid-twentieth century development. However, the city has had a full-time mayor elected by the public for several decades.

The study period extends over 38 years, from 1921, the year in which the Chest was organized, to 1958, the year this study was authorized.

The study population consists of 231 Chest Board members and 235 Council board members who held formal membership positions on the respective boards during the study period. A list of board members for each year of the study period was obtained from official records of the Chest and the Council. Residential and business addresses were recorded when available. City directories and directories of the Manufacturers Association of Syracuse, the New York State Commerce Department, and the New York Telephone Company were consulted about each board member's occupation, place of employment, name of employer, type of business, and rank within company organization. Also, officials of the Chest and Council and long-time residents of the community were interviewed to obtain additional unrecorded information about board members. Industrial and occupational categories of the U.S. Census Bureau were used in classifying business affiliations of board members.

The Community Chest was organized in Syracuse and Onondaga County, New York in 1921, as a successor to the old War Chest. A committee of the parent corporation was the Council of Social Agencies, organized in 1930. Although historically a single corporation, the Chest and the Council have separate officers and elect separate boards of directors. Every year one-third of these are elected from the community-at-large or from social agency staffs and boards for a three-year term of office. (As of August, 1960, the Community Chest and the Council of Social Agencies were merged into a single integrated organization with a single Board of

Directors known as the United Community Chest and Council of Onondaga County, Inc. This study is limited to the period when the Chest and Council operated as separate organizations.)

Although the Chest and the Council operate as separate entities, they complement each other in function. The Council plans and coordinates community social services while the Chest raises and allocates funds for their support. Members of the Board of Directors of the Chest and of the Council together hold formal positions of authority that can influence the growth and development of health and welfare services in the local community voluntary system.

The characteristics of leaders in the voluntary system during their first year of service on the Chest or the Council board are analyzed in this study. Chest and Council boards are analyzed together and separately. The purpose of the joint analysis is to identify the kinds of persons who hold formal positions of leadership in the community voluntary system of health and welfare services. The purpose of the separate analysis is to determine the differences, if any, in the characteristics of community leaders active in the planning or in the funding of community social services.

## Analysis of Combined Chest and Council Boards

The total number of persons filling positions on the Chest and Council boards varied through the years. There were 36 persons on the Chest board in 1921, the year of organization, and 29 in 1958, the last year included in this study. Fifteen persons were members of the Council board in 1930, its first year of existence, and 45 in 1958. A total of 422 different persons served on the Chest and Council boards during the 38-year study period.

About three-fourths of the total number of Chest and Council board members are male and one-fourth female. Thus, men outnumber women four to one as community leaders in the voluntary system for health and welfare services.

Most of these leaders are active in the labor force with full-time jobs. Eighty-five per cent of Chest and Council board members are employed. The remaining proportion consists largely of housewives. Seldom are retired persons or single women recruited to positions of leadership in the voluntary system.

Business and professional persons are the main source of formal community leadership for the planning and funding of health and welfare services. A majority, nearly 60 per cent, of the combined board members earn livelihoods in business. Another one-third are professional or technical workers. Although few, if any, skilled, semiskilled workers, service workers or laborers serve on Chest and Council boards, one or two part-time labor officials with full-time blue collar jobs have been members. Only one blue collar worker who was not a labor official has ever served on one of the boards. There has been almost continuous representation of a limited number of full-time labor officials during the last two decades of the study period, and they are classified as professionals.

Leadership is recruited largely from leaders in business, industry, and community agencies. Nearly one-third are president or vice-president of a corporation; another third are manager, director or administrator of a business or community agency. Most of the remaining leaders are scattered among the self-employed. There are few persons with nonadministrative responsibility on Chest and Council boards. Persons of high status in their respective organizations and in control of the activities of others occupy most board positions.

Professionals represent about one in every three Chest and Council board members. About one-third of all professionals on the boards are social workers affiliated with a social service agency. Approximately one-fourth are lawyers. About ten per cent may be classified as physicians or nurses, affiliated, in most instances, with health agencies or medical educational institutions. Less than ten per cent of the board members have been public administrators. About five per cent have been educators, including college administrators and professors and public and parochial school officials and teachers. Less than three per cent have been clergymen or religious workers. The remainder are from a number of different professions.

Few systems other than business have been represented by large numbers of persons serving on boards of the Chest and Council. Although by charter some Council board members are recruited from agency staffs and boards, only one-sixth of the persons who have served in this high decision-making structure of the voluntary system are social workers. Especially observed is the small representation of clergy leaders of the religious system of the community, a system, incidentally, that is closely related in ideology to voluntary health and welfare services. In general, professionals have not served in great numbers on Chest and Council boards.

By residential area, leadership has come largely from the city during the 38-year study period, and not from the suburbs. Only one-fifth live outside the city. About one-third of all persons who have ever served on Chest and

Council boards have lived in two areas. These are the Sedgwick Farms neighborhood on the North Side and the University Section on the East Side of the city.

Actually, about one of every five formal leaders in the voluntary system has lived in the Sedgwick Farms neighborhood. According to a 1950 study, it is an upper-class neighborhood less than two miles from the center of the city and within walking distance of it.[5] It does not extend to the city periphery and is surrounded by neighborhoods with property of lower value. During the first half of the nineteenth century, large mansions, many with ballrooms and carriage houses, were erected along upper James Street. Because of these and the gracious living of the residents, it achieved a reputation as a high status neighborhood. These homes were occupied by founders of some of the nation's larger industries such as the old L. C. Smith Typewriter Company which had a main plant in Syracuse for several years. In many respects, the Sedgwick Farms neighborhood is like Beacon Hill in Boston.[6] It has reputation and tradition, especially a tradition for community service, and has managed to maintain them through the years. As old industrial leaders have passed away new leaders are attracted to Sedgwick Farms because of its tradition and symbolism. Part of that tradition is service in the community system of social welfare problems. It would appear that new residents of the neighborhood have adopted this tradition.

## Analysis of Separate Chest and Council Boards

Although the Chest and the Council are legally a single corporation and are directing their efforts toward a single goal—that of planning and providing for necessary health and welfare services—they have different functions. The Chest is concerned with the funding, and the Council with the planning of community services. It is probable that the kinds of leaders recruited for financing activities differ from those for planning activities. This probability is set forth as an hypothesis. A comparative analysis of Chest and Council boards is made to affirm or cast doubt upon it.

A total of 891 different persons have served on the board of the Chest during its 38-year existence from 1921 to 1958, and 235 on the board of the Council between 1930 and 1958. Forty-four persons served on both Chest and Council boards during the study period. Except for about ten per cent who served the two organizations, these data indicate that the kinds of leaders for the Chest and Council are mutually exclusive.

In numbers, men dominate both Chest and Council boards. But the proportion of female Council board members is twice that of the Chest. Fully one-third of the Council board is female.

Possibly the greatest difference between Chest and Council boards is the occupations of their members. A majority of Chest board members are businessmen, most of whom ar affiliatied with manufacturing industries. Although nearly 40 per cent of the Council board is in business, the majority is employed in the professions. Unlike businessmen on the Council board, professionals do not run a close second on the Chest board; they account for only twenty per cent of total board membership.

In terms of rank within company structure, the Chest board consists largely of corporation officials, and the Council board consists primarily of managers, directors and administrators. About 60 per cent of the Chest board and less than 15 per cent of Council members are corporation presidents, vice-presidents, secretaries or treasurers. On the other hand, more than 15 per cent of the board members of the Chest and nearly 50 per cent of the Council are managers, directors and administrators. Thus, officers of highest status tend to participate in Chest decisions while persons at the managerial level or below, in various business and agency enterprises in the community, make Council decisions.

One similarity between these two boards is the absence of manual workers in this decision-making structure. One skilled workman (a foreman) served on the Chest board but no blue collar workers have served on the Council board, although full-time labor officials from crafts and industrial unions have rotated on and off the two boards and have served continuously since the end of World War II.

The greatest similarity between these two boards is the setting in which their members live. Slightly more that 75 per cent of the Council board and a little less than 85 per cent of the Chest board live within the city. Moreover, the highest proportion of members on these two boards is concentrated in two neighborhoods; 45 per cent of the Chest board and 30 per cent of the Council board live in the Sedgwick Farms and University Section neighborhoods of Syracuse. A plurality of Chest board members live in the Sedgwick Farms neighborhood while a plurality of Council board members live in the University Section. As mentioned earlier, the Sedgwick Farms neighborhood ranked among the highest in the city in 1950; the University Section ranked among second level neighborhoods in a five-level socioeconomic status scale. In this respect, a minor difference is seen in residential address of Chest and Council board members.

# The Community Voluntary Health and Welfare System

*Conclusions and Discussion*

On the basis of data analyzed, several conclusions are made:

*1.* Community leadership in the voluntary health and welfare system is basically a male affair, with men outnumbering women four to one. Men are involved both in planning and funding decisions. But the leadership of women is limited largely to planning.

*2.* Community leadership in the voluntary health and welfare system consists largely of business and professional persons, with business persons outnumbering professionals two to one. Professional persons participate primarily in the planning of services, while businessmen give leadership both in planning community services and in raising and allocating funds for their support.

*3.* Community leadership in the voluntary health and welfare system consist of persons who occupy positions of high prestige in their work organizations, and control or influence the distribution of its resources.

*4.* Community leadership in the voluntary health and welfare system is an activity of city dwellers. Few suburban residents of the metropolitan area participate in decision-making on local community social services.

*5.* The decision-making structure of the voluntary health and welfare system is connected, through the vocations of its board members, with the economic system and moderately or tenuously with others, including governmental, educational, and religious systems.

The extensive involvement of business executives and of men as formal leaders in the decision-making structure for community health and welfare services indicates their dominant influence. Professionals and women who contribute leadership in planning but not in the funding of these services have a subdominant influence. Two significant categories of community leadership, therefore, are identified—dominants and subdominants.

These two categories complement each other. Subdominants are no less real community leaders than the dominants. But they have different functions. The dominant category consists of people with access to the community's wealth and other resources, while subdominants have knowledge of the sentiments and sanctions of the people. Leadership structures containing both categories are best for decisions about community health and welfare services.[7] Adequate funding is not enough in planning for community services. Sentiments and sanctions prevailing in the community also are variables that must be considered. It may be necessary to program

*213*

# Charles V. Willie

methods of changing sentiments as well as of raising money. Each requires careful consideration. A leadership structure of diversified persons is partial insurance that problems involving sentiments and sanctions as well as financing will be brought to attention for decision.

## NOTES

1. Charles V. Willie, "A Success Story of Community Action," *Nursing Outlook,* 9 (January, 1961), 20.

2. Floyd Hunter, *Community Power Structure,* Chapel Hill: University of North Carolina Press, 1953, p. 248.

3. Mirra Komarovsky, "The Voluntary Association of Urban Dwellers," *American Sociological Review,* 11 (December, 1946), 698.

4. Robert K. Merton, *Social Theory and Social Structure,* Rev. New York: Free Press, 1957, p. 398.

5. Charles V. Willie, "Socio-Economic and Ethnic Areas in Syracuse, New York." Unpublished doctoral dissertation, Department of Sociology and Anthropology, Syracuse University, 1957.

6. Walter Firey, "Sentiment and Symbolism as Ecological Variables," in Paul K. Hatt and Albert J. Reiss, Jr., eds., *Reader in Urban Sociology,* New York: Free Press, 1951, pp. 233–43.

7. Charles V. Willie, *Nursing Outlook, op. cit.*

# 16. Factors Associated with Community Attachment

DAVID GOLD, FRANK N. MAGID, AND
NICHOLAS G. FOTION

THIS IS A REPORT ON COMMUNITY SATISFACTION. Thus far, we have completed one study, and others are in process. The data are collected by interviews of an area probability sample, modified by replacements for those not available at initial contact. The interview schedule stresses open-ended questions.

In each of these communities we know that community satisfaction is low, at least among the businessmen. For it is they who requested these studies and provided modest amounts of money for them. It is not difficult to trace the source of their dissatisfaction; business is not as good as they think it should be. Influenced by notions of "hidden persuaders," they feel that if they could discover who the unhappy people in the community are, and why—it is interesting that they do not see themselves as unhappy—they should then be able to induce people to spend more money in the community. Common sense notions (and, incidentally, theoretically respectable) relating spending to such mundane factors as income level are passé to them. We have capitalized on this opportunity to explore some matters of interest to us and we have focused on community attachment, whether or not this represents an accurate translation of the worried businessman's interest.

We shall not discuss here the exploratory work and theoretical considerations that led us to select a general indication of community attachment for primary attention rather than more explicit indicators of satisfaction or dissatisfaction with the community.[1] It is our notion that a person's degree of attachment can most readily be determined by his willingness or unwillingness to remain in a community. We devised a series of interlocking questions and found that the responses by ninety per cent or more of the respondents clustered into three more or less "natural" patterns.[2] The basic questions are:

Would you like to live in Rivertown the rest of your life?

Have you ever seriously thought about leaving Rivertown?

If the opportunity arose, would you consider leaving Rivertown?

These questions are probed for both YES and NO answers.

The following patterns emerged:

1. There were those who accepted without qualification the notion of living in the community the rest of their lives; they reported that they have never "seriously considered leaving Rivertown"; and asserted that they would not leave even if the opportunity arose. These are the "hard-core" residents of the community. At least, at the verbal level, they will not entertain the notion of leaving the community. In Rivertown, one-fourth of the respondents fall into this "strongly attached" category.

2. There were those who can be classified as somewhat less committed to the community because they reported that, if the opportunity arose, they would consider leaving. These people are "attached" to the community— they say they would like to live there the rest of their lives and have not thought seriously about leaving, but are at least willing to entertain the possibility. In Rivertown, one-third of the respondents fall into this "attached" category.

3. Finally, there are those respondents who reject the idea of living in the community the rest of their lives and/or describe in detail a specific period when they were thinking seriously about leaving, and give the reasons. It must be noted that some of the respondents classified in this "not attached" category responded affirmatively to the question about living in the community the rest of their lives. However, in relation to all the demographic and attitudinal variables of interest, we found no substantial differences between the respondents who said they wanted to live in the community the rest of their lives but had seriously thought about leaving, and those who said they did *not* want to stay there. It is significant that practically all respondents in this latter group could also provide a detailed description of their thinking about leaving. In Rivertown, two in every five respondents fall into the "not attached" category.

There is a crucial distinction between the first two "attached" categories and our third "not attached" category: thinking about leaving in more than casual terms. The richness of the response to probes suggests that we had tapped an important life concern for many respondents, and one that they were accustomed to discussing. Thus, the distinction between those who reported that they have thought seriously about leaving the community and those who stated that they have not can serve as a simple dichotomous measure of community attachment.

For a more refined measure of community attachment, a distinction can be made among those who say they have *not* thought seriously about leaving. In terms of systematic variation of associations, there are the respondents who, when urged by the interviewer to think of the most favorable inducements, will not consider the notion of leaving and there are those who will. These latter, less attached members of the community (our second category), though differing systematically from the more strongly attached, differ more from the "not attached"—those who report thinking about leaving. Assuming that the responses to our questions are valid, we are using a behavioral criterion as the basic indicator of community attachment, and we are using an attitudinal criterion as a secondary measure.

At this point in our studies we obtain a quick, rough measure of community attachment in survey research by asking the respondent if he has thought seriously about leaving the community. An affirmative reply merits confidence. But a negative reply may represent the individual's unwillingness to "admit" having thought about leaving. This in itself may be an indication of more feeling for (attachment to) the community than an easy affirmative reply.

## Rivertown

This report will be confined to one community, Rivertown, population 35,000. It has a modest amount of industry, which developed rapidly during World War II. Now it suffers the highest unemployment rate in the state of Iowa. Contrary to expectation, we discovered no relationship between employment status and community attachment. Those who were unemployed or unhappy with their employment status were no less apt to be attached to the community than those who were satisfied (Table 1). In addition, we found only a small relationship between attachment to the community and estimates of "job opportunities" in Rivertown. Respondents who thought "job opportunities" and "chances for advancement" were poor in Rivertown showed only slightly less attachment than those who thought "things are pretty good" (Table 2). It is clear in these data

## David Gold, Frank N. Magid, and Nicholas G. Fotion

that employment status and beliefs about employment in Rivertown cannot be offered as a possible explanation of attachment.

### Table 1—Community Attachment and Feelings About Own Employment Status[a]

| | EMPLOYMENT STATUS, PER CENT | |
|---|---|---|
| Attachment | Satisfied | Dissatisfied[b] |
| Strong | 25 | 25 |
| Moderate | 31 | 29 |
| None | 44 | 46 |
| Total | 100 | 100 |
| | (228)[c] | (93) |

[a] If the respondent was not the principal breadwinner in the household, he (she) was asked about the principal breadwinner. Excluded from this table are 37 pensioners.
[b] Included are unemployed who are in the labor force.
[c] In this and all subsequent tables, numbers in parentheses are bases from which per cents have been calculated.

### Table 2—Community Attachment and Estimate of Job Opportunities in Rivertown

| | JOB OPPORTUNITY, PER CENT | | |
|---|---|---|---|
| Attachment | Good-Fair | Poor | Total |
| Strong | 31 | 25 | 27 |
| Moderate | 26 | 33 | 31 |
| None | 43 | 42 | 42 |
| Total | 100 | 100 | 100 |
| | (143) | (215) | (358) |

It is worth noting that only when we include the attitudinal dimension in the measure of community attachment is there any relationship between attachment and views of job opportunities in Rivertown. There is no relationship at all if we use the dichotomous measure, based upon whether or not respondents have seriously thought about leaving. However, among those who say they have *not* seriously thought about leaving, a greater proportion of those who see job opportunities as poor can be pushed to an assertion that they would leave if the opportunity arose. Thus, it may well be that an unfavorable view of the job situation can provide the "opening wedge" against community attachment, but it takes something more to get persons seriously to consider moving to some other community. Another possibility is that the length of time persons hold these unfavorable views is the crucial factor. The objective fact is that the unemployment situation in Rivertown has become marked only within the past year. It could be that if people continue to hold negative views about the job situation over a longer period of time, they will indeed become less attached to the community; they will then begin to think seriously about moving someplace else.

We found in Rivertown two demographic factors which showed marked association with community attachment—age and length of residence in the community (Tables 3 and 4). Those who have lived more than twenty years in Rivertown are over three times more likely to show "strong attachment" to the community than those who have lived there five years or less. There is not a great deal of difference between those who have lived in the community five years or less and those who have lived there six to twenty years, and these latter respondents actually show a greater proportion "not attached" to the community. The major break seems to be at more than twenty years, which, significantly, includes any respondents who have lived in the community all their lives. The variation on attachment is more marked and systematic by age than by length of residence. The proportion of strongly attached increases systematically from one in nine in youngest age grouping (21 to 34) to one in two among those over 55; and the "not attached" decreases with increasing age from one-half to one-fourth.

### Table 3—Community Attachment and Length of Residence in Rivertown

YEARS OF RESIDENCE, PER CENT

| Attachment | 5 or less | 6-20 | More than 20 |
|---|---|---|---|
| Strong | 10 | 13 | 38 |
| Moderate | 44 | 33 | 26 |
| None | 46 | 54 | 36 |
| Total | 100 | 100 | 100 |
| | (39) | (111) | (208) |

### Table 4—Community Attachment and Age

AGE, PER CENT

| Attachment | 21–34 | 35–54 | 55 plus |
|---|---|---|---|
| Strong | 11 | 19 | 50 |
| Moderate | 38 | 31 | 23 |
| None | 51 | 50 | 27 |
| Total | 100 | 100 | 100 |
| | (103) | (134) | (121) |

*219*

David Gold, Frank N. Magid, and Nicholas G. Fotion

Two common-sense explanations come to mind. Perhaps younger people tend to be less contented wherever they are, less ready to commit themselves to a place for the rest of their lives. Perhaps a person has to live in a community for a long time before becoming committed to it. However, since age and length of residence are associated, it may be possible to explain one of these associations with community attachment in terms of the other independent variable, i.e., the association between age and attachment may tend to disappear with length of residence constant, or the association between length of residence and attachment may tend to disappear with age constant. In the Rivertown data, there is a systematic reduction in the size of the association between length of residence and attachment, with age constant. However, the reduction is notably greater among the younger residents than among the older, among whom the reduction is slight. Therefore, the association between length of residence and attachment is inconclusive. We cannot rule out the possibility of interaction. A substantial proportion of the younger respondents who can be classified as long-time residents have lived in the community all their lives, and we might well expect them to have notions about getting out into the world no less, perhaps even more, than other young people. On the other hand, for older persons, the longer they have lived in a community, the greater the "wrench" would seem to be. It may well be that many of these older long-time residents who are strongly attached (by our measure) to the community are simply expressing their "resignation" to living in Rivertown the rest of their lives; they have given up the thought of ever leaving, and to protect their egos they assert that they "want" to continue to live in Rivertown, come what may.

There is some relationship in Rivertown between sex and attachment to the community (Table 5). The women distributed themselves almost equally in each of the three categories of attachment, while half of the men could be classified as "not attached." This, we suppose, might be indicative of a small tendency in our society for men to be more oriented toward mobility.

### Table 5—Community Attachment and Sex

| | SEX, PER CENT | |
|---|---|---|
| Attachment | Male | Female |
| Strong | 22 | 30 |
| Moderate | 25 | 35 |
| None | 53 | 35 |
| Total | 100 | 100 |
| | (158) | (200) |

220

# Factors Associated with Community Attachment

There is also some relationship in Rivertown between income and community attachment, but this is by no means a simple linear one (Table 6). Among those with incomes of $5,000 or higher—the modest and the high income groupings—one in six or seven were "strongly attached" to the community. This ratio goes up to one in three among those with incomes less than $5,000; and up to three in five among those on pensions, who are almost all in the very low income group. There is little variation in the proportion "not attached," excluding the pensioners. On the whole, it may be said that there is an inverse relationship between income and community attachment, but it is neither striking nor systematic. As might be expected, the concomitants of income—education and occupation— roughly mirror these findings. Our guess is that this inverse association represents the more limited outlook on the world of people with lower income, less education, and more restrictive jobs.

### Table 6—Community Attachment and Income

| Attachment | INCOME, PER CENT | | | |
| --- | --- | --- | --- | --- |
| | Pension | Below $5,000 | $5,000–7,500 | Over $7,500 |
| Strong | 59 | 31 | 17 | 15 |
| Moderate | 14 | 29 | 34 | 40 |
| None | 27 | 40 | 49 | 45 |
| Total | 100 | 100 | 100 | 100 |
| | (37) | (153) | (135) | (33) |

During the course of the interview, each respondent was given the opportunity to comment upon thirty specific aspects of Rivertown. Some of the questions were structured and some were open-ended, but in each instance the respondent could give a favorable, unfavorable, or neutral response. These questions ranged through such varied matters as schools, recreational facilities, police, streets, stores, location on the river, size, etc. Opinions about most of these specific items proved to be unrelated to community attachment. For example, those who were unhappy about the streets in Rivertown were no less attached to the community than those who were satisfied with the streets, or those who thought business and industry were not doing as much as they should for the welfare of the community were no less attached than those who thought business and industry were doing "good" for the community. Opinions on a few of these matters were related to attachment in the expected direction, i.e., those who made unfavorable comments were less attached. For example, those who were unhappy about the stores in Rivertown were less attached than those who thought the stores were all right; or those who thought the schools in Rivertown were average or below average were less attached than those who thought the schools were above average. Thus, if we view attachment as possibly determined by attitudes toward specific aspects of the community, we must conclude that no one of these is important enough to affect attachment very much.

However, we decided to form a "gripe index," by counting the number of times a respondent volunteered an unfavorable comment among the thirty opportunities offered during the interview. This index of dissatisfaction is markedly related to attachment (Table 7). Breaking the distribution on the index into quarters as nearly as possible with discrete measures, we find a systematic decrease in "strong attachment" from the most satisfied quarter (7 or fewer negative comments) to the most dissatisfied quarter (15 or more negative comments); 51 per cent of the most satisfied are strongly attached and 7 per cent of the most dissatisfied are strongly attached. Or, 24 per cent of the most satisfied are "not attached," and this increases systematically to 68 per cent among the most dissatisfied. These attitudes toward specific aspects and facilities of the community appear to have a cumulative effect upon community attachment.

#### Table 7—Community Attachment and Index of Dissatisfaction with Rivertown

| Attachment | NUMBER OF DISSATISFACTIONS, PER CENT | | | |
|---|---|---|---|---|
| | 0–7 | 8–11 | 12–14 | 15–30 |
| Strong | 51 | 29 | 18 | 7 |
| Moderate | 25 | 45 | 24 | 25 |
| None | 24 | 26 | 58 | 68 |
| Total | 100 | 100 | 100 | 100 |
| | (92) | (100) | (85) | (81) |

This association does not "wash out" with the introduction of any demographic controls. Indeed, we found only one possible pattern of interaction, age, which we found to show an important association with attachment. It is also related to cumulative dissatisfaction, younger persons manifesting considerably more dissatisfactions. And the interaction of age and dissatisfaction affects attachment. Among older people, the differences in degree of community attachment between those who have few dissatisfactions (the lower 50 per cent) and those who have many dissatisfactions seem to be somewhat smaller than those among younger persons. Or, holding dissatisfactions constant, the differences in attachment between the younger and older are more than twice as large among those with many dissatisfactions than among those with few. In general, the younger people in Rivertown have a greater number of specific dissatisfactions with the community than older people. But the younger people who have few dissatisfactions tend to be no less attached than older persons in general and only slightly less attached than older persons with few dissatisfactions. It is our conclusion, at this point, that age and cumulative dissatisfactions are two important variables which interact to affect community attachment. The variation in terms of these two variables in Rivertown is most marked, going from 77 per cent attached among older persons with few dissatisfactions to only 29 per cent attached among younger persons with many dissatisfactions (Table 8).

### Table 8—Community Attachment, Index of Dissatisfaction, and Age

| Many Dissatisfactions (12–30) | Per cent Strongly and Moderately Attached to Community | |
|---|---|---|
| Young[a] | 29 | (99) |
| Old | 55 | (67) |
| Few Dissatisfactions (0–11) | | |
| Young | 67 | (78) |
| Old | 77 | (114) |

[a] Less than 45. This is approximately a median break on age in this sample.

It will be recalled that length of residence was associated with attachment. We found that length of residence was not associated with the measure of cumulative dissatisfactions; and that it does not affect the relationship between dissatisfactions and attachment.

In the Rivertown study, we had the opportunity to check upon only one possible consequence of degree of community attachment. We were able to classify respondents in terms of the amount of shopping outside the community. In our other studies we are investigating possible relationships between attachment and other forms of community behavior, such as voting on various issues and participation in general community activities. We are particularly interested in discovering whether degree of community attachment can explain to some extent the position individuals take, for example, on a bond issue to build a new schoolhouse or a community center. Meanwhile, our one measure of the possible effect of community attachment does show the expected positive association. The proportion of those going outside Rivertown to shop increases consistently with decreasing attachment, from 21 per cent among the "strongly attached" to

## David Gold, Frank N. Magid, and Nicholas G. Fotion

45 per cent among the "not attached" (Table 9). Since age and income are related to shopping outside Rivertown, we controlled for these variables. The association between attachment and shopping outside the community proved to be unaffected by these controls, nor was there any hint of interaction.

### Table 9—Community Attachment and Shopping Outside of Rivertown

| Attachment | Per cent of Significant Amount of Shopping Done Outside of Rivertown | |
|---|---|---|
| Strong | 21 | (97) |
| Moderate | 35 | (109) |
| None | 45 | (152) |

Finally, we should like to report upon our exploration of one other factor that may affect community attachment. Because we had not anticipated it, the data from Rivertown on this variable are not as rich as they will be in our other community studies. We mentioned earlier that all responses to the attachment questions were probed. The respondent was free to choose any terms he wished for his answers. In attempting to categorize these responses in some meaningful fashion, we, like many social researchers recently, "rediscovered the primary group."[3] In particular, we found that those who wanted to remain in Rivertown the rest of their lives invariably gave as reasons family, friends, and people they know. On the other hand, those whom we classified as "not attached," who did not want to live in Rivertown the rest of their lives and/or had thought seriously about leaving, rarely mentioned family and friends as a reason for not having left Rivertown. These latter respondents were much more apt to rationalize their remaining in "economic" terms. Since the focus for these "not attached" respondents is upon leaving, perhaps it is somewhat more "natural" in our society to think in terms of economic costs—jobs, owning a home, etc. Nevertheless, it is striking that hardly any of the "attached" respondents referred to their jobs or owning a good home as a reason for wanting to remain; and it is also striking that hardly any of the "not attached" suggested "all my friends are here" as a factor which has prevented their leaving. Presumably they, as well as the more attached respondents, have family and friends in Rivertown. Unfortunately, we do not have data on the quantity of primary group relationships in Rivertown. It is currently our notion that the *quality* of the primary group relationships, and not the quantity, may differ considerably between those who are more attached and those who are less attached to the community.

224

## NOTES

1. We view community attachment and community satisfaction as more or less independent variables. Some people with high community satisfaction have little sense of attachment to the community and vice versa. We see community satisfaction as only one of several factors that can affect community attachment.

2. In this study, about 9 per cent of the respondents could not be definitely classified into one of the three attach-

ment patterns; but at least half of these cases were due to failure to obtain a complete response on each of the three questions. The 358 cases which are used in the analysis represent unambiguously the described patterns of response on community attachment.

3. Elihu Katz and Paul F. Lazarsfeld, *Personal Influence*, New York: Free Press, 1955, pp. 34–42.

# 17.   Mediating Leadership and Community Interaction

RITCHIE P. LOWRY

## The Community Setting

THIS REPORT IS BASED UPON SELECTED FINDINGS from a four-year study of a rapidly changing small community in northern California.[1] The initial study was prompted by an interest in leadership problems that resulted from the increasing impact of larger urban society.

The California community of Micro City represents a blending of rural and urban social and cultural characteristics. The over-all population includes about 14,000 within the city limits and an additional 15,000 or more on the fast-growing unannexed fringes. The community is a Protestant, white-collar, middle-class service center for a northern California region of six to nine counties. The bulk of Micro City's residents are doctors, lawyers, teachers, private and public welfare workers, salesmen, and technicians in service industries. The community's largest single industry is a five-year college, part of the California state college system, with a student body of 3,500 and a faculty of 250.

Physically, Micro City is one of the most attractive of the many towns and cities in California's great agricultural central valley. Farming in the surrounding region is large-scale, and the basic crops are almonds and rice. The community was founded in 1850 by one of California's original settlers of the northern gold country. The founder's wife died in 1918, and there are still old-timers in Micro City who remember playing as children in her home.

Since the end of World War II, the growth of population and business has been steady, though moderate for the state. In the decade of the 1950's the population of the city proper increased 12% and the township 35%, in contrast to 26% in the county and 40% in the state. Future expansion will probably exhibit the same steady trends, since Micro City lacks the physical and demographic bases for explosive industrial development.

The community has a city manager–council form of government, and local political activity is manifestly nonpartisan. However, elective and appointive positions have been dominated for over thirty years by Republicans, Masons, and downtown business interests. Campaigns are devoid of debate or discussion of issues and problems, and are characterized by personal appeals through informal contacts in civic and social groups. Support by Micro City's one community newspaper generally guarantees a candidate's success at the polls. In national, state, and local affairs the community's political and social stance has been traditionally conservative and provincial. Leaders of the community and individual citizens alike consider maintenance of the comfortably affluent status quo the most important norm for local social and political behavior.

Nevertheless, in recent years increasing voices of discontent have been heard in community affairs. These have come from the liberal arts faculty at the state college, a handful of Protestant ministers, and several businessmen and citizens. These critics have begun to question the traditional rural and conservative basis of community life and have played an increasing role in Micro City's leadership structure.

Micro City, then, is a changing small community with strong roots in rural and historical tradition and, at the same time, increasing contacts with urban society. It has experienced considerable population and technological growth while remaining relatively homogeneous and stable. The community lacks the severe problems of crime, delinquency, personal deviance, poverty, congestion, and so on, which characterize many larger cities. This unique mixture of simultaneous stability and change, rural and urban ways of life, makes Micro City an ideal case for testing theories about leadership structure in the changing small community.

## Typologies of Leadership

For analyzing the structure of community power and leadership, one of the most useful and provocative concepts is Robert Merton's distinction between "Local" and "Cosmopolitan" influentials.[2] In general ideological orientation the Local leader is parochial and provincial. His attentions are directed mainly toward the problems and issues of the small community as an isolated grouping within the context of larger society.

The Cosmopolitan leader, on the other hand, is ecumenical and sophisticated. His significant reference groups and affiliations transcend the local community in the form of professional or large-scale ties and allegiances, and, as a result, his primary frame of reference is the world outside the community.

The Local leader is one who has either been born in or has lived in the community most of his life. He is proud of the fact that he knows many people intimately and reflects this basic attitude by joining voluntary organizations solely to make contacts or have fun. Thus, the Local's influence in the community power structure is a function of whom he knows, rather than what he knows. In contrast, the Cosmopolitan leader is a highly mobile individual who has been in the community a relatively short period of time. He tends to be a trained specialist who possesses influence because of his particular skills and knowledge. Hostilities and antagonisms between Locals and Cosmopolitans often arise because the latter are younger, more formally educated, and highly mobile, socially and economically.

It was apparent from the outset of the study of Micro City that these typologies would be relevant to the community's changing leadership structure. It was, however, equally evident that such a classification was in many instances too simplistic. First, there is an implicit assumption in Merton's types that the Locals would tend to be more parochial and conservative in their total cultural views and perspectives and the Cosmopolitans more sophisticated and liberal. Interviews with Micro City's leaders indicated that this was not necessarily the case. Many of the community's leaders had cosmopolitan orientations toward the local community but were also predominently conservative in their larger political and social beliefs. A second small group of leaders evidenced nonconservative and, often, radical frames of reference for their actions but participated actively in many forms of purely local activities. Still others expressed local attitudes about some community problems and cosmopolitan attitudes about different issues.

Second, Merton has suggested that some community influentials can be identified as monomorphic and others as polymorphic. That is, some leaders possess single areas of influence within the total life of the community, whereas others have multiple influence in social, economic and political life.[3] However, in his original study of the community of Rovere, Merton never explicitly indicates how these two kinds of influence are related to the typologies of Local and Cosmopolitan leaders. As a matter of fact, each seems to be monomorphic in separate areas of influence.

Third, the Local–Cosmopolitan classification leaves an empirical gap and raises serious practical questions about effective leadership in the changing small community. Merton's analysis concentrates upon the conflict between these two groups caused by the vast ideological and social distance between them. Locals and Cosmopolitans do not share the same frame of reference, nor do they generally confront one another in the group activities of daily life. Differential status and prestige are marked. Locals control the electoral process through informal association and contact.

If this is the situation which faces any small community as it comes into contact with the larger world, how is it possible to maintain a dynamic leadership process? On what social and cultural levels could Locals and Cosmopolitans conceivably interact? Merton's typology provides no answer.

A primary purpose of the study of Micro City, therefore, was to devise a typology of leadership based upon the traditional notions of local and cosmopolitan influence, including the question of effective leadership interaction. Two major variables were used in constructing this typology: (1) the cultural orientation of the leaders and (2) their place in the community social structures as determined by their participation in daily group life. An analysis of community ideology indicated that the cultural orientation of Micro City's leaders could be classified as Conservative or Utopian. These concepts were adapted from Karl Mannheim's distinction between ideology and utopia.[4] By utopia, Mannheim means those particular belief systems which transcend reality and are, therefore, fundamentally challenging to the prevailing social system. Conservative ideologies, on the other hand, are belief systems which attempt to represent culturally the reality of a social system and serve the function of maintaining the status quo. According to the second variable of participation in the group structure of community life, it was found that leaders may be designated as Locals, Cosmopolitans, or Mediators.

In the case of Micro City, although the leadership conflicts suggested by Merton do frequently arise, it was also evident that there was a good deal of meaningful interaction among leaders about specific community issues. In some instances of community conflict, local and cosmopolitan groups joined together in promoting a specific cause. Decision-making processes at these times were usually the result of a dynamic and meaningful confrontation of opposing interest groups.[5] The key to such interaction lay in the emergence of a "mediating" leader.

The sociological concept of a "mediating group" has been used to designate the unique structural function of heterogeneous, special-interest groups in the context of mass society, bureaucratic organization, and large-scale groups.[6] Rarely, however, has this notion been employed in small community research. In addition, the special role of the mediating leader

*229*

# Ritchie P. Lowry

in mobilizing group interaction is often overlooked. Questionnaire data, interviews, and observation of situations of community conflict in Micro City suggested that these concepts are also crucial in understanding effective leadership in the small community.

### Table 1—A Typology of Community Leadership

|  | CULTURAL ORIENTATION | |
|---|---|---|
| *Participation in the Structure of Group Life* | Conservative | Utopian |
| Local | C-L | U-L |
| Mediating | C-M | U-M |
| Cosmopolitan | C-C | U-C |

Table 1 illustrates this sixfold typology of leadership.

Extensive analysis (Table 2) of 77 of Micro City's leaders disclosed the following kinds of profiles for each leadership group. In general, both

### Table 2—Selected Characteristics of 77 Local, Mediating, and Cosmopolitan Leaders

|  | Locals | Mediators | Cosmopolitans |
|---|---|---|---|
| *Number* | 24 | 28 | 25 |
| *Mean Age* | 57.0 | 42.7 | 45.4 |
| *Mean Years Residence in Micro City* | 37.0 | 12.9 | 13.2 |
| *Modal Education* | Some college | College graduate | Postgraduate |
| *Birthplace or Former Residence:* | | | |
| Micro City | 8 | 2 | 1 |
| Northern California Community | 6 | 1 | 0 |
| Other Small California Community | 3 | 4 | 1 |
| Other Small Community | 2 | 3 | 1 |
| San Francisco Area | 2 | 10 | 9 |
| Los Angeles Area | 1 | 3 | 3 |
| Other Metropolis | 2 | 5 | 8 |
| Foreign Country | 0 | 0 | 2 |
| *Occupations:* | | | |
| Housewife | 8 | 4 | 3 |
| Farmer/Rancher | 5 | 0 | 1 |
| Small Business | 3 | 8 | 0 |
| Civil or Public Agency | 1 | 4 | 7 |
| Professional | 4 | 6 | 9 |
| Large Business | 2 | 6 | 5 |
| Other | 1 | 0 | 0 |

# Mediating Leadership and Community Interaction

Conservative and Utopian Locals (C-L and U-L) are similar to Merton's concept. This leader is a long-time resident of the community, and most often he can trace his family lineage by birth or marriage back to the original settlers of the area. He possesses power and influence in Micro City because he represents stability, permanence, and tradition. Individually, the Local leader exhibits great occupational and educational diversity, although many are part- or full-time farmers and most have only a high school education. Locals exercise power in contemporary Micro City mainly through social groups such as Masonic affiliations, Daughters of the American Revolution, Veterans of Foreign Wars, Lions, Eastern Star, the county Historical Society, Omega Nu, and so on. What few direct political allegiances the Locals have tend to be confined to state and national politics and, within the local community, to a few minor appointive positions.

The Utopian Local differs from the Conservative Local in that he adopts a liberal or radical social and political philosophy. In Micro City, a Utopian Local comes from the lower social, economic, and educational groups in the community; for example, from a small Negro subcommunity or labor. He looks upon the local community as his permanent home and, therefore, restricts his local participation; he rarely translates his radical beliefs into concrete local action. On the state and national level, the U-L maintains nominal membership in the NAACP, labor union organizations, peace groups, and radical political parties.

At the opposite end of the continuum of social structure we find the Cosmopolitan leader. He is usually younger than the Local, more mobile, and extremely active in regional, state, and national organizations. Occupationally and professionally, the Cosmopolitan is a highly trained specialist who earns his living either working for a large-scale organization or as an independent professional. Conservative Cosmopolitans include physicians, lawyers, college staff and faculty, or businessmen from the few larger industries in Micro City or from public service institutions such as the gas, electric, and telephone companies. Utopian Cosmopolitans are drawn from the community's social welfare agencies, the liberal arts faculty at the college, and the local offices of national service groups. As a consequence, Cosmopolitans have an advanced degree of formal education from universities and colleges. Most migrated to Micro City from large metropolitan areas and tend to judge local problems and issues in purely professional terms. The Cosmopolitan has membership in few local groups and is most active in professional and allied organizations on a regional, state, and national level. Both Conservative and Utopian Cosmo-

*231*

politans are highly critical of the local community; few hold either elective or appointive positions in local government. Most Cosmopolitans become interested in local issues only when their profession or family circumstances are affected (for example, local education, medical, or welfare problems).

The Mediating leader is so termed because he is polymorphic, possessing overlapping memberships and informal relationships in both Local and Cosmopolitan groups. The Mediator may come from a diversity of occupational fields: small business, public service, education, politics, religion, social welfare, or the mass media. However, all of these occupations provide him with a common orientation—an interest in larger social processes and their implications for the local community. The Conservative Mediator is usually a businessman who considers himself a semiprofessional (for example, real estate broker, insurance broker, or pharmacist). He is middle-aged and has lived in the community an average of 10 to 15 years. Many C-M's are either second generation or marital relatives of old Micro City families. As a result, they are in the unique position of being able to exercise power and influence in the community on the basis of both ascribed and achieved characteristics. In Micro City, the C-M dominates the top elective and appointive positions of influence and controls the electoral process through informal contacts in Rotary, Kiwanis, Masons, and the Chamber of Commerce.

The Utopian Mediator may be a college professor, minister, attorney, housewife, or businessman. He, too, is middle-aged and has lived in the community about 10 years. He is extremely active in professionally oriented local groups such as the Family Service Association, the Mental Hygiene Board, Parent-Teacher Associations, Micro City Council of Social Agencies, American Association of University Women, League of Women Voters, and Micro City Council of Churches. The U-M in Micro City rarely occupies a top position of community leadership in the structure of formal government, but he often serves in an advisory capacity in appointive positions.

## Leadership Interaction

Theoretically speaking, the dynamics of leadership in the community—that is, the channels of influence and communication among various leadership groups—would be expected to follow the pattern suggested in Figure 1. As can be seen, Mediating leaders play a key role.

## Mediating Leadership and Community Interaction

First, it is through these key Mediating leaders that extreme and opposing ideological groups may confront one another directly. Without an interpersonal mediating influence, opposing interest groups would tend to confront one another infrequently and only in an impersonal manner. Interaction would take place only through the secondary means of mass media or an occasional and highly formal group (for example, at a public forum).

*Figure 1. Typical patterns of leadership interaction: Solid lines depict primary and intimate lines of leadership interaction. Dashed lines depict secondary interaction and contact.*

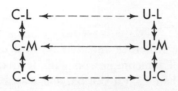

Second, by utilizing the mediating-group experience, Mediating leaders can supply diverse interest groups in the community with a common frame of reference, a meaningful sense of contemporary community interest. The groups of which the Mediator is a member have such potential because they possess ideological and social roots in both the local community and the larger society. In addition, several of these groups (in Micro City, for example, the Family Service Association, the League of Women Voters, and Rotary) have memberships which represent each of the different leadership groups of the community. It is only when individuals share, to some extent, the same continuing environmental frame of reference that there can be effective interaction of contrasting beliefs and interests.

Third, through the group experience, the Mediator can provide the effective leadership necessary to mobilize and encourage community interest and action. In the context of large-scale, mass society, mediating groups sustain interest and participation by relating individuals on a daily face-to-face basis. In the small community these mediating groups serve an additional and dichotomous purpose. Because everyone's life is something of an "open book", most leaders are reluctant to confront one another on a purely personal basis. In the small community, personal antagonisms and vindictiveness are long-lasting. As one leader described it, leadership "continually operates in a fishbowl." The mediating group provides the psychological protection necessary to encourage vigorous and dynamic leadership by ameliorating and attenuating the personalized aspects of interaction. One may speak out as a college professor, a Republican, a Democrat, a member of the League of Women Voters, or a minister without running the risk of immediate public censure.

In other words, the effective leader may act in terms of his role as a member of a concerned community group. The mediating group, then, stands as a buffer between this leader and potential criticism from others in the community. It is the job of the Mediating leader to provide the community with the group channels through which special and conflicting interests may confront one another in an impersonal yet productive, dynamic manner.

## Conclusion

This concept of the structure and dynamics of community leadership can be used as a model for comparison with leadership interaction in a specific community. When such a comparison was made in Micro City, it became evident that not only is the Mediator the key to effective leadership, but the processes of leadership interaction frequently break down. The community's Mediating leaders share with others the prevailing ethic of maintenance of the status quo. As a result, they often consciously avoid situations of community debate and confrontation, particularly in matters of local politics. The Mediator, too, becomes content to maintain community harmony at all costs.

Secondly, the Mediator is particularly susceptible to a unique form of alienation from meaningful community participation.[7] He may become so involved in the routine and demanding tasks of daily leadership in Micro City's multiple subgroups that he no longer has the time or inclination to provide an ideological orientation for such action. One leader complained that the community's leadership is ineffective because "we tend to wear out our good men on minor and unimportant jobs."

Thirdly, most of the leaders in Micro City's heterogeneous interest groups are totally unaware that their organizations have the vital psychological function of mediating in local community life. Businessmen from large-scale organizations are formally prohibited from engaging in "local politics". Groups such as the League of Women Voters and American Association of University Women frequently claim to be interested only in "nonpartisan" local issues. Local labor unions and political parties are active only in state and national affairs. The state college administration formally and informally censures its professors and staff when they become involved in local disputes which oppose the interests of the downtown business leaders. Ministers meet great resistance from their congregations if they attempt to combine religion and community action. Each group in Micro City seems content to leave the job of vigorous leadership to some other group.

As a consequence, potential Mediators themselves tend to limit or restrict their local social activities. Only a few Utopian Mediators are members of civic clubs, the informal power groups of the Conservative Mediator. Rarely are they asked to join, and usually they refuse such offers because of lack of interest in the social activities of these groups. On the other hand, not one Conservative Mediating leader belongs to utopian mediating groups such as the Micro City Council of Social Agencies. Informal patterns of socialization depict the same processes. College personnel and townspeople do not travel in the same social circles. Micro City's physicians form a tightly knit in-group of their own. Potential Mediators tend to interact only with those who share the same perspectives and interests, and, therefore, cannot carry out their ultimate function.

In summary, we can see that the increasing differentiation of the small community's leadership structure is a direct result of social change brought about by the impact of larger society. This very differentiation serves as a basis for leadership that is potentially meaningful and dynamic. Confrontation of conservative and utopian interests can effect needed change, but within the context of orderly, traditional patterns of community action. Confrontation of local and cosmopolitan interests can relate the small community to the larger society while, at the same time, preserving a local sense of community.

Only the Mediating leader can facilitate this leadership interaction. If he does not do so, the differentiation can cause ineffective and disruptive community leadership processes. Only a few of Micro City's leaders are aware of this situation and of the need for vigorous mediating leadership. As other small communities of the country undergo similar social change and Locals are confronted by the challenge of Cosmopolitans, and Conservatives by Utopians, the Mediating leader, facilitating and sustaining leadership interaction, can be expected to exhibit similar trends as in the case of Micro City.

## NOTES

1. This article is a revised version of a paper presented to the Committee on Community Research and Development at the annual meeting of the Society for the Study of Social Problems, St. Louis, Missouri, August 1961. Data are taken from *Who Runs This Town? A Study of the Quality of Public Life in a Changing*

# Ritchie P. Lowry

*Small Community* (Unpublished Ph.D. Dissertation, Department of Sociology, University of California, Berkeley, 1962).

2. Robert K. Merton, *Social Theory and Social Structure,* New York: The Free Press of Glencoe, 1957, pp. 387–436.

3. *Op. cit.*

4. Karl Mannheim, *Ideology and Utopia,* New York: Harcourt Brace and Co., 1949.

5. For a description of several specific incidents of community conflict (a freeway dispute, Negro-White tensions, and Un-American Activities Committee investigation, etc.) see: Lowry's "The Myth and Reality of Grass-Roots Democracy,"

*International Review of Community Development* (journal of the International Federation of Settlements and Neighbourhood Centres, Rome, Italy), 12 (1963).

6. This literature includes works by Elton Mayo, Rothlesberger and Dicksen, and David Riesman. A more recent consideration of the theoretical implications of mediating groups in mass society can be found in William Kornhauser's *The Politics of Mass Society,* New York: The Free Press of Glencoe, 1959.

7. Various forms of community alienation and their consequences are discussed in the author's "The Functions of Alienation in Leadership," *Sociology and Social Research,* 45 (July, 1962), pp. 426–35.

# 18.   Where is the Metropolitan Problem?

SCOTT GREER

A DECADE AGO THE "METROPOLITAN PROBLEM" rose on the horizon of public concern. A large number of journalists on the "metropolitan beat" ran feature articles on local versions. Citizens' groups organized to consider it. The editors of *Fortune* published a lively and profitable book on the subject, and the entire enterprise was given the Good Housekeeping seal of approval—that is, many substantial foundation grants were made for the purpose of solving the problem. Eventually, the Public Administration Service published a survey of metropolitan surveys listing almost a hundred investigations of the problem.[1]

The question arises: what is this problem? The question may seem superfluous—most cities appear to be disorderly, schismatic, conflict-ridden, dirty, rackety, and not ordered the way a beneficent God or social system would order them. However, in this respect they differ not at all from many other aspects of our lives and works. What is peculiarly problematic about the metropolis? As a first approach to the question, I wil try to summarize, impressionistically, the kinds of concerns implicit in statements of the problem.

## I.

In 1957 the *St. Louis Post-Dispatch* published a cartoon of the St. Louis metropolitan area as Gulliver, bound flat on his back by the myriad

This paper is a side-effect of research work carried out by the author (1) as Chief Sociologist of the Metropolitan St. Louis Survey in 1956–57; (2) as Director of the Center for Metropolitan Studies (Northwestern University) during the course of a study of the referendum for a metropolitan district government in St. Louis in 1959. Both studies were supported by the Public Affairs Division of the Ford Foundation; the first was also supported by the McDonnel Aircraft Company Charitable Trust.

*237*

tiny threads of diverse local governmental units. The implication is that
the metropolis is organically united, but unable to act because of political
fragmentation. The *Post* also published a cartoon showing Tweedledum
and Tweedledee (two simpering fat boys) labelled as central city and
suburbs. The implication is that halves of an identity have become split
and separate. These cartoons correspond to the most common slogans of
metropolitan governmental reform; both deplore "the crazy-quilt of local
government in the "metropolis," and "the Chinese wall between city and
suburbs." Rift and fragmentation seen as vitiating the polity—this is one
important element in the picture.

The division of government, in turn, is held accountable for many other
losses and lacks. The policy power is divided with a resulting loss of communication and surveillance; land-use planning is impossible with 149
units as in St. Louis (or 1467, as in the New York area); development
and maintenance of an adequate circulatory system is hamstrung by divided jurisdiction over roads; even the disposal of waste, sewage and
garbage and noxious gases, is difficult when one watershed and one atmosphere are so divided, while such esoteric governmental tasks as preventive public medicine and standby organization for disaster control are
all but impossible. And, as the argument goes, traffic, crime, disease and
air pollution, tornadoes and hydrogen missiles, are no respecters of our
divided jurisdictions.

A further argument might be called the local patriot's concern. "This
is a great old City," remarked a leader in a recent metropolitan reform
movement, "The only trouble is it's *dying*." Newspapers hammer on the
theme of "Progress or Decay," with the implication that the economic future of the area depends upon solving the problem of metropolitan government. As a variant of this, many are concerned with the very shape of
the city . . . "the death of Downtown," the "sprawl of suburbia," the
disappearance of surrounding countryside and forest, the decline of the
central city as "symbol and hub of the metropolitan area" (in the words
of Philadelphia's City Administrator). In short, the city is seen as changing, and in a direction which is foreboding.

Metropolitan surveys, varying in scope and resources, have tended to
a common solution: governmental integration of the urbanized region. I
will quote from the official charter of the Metropolitan St. Louis Survey:
Since "the governmental pattern . . . gravely impairs efficiency and di-
lutes responsibility . . . impedes the orderly and healthy development of
the expanding community . . .(while) many major needs of the people
. . . are not being uniformly met and cannot be met adequately by unco-

# Where is the Metropolitan Problem?

ordinated, piecemeal local action," (it is necessary) "to prepare . . . alternative proposals for action designed to remedy some or all of the major ills arising out of the present pattern of government . . ."[2] And the Survey recommended a metropolitan district government, as the Cleveland survey recommended an Urban County government, and the Dade County survey, something in between.[3]

The consistency of such findings and recommendations may be evidence of convergence in our knowledge of the nature of things—that happy state of a mature science. It may, however, only bear witness to the weakness of our scientific tools, the uncontrolled nature of our inferences, and the consensus among us on certain values. For this reason it is important that we examine the thoughtways of the various actors involved. These include the rank and file citizens, the civic leaders of the area, the staff experts of local government, and social scientists.

A social problem has been usually defined, by sociologists, as a social situation departing from existing norms and therefore presenting a task to the actors. Thus, it is useful to ask, "What bothers different people about government in the metropolis?" There is a wide array of answers. For the general public, as reflected in sample surveys, it is the bread and butter issues—the amount and quality of consumption items provided by local government. Dissatisfaction clusters around such matters as the transport system, the maintenance of streets and sidewalks, parks and playgrounds, and the sewage-disposal system. Concrete and discrete items in the housekeeping of the area form the typical agenda of discontent.[4]

For the civic leaders who are involved, however, dissatisfaction focuses upon governmental structure. The various concrete items are seen as symptoms of a basic weakness, inefficiency, and disorder. Such leaders speak of the effects of government upon the good life of its citizens and, at another level, speak of the City's future, with an emphasis upon the economic losses caused by metropolitan fragmentation. These leaders, economic dominants, members of the Chamber of Commerce and Committee of 57, elected officials from the business or professional strata, assume responsibility for an area as a unit.

The staff experts of local government are earnestly committed, for the most part, to a particular and limited task in a functional segment of the society. The police administrator, public health officer, county school supervisor, traffic commissioner, head of the city plan commission—each, in his way, faces the consequences of metropolitanization. And the resulting problems are similar: to get hold of enough legal power, over a broad enough area, and enough money, to do the job at hand. In the main, such officials are in favor of extending jurisdictions and tax resources: they need them.

These positions coincide with the problem as seen by the social scientists, who might be defined as staff experts of the community as a whole. The social scientist, interested in metropolitan affairs, typically speaks of the disjuncture between social city and political city, or he emphasizes overlapping jurisdictions, waste, inefficiency, conflicting hierarchies of power, incompetent personnel, inadequate revenue, and unable government. Derived from the public administrative approach to local government, the definition focuses upon all those gaps in the system of control which should be filled in to produce an effective task-performing organization.[5]

These are cogent arguments. However, if one steps back a moment and recalls some competing ideas, their plausibility suffers. While the people may be dissatisfied with some local services, they usually turn down proposals to right the wrongs done them. They vote against metropolitan government, they oppose annexation, they trim bond issues and tax levies, and they turn Urban Redevelopment programs into baseball lots for big league clubs. It is possible, of course, to simply say: The people are dumb.[6] This is a very damaging admission if one's argument for a problem's existence depends upon "widespread public discontent" (as in one foundation proposal). Furthermore, it is at least possible that the voters are committed to the present loose governmental congeries. In the central city, governmental autonomy may represent control of their own destiny by the working class and the ethnics, through the Democratic party. To those in the suburbs, their small neighborhood enclave bounded by governmental walls may be the "republic in miniature," offering some control over the collective fates of their treasures.[7] If such were the case, it would not negate dissatisfaction with governmental services, even those which seem to demand area wide control. Beyond the "bitch function" of the democratic sample survey may lie real dissatisfactions,—endured, however, as the price of maintaining other normative structures.

Looking at the metropolitan problem as defined by experts and elites in the light of such considerations, leads one to question the validity of the approach. Estimates of the consumption norms for governmental goods may be correct; the discrepancy between what is and ought to be is indeed existent; weakness of governmental structure may even be an adequate explanation for this discrepancy. This weakness is not, however, just a simple, accidental result of unplanned change; it also reflects interests, organized by ideology. These in turn grow out of the differentiation, stratification, and social organization of the metropolitan population.[8]

## Where is the Metropolitan Problem?

In a sense, all definitions of the "metropolitan problem" are folk-thought. Uncontrolled by systematic theory and unsupported by observation at the crucial points, they are forms of cautious utopianism masquerading as scientific analysis plus common sense.

## II.

We have identified the metropolitan problem by pointing. It would be more useful to identify it within the structure of sociological thought: this I will attempt in the remainder of the paper.

If the metropolitan situation is a problem, then it is an indeterminate situation to which the definer is committed, and one about which something basic is unknown. If it is, further, a *social* problem, it is one in which some aspect is socially indeterminate—i.e., the direction of social action is not clear. Typically arising as a discrepancy between what exists and what should exist, such indeterminacy may be of ends (what do we want?) or of means (how should we get it?).

Such problems imply questions about the nature of what is, and what should be, as well as interactions between them. The question of what is, the empirical nature of the situation, is formally simple—though practically very difficult, with anything as complicated as a metropolitan complex. What is required is a map of the way the thing lies and operates, tested at key points by logic and observation, grounded in a universal theory of human behavior. The question of what ought to be is the real difficulty. If, however, we focus upon the observable social world we can say that a *socially effective* definition of what ought to be is always an application of a norm—a groupwide consensus on what should be done.[9] Such norms are always specific to a social collective; in contrast to the various images flowing through a given nervous system, they are *social* fact.

To be sure, the occasional nonconformist may propose new normative concepts, importing them from outside the group discourse, or inventing them through logical extension and individual conception. In contemporary large-scale society, the introduction of new normative concepts to given groups is an everyday phenomenon. The sheer mixture of cultures and sub-cultures, as well as the emphasis upon cultural innovation (institutionalized in such organizations as university departments of planning and public administration), guarantees a wide range of concepts, while the winds of the mass media broadcast all kinds of seed in all directions. To take root and grow, however, they must be couched in the conceptual language of the group, which sieves individual conceptions through the flow

*241*

of communication, limiting them to what may be understood. They will be effective only as they take a place within the organizational language of the group—the role system, and the normative system.

The available range of definitions of the metropolis and its problems is wide. There are those who think that what exists conforms to what ought to be. Then there are the deviants, the nonconformists who want more of the services provided and evaluate the system in these terms (the pragmatic reformers), and the nonconformists who want a new system. The latter compare their city with other cities—typically, the bright, new, rapidly growing cities. Or they compare their city with its own "golden age"— and derive radical proposals for change. In short, they contrast the Earthly City with the Heavenly City, and are dissatisfied. Many of their notions of what ought to be, and how to achieve it, are derived from what might be called the professional intellectuals of local government—the National Municipal League, the Public Administration Service, the professional planners, the political scientists, or columnists on the metropolitan beat. The new models for the city, growing within such circles, spread more widely through the public print. They are based upon such common norms as "efficiency," local patriotism, and boosterism. They imply a change in the structure of the polity.[10]

The basic effort then is revolutionary. But to make such an effort is to threaten a whole existing system, and resistance to change is one way we know there *is* a system. The intellectuals of local government, having made the existing order problematic through use of alternative norms, seek to make it objectively problematic for those who accept it. In the process they encounter violent counterattacks—from the Mayor and City Hall, the politicians and the unions, the Negroes and other ethnics of the central city; from the community press and elected officials, municipal attorneys and small businessmen, the tax payers leagues of the suburbs. Because the proponents of metropolitan government use a normative system derived from the intellectuals of local government, and because they frequently base their proposals upon a "scientific survey's recommendation," they seem to themselves to stand for the unvarnished, scientific truth. To their opponents, however, they may seem only irresponsible "do-gooders," or salesmen of "big government." It becomes clear in the heat of battle that the authority of social science is not adequate to convince opponents of metropolitan government.[11] It is my position that it should not. The reasons, I believe, go as deep as the roots of normative theory. To make the point clear, another brief detour is necessary.

By normative theory is meant the more or less systematic formulations of what ought to be in human society. Since what can be logically limits what ought to be in any practical sense, normative theory always subsumes a degree of empirical theory; it is constrained by notions of what is inexorable, but only within very broad limits. At the simplest level, if we inferred the normative order of a small group from observable behavior, we should particularly attend the sanctions used, and the inferred grounds for these sanctions we would designate as the construct "norm." The order internal to a collection of norms held by a specific group and effective in ordering behavior, we should call the "folk" normative theory of the group—something very similar to what anthropologists call "ideal culture." It is the effective consensus as to what ought to be done, given the nature of what is believed to be empirically true, as the complex is inferred and ordered by an observer.

The construction of a theory of the normative system in a group is an acknowledged task of social science. It is a construct; further, it is only a part of the explanatory apparatus of the social scientist. For example, he can foresee conflicts between what "is" and what "ought" to be, and he should be able to predict outcomes—modifications either of what is or what ought to be. Should he not command a theory larger than and inclusive of the normative order in the group, he is as culture-bound as the subjects he studies. Many experts in local government fall into this position; their recurring assumption of a rational voter, who remarkably resembles a public administrator, is one indicator of their endogenous relation to the system.[12]

What, however, of the claim for a scientific normative theory? Such claims have been made by classical political theorists, by neo-positivists in sociology, and by philosophers. The answer seems implicit in the above discussion of norms. If a normative theory is anything besides a dispassionate mapping of the notions of what ought to be in a specific collective's behavior, then it is simply a reflection of the social scientist's own role within a normative order. It may be more or less logically consistent, more or less possible in terms of known empirical limits. But if it has any social legitimacy, it rests upon the uniformity of response from other actors. As Wirth remarks, "there is no value apart from interest and no objectivity apart from agreement."[13] The objectivity of normative theory always rests upon shared interests and definitions; it can be extended only by persuasion, for the necessary assumptions are optional and have neither logical nor empirical coerciveness. They are given not by nature, but by the significant others who maintain the specific order.

The reason for the unauthoritative nature of the arguments for metropolitan government is clear. The authority in question was basically inappropriate to the subject. Normative theory, indicating "What kind of a city we ought to have," is not intellectually coercive, even when called scientific, for normative problems cannot be settled by scientific authority. Nor can they be *finally* settled by any authority. Normative theory is a means for group mobilization to achieve group ends. The area within which such ends are achieved is the polity. Indeed, this is the reason for the inescapable necessity of politics—there is no other means of resolving such questions.

Within the polity are forged the temporary validities of norms. The possible norms are limited as a control of behavior only by the nature of what is. Within these broad limits (for the flexibility of man, his collective opportunism, is notorious) the normative theory internal to a group can be neither "true" nor "false." It can be dominant, declining, recessive—but not incorrect. As a social scientist, one can do no more than describe it, analyzing its antecedents, structure, and consequences. This task, of course, may be highly valued—but it does not, logically, dictate choice. We may be able to point out the costs of alternative means, in scarce values and in side-effects, but the rank order of cost-benefit ratios still remains a product of a polity.[14] Of course we may, as social actors with commitments to interests, groups, and norms, violently reject, tolerate, or vigorously espouse given normative concepts. Any member of the collective can do so with equal intellectual authority, however, for such choice is inherently political.

## III.

Returning then to the metropolitan problem, we may view it as a struggle among sub-units of a collective to formulate the normative system of urban life. Thus, it is clear that this normative system is, at least in part, problematic to some groups. Wherever such situations occur, we infer change in the normative or empirical order, or in both. The latter seems to be the case in contemporary settlements.

The empirical situation in our cities has shifted with broad trends in the total society. For example: (1) the space-time ratio within the city has altered radically, making a much wider geography available for action; (2) the way of life of the population has changed, with increasing social rank and familism the trends; (3) from the interaction of these we have the rapid growth of familistic suburbs in the middle socioeconomic range, and increasing segregation of working-class ethnics in the central city. For another example: (1) we have an increasing dominance of the local population by the national society, as the network of interdependence extends and communication and control follow; (2) we have a new use for municipal government as a barrier to invasion by certain aspects of the larger society, and a consequent reinforcement of the sacrosanct status of local units; (3) from the interaction of these, we have a conflict between the consumer norms for government, which require large-scale organization and finance, and the governmental norms which perpetuate the governmental enclaves—the villages, towns, cities, of suburbia.

These changes in the society as empirically determined are accompanied by changes in the normative order. The metropolis contains many functionally concentrated and/or segregated groups. Through interaction within groups and segregation between them, new concepts are formed, stabilized in the ongoing normative language of the group, and creating normative order within subsystems, diversity between them. Planners and architects, machine politicians, Negroes, suburban neighbors—these are specimen cases. Thus in some areas of the institutional order we have growing diversity. However, the mass media and mass education are powerful channels for broadcasting some norms to almost all groups. In other areas we observe growing similarity.[15]

Such a situation is conducive to throwing up new versions of old normative concepts, of pseudo-norms, ideologies, and utopias. Some ideologists are critics of what is, or what is projected to be, against the normative standards drawn from a golden age when the city was young; for them the central city is hallowed ground. Others find what is, is for the best, in the best possible world. Though concentrated in positions which benefit from the *status quo,* such persons find broad support among those whose slogan is "leave well enough alone" or "better the evil that is known." Still others are oriented toward an invented image of the future. Utopians struggle for the greenbelt principle, the shopping mall, the new concept in transport, the ideal size city. They are chiefly intellectuals of local government—planners, engineers, political scientists and that ilk, who wear the mantle of expertise and broadcast images of a city transformed. In short, the ordinary literate citizen has a plethora of normative theories to choose from.

There is little evidence that many citizens respond with enthusiasm to either ideology or utopia. For many, the response is profound apathy, hardly taking one to the polls; for others, it is a peripheral concern, leading to little light and less heat. It has been proposed that, over the long haul, discrepancies between what is and ought to be are resolved by change in one or the other. Looking at recent results of failure on the metropolitan front in St. Louis and Cleveland, it appears likely that the normative theories will change. Failure leaves, among the significant actors, acceptance of public disinterest as a limiting factor in any possibility for change. Thus, developments to be expected are those required to perpetuate the given system with less friction—*ad hoc* integration by administrative fiat where possible, the formation of *ad hoc* special district governments, the *ad hoc* extension of State and Federal aid.[16]

Meanwhile, it is possible that the very concept of a city has changed under our discourse for many of us. Instead of a centralized community with the Downtown as hub and symbol of the metropolis, the picture is becoming one of a scattered, variegated set of low-density neighborhoods, looped together by freeways, which bind them also to the centers of production and distribution. Such a city would allow wide choice among residential areas with respect to location, house type, neighbors, governmental facilities, and price. It is a picture congruent with the new metropolis— that of the West Coast and the Southwest, but it can be found at the suburban growing edges of all our cities. If such is the new notion of a proper city, then the "metropolitan problem" is that of working out the details in the maintenance of that order. It is also the death rattle of an older normative theory.

## NOTES

1. The Editors of *Fortune, The Exploding Metropolis,* New York: Doubleday, 1958; Governmental Affairs Foundation, *Metropolitan Surveys: A Digest,* Chicago: Public Administration Service, 1958.

2. These quotations are from the proposal for the Metropolitan St. Louis Survey (1956).

3. See, for example, *Path of Progress for Metropolitan St. Louis,* The Metropolitan St. Louis Survey (University City, Mo., 1957).

4. See *Path of Progress for Metropolitan St. Louis, op. cit.;* see, also, the forthcoming research report of the St. Louis Survey, projected for 1961, University of California Press, Berkeley and Los Angeles.

5. I have discussed this intellectual tradition at greater length in "Dilemmas of Action Research on the 'Metropolitan Problem'," in Morris Janowitz, ed., *Community Political Systems,* Glencoe: Free Press, 1961.

6. This definition is stated clearly in "Resistance to Unification in a Metropolitan Community" by Amos H. Hawley and Basil G. Zimmer, in *Community Political Systems, op. cit.*

7. An intensive study of one such campaign is Scott Greer (with the advice and assistance of Norton E. Long), *Metropolitus: A Study of Political Culture,* New York: John Wiley and Sons, 1963. Other relevant observations are found in "Decision Making on a Metropolitan Government Proposition: The Case of

# Where is the Metropolitan Problem?

Cuyahoga County, Ohio, 1958–1959," by Matthew Holden, Jr., unpublished Ph.D. dissertation, Northwestern University. See also, Robert C. Wood, *Suburbia, Its People and Their Politics,* Boston: Houghton-Mifflin, 1959, and Scott Greer, "The Social Structure and Political Process of Suburbia," in *American Sociological Review,* August, 1960, pp. 514–26.

8. For a discussion of the consequences variable social position has for problem definitions, see Scott Greer, "Traffic, Transportation, and the Problems of the Metropolis," in Robert K. Merton and Robert A. Nisbet, eds., *Contemporary Social Problems,* New York: Harcourt-Brace and World, 1961.

9. This conceptual framework is spelled out in greater detail in Scott Greer, *Social Organization,* New York: Random House, 1955.

10. For the Metropolitan St. Louis Survey, see "Dilemmas of Action Research on the 'Metropolitan Problem'," *op. cit.* I should also acknowledge a general debt to Karl Mannheim, for notions first clearly presented in *Ideology and Utopia,* International Library of Psychology, Philosophy and Scientific Method, 1936.

11. Our follow-up study of the referendum election in St. Louis indicated that voters on both sides of the issue categorized those who voted differently as "uninformed, incompetent, irresponsible, or immoral."

12. On the irrational (or other-rational) approach of the voters, see the two previously cited articles in *Community Political Systems.*

13. "Preface," *Ideology and Utopia* (Harcourt-Brace Harvest Books edition, undated), page xxv.

14. These uses have been stated unforgettably, for this writer, by Max Weber in "Science as a Vocation," in H. H. Gerth and C. Wright Mills, eds., *From Max Weber: Essays in Sociology,* London: Routledge and Kegan Paul Ltd., 1948, pp. 150–152. For a clear and useful recent discussion see W. H. Werkmeister, "Theory Construction and the Problem of Objectivity," in Llewellyn Gross, ed., *Symposium on Sociological Theory,* Evanston: Row, Peterson and Company, 1959. In a recent statement Merton is in substantial agreement, although his emphasis is upon the positive value of social scientific inquiry for normative theory (see "Social Problems and Sociological Theory," Robert K. Merton, in *Contemporary Social Problems, op. cit.*)

15. These arguments, presented in such a cursory fashion, are developed in an expanded and systematic form in *The Emerging City: Myth and Reality,* New York: Free Press, 1962.

16. No adverse judgment of *ad hoc* structural development is implied. After all, the British government is a gigantic product of such social invention. Such piecemeal, experimental development might well be called "organic," "continuous," and other good things: it is, however, very different indeed from a master plan or a simultaneously conceived blueprint.

# 19.    Age at First Marriage

JOHN MOGEY

Marriage in all societies must be distinguished from sexual activity: in no society is sex entirely controlled by marriage. The relations between age at marriage and age at puberty are never simple and obvious. As a sociological phenomenon, marriage is essentially a license to a conjugal pair guaranteeing a legitimate claim to social status to the offspring of the woman. Age at first marriage, therefore, reflects the status conferring system of the society and, within this set of rules, the locus of control over entry to status. In highly traditional societies, the existence of marriage classes and prescribed mates gives control over status and succession to the society as a whole: such are the elaborate *kariera* rules of some Australian aboriginal tribes. Wherever family control over property is vital to continuity and stability, parental controls over the marriage of their children are strong. Two consequences follow for age at marriage: *either* children may be betrothed or married in infancy before they can object, *or* a child may be given in marriage to an adult. In feudal societies, marriages between an old man and a young girl, or between a boy and a woman old enough to be his mother, are well known. Some writers, indeed, derive our present conception of romantic love from the attachments formed between late medieval troubadors and the child wives of the palaces of Provence. (Duplessis, 1954).

Industrial, urban societies, where large numbers depend on wages for a livelihood, have been characterized by freedom to choose a mate. In the present century, direct family control over the choice of a mate appears to have decreased even among property owners. Whatever the explanation, the figures for marriage rates are dramatic. Since 1900, age at first marriage has declined from around 26 years for men and 22 years for women to around 22 for men and 20 for women in 1950. This reduction in age has been most dramatic in the U.S.A. but it affects most countries of western Europe. In Denmark and Great Britain, age at marriage is declining at the (tremendous) rate of 0.1 year per annum. Parallel to this statistical trend is an increase in the total number of marriages. Since 1940, the proportion of single persons above the legal age to marry has gone down sharply, except in France and Luxembourg. (Hajnal, 1953). All of this is well known and carefully documented.

## Age of First Marriage

One sociological regularity in this process seems important. Apart from the regular reduction in marriage age and the increase in the proportions of people getting married, the age of entry into marriage is extraordinarily uniform. American men contract marriages today for the most part between the age of 21 and 22: American women between the age of 18 and 19. The age range for 75% of all first marriages is 21, plus or minus 3 or 4 years. Within an eight year period of a life span now approaching 80 years, our young men and women feel an overwhelming urge to obtain a license to live together.

My problem is to explain why 60% of all first marriages occur within a 4 to 5 year period, and 75% within an eight year period.

At the outset of this paper other statistical regularities related to age at first marriage should be presented. Firstly, this is a national norm, color makes little difference to age at first marriage. Remarriage is a different matter, but this is beyond the scope of my present investigation.

Secondly, educational level shows a curvilinear relationship to age at marriage: those with no high school education, as well as those with a college degree marry above the median age. People who marry early tend to be the group that drops out of high school. Relations of this type are obviously more complex than straight line relationships and without specific empirical studies, I doubt that we can clarify this. However, age at leaving school is not the important aspect in this factor: on the average, laborers leave school five years earlier than professional people, but are only two years apart in age at marriage.

Thirdly, occupation shows a straight line relationship. Those in the lowest occupational strata marry earlier than those in any higher strata, while those in professional and executive occupations marry oldest of all.

Fourthly, there is no simple relationship between income in the years following marriage and age at marriage. The same source reports that men who never marry spend all their lives low on the income scale, men who marry before 25 have low incomes in these years, men who marry between 25 and 29 have higher than average incomes while those who do not marry until 30 or over enjoy only intermediate incomes. Only 15% of the men postpone first marriage so late in life and only 10% of women. The relationship of income to the weekly maximum expected in a lifetime rather than to the total distribution may of course be important.

Fifthly, the differences between urban and rural populations are slight. Urban women marry one year later than rural women, on the average.

Sixthly, only 20% of first marriages do not set up a separate home in the first year of marriage; 80% practise neo-local residence.

Lastly, the birth of the first child is normally between one year and 2½ years after marriage.

These last two facts reinforce our early statement that, empirically, marriage represents a license to live together. It does not in itself show a desire for the initiation of sexual relations or for parenthood. (Glick, 1957)

## Factors Limiting Marital Choice

These facts come from gross national figures which might apply to a state of *panmixia,* where everyone had an equal chance to marry any other person. There are several limiting factors which divide the population into quasi-endogamous subgroups. I should now like to refer to these to see if any of them explain age regularities at the time of marital choice.

The first is the incest taboo not only in the immediate family but to the first consanguine and collateral relatives. One way to measure this is to compute the ratio of marriages between first cousins to all marriages. This group of intermarrying families gives a population statistic called the "isolate." In the United States this type of marriage is completely unimportant: first cousin marriages are less than 0.1%. This may be compared with over 2% for Brazil, and around 1% for Europe. Some villages in Scotland, in Germany and in Switzerland report first cousin marriages as high as 15%. (Dahlberg, 1948: Freire-Martin, 1957: Sutter and Tabah, 1951) Conformity to the established norms in this area raises no difficulties. More effective endogamous barriers surround (1) race:

Negro-white intermarriage is so infrequent it may be ignored—this type of restriction is very effective, (2) religion: Jewish groups show a tendency to prefer intramarriage and to a lesser degree so do Catholics. (Monahan and Chancellor, 1955)

Other major studies using the concept of endogamy lay stress on social class and this is a factor that may have critical relevance. The straight line relationship between occupation of the husband and age at marriage was mentioned as one of our basic facts. Burchinal gives an impressive table which supports the importance of this limitation.

### Table 1—Occupational Status Distributions of Grooms by Ages of Brides and Grooms

*Iowa, White, Primary Marriages (1953–1957)*

| Occupational Status of Grooms[a] | AGES OF BRIDES | | | | |
|---|---|---|---|---|---|
|  | 17 or Below | 18 | 19–22 | 23–29 | 30 or + |
| High | 26.1 | 28.8 | 43.9 | 51.1 | 46.1 |
| Middle | 19.3 | 21.5 | 20.9 | 24.4 | 29.2 |
| Low | 42.8 | 36.4 | 23.9 | 18.6 | 22.6 |
| Armed Forces | 11.8 | 13.3 | 11.3 | 5.9 | 2.1 |
| N | 11,088 | 15,736 | 37,019 | 10,394 | 2,198 |
|  | AGES OF GROOMS | | | | |
| High | 34.4 | 27.7 | 34.4 | 45.8 | 49.2 |
| Middle | 16.3 | 19.6 | 19.4 | 24.1 | 26.6 |
| Low | 40.2 | 38.7 | 30.2 | 24.6 | 22.3 |
| Armed Forces | 9.1 | 14.0 | 16.0 | 5.5 | 1.9 |
| N | 2,580 | 4,404 | 35,951 | 28,771 | 4,727 |

[a] High occupational status occupations included professionals, managers, farm operators and owners, officials and proprietors; middle status occupations include clerks, sales and operatives; low status occupations include domestics, farm laborers and other laborers (Burchinal, 1960).

The next type of endogamy used to define limitations in marriage choice rests on residential propinquity. This concept is parallel to, rather than convergent with, the demographic concept of the isolate, used in the paragraph on the incest taboo. It defines the field within which a marital choice is made by distance between the homes of the spouses. However, since residential areas are often segregated by color, religion, and social class, it is a very complex variable. (Katz and Hill, 1958)

Finally, I would refer to endogamy enforced by value considerations. Formerly, parents in certain social classes were able to make marriage difficult by using the norm that a man could only marry when his material circumstances assured economic stability to the new marital pair and their family. (Davis, 1949)

The question now is: do these evidences of restriction in individual marriage choice suggest that our original simple statistic about age at marriage obscures more than it reveals? Since ages at marriage are similar both for white and nonwhite, and for urban and rural, the national average seems to be meaningful in these areas. In the absence of data about the ages of Catholics at marriage and in view of the evidence for a high rate of intermarriage, I shall assume that they are not very different from those of the general population. In spite of barriers to absolute equality of marital choice between age grades, it seems then that the national data can be applied generally to all groups in the population.

## The Process of Marital Choice

In the U.S.A., the decision to marry now rests on the free choice of both parties: the factors that enter into this decision may differ for men and women. Even though pressures may be brought to bear on the parties involved, this personal decision is vital. No one should coerce them, neither parents, nor peer group, nor any institutionalized group.

If this free choice is to be effective, children must be emancipated from their families. This is the structural explanation for the emergence of a youth culture. "The period of youth in our society means . . . turning one's back on the security both of status and of emotional attachment which is engaged in the family of orientation. It is structurally essential to transfer one's primary emotional attachment to a marriage partner who is entirely unrelated to the previous family situation. In a system of free marriage choice this applies to women as well as men." (Parsons, 1954)

This choice means living with a strange woman in a strange house, for 80% of first marriages choose neolocal residence. Evidence for the existence of such a period of emancipation comes in papers that report the dominance of peer group norms over parental norms at the entry into marriage. The fact of a period of emancipation is attested by many descriptive studies in addition to those focussed on marital choice. (Burchinal, 1959: Davis, 1940: Moss and Gingles, 1959: Freeman, 1955)

The importance of the peer group is more general than that of education. The median adult today has completed high school, but age at marriage is not related to age at leaving school. Consequently, peer group interaction has more relevance to marital choice than does formal education.

During this period of emancipation the youth learn how to define the field of eligibles through the combination of familial and age grade norms. The meaning of romantic love as a criterion in choice of mate is continually refined until at the time of decision sexual love and affection are only one factor in the complex that makes up romantic love. The evidence is strong for similarity in social class interests and in earning ability of wives and husbands. This part of the cycle which leads to a marital decision is adequately explained by the reformulation of the residential propinquity theory into a norm-interaction theory by Katz and Hill. However, even in its new and more elegant statement this theory explains only the process. To account for the national pattern of decisions we must know which norms are dominant and how much interaction is needed to result in this decision. These empirical problems are still awaiting attention.

Parenthetically, if a requisite of all free marriage is a youth phase independent of parental pressures, a retreat phase immediately after marriage is also necessary so that the youths may practice their new roles of husband and wife free of interference by parents and peers. I have still to find a good study of the honeymoon in the literature of American families, although its functional significance seems clear.

No consistent relationship was found between age at marriage and education, nor between age and income, but a straight line relationship did hold between age at marriage and occupation. This suggests that a look at work experience may explain the rush toward marriage licenses.

## Occupational Role

What aspect of occupational roles is likely to affect this form of behavior? It cannot be income alone, since there is no direct relationship between income level and age at marriage. It must, however, be a dimension as common to all occupational roles as income is, or it will not account for this mass phenomenon. The most general frame for the analysis of all roles is the pattern variables proposed by Parsons. This framework is still being developed, but the variables are four in number: specificity—diffuseness; affectivity—neutrality; universalism—particularism; quality—performance. Work roles vary in their position on several of these dimensions and only those clustered at one end of the dimension are likely to be useful in our analysis. Only one pattern variable fits all these

*253*

conditions: affectivity—neutrality. I shall call this role aspect impersonality; even roles which involve handling people require that this be done in a professional way, so that the neutrality aspect of the role interaction is valued.

If we establish empirically that the sequence of events leading to marriage is: youth–peer group—occupation—marriage, I believe we have an explanatory variable in the impersonality of the work role. In this interpretation, it will be noticed that I have added an extra step to the established sequence of the residential propinquity theory of youth–peer group–marriage. The importance of the peer group identification is clearly shown in the literature. So far as age at marriage is concerned, we may consider the peer group as a set of primary supportive relations. Entry into an occupation breaks this bond and, consequently, we should expect a search for a new type of supportive relation to follow this deprivation.

If this new sequence can be shown to hold generally, we should still have to explain why young males, influenced by the impersonality of the job, seek marriage. If this contention is correct we can assume that they marry for affection. The expressive role of the wife in the family role constellation satisfies this need, and we know that this holds true for all nuclear families in all societies. (Zelditch, 1960)

So we may conclude that the young male marries for love and gives status to his spouse.

Young women are subject to different constraints. Their work experience should also be impersonal and drives them to seek love in a marital relation. However, two consistent findings about first marriages complicate this interpretation: Firstly, women are nearly always younger than their mates and secondly, women take over their husband's position in the social class hierarchy. The normal process differentiating the sexes in biological maturing may account for the first of these. It is clear, too, that before marriage women spend less time in the labor force than men; so, impersonality on the job will have less influence on them. There may be sex differences in tolerance along this dimension, but, in the absence of evidence, it would be unwise to rely on this as an explanation. The second is sociological rather than biological. In contrast to the male, women seem to marry for status and give love to their spouse. The status they seek lies often in the future of the family.

There is another aspect of the interaction of family and occupational status. Our society considers it normal for adults to live in "nuclear families," and the local pressures to get into a family group are very strong. In class societies, a wife takes on the social class of her husband, providing him with an acceptable base for job mobility. Occupations which do not permit a man to support a wife and eventually a family at an adequate standard are severely disvalued in the occupational status hierarchy. The fact that these tasks are favored by mass (nonclass oriented) entertainment, and are, therefore, highly visible and known, does not lead to a rush toward such occupations as cowboys, divers, gamblers, and hobos.

The supply of houses is important in hastening or delaying the decision to marry. Yet it should not be over-emphasized, for we know that absence of housing is no barrier to marriage in the early years of war. In special populations such as undergraduate students, the provision of adequate housing by universities would probably precipitate many marital decisions. For the population at large, this type of provision is lacking. It would be interesting to compare age at marriage for European countries in the light of the stock of houses available for newly wed couples. It may be that some part of the differential in age at marriage could be explained by this factor.

### SUPPORT FOR THIS THEORY

One study has been found which relates impersonality in occupational role expectations to family role patterns. It finds a strong positive relationship between occupations rated high in impersonality and a collective orientation within the family. This shows that affective relations not met on the job are sought in the family. (Podell and Aske, 1960)

We should predict that occupational roles high on impersonality would be the most married section of the community. Such roles may be technical or executive: they should contrast in their marital sequence with occupational roles that emphasize handling people or groups. Family sociologists should also work on a classification of jobs by impersonality orientations, according to the length of time a worker can stand the occupation before he rushes for a marriage license.

Some European studies have tried to relate satisfaction at work with satisfaction at home or in the local community. Some degree of relationship has been reported from Holland and Finland. (Gadourek, 1956; Siipi, 1954) The relationship is not very straightforward, for skilled workers behave differently from unskilled even though their job satisfaction rates remain constant. In England, I noticed that workers interviewed at home were reluctant to talk about work conditions. Independently, Banks found them equally reluctant to talk about home conditions when interviewed at their work place. (Banks, 1957; Mogey, 1956)

*255*

# John Mogey

## *Youthful Marriages*

Since 1890 there has been a trend toward marriages at earlier and earlier ages, and this process has accelerated since 1945. Yet, we should not exaggerate the extent of this movement: only a small proportion of high school age students are married; most youthful marriages involve the 18 and 19 year olds. Most of the marriages in this age-grade affect girls rather than boys: 33% of females in 1959 were married at 18–19 as compared with 8% of males. These women marry men of an average 3 years older than they are. If they marry for status, our explanation is apt.

In the second place, these youthful marriages are not elopements. They have conventional weddings: in 84% to 92% of cases reported in Iowa and Kansas the marriage was performed in church by a clergyman. Two factors account for many of them: (1) they are among the working class where age at marriage has always been lower than for any other group in the population; (2) one-third to one-half of the brides were pregnant on their wedding day. These two factors overlap and probably account for 40% of youthful marriages.

The rest are still to be explained and so also is the general trend to lower marriage age throughout the century. From our account of the processes behind marital choices, we should look for an explanation in the work situation.

Since 1890, there is no doubt from the studies of industrial sociologists that a higher and higher proportion of the labor force is being employed by large bureaucratic corporations. This phenomenon has also been called "the transfer of the labor force to tertiary occupations." A prime characteristic of such organizations is that work becomes more and more specialized, each task more and more fragmented, and the work process continuously more impersonal. An empirical link should be sought between these developments and the age of the man at marriage. This will not be a simple matter since impersonality of work is a complex role attribute, and in a highly individual matter such as a free-choice marriage decision, no simple one–to–one relationship should be expected. None the less, I think these arguments give a new direction to the problem of the uniformly decreasing age at marriage.

When we consider occupational changes during this century, the question also arises of the influence of women in the work force on age at marriage. Two aspects of the increase in numbers of women at work may be important: Firstly, the sociological consequences of two incomes, since marriage rates are well known to vary with economic booms and depressions. Comparisons of age at marriage in areas of high unemployment and of low unemployment should throw light on this factor. Secondly, the effects of social interaction at work on the propensity to marry should be considered. If impersonality on the job is important, we could expect few marriages among work-mates employed in the same factory.

I should refer at this point to another change in the norms of this century: the increasing freedom of sexual experimentation among the youth. There has been, so far as I can judge, no corresponding change in the desire for exclusive sexual privileges. Women are no longer expected to be virginal at marriage, but intolerance of promiscuity is still exceedingly strong. Given a drive toward sexual activity and a parallel drive toward exclusiveness, we should expect an increase in youthful engagements and marriages.

### HIGH SCHOOL MARRIAGES

There remain, as a residual category, marriages within the high school population itself and between those who enter but never complete their high school career. Some evidence is presented by Burchinal that high school marriages involve a high proportion of those who reject parental norms and relations and who *also* are poorly integrated into their peer group. Girls who remained single scored more favorably in various tests for social adjustment than girls who married while in high school. It is this group of marriages that should be expected to contribute more highly than others to the low stability of youthful marriages. A poor prognosis should be associated in our society with the transition from childhood to marital relations, giving a minimum of time in the youthful peer group for emancipation from previous sets of role prescriptions.

An alternate proposition could be advanced to explain the recent decline in marriage ages. Consider first the definite break between parents and their children in adolescence: this may be interpreted as a loss of parental responsibilities. Now consider the mounting evidence that youthful marriages are entered into with parental consent and often financial support. We can interpret this as one way in which parents, having "lost" their children as adolescents, can legitimately claim them as adults. From the point of view of the adolescent, too, he can accept parental help at marriage with no loss of adult status and responsibility; it is a legitimate form of assistance and not counted as interference. Parents of girls who cannot control their children's activities in adolescence, might be expected to encourage early marriage: once the right boy appears, marriage is desirable, for illegitimate births still carry a social stigma to both families.

If the man's work experience generally precedes the decision to marry, the parents' role must be passive and dependent.

It is possible, of course, that the next decade may see a whole population of newlyweds going through high school. So far as I can see, the evidence for such a prediction is lacking. We are still in a phase of society where new entrants to the labor force reach back into their peer group for their brides: those most eager to leave this group are least integrated into it.

## Conclusions

Much remains to be done to test these propositions. The existence of a substantial national uniformity in age at marriage should be verified by an examination of the most recent Census figures. Age at marriage varies between urban and rural, upper class and lower class, higher education and lower education. Whether the differences prove more vital than the similarities is statistically uncertain.

Secondly, the independent variable, occupational affectivity, must be further refined and measurement instruments devised. Whether this can be done can only be discovered by working at the problems.

Lastly, the stubborn fact remains that there *is* a great sociological uniformity here and, if this approach proves inadequate, another attempt will have to be made to solve it.

## NOTES

Banks, J. A., "Group Discussion as an Interview Technique," *Sociological Review*, 5 (1957), pp. 75–84.

Burchinal, Lee G., "Adolescent Role Deprivation and High School Age Marriage," *Marriage and Family Living*, 21 (1959), pp. 378–84.

Burchinal, Lee G., "Research on Youthful Marriages," *The Family Life Coordinator*, 1960, pp. 6–24.

Davis, Kingsley, "The Sociology of Parent-Youth Conflict," *American Sociological Review*, 5 (1940), pp. 523–34.

Davis, Kingsley, *Human Society*, New York: Macmillan, 1949.

Dahlberg, G., *Mathematical Methods for Population Genetics*, New York: Interscience Publishers, 1948.

Duplessis, G., *Les Mariages en France*, Paris: Colin, 1954.

Freeman, Linton, "Homogamy in Inter-

Ethnic Mate Selection," *Sociology and Social Research*, 39 (1955), pp. 369–77.

Freire-Martin, N., "Inbreeding Levels in Different Countries," *Eugenics Quarterly*, 1 (1957), pp. 127–38.

Gadourek, I., *A Dutch Community*, Leiden: Steinferte Kroese, 1956.

Glick, P. G., *American Families*, New York: Wiley, 1957.

Hajnal, Jan, "Age at Marriage and Proportions Marrying," *Population Studies*, 7 (1953), pp. 111–36.

Katz, A. and Hill, R., "Residential Propinquity and Marital Selection: A Review of Theory, Method and Fact," *Marriage and Family Living*, 20 (1958), pp. 27–35.

Mogey, John, *Family and Neighbourhood*, Oxford: Oxford University Press, 1956.

Monohan, T. F. and Chancellor, *Eugenics Quarterly*, 2 (1955), pp. 162–73.

Podell, L. and Askern, F., "Occupational and Familial Role Expectations," (unpublished) City College, New York, 1960.

Siipi, J., *Pulkaty ovaen Viihtyryys* (Worker's satisfaction with their place of residence) Doctoral Thesis, University of Helsinki, 1954.

## 20. Are Industrial Societies Becoming Alike?

ARNOLD S. FELDMAN AND WILBERT E. MOORE

To MANY SOCIOLOGISTS THE ANSWER TO OUR TITU-lar question is so clearly affirmative that one might simply say "Yes," and let us proceed with suitable dispatch to the next question. In behalf of an affirmative reply, one could note the marked extension of merit-based educational opportunities in England, the increased incidence of marital choice based on romantic love in urban France, and the ubiquity of organization men in Soviet industry. But let us not be too hasty. We must also concede the durable qualities of one-party government in Russia, the alternation of multi-party instability and charismatic political unity in France, and the hardy survival of parliamentary government in England. No trends now in evidence would lead us to expect a convergence of political systems, unless one truly accepts the hopeful or dire prediction of eventual Communist victory for the entire world.

Our answer, then, must be "Yes and No," and the clarification of the ambiguity may justify a continuation of the discussion. In what follows, brevity imposes on us a mode of presentation that is more taxonomic and dogmatic than would otherwise be tolerable in polite discourse.

Much of the support for the common structural characteristics of industrial societies derives, in fact, from analysis of the industrialization process, particularly in the contemporary context. These analytical studies typically ask, what are the social changes that can be expected to accompany and follow successful industrialization? Implicitly or explicitly, some salient structural features of industrial societies are identified as the terminus of a path of progress, and resistances, tensions, and strains in the transformation of the pre-industrial social order to an industrial one are then identified and appraised.

The degree of functional determinism, that is, the extent of the requiredness of elements in an industrial social structure, differs from one interpreter to another. Nonetheless, virtually no one rejects the notion that industrial societies share a core set of social structures that together provide a kind of extended operational definition of industrialism itself. This core would include the factory system of production, a stratification system based on a complex and extensive division of labor and hierarchy of skills, an extensive commercialization of goods and services and their transfer through the market, and an educational system capable of filling the various niches in the occupational and stratification system. If one goes much beyond this list, the degree of requiredness or variability becomes distinctly controversial.

Now we do not reject this mode of interpretation, and have ourselves recently indulged in it in our chapters in the volume on *Labor Commitment and Social Change in Developing Areas*. However, there are two major difficulties in extending this analysis to all elements and features of social systems, and to a prediction of a growing and enduring convergence among industrial societies.

Let us take first the industrialization process. From what has been said so far our titular question, taken literally and restrictively as concerned with *industrial* societies, could not be answered. Rather, one could say, all societies will become more alike as they become industrial, and at least with respect to core structures this is clearly true. But it does not follow that no variability of any consequence remains. The sources of that variability we can deal with at least taxonomically, although without full explication and illustration.

For convenience, let us distinguish three principal sources of variability, although these can and must be subdivided. The first is the character of the pre-industrial social structure and its influence on subsequent social states. The second is the route or trajectory of industrialization. The third is the structure of industrial societies, structure being used in a loose and extensive sense. The last of these gets close to the heart of our initial question, and in proper fashion of manufacturing suspense, we shall discuss it last.

*261*

## Arnold S. Feldman and Wilbert E. Moore

One certainly need not enumerate here the ways in which historians, anthropologists, and sociologists have documented cultural diversity. The principal critical issue is one of relevance to economic development or industrialization. For the true functional determinist, the question of relevance does not arise. It is a matter of faith and conviction that everything is related to everything. And anthropologists and sociologists are generally most impressive when they trace out the connections between, say, a given change and a consequence in some seemingly remote aspect of culture or social action. Yet, surely the examples are a radically unrepresentative selection from among the myriads of variations and changes that are essentially inconsequential. What still remain to be codified are the necessary or highly probable routes and mechanisms of systemic articulation, and, conversely, the kinds of variability that barely escape the derogatory designation of "chance," if they escape it at all.

We are essentially forced back to a minimal position. Some elements of any pre-industrial culture or social system cannot accompany industrialization. These represent impediments or required changes. The inconsistent elements of pre-industrial systems do not simply disappear, lost without trace. Rather, if industrial development does continue, they become attenuated, partially suppressed, partially adapted to changes in the core structure. But by their persistence, they constitute a continuing source of tension, a focus of social problem solving, a challenge to scholars and administrators alike who want the system tidy. The solutions, we suggest, are always partial, and always have further consequences that in turn provide new points of tension. For example, an industrializing economy may face labor shortages, either absolute, or because of structural and motivational impediments to mobility. Any solution, ranging from coercive tactics to the offering of exceptional inducements, will have enduring consequences, and, to repeat, new solutions will provide their own new problems.

Now let us turn to the question of route or trajectory. The first point to be noted is that in some situations history itself prevents its own repetition, for its lessons and results become the basis of new social actions. The simplest illustration of this is the lack of necessity for a newly developing economy to repeat either the timing or sequence of technological change. More fundamentally, there now exist a number of advanced industrial economies, which, whatever the answer to our initial question, *still* provide alternative models of ideology, political control, and peripheral or noncore structural features. The available models permit a degree of choice to the developing area that earlier innovators did not have.

Here, however, we find an unexpected dividend for the believers in

*262*

growing homogeneity. All industrial societies, and perforce all industrializing societies, exhibit a degree and extensity of deliberate and administered social change that is historically unmatched. The attempt to predict and control secondary and tertiary results—to reduce the number and salience of unanticipated consequnces—will not, we believe, finally succeed in a perfectly manipulated system anywhere, and there is no reason to expect the failures or inhibiting costs to be uniform. So we have a second foretaste of our final answer.

Trajectories of industrialization do differ, not so widely as to make them randomly variable or incomparable, but enough to caution against singular generalization. In form, social change may vary in *sequence*—the order in which different components change, in *rate*—the relative rapidity of change in one or another systemic component, and in *timing*—a special attribute of rate calling attention to intervals among component changes, and especially the phenomena of leads and lags. In context, societal change will vary in *historical era*, as just discussed, in *relationship between a given society and others*, and rather importantly, in the *kind of economic regime* directing any program of change.

Although each of these variables might be discussed somewhat extensively, we shall concentrate here on questions of sequence. This has been an arena of somewhat inconsequential conflict among adherents of various determinisms or "key strategies," and between all of the single-factor proponents and those who argue for the simultaneous change in everything.

The initial difficulty in the search for the magic key is that not all doors have the same locks. Less figuratively, any pre-industrial society has a somewhat different array of resources and shortages, of facilitating and impeding elements in the social structure, of bottle-necks and overfull vats, of leads and lags. The second difficulty is that the sequence of change does involve allocation priorities, whether or not these are consciously made. Thus, in some sense all positions are equally right or equally wrong, since any sequence involves costs and will be disequilibrating.

Those who argue for simultaneity of change have a kind of correct premise and the wrong conclusion. It is true that anything short of simultaneity will adversely affect some institutions in that their energy and resource allocation will be lessened. It is also true that eventually the disparity between "leading" and "lagging" sectors can threaten seriously an industrialization program. Nevertheless, this is exactly the sequential route that societies undergoing industrialization will experience.

In other words, equivalence of change in major institutions is impossible, but failure to achieve it will introduce profound strains and tensions. This is intrinsic to industrialization. Thus the sequential order involves shifting rates and intensities of change. Modernization may begin in any one of various spheres of a society—the work place, the market, political structure, or others. It will proceed by various leads and lags, but no single sphere will predominate throughout. (Technology, for example, will often be substantially behind a change in goals or their priority.) The sequence will reflect shifting leads, since continued advances in any one sphere will require some approximation to equivalence in other spheres.

Questions of rate and timing essentially provide multipliers or divisors for the basic question of sequence. Sequence, as a matter of fact, is more often characterized by differential rates of change than by a singular dynamic element and a residue of static ones.

Industrialization, then, does have a partially specifiable and common destination, but reaches that destination from different starting points and follows different routes or trajectories. Neither pre-industrial societies nor the modes of social transformation are randomly or uniquely variable. We do not have to abandon ourselves to the exaggerated particularity of history or descriptive ethnography. But restraints imposed by systemic characteristics, by a kind of functional determinism, are less precise and less predictive than seekers of simplicity would wish.

Now this finally brings us to the question of the increasing similarity of industrial societies. Here our basic theoretical position, with readily manifest empirical grounding, has far-reaching interpretive consequences. Stated baldly, the crucial fact is that there is no stable and enduring terminus to the industrialization process. In general, the rate of change increases at an accelerating rate. This casts in doubt, to put it mildly, all the conventional notions that the similarities of all industrial societies, and all industrializing ones, will become virtually complete, if, like mystical Marxists or millennialist Christians, we are content to wait.

Let us recapitulate the persistent sources of difference. Societies start a process of industrialization from different antecedent conditions. Part of those conditions will constitute problems or barriers, a typology of which can be constructed. But the problems are never finally solved, for even victory carries with it its own train of peculiar consequences. Societies undertake economic development with a high quotient of deliberate change, including the kind of problem solving required to overcome impediments. Deliberate change, however, can scarcely be complete and completely controlled, if for no other reason than the lack of infinite resources for knowing, predicting, and controlling everything. Among the unanticipated changes will be some that are continuously consequential, although others may constitute rather random or chance variability or "noise."

Persistence and its consequences and deliberate change and its consequences constitute the first two orders of variability in industrial societies. They lead to a third, which is a very familiar one when restated. It is the lack of close, organic, functional integration in social systems. The tracing out of relationships, in terms of a sort of scale of requiredness, limited ranges of viable variability, and wider degrees of random or only historically explainable variation, is still an unfinished and worthwhile investigative enterprise. But it must be faced with an open mind, and not from a partisan position of functional determinism.

The final source of variability, however, is of crucial relevance for any attempt at functional interpretation. This is the essential and inherent instability of the core elements and their first-order associated variables. Industrialism generally increases the comparability among societies and their principal structural elements, but does not necessarily increase their operating similarity. The problems may be typologically standard but the solutions somewhat more variable, if for no other reason than the differences in starting points and trajectories. It was not accidental that the examples of persistent dissimilarity noted at the beginning of this paper were political. The political order, almost by operational definition, is the residuary legatee of unsolved social problems. Because a viable polity is essentially a tension-management system, and tensions are not the same or likely to become the same, there is no reason to expect greater and greater convergence of the tensions of industrial societies, or their ideological rationalization, or the political and other modes of partial containment. Surely most of the changes in industrial societies, and certainly the major ones by any crude scale, are disequilibrating rather than equilibrating.

We have not retreated to the womb of relativistic particularity, for both structural and dynamic generalization is possible. But we do think the leverage provided us by comparative statics is rather less than had been hoped, because the place to stand turns out to be moving at high speed and is very shaky in transit. It is not simply our deepened understanding that makes the world complex. It really is.

# 21.    Social Science Approaches to Peace

KATHLEEN ARCHIBALD

THIS PAPER ATTEMPTS TO DELINEATE SOME OF THE problems and issues in the application of the social sciences to problems of peace and international conflict. Although they are assumed to have an important and distinctive contribution to make in achieving peace and world order, this is not a call to arms. It is rather an effort to spell out factors affecting the social scientist's role in this policy area. This discussion is based on material from three sources: (1) intensive, semi-structured interviews with a small number of the more prominent contributors to the war/peace discourse;[1] (2) less systematic interviews and discussions with a number of other social scientists involved in peace research; and (3) observations made at meetings, conferences, and seminars on peace research.

Although it is generally recognized that there are difficulties in utilizing the social sciences for informing and shaping public policy, interpretations of these problems vary. Some writers see them as warning signs and suggest proceeding with caution, if at all, when confronting policy areas; others view the problems as challenges and point out a need for greater effort.

Despite the warning signs—or because of the challenges—social scientists are becoming increasingly involved in policy-oriented research. Questions of international development and foreign aid have interested social scientists for several years and, more recently, they have invaded the area of peace and international security.

*"Peace Research" and the Social Scientist*

Although there has been growing talk of "peace research," and even of a peace research movement, it is not easy to define what the terms means. On the one hand, some of the most visible material carrying this label[2] has not been research at all, as many social scientists would define "research." On the other hand, if any study which has a bearing on problems of peace and security is considered to be peace research, then a fair amount of the literature in any of the social sciences would in fact be peace research.

In the view of some, much creative peace research has been sponsored by the Department of Defense;[3] in the view of others, peace research, by definition, cannot be sponsored by the military establishment. There is also a question as to whether peace research refers only to work with a social science orientation, or whether it refers to any intellectual attack on the problems involved.

A further confusion is that there are many, among those often called peace researchers, who shy away from the term altogether. They substitute such terms as arms control research, war/peace research, conflict-systems studies, etc.; but each of these terms has its own denotative and connotative problems, just as does "peace research."

For particular contexts, one term may be more appropriate than another but, for general usage, no one label stands out as being clearly more suitable. Therefore, the various terms will be used more or less interchangeably in this paper to refer to *intellectual or scientific work that is seen by the person doing such work as having implications for the avoidance of war and/or the attainment of peace*. Some particular attention, however, will be paid to the ambiguities and arguments as to what "peace research" is. Since this is the most commonly used term, confusion about its referent affect both the role of the social scientist in the area and the evaluation of his contributions.

It should be noted that the area of work is defined above in terms of an orientation to a particular set of practical problems, and not in terms of substantive topics, generalized concepts, or methodology. Although this seems to be the most adequate way of defining an area of applied social science,[4] it has its difficulties in that there is little agreement among researchers on what problems or goals peace research should be directed towards. The fact that everyone is for peace is no guarantee of any agreement on how to achieve it. A sharp distinction is sometimes made between the "war thinkers" (for instance, RAND strategists) and the "peace thinkers," even though "war thinkers" may study the deterrence of war rather than the winning of it and "peace thinkers" may talk about ways of winning the "real war" with Communism. For instance, Rapaport has recently argued that those who are interested in "waging peace" have little to gain from attempts to communicate with those who are concerned with "avoiding war."[5] In the definition above, however, the avoidance of war and the attainment of peace are considered as dual goals delineating one area of applied research, on the grounds (a) that the kinds of practical problems studied under each banner are more similar than they are different, and (b) that although differences in values and assumptions among those working on problems of international conflict are indeed great, the differences range along a variety of values and assumptions so that it is difficult to classify people in terms of only two categories.

### CRITICISMS OF THE RESEARCH APPROACH TO PROBLEMS OF PEACE

There are two major schools of criticism of a research approach to problems of peace and international conflict. One school suggests that doing peace research indicates *a lack of responsibility as a citizen or as a human being;* the other, that it indicates *a lack of responsibility as a scientist.*

There are several varieties of the first school of criticism, although there is agreement on the assumption that there is no need for more research or, at least, that research is not essential. The views vary with respect to their charity in explaining the motives of those people who choose to do research on the problems of peace.

The least charitable branch of this school sees peace research as a compromise course chosen by the intellectual who wants to contribute something to the cause of peace—but who is not willing to voice militant, public dissent from current policy for fear of endangering his career. Another branch tends to see peace research as just another example of the ivory-tower orientation of academia; professors poking their noses into books and data, for whatever reason, instead of using their intellects for the betterment of society. Others feel that research is just not needed or is not effective; that it will not make any difference in either the long or short run because achieving peace is a matter of will, not of knowledge. Still another group sees the peace researchers differing from themselves only in the sense of urgency. These people feel that there is no time to wait for the results of research, and particularly for the basic research which is favored by many peace researchers; that something more direct, more active, more political must be done in the here and now if anything is to be done at all.

The other major school of criticism, and undoubtedly the predominant one *within* social science, sees peace research as a somewhat improper scientific activity. To these critics, the peace researcher is *too concerned* with the major problems of his time, and they assume that this lack of detachment will have adverse effects on his scientific activity. Again, views within this school vary with respect to charitableness; from those who fear only that the social scientist will not do as creative work in the peace area as in other areas where he is motivated by more "objective" concerns, to those who expect that peace research will lead the social scientist astray into distortions of his findings and other prostitutions of his science.

The least charitable interpretations within each school of criticism are undermined by the very fact that they both exist. The view that peace research is an improper scientific activity suggests that it is not altogether protective of one's career to become visibly involved in it. The view of peace research as a way to sidestep taking a strong policy stand suggests that objectivity is not altogether forgotten.

Critics on both sides can cite examples to support their positions. Some peace researchers are victims, hapless or otherwise, of academic seduction. Once this problem area has been selected, the norms and rituals of accepted "basic" research take over and considerations as to the utility of the research are forgotten. Others fall from virtue in the opposite direction. Their desire to make a difference on matters of policy leads them, with or without awareness, to bias their research design, to go beyond their findings in interpretation, or to forget findings that do not support their value position. Knowing that such things happen is useful, not for passing judgment on the area as a whole, but for placing warning signs beside possible pitfalls.

### IMAGES OF PEACE RESEARCH

These two opposing criticisms of peace research confront the social scientist who becomes concerned about the international situation. If he decides in favor of activities *as a citizen* (signing newspaper advertisements, writing letters, joining a "peace action" group), he is not particularly vulnerable to *either* kind of criticism. Some may think he should be doing more, others may think what he is doing is somewhat unseemly—but little more than this. However, if he considers doing peace research, which tends to happen if his concern is wedded to a belief that social science has some remedial contribution to make, he is vulnerable to both kinds of criticism.

It is the view that peace research is an improper scientific activity that most often gives pause to a social scientist. His concern simultaneously suggests involvement in and avoidance of the area. Even if he believes that one's values should have some effect on choice of problems, the peace area poses extra difficulties because it looks as if the issues are so shaped by emotions and values that the research process itself would inevitably be contaminated.

"Peace," while no longer a dirty word, still has somewhat radical connotations and tends to conjure up pictures of peace walkers, petition signers, and pacifists. Peace research and peace action may appear quite indistinguishable to the outsider, and to some insiders. Many people are involved in both activities. There is a National Research Council on Peace Strategy and a Gradualist Faculty Council; both visibly link the intellectual and scientific community to the political activities of the peace movement. While one may be very much in favor of these activities, they tend to blur the line between research and opinion, between knowledge and action. This is upsetting to social scientists who feel that their disciplines have only quite recently started reaping the benefits of a long, hard fight to eradicate those biases which arose out of normative orientations to a subject matter.

A related issue, involving the identity of social scientists as scientists, is the commitment of many to "hard" empirical research, to the rigorous methods and quantifiable data which help justify the claim to being a science. The increasing involvement of the intellectual and scientific community, and the increasing use of the term "peace research" by respectable individuals and organizations, seems to have helped make "peace" more respectable but, unfortunately, it may also be helping to make "research" on peace more disreputable. Much of what is called peace research is, to many social scientists, discussion, analysis, opinion, speculation, or what have you.[6] Labeling a think piece or analytic essay, which may be "good social science," as research will bother many social scientists; while labeling *opinion* as research may lead to a deprecation of the whole area as one in which no one does objective work.

These images of peace research—that it is not objective or not "research"—become part of the gestalt in which decisions about evaluating, or embarking on, such work are made. However, they are important as images, not as issues; and critiques on this general level tend to obscure more interesting and significant questions related to objectivity and researchability.

Objectivity need not present serious problems when considering *how to do* research; but it often does when considering *what to do with* research. There are methods for guarding against bias in any investigation, and there are also additional safeguards available if it is felt that emotions and values may enter unnoticed despite the best of intentions.[7] Objectivity can probably be approached as closely in applied as in pure research. However, when the *utilization* rather than the *execution* of the study is considered, a number of serious issues related to objectivity come into focus. One way of differentiating utilization from execution problems is to make a distinction between the professional and the scientific roles of the social scientist. As a scientist, he does the research; as a professional, he decides what to do with it. It is the latter role that poses the most difficult conflicts for scientists engaged in peace research.

With respect to the *image* of peace research as not "research," the primary problem seems to be a semantic one; research means different things to different people. There is peace research that is "real" research in the sense that it is experimental[8] or involves analysis of quantifiable empirical data.[9] There are, however, a number of issues concerning the interrelation between the practical significance of a problem and its researchability, or more generally, between "useful" science and "good" science.

## The Question of Utility

Applied social science raises questions about the relationship between practical significance and scientific significance, that is, questions for *science*. It also raises a related set of questions for the *scientist;* the wish to do useful research may conflict with other wants and needs.

### ISSUES FOR SOCIAL SCIENCE

In considering how war/peace research relates to the social science endeavor as a whole, one must ask: Compared to alternative kinds of efforts, what will be its contribution to the development of social science? The assumption that science develops more rapidly if scientists are motivated purely by intellectual curiosity or by a desire to develop their science is often accepted unquestioningly. The evidence seems to permit no more than an agnostic position. Rapid scientific development has found its wellspring in "pure science" motivations, but also, and this may be particularly true of the social sciences, in "practical" concerns and worries. Freud and Durkheim are two examples; other examples can be cited from the war/peace area itself. Out of applied research efforts during World War II came the culture-at-a-distance approach in anthropology, Guttman scaling, advances in psychological testing, operations research, and computer technology. Evaluations of these as contributions to the development of social science may vary, but it would be difficult to claim that they are all insignificant. Currently, the development of a theory of conflict, a development that is drawing the interest and praise of scholars in many disciplines, is being pressed forward by men concerned about the international situation.[10]

A concern with practical problems can find expression in many different kinds of scientific effort. Among those who are worried about the dangers posed by nuclear technology, there are a number of basic theory advocates. This is an *applied* social science position in that it is concerned with practical goals and is well stated by Boulding.

The origin of this book in my own mind can be traced back to a passionate conviction of my youth that war was the major moral and intellectual problem of our age. . . . [The book] is driven by that practical curiosity which inspires applied science. Nevertheless, it is a work of pure theory, that is, of the abstract imagination. It gives no easy recipe for the abolition of war or for the general control of conflict, though it does, I hope, demonstrate exactly why in our age these tasks have become a necessity . . . it has been inspired not only by a practical end but by the belief that applied science cannot succeed unless it guides its empirical study by reins, however loose, of pure abstract theory. In particular, this work is the result of a conviction that the intellectual chassis of the broad movement for the abolition of war has not been adequate to support the powerful moral engine which drives it and that the frequent breakdowns which interrupt the progress of the movement are due essentially to a deficiency in its social theory.[11]

Parsons, in speaking of the conflict between a "concern for the practical world and the ethos of science," warns that the "attainment of high levels of analytical generalization . . . tends to be impeded by a too intensive concentration on problems at particular empirical levels."[12] But intensive concentration on particular empirical levels does not necessarily flow from a concern about practical problems. In fact, in the war/peace area, the pressure has been in quite the opposite direction. Because there are serious problems in testing hypotheses at the international system level, social scientists have bundled their favorite hypotheses off to more hospitable environs and are now using experimental games and simulation approaches to study conflict.[13] Meanwhile, the theoretical work on conflict, concerned with the generalizability of hypotheses, is paying increasing attention to the similarities and differences among system levels.[14]

So far, illustrations have been drawn from kinds of war/peace research that are, comparatively speaking, in the mainstream of social science. Other kinds of work in the area are more removed from the usual concerns of academic social science. They seem to have immediate practical payoff, but apparently have little or nothing to offer to the development of science. A hypothesis, that has already been confirmed and reconfirmed several times over, may be tested in a particular substantive area merely for the persuasive value of such a test. Practical needs may call for a quick and simple descriptive or how-to-do-it study when the most interesting scientific questions are analytic ones which could only be explored in longer and more complicated studies. Those who argue that this is not the kind of work that a social scientist should be wasting *any* time on, have to consider two queries: (1) Whose kind of work is it? (2) Since science is the goose that lays the unanticipated golden eggs,[15] can it be convincingly argued (keeping the Hawthorne studies in mind) that there is little likelihood of serendipitous findings in research of this sort?

Although it is often assumed that policy makers are primarily interested in studies which will shed light on their immediate problems this is not necessarily the case, at least in the war/peace area.[16] There are a number of questions important for policy that call for speculative, long-run thought and analysis. What would the consequences and ramifications of a particular policy move be? What policy alternatives are possible and what should be taken into consideration with respect to each? What is the range of relationships that might exist between the United States, the Soviet Union, and Communist China in twenty years, and what implications would each of these have for American policy? What would a disarmed world look like? Such questions do not appear to be particularly researchable to most social scientists, but often a research handle can be found if the questions are rephrased or broken down. Further, while the scientist may be aghast at the idea of engaging in "sheer speculation," much of what is required is not too different from approaches to analysis and theory-building that are well established. For instance, Walter Millis has set himself the task of outlining what a world without war would look like. In essence he is doing a functional analysis, asking what functions are served by the military institution and what alternative structures could fulfill these functions.[17] Similarly, one of the debates that Kahn's work[18] has set off is concerned with the functional prerequisites of society; how much and how many could be destroyed in a nuclear war without doing irreparable damage to the fabric of American society? Thus old and respectable questions in sociological theory have now become questions of quite vital significance in the planning of national policy.

Yet those whose stock in trade are these very questions, the sociologists, have contributed very little to their revivified discussion. It is the same in other areas. A sociology of conflict is being constructed without benefit of sociologists. Notions of stability are used as underpinnings in planning both weapons systems and disarmament proposals, but sociologists have not examined these uses of the stability concept. Exchange, bargaining, and reciprocity are becoming important concepts in sociology, and they have also become important concepts in the war/peace area; but there has been little or no conjoining.

Sociology and political science, the two social science disciplines seemingly most relevant to problems of war and peace, have contributed less to the discourse than psychology or economics. Why is this? The criticisms and negative images of peace research have already been referred to and perhaps these affect some disciplines more than others. Economists are more at home in a policy-informing role than other social scientists; psychologists may also be more comfortable than others in advisory roles. But these factors alone do not seem to explain what appears to be an underrepresentation of the most relevant disciplines. Other factors can be explored by turning attention to peace research and the social scientist, as distinct from peace research and social science.

### PROBLEMS FOR THE SOCIAL SCIENTIST

The very relevance of sociology and political science to war/peace problems may, paradoxically, be a factor explaining why relatively few of their adherents have become involved in these problems.

The dynamics of commitment often work in a roundabout way. The most usual path into war/peace research starts with a decision to do some work on a spare-time or *pro tem* basis. The more distant peace research is from one's specialty, the easier it is to see it as a side-line. If one's specialized skills and knowledge are not particularly relevant, the possibility of moving full-time into the study of international conflict appears to be out of the question. So the psychologist (or the physicist) can take the first step without feeling that all his previously-made career plans are threatened. The political scientist or sociologist may be aware of the fact that his expertise could be completely diverted and rechanneled into the study of international conflict and peace.

Once into the area, the conflicts and problems are quite similar no matter what the discipline of the social scientist. Pressures toward an all-or-nothing commitment become evident,[19] as do pressures toward an interdisciplinary approach. There is widespread agreement that the most productive research on international conflict, whether directed toward long or short run practical payoffs, will be interdisciplinary. Certainly many of those now working in the area have crossed disciplinary boundaries; Boulding and Schelling are not talking like economists, North is not talking like a political scientist.[20]

Many social scientists already feel they are running a losing race in trying to keep up with the literature in their specialty. To take on a whole new area, that involves an extensive policy and multidisciplinary literature, is a formidable task. It may mean estrangement from favored variables and concepts. It may lead to a neither fish-nor-fowl professional identity; a reduced role in the ongoing discourse of one's own discipline and the risk of being called naive by specialists in other disciplines. It may mean participation in team research with its attendant interpersonal and inter-intellectual frustrations.[21] Although the excitement and challenges of an interdisciplinary area often provide adequate compensation for these conflicts and frustrations, moving into an interdisciplinary area involves a major transition that is not taken lightly by many. But the change can, like other commitments, be entered upon with varying degrees of awareness. From the vantage point of some disciplines the path to commitment initially looks like an interesting side trip; while from the vantage point of others, it has the look of a permanent detour.

Often sociologists and political scientists think the psychologist naive in his approach to the study of conflict and problems of international security.[22] Their own hesitance to move into the area may be a function of their recognition of the immensity and complexity of the problems involved. They may consider it next to impossible to do worthwhile research on questions of such magnitude.

When a social scientist says that worthwhile work cannot be done or that a particular question is not researchable, he may mean a number of things. He may only be saying that *he* does not like doing the "messy" kind of work that is required. Messy may mean that there are too many variables to be considered, they are too difficult to measure, the important questions cannot be formulated in terms of one-tailed hypotheses, the required conceptual framework cuts across the boundaries of specialties and disciplines. Or it may mean that the problem is so large that it would require team effort to make any headway.

Or the social scientist may mean, when he says that worthwhile research cannot be done, that it is impossible to predict with any degree of confidence what kinds of work will be useful, particularly in a complex area. He may mean that he does not know what questions are of real practical significance and that, even if he did, anything he could contribute to them would be inconsequential. He may feel that he would not have sufficient confidence in the results of any research that could be done to make any practical recommendations. Or he may feel that no matter how useful a piece of research is, it will go unheeded by the decision-makers who could put it to use, particularly if it questions accepted policy. Thus considerations of utility may represent an insoluble puzzle that prevents any attempt at applied research.

By being content with research that is *relevant,* some social scientists have avoided ever coming to grips with the difficult question of utility. Research that is very *relevant* to practical problems may have no *practical significance* whatsoever if, for instance, none of the variables studied are subject to control or manipulation.[23] In doing relevant research, practical concerns tend to determine only the choice of problem *area;* other criteria then take over and determine the rest of the study. It gets published in a social science journal and is read only by colleagues. If one wants to do good disciplinary research for such an audience, then there are far better grounds for the testing of hypotheses than the war/peace area. If, however, one wants to contribute to the avoidance of war or the waging of peace, then the question of utility must be considered throughout the research process, up to and including the communication of the results. This is saying nothing new; applied research has been recognized as something to be approached differently from pure research for quite some time.[24] But whether it is the feeling of urgency about the international situation, the pressure of an already overburdened schedule of research and teaching, or the problem of discerning what is practically significant, many social scientists seem to embark on projects they see as peace research without ever taking the time to ask: How are the results of this study going to be useful? Who will they be useful to?

## The Social Scientist's Relationship to the Users of His Research

To raise the question of utility automatically raises the question: Useful to whom?

The social scientist interested in peace and security has a choice of audiences. He may choose to communicate only to his colleagues; but to the extent that his work has implications for practical problems other audiences will pay attention to it, and to the extent that he is concerned about practical payoffs he will pay attention to these other audiences.

The social scientist's role vis-á-vis the potential clients, audiences, and targets of his research, whether they be the general public, peace groups, or policy-makers in government, presents a number of issues. This relationship has been referred to earlier as a professional role, a role at least analytically distinct from the scientific role. A distinction is thus possible between activities related to the utilization of research and those related to the execution of research.

It was also stated that there is little problem in doing objective work in the war/peace area as long as one *wants* to do objective work. This is not to say that there are not strong motivations to "forget" about guarding against bias and interpreting findings meticulously if a social scientist becomes too concerned about communicating to a lay audience. The problem is the same as that for any profession where an expert deals with clients or audiences who cannot evaluate the adequacy of his work. It is not a solution to say that the social scientist has no business trying to influence the general public or advise policy-makers, as this will not prevent abuses. The only effective safeguard is for social scientists to have both some ability to monitor, and some interest in monitoring, their colleagues' communications to lay audiences.

But there is still a problem as to what standards should be applied. It would be difficult to argue that research should be reported to a policy-maker exactly in the same way as it is reported to colleagues, unless the policy-maker has had some training in the social sciences. How much simplification is justified? If all the caveats and qualifications are spelled out in detail, might not this dilute the impact so much that the policy-maker will decide that this research gives him no dependable information? If they are not spelled out in detail, are the findings being misrepresented? And what of the cases where the social scientist has not done any research on a particular problem, but is speaking as someone who has expert knowledge? How confidently should he express opinions, judgments, and predictions under these circumstances?

It is often felt that questions such as these are of particular concern to the social sciences but not to the physical sciences, either because the physical sciences have knowledge that is more dependable and has fewer value implications or because engineers handle all the applied problems for the physical sciences. When one looks at the role that physical scientists have played in the peace and security area in recent years it is not apparent that either the maturity of their disciplines or the existence of engineers has provided unambiguous answers to client-relation questions.[25] Van Allen's role in the controversy as to whether or not the United States should conduct high altitude nuclear tests provides a recent example.

*277*

To illustrate the utility of making a distinction between the scientific and the professional role of the scientist, and the need for social scientists to come to grips with the latter, three hypothetical examples will be used to raise a series of questions. Although examples could be drawn from war/peace problems, the points can be made more clearly in a less complex area. The examples will refer to a hypothetical social scientist who believes that capital punishment should be abolished because it is an ineffective deterrent and is immoral.

1. The social scientist believes that a majority of people in his state are against capital punishment, so he decides to do a survey to demonstrate this. His study is well-conceived and rigorous and, as well as collecting descriptive data, delves into interesting analytic questions. In other words, he performs well as a scientist. But let us say he was wrong in his estimate of public opinion and he finds that 65% of the sample are in favor of capital punishment, 25% against, and 10% don't know or don't care.

If he had initially intended not only to publish in a scholarly journal but also to seek general publicity for the findings, does he now have a responsibility to disseminate the results to the general public even though they did not come out in the direction desired? There is a bill to abolish capital punishment scheduled to come up before the State Assembly in six months; would he be justified in postponing *any* publication of the results until after the vote on the bill?

Say he had done the work for an organization that wanted to use the results to plan a campaign against capital punishment. He was not paid but has done the study because he is in sympathy with the organization's goals. He explains the findings to the executives of the organization knowing that they will make use of them in their campaign but will not publicize them. Does he have a *responsibility* to make the results generally available if he knows the press will immediately pick them up and publicize them? Does he have a *right* to?

What if a pro-capital-punishment organization has heard about the research, has not been able to get any information from the organization that initially requested it, and so asks the social scientist for a report of the findings. Should he give it to this organization, whose goals he disagrees with? Does he have a right, or a duty, to keep it "classified"?

What difference would it make if the anti-capital-punishment organization had paid him. Suppose it had specified no restrictions on publication initially, but then asks the social scientist to keep quiet about the results until after the vote on capital punishment in the State Assembly. Is this an improper request?

2. Again the hypothetical social scientist decides to do survey research but this time he is less confident about public attitudes. He includes the following question:

The governor of our state and the head of the state penitentiary believe that capital punishment should be abolished because it does not prevent people from committing murder. Do you agree that capital punishment should be abolished?

He finds that 75% of the respondents say "yes," 15% say "no," and 10% don't know. It is true that both the governor of the state and the head of the state penitentiary are against capital punishment.

Is the investigator asking a biased question? Citing authority figures in favor of a position often biases answers in the direction of agreement with that position. But if one wants to know what public support the governor could get in a campaign against capital punishment, is this not the way to find out?

But what if the people who will use or be influenced by the results do not understand this distinction and will simply interpret the question as indicating the percentage against capital punishment? How much responsibility does the social scientist have to make the distinction clear?

Say the social scientist finds out that the results of this question have been misrepresented, that it has been reported in the State Assembly that 85% (the "yeses" and the "don't knows" have been combined) of the people in the state support the abolition of capital punishment. Should he attempt to correct this distortion? Would he go out of his way to correct a misrepresentation that overestimated the number of people *in favor* of capital punishment?

3. In this final hypothetical case, the anti-execution social scientist does a study on the effects of capital punishment. He manages to show that capital punishment not only does not deter crime but actually tends to increase the incidence of murder. It is a good study and is lauded by colleagues when published in a journal. But the press does not pick it up, and decision-makers do not hear about it.

The social scientist sends reprints to those he thinks are key decision-makers in the state but as far as he can tell the reprints are not read or else the implications of the study were not clear to the reader. What should he do now? Does he have a responsibility to push it further? If he does, is this a responsibility as a scientist, as a citizen, as a human being, or as a professional having expert knowledge that significantly affects people?

Suppose he has strong evidence, but it is not *completely* conclusive. Is he then justified, in speaking to the public or to policy-makers, to say categorically that capital punishment does not deter crime but increases it? Can he use the categorical imperative and tell them they *must* abolish capital punishment? Would it make any difference whether or not pro-capital-punishment experts were talking in categorical terms?

In the first and third examples, "good" objective research is completed before any of the questions arise.[26] The second example appears, at first glance, to raise questions about the objectivity of the research itself, but this is not the case. In each instance, the issues can be defined only when utilization is considered.

No attempt will be made to answer the questions raised by these hypothetical examples. The point is only that the ethics of science do not provide adequate guidelines to define the role of the scientist vis-à-vis the users of his research. Social scientists have an audience, whether or not they like it. Waldo has summarized his view of this situation with some vigor:

> Now I submit for consideration the proposition that social science has and will have, to the extent that it explains and justifies our policy choices, not just a clinical and a rejective function, but a *symbolic*, a *legitimatizing*, and an *ideological* function. I argue, in other words, that in the sociological-anthropological perspective social scientists will have *religious* and *political* functions. We may protest in all honesty and with deep conviction that this is not our intent or desire, that we wish to function as scientists, pure and simple—but if old legitimacies crumble in the modern 'crisis of authority,' does not science itself raise a claim to legitimatize decision? I believe there is no denying that the social scientist will exercise much the same social role and function as the Roman priests in the temple who read the future from the entrails of oxen—though the social scientist reads it from graph, from report, from computer.[27]

It can be argued that the scientist doing basic research has every right to disclaim a professional role. However, if he is doing *applied* research and chooses to leave his professional role largely undefined, then he is walking toward his goal blindfolded. If he does not define the additions to his scientific role, others will define them for him. If he does not make it clear how his knowledge and prestige are to be used, others will use them for him. If he does not define his professional responsibilities, he will find he has none.

This is not a matter of saying that social scientists should exert greater or less control over the uses to which their applied efforts are put. It is a matter of saying that the applied social scientist does a disservice to his practical goals if he commutes between the horns of these ethical dilemmas, or ignores their existence, rather than making a considered choice between various alternatives.

## Summary

An attempt has been made to enumerate and clarify some of the factors affecting the contributions of social science to, and the role of the social scientist in, the peace and international security area. A concern with practical problems does not *necessarily* hinder the development of social science and certain kinds of applied efforts may in fact facilitate it. However, social science approaches to problems of peace and conflict may be disconcerting to the social scientist even if harmless to his science. Issues related to the criteria of practical utility, and to the role of the social scientist vis-à-vis the users of his research, pose the most difficult conflicts and problems for him.

The war/peace area tends to demand, of any social scientist who wishes to make a significant contribution, an all-or-nothing commitment and major changes in the direction and nature of his work. The development of research that will meet the criterion of utility, as well as other important criteria (for instance, is the research also of intrinsic interest to the investigator and manageable in terms of his training and talents), is particularly difficult in the war/peace area because the complexity of the practical problems complicates the task of anticipating what will be useful.

A distinction has been made between the scientific and the professional role of the applied social scientist; as a scientist he does research, as a professional he decides what to do with it. Several hypothetical examples are used to suggest that problems for the social scientist do not arise as much from a conflict between these two analytically distinct roles as from the fact that the professional role is largely undefined. While applied research need not conflict with the values and ethics of science, the applied researcher cannot depend on these values and ethics alone. They do not provide adequate guidelines for the conduct of his professional role.

## NOTES

1. These 13 interviews, mostly with social scientists, as well as interviews with personnel of the U.S. Arms Control and Disarmament Agency, were collected for a doctoral dissertation (for the Department of Sociology & Anthropology, Washington University, St. Louis, Mo.) examining the utilization of the social sciences in policy-making. I would like to express my appreciation to Mrs. John A. Semmelmeyer, Jr., and to the Society for the Psychological Study of Social Issues for their support of this phase of the work.

2. Charles E. Osgood, *An Alternative to War or Surrender*, Urbana: University of Illinois Press, 1962; Amitai Etzioni, *The Hard Way to Peace*, New York: Col-

lier Books, 1962; Arthur I. Waskow, "The Shelter-Centered Society," A Report of a Peace Research Institute Conference on Potential Implications of a National Civil Defense Program, Washington, D.C.: Peace Research Institute, 1962.

3. For instance, the variety of studies related to deterrence that are being supported by Project Michelson, under the direction of Thomas Milburn, Naval Ordnance Test Station, China Lake, Calif. For a general review of the peace research area, see Donald N. Michael, "Basic Research for Peace," *The Nation*, 195 (September 1, 1962), pp. 83–86.

4. Cf. Alvin W. Gouldner, "Theoretical Requirements of the Applied Social

Sciences," *American Sociological Review,* 22 (February, 1957), pp. 92–102.

5. J. David Singer and Anatol Rapaport, "The Armers and the Disarmers: Is Debate Useful?", *The Nation,* 196 (March 2, 1963), pp. 174–177, 188. (Singer takes the "pro" position; Rapaport, the "con.")

6. There seem to be a number of reasons for this use of the term "research." One is simply the difficulty of finding a better term. "Peace studies" (or "conflict studies") is an alternative, but it obscures one of the implicit connotations of "peace research," one of the distinctive features of this new surge of activity on problems of international conflict. Kenneth Boulding has spoken of an ongoing transition in policy thinking from a "wisdom orientation" to a "research orientation." To call something "peace *research*" is a way of distinguishing it as material based on a scientific *approach* (although not necessarily on scientific findings) rather than on the wisdom and intuition of the humanities or practical experience. Another reason is undoubtedly related to the very general usage that "research" has within the government; within the State Department, "research" can mean anything from a summary of a New York Times article on up, or down.

7. One research group in the San Francisco Bay Area, The Committee for the Application of the Behavioral Sciences to the Strategies of Peace (ABSSOP), has adopted a policy called the "balanced bias." In studying a topic on which there are strongly held and conflicting opinions, an attempt is made to have the conflicts represented on the research team. For instance, in a study of a peace group and a shelter group in a suburban community, the research team was composed of psychologists who differed in their attitudes about civil defense and peace groups. The research design, the instruments used to collect data, and the interpretations of

findings had to be approved by the whole team. Cf. Paul Ekman *et al.,* "Divergent Reactions to the Threat of War," *Science,* 139 (January 11, 1963), pp. 88–94.

8. For instance, Morton Deutsch and Robert M. Krauss, "Studies of Interpersonal Bargaining," *The Journal of Conflict Resolution,* 6 (March, 1962), pp. 52–76.

9. For instance, see Ekman *et al., op cit.,* and Snell Putney and Russell Middleton, "Some Factors Associated with Student Acceptance or Rejection of War," *American Sociological Review,* 27 (October, 1962), pp. 655–667.

10. Kenneth E. Boulding, *Conflict and Defense,* New York: Harper & Brothers, 1962; Anatol Rapaport, *Fights, Games and Debates,* Ann Arbor: University of Michigan Press, 1960; Thomas C. Schelling, *The Strategy of Conflict,* Cambridge: Harvard University Press, 1960.

11. Boulding, *ibid.,* p. vii. Schelling takes a similar position: "In my own thinking ['pure' and 'applied' research] have never been separate. Motivation for the purer theory came almost exclusively from preoccupation with (and fascination with) 'applied' problems; and the clarification of theoretical ideas was absolutely dependent on an identification of live examples. For reasons inherent either in the subject or in the author, the interaction of the two levels of theory has been continuous and intense." Schelling, *ibid.,* p. vi.

12. Talcott Parsons, "The Role of the Behavioral Scientist in the International Situation," Abstract of paper read at the Annual Convention of the American Orthopsychiatric Association, March 6–9, 1963, Washington, D.C., *American Journal of Orthopsychiatry,* 33 (March, 1963), p. 224.

13. For instance, some of Osgood's propositions on "graduated reciprocation in tension-reduction" are being tested in experimental game situations: Jack Saw-

yer, "The Interaction Screen: An Electronic Representation of Interpersonal Conflict," research in progress, University of Chicago; Kellogg V. Wilson and V. Edwin Bixenstine, "Effects of a Third Choice on Behavior in a Prisoner's Dilemma Game," uunpublished manuscript. Richard A. Brody has used simulation to test hypotheses concerning the spread of nuclear weapons; *Some Systemic Effects of the Spread of Nuclear Weapons*, Evanston, Ill.: Program of Graduate Training and Research in International Relations, February, 1963. (Also in the December, 1963, issue of *The Journal of Conflict Resolution*.) For a recent review of simulation approaches, see Harold Guetzkow, Chadwick Alger, Richard A. Brody, R. Noel, and Richard C. Snyder, *Simulation in International Relations: Developments for Research and Teaching*, Englewood Cliffs, N.J.: Prentice-Hall, 1963.

14. See Boulding, *op. cit.* Robert C. North and Charles E. Osgood are currently working jointly on an analysis of the interrelation between system levels and the applicability of propositions across system levels.

15. This apt phrase is from Parsons, *op. cit.*

16. However, there may be a gap between the kinds of research that federal policy officials are interested in and the kinds of research that federal policy agencies feel able to support. For a review of a number of long-range policy-oriented problems see Richard J. Barnet, "Research on Disarmament," *Background: Journal of the International Studies Association*, 6 (Winter, 1963), pp. 3–15. Mr. Barnet was with the U S Arms Control and Disarmament Agency at the time the paper was written.

17. Walter Millis, "A World Without War" and "Permanent Peace," in Millis et al., *A World Without War*, New York: Washington Square Press, 1961, pp. 53–144.

18. Herman Kahn, *On Thermonuclear War*, Princeton: Princeton University Press, 1961.

19. There are several reasons for this: (1) the large and rapidly growing body of literature; (2) the intellectual fascination of many of the problems; (3) the desire to "make a difference" on a huge problem, a motivation that not only pushes toward full-time scientific work in the area but also leads into various other time-consuming activities, such as public speaking, attempts to inform and/or influence policy officials, assorted meetings and workshops, etc.; (4) the feeling that it is particularly important to keep at it in a crisis period because war may be just around the corner, and equally important to keep at it in a non-crisis period because a breakthrough to peace may be just around the corner.

20. Robert C. North is Director of the Studies in International Conflict and Integration, Stanford University; for a sampling of this project's work, see Dina A. Zinnes, Robert C. North, and Howard E. Koch, Jr., "Capability, Threat and the Outbreak of War," in James N. Rosenau, editor, *International Politics and Foreign Policy*, New York: Free Press of Glencoe, 1961; and the special issue "Case Studies in Conflict," *The Journal of Conflict Resolution*, 6 (September, 1962).

21. Warren G. Bennis, "Some Barriers to Teamwork in Social Research," *Social Problems*, 3 (April, 1956), pp. 223–235.

22. J. David Singer, "Peace Research, Peace Action," *Bulletin of the Atomic Scientists*, 19 (January, 1963), pp. 13–17.

23. Gouldner, *op. cit.*, pp. 96–98.

24. For instance, see "The Application of Social Research," Chapter 13 in Claire Selltiz, Marie Jahoda, Morton Deutsch, and Stuart W. Cook, *Research Methods in Social Relations*, revised one-volume edition, New York: Henry Holt, 1959.

25. For a recent discussion of some of these questions, see Albert Wohlstetter,

"Scientists, Seers and Strategy," *Foreign Affairs*, 41 (April, 1963), pp. 466–478.

26. This is not to say that the questions *should* be raised only after the research is completed. The author's position is that these kinds of questions should be considered before the research is *started*.

27. The Brookings Institution, *Research for Public Policy*, Brookings Dedication Lectures, Washington, D.C., 1961.

22.   Law as an Instrument

of Social Change

WILLIAM M. EVAN

IN IMAGINARY SOCIETIES, SUCH AS SOME AUTHORS of utopias have depicted, there is such a high degree of social harmony and tranquillity that no law is necessary—and no lawyers either. Such societies enjoy a perfect state of social equilibrium because there is a perfect degree of congruence between the ideal prescriptions and proscriptions of behavior and actual behavior. The free and frictionless association among all citizens makes the state superfluous as the source of law and as an instrument of social control.

In all real societies, whether "primitive" or "civilized," such an ideal state is not to be found. In fact, we can argue that in principle it is impossible for human beings ever to attain that blissful state of equilibrium which would not require law or some form of legal system. Disequilibrating forces are generated from both outside and inside a society. These pressures for change stem in part from the impossibility of achieving perfect congruence between the ideal cultural blueprint of a society and the actual social reality. A certain amount of social deviance occurs in all societies, if only because the socialization process through childhood as well as through the rest of the life cycle can not possibly be uniform and perfectly successful. As a consequence, in all societies of any appreciable size, there is a tendency for law to emerge distinct from "the cake of custom." Law in this context does not necessarily refer to a written statement of a rule of conduct, since in nonliterate societies this cannot occur, but rather to a particular social status—such as that of a tribal chieftain or a judge—the incumbent of which has the authority to assert a norm, resolve conflicts, and bring to bear the coercive power of the community against those guilty of violating a norm.

## Contrasting Conceptions of the Function of Law

Law emerges not only to *codify* existing customs, morals, or mores, but also to *modify* the behavior and the values presently existing in a particular society. The conception of law as a codification of existing customs, morals, or mores implies a relatively passive function. On the other hand, the conception of law as a means of social change, i.e., as a potential for modifying behavior and beliefs, implies a relatively active function.[1]

The passive law, namely, that one cannot legislate mores and people's behavior, is rooted in the 19th century philosophies of Social Darwinism and historical jurisprudence. At the turn of the century, William Graham Sumner articulated this conception of the law. It assumes that law is a passive, rather than an active social force, which gradually emerges into a formal or codified state only after it has taken root in the behavior of the members of a society. Whenever an effort is made to enact a law in contradiction to existing folkways and mores, conflicts arise which result in the eventual undoing of the law. Since Sumner claims there is a "strain toward a consistency of the mores," he concludes, in effect, that "stateways cannot change folkways." An implicit assumption of this view is that the exclusive function of law is to reinforce the mores and to provide a uniform and predictable procedure for the evaluation and punishment of deviance. That is to say, the function of law is social control and the major problem is one of designing legal sanctions to minimize deviance and maintain social stability.

A contrary view is that law is not merely a reflection of existing customs, morals or codes, but also a potentially independent social force which can influence behavior and beliefs. As an instrument of social change, law entails two interrelated processes: the institutionalization and the internalization of patterns of behavior. In this context, institutionalization of a pattern of behavior means the establishment of a norm with provisions for its enforcement,[2] and internalization of a pattern of behavior means the incorporation of the value or values implicit in a law.[3] Law, as has been noted by others, can affect behavior directly only through the process of institutionalization; if, however, the institutionalization process is successful, it, in turn, facilitates the internalization of attitudes or beliefs.[4]

### A CONTINUUM OF RESISTANCE TO LAW

These opposing views of the function of law suggest a hypothetical continuum of the amount of potential resistance to the enactment of a new law. When there is likely to be zero per cent resistance to a law, one would obviously question the need for it, since complete agreement between the behavior required by the law and the existing customs or morals apparently exists. In this situation, there would be no need to codify the mores into law. At the other extreme, when there is likely to be 100 per cent resistance to a law, one would expect the law to be totally ineffective, because nobody would enforce it and the authority of the lawmaker would be undermined.[5]

No law would ever emerge if these two extremes existed at all times. Between these ends of our continuum, there are evidently two important thresholds involved in lawmaking. Somewhere at the lower end of our hypothetical continuum of resistance, where a certain degree of nonconformity or deviance from existing mores is reached, society acts to control it by codifying mores. What this threshold of nonconformity is for different societies, we do not yet know. Similarly, somewhere at the higher end of our continuum there is a threshold of such massive resistance to a new law that enforcement is impossible. At what point on this continuum a new law provokes the overwhelming majority of the citizenry to violate it so as to nullify it, we also do not know. Civil wars and revolutions approximate this form of massive resistance to law culminating in its "decodification".[6] Thus, in considering the social functions of law, we have to focus on the intermediate portion of our hypothetical continuum of resistance to law.

Whenever a law is enacted in the face of any appreciable resistance, that is to say, whenever it falls somewhere in the middle of our hypothetical continuum, the legal system becomes involved in an educational as well as in a social control task. If the educational task is not accomplished, a situation exists in which individuals are obligated to obey a law at the threat of punishment, while, in fact, not believing in it. This situation produces what Festinger calls "forced compliance", viz., a discrepancy between public behavior and private belief.[7] So long as behavior involves forced compliance, there is no internalization of the values implicit or explicit in a new law. The resulting tension may lead to disobedience of the law, depending on the nature of the sanctions and the consistency and efficiency of enforcement. If law is to perform an educational function, it is necessary to convert *forced* compliance into *voluntary* compliance.

## Necessary Conditions for Law Performing an Educational Function

Under what conditions can law succeed, not only in institutionalizing a new pattern of conduct, but also in generating the internalization of new attitudes implicit in the conduct required by the new law? The failure to specify these conditions leaves the theoretical problems of the relation of law to social change unanswered. It also leaves unsolved the administrative problems of the conscious use of law as an agent of social change. As a first approximation to an answer to this problem, we shall consider seven necessary, though perhaps not sufficient, conditions for law to perform an educational function.

The first condition is that the source of the new law be authoritative and prestigeful. This condition may at first appear to be trivial, since law, by definition, connotes an authoritative or legitimate action. There are, in fact, four authoritative lawmaking sources in our society: legislative, executive, administrative, and judicial. It is hypothesized that they differ not only in their reputed authoritativeness and prestige in exercising a lawmaking function, but also in their effectiveness in performing an educational function. A law enacted by a legislature—rather than issued as a decision by a court or an administrative agency, or as an executive order—probably lends itself more readily to performing an educational function. For, in the minds of the average citizens, legislatures—whether at the local, state or federal level—are probably perceived to be the proper and legitimate forums for the enactment of new laws. This perception may be due to the fact that legislatures are more sensitive to public pressures and sentiments than are the other sources of lawmaking.[8] Second in the perceived rank order of authoritativeness and prestige are probably executive orders, followed by the decisions of administrative agencies; and lastly, in all likelihood, are the decisions of the courts.

This hypothesis about the differential in perceived authoritativeness and prestige of lawmaking sources leads us, in turn, to the hypothesis that the more drastic the social change to be effected by law, i.e., the higher the proportion of potential resistance on our hypothetical scale, the more authoritative and prestigeful the lawmaking agency should be to effect the change. In other words, when there is a low degree of consensus regarding the norms involved in a law, "legislative lawmaking"—the most authoritative and prestigeful source of law—is apt to be more effective than "judicial lawmaking," the least authoritative and prestigeful source of law.[9]

The Supreme Court's decision to desegregate the public school system is generally acknowledged as representing an effort to effect a drastic social change. Consequently, we venture to suggest—in light of the hypothesis stated above—that Congress would have been a more effective lawmaking source in this instance. To be sure, had the Supreme Court in 1954 declined the opportunity to revise its 1896 doctrine of "separate but equal" treatment, enunciated in *Plessy* v. *Ferguson*, it might have taken many years for Congress to enact a desegregation law in view of the monumental resistance of the Southern pressure group.

The second condition is that the rationale of a new law clarify its continuity and compatibility with existing institutionalized values.[10] The fulfillment of this condition helps to overcome possible objections to a new law and establishes its legitimacy in the eyes of the citizenry. Such a rationale is readily imaginable in the desegregation decision. The Thirteenth and Fourteenth Amendments, as well as the Declaration of Independence and various judicial decisions in the preceding decade, clearly establish the rights of all citizens of this country to equal treatment by the law, including agencies of the state, such as the public school system. Thus, a legislative enactment of school desegregation could have drawn on prior legal support, quite apart from general cultural and historical justifications.

The third necessary condition for making law an educational force is the use of models or reference groups for compliance. This could involve several possible actions by a lawmaking body. It might single out a group or a community in which the proposed pattern of behavior already exists without any observable adverse effects. Thus, for instance, it would have been possible in our hypothetical "legislative law" on public school desegregation to have included statements that in various countries with which we identify politically, desegregated schools operate smoothly. Moreover, it would have been possible to point to any number of communities in this country where desegregation has been in effect for many years without any known untoward effects on either whites or Negroes. Also relevant would have been a reference to the successful desegregation in the armed services in both Northern and Southern installations. The examples cited of models for compliance may not have proved adequate for the law in question. The idea, however, of deliberately upholding a pragmatic model which is visible and the likely object of admiration by potential recalcitrants might contribute to overcoming resistance to a proposed change.

The fourth condition is that law make a conscious use of the element of time in introducing a new pattern of behavior. This is essential for breaking an old pattern and instituting a new one. To be sure, the Supreme Court took the time element into consideration when it resorted to the intentionally ambiguous phrase "with all deliberate speed" in its desegregation decision.

It may be hypothesized that if a significant pattern of social behavior is to be changed, the less the transition time, the easier—rather than the harder—the adaptation to the change.[11] The rationale for this proposition is that the reduction of time delay minimizes the chances for the growth of organized or unorganized resistance to the projected legal change. The possible validity of this hypothesis depends on at least two conditions, to which we now turn.

The first of these, our fifth condition, is that the enforcement agents must themselves be committed to the behavior required by the law, even if not to the values implicit in it. Any evidence of hypocrisy or corruptibility on the part of the personnel of the legal system, whose task it is to implement the law, undermines the chances of its being effectuated. One of the major reasons for the failure of the Prohibition Amendment was the disrespect for the law evidenced by enforcement agents, particularly local police, on whom the major task of enforcement devolved.[12]

The sixth condition, which also bears on the time factor mentioned earlier, is that as resistance to a new law increases, positive sanctions are probably as important as negative ones.[13] Legal sanctions are almost invariably negative in character, e.g., fines and/or imprisonment. As the severity of the punishment increases, compliance does not necessarily increase.[14] Severe punishment often affords people the opportunity to neutralize any guilt experienced for their wrong-doing with what feels like justified resentment against punishment. To encourage the learning of a new pattern of behavior and a new attitude, some positive reinforcement is required, as learning theorists have found experimentally. We would speculate that as the proportion of potential resistance to a new law increases, the need for including some positive sanctions or rewards for compliance also increases. In the case of the school desegregation decision, such rewards might have consisted of a special Federal school subsidy for teachers' salaries and school construction, and possibly even a rebate on Federal income tax for a given length of time for the people in those communities complying with the law. Although the Anglo-Saxon legal system generally does not provide for positive sanctions, there is no reason to doubt their value when law is used as an instrument of social change, particularly of a significant magnitude.

The seventh and final condition under which law performs an educational function is that effective protection be provided for the rights of those persons who would suffer if the law were evaded or violated. If an individual is required, because of the legal doctrine of "standing" in court, to vindicate his rights against those of an organized entity, public or private, whose resources are infinitely greater, his rights are, in fact, unprotected. Only if the law should provide that he have the aid of a public organization, such as an administrative agency charged with the enforcement of the law, or the aid of a private organization of his own choosing, does he stand a chance to obtain justice.

In the case of our hypothetical "legislative law" on public school desegregation, parents of Negro children who are barred from admission to white schools should not have to fight boards of education alone; rather, they should, if they wish, have the support of either a public agency, such as the Civil Rights Commission, or of private organizations. In the latter case, such organizations should not run the risk of being accused of the crime of barratry, as has occurred in recent legal conflicts in the South.[15] Adequate provisions to protect the rights of those affected by a law presuppose that special and suitable efforts be expended to inform people of their rights under a new law. The problem of informing people of their legal rights appears to be endemic in all known legal systems; appreciably more effort is devoted to informing people of their duties than of their rights.[16]

## Conclusion

In short, we are suggesting that law can potentially act as an educational force in changing people's behavior, even in the presence of appreciable opposition to the projected change implied by the law, if it meets the following seven conditions:

1. The source of the law is perceived to be authoritative and prestigeful,

2. The rationale for the new law is articulated in terms of legal, as well as historical and cultural continuity and compatibility;

3. Pragmatic models for compliance are identified;

4. A relevant use of time is made to overcome potential resistance;

5. The enforcement agents are themselves committed to the behavior

required by the law, at least to the extent of according it legitimacy if not to the extent of internalizing the values implicit in it;

6. Positive, as well as negative, sanctions are employed to buttress the law; and

7. Effective protection is provided for the rights of those persons who would suffer from evasion or violation of the law.

In our large and heterogeneous society, laws are designed with an educational as well as a social control function. The existence of many organized groups devoting considerable resources to promoting or obstructing new laws means that an appreciable portion of the population will resist a new law if it conflicts with their interests and values.[17] Hence, of necessity, laws of this character must have built-in provisions for performing the educational function which we have been concerned with in this paper. In other words, it is necessary to institutionalize a new pattern of conduct so as to maximize the chances for the internalization of values implicit in it.

Resistance to law, organized and unorganized, is the price we must often be prepared to pay for living in a pluralistic and rapidly changing society. Greater knowledge of the means of overcoming resistance to laws seeking to effect social change will probably increase the chance of law performing an educational, rather than merely a social control function.

As Morroe Berger has put it, law is "one of the great movers and changers of basic institutions of all kinds, and helps in establishing the conditions which favor group equality in a free society."[18]

## NOTES

The author wishes to express his indebtedness to Harold B. Gerard for much help in preparing this paper.

1. Cf. Arnold M. Rose, "Sociological Factors in the Effectiveness of Projected Legal Remedies," *Journal of Legal Education*, 11, 4 (1959), pp. 470–481; Will Maslow, "The Uses of Law in the Struggle for Equality," *Social Research*, 22 (Autumn, 1955), pp. 297–314; Robert M. Hutchins, "The Corporation and Education, Ethics, and Power," in Melvin Anshen and George Leland Bach, eds., *Management and Corporations 1985*, New York: McGraw-Hill Book Co., 1960, pp. 183–196.

2. Ernst Borinski, "The Litigation Curve and the Litigation Filibuster in Civil Rights Cases," *Social Forces*, 37 (December, 1958), pp. 142–147.

3. Cf. Herbert C. Kelman, "Compliance, Identification, and Internalization: Three Processes of Attitude Change," *Journal of Conflict Resolution*, 2 (March, 1958), pp. 51–60. For an analysis using the concepts of institutionalization of norms as well as internalization of norms, see William M. Evan, "Due Process of Law in Military and Industrial Organizations," *Administrative Science Quarterly*, 7 (September, 1962), pp. 187–207; and "Due Process of Law in Formal Organi-

zations: A Comparative Analysis" (forthcoming).

4. See, for example, Morroe Berger, *Equality by Statute,* New York: Columbia University, 1948, pp. 170 ff.; Kenneth B. Clark, "Desegregation: An Appraisal of the Evidence," *Journal of Social Issues,* 9, 4 (1953), pp. 72–6.

5. Cf. Berger, *op. cit.,* p. 4.

6. The formidable difficulties of studying the "decodification" of laws historically as it relates to the degree of resistance to law suggests that one heuristic strategy is to design laboratory experiments on the conditions under which norms become codified and those under which they become "decodified." Such experiments would simulate macroscopic processes in society as a whole as well as microscopic processes in such social structures as formal organizations.

7. Leon Festinger, "An Analysis of Compliant Behavior," in M. Sherif and M. O. Wilson, eds., *Group Relations at the Crossroads,* New York: Harper & Bros., 1953, pp. 232–256; *A Theory of Cognitive ·Dissonance,* Evanston, Ill.: Row, Peterson and Co., 1957, pp. 84–122.

8. Cf. John C. Wahlke and Heinz Eulau, eds., *Legislative Behavior: A Reader in Theory and Research,* Glencoe, Ill.: The Free Press, 1959, p. 6.

9. Cf. Robert A. Leflar, "Law of the Land," in Don Shoemaker ed., *With All Deliberate Speed,* New York: Harper & Bros., 1957, p. 1.

10. Cf. H. G. Barnett, *Innovation: The Basis of Cultural Change,* New York: McGraw-Hill, 1953, pp. 329 ff.

11. Clark, *op. cit.,* pp. 44–7.

12. Cf. Clark Warburton, "Prohibition," *Encyclopedia of the Social Sciences,* New York: Macmillan, 1933, p. 505.

13. Rose, *op. cit.,* p. 472.

14. See, for example, Frederick K. Beutel, *Some Potentialities of Experimental Jurisprudence,* Lincoln, Neb.: University of Nebraska Press, 1957, pp. 400–401.

15. Borinski, *op. cit.,* p. 145.

16. Cf. Evan, "Due Process of Law in Military and Industrial Organizations," *op. cit.*

17. Cf. William M. Evan and Mildred A. Schwartz, "Law and the Emergence of Formal Organizations," *Sociology and Social Research,* 1964.

18. Berger, *op. cit.,* p. 186.

# 23.    Trial by Jury:

# A Critical Assessment

RITA JAMES SIMON

Iɴ ɪᴛs ʙᴇɢɪɴɴɪɴɢs ɪɴ 11ᴛʜ ᴄᴇɴᴛᴜʀʏ ᴇɴɢʟᴀɴᴅ, ᴀ trial before a jury was quite different from present-day courtroom practice. The early jury was a group of the defendant's neighbors who were called in to answer questions from their own knowledge. Thus, the jurors were both witnesses and triers of fact. It was not until the end of the 15th century that jurors ceased to serve as witnesses and came to function exclusively as triers of the facts.

In the United States, the right to a trial by jury is guaranteed in the Federal Courts by the Sixth Amendment to the Constitution which states:

In all criminal prosecutions, the accused shall enjoy the right to a speedy and public trial by an impartial jury of the state and district wherein the crime shall have been committed.[1]

From the earliest jury trials until now, the practice of trial by jury has caused considerable controversy and evoked much criticism.[2] Some members of the bench and bar have sought to abolish completely the institution of jury trials. Others have tried to introduce major and strategic changes in its present form.[3] Interested lay persons have crusaded for alterations from time to time. Representatives of professional groups, who have served as expert witnesses and have had limited, but unpleasant contacts with the courts in general, and with trials before juries in particular, have argued for changes in the court procedure.

Critics generally have attacked one of two aspects of the system. The first pertains to the method of selecting members for the jury. Selecting a jury is locally determined, and may lead to panels that are heavily weighted in favor of one social, ethnic, or racial group. Critics argue that the phrase "a jury of one's peers" is without meaning in some localities. In *Smith v. Texas* and in *Glasser v. United States,* the Supreme Court heartily affirmed the principle of representativeness. Justice Murphy, speaking for the court said:[4]

The exercise of the duty of selection must always accord with the fact that the proper functioning of the jury system requires that the jury be a body truly representative of the community and not the organ of any special group or class. The deliberate selection of jurors from the membership of particular private organizations definitely does not conform to the traditional requirements of jury trial.

The critics argue that the system of jury selection leads to the exemption from service of many persons who might perform most effectively: for example, professional men and women in almost every American jurisdiction. One critic claimed that:[5]

The democratic process itself seems designed to ensure the legislative exemption of persons most capable of resolving factual disputes. Jury service often involves bearing economic sacrifices, especially for those persons whose daily incomes are in excess of the per diem pittance meted out to jurors. It is only natural to expect that groups possessing substantial influence will utilize it for the purpose of securing legislative exemption. As the groups which can exert such pressures must possess a relatively small membership, the usual result is the exemption of doctors, lawyers, dentists and educators of every grade and description.[6]

A second group of critics attack the system per se. They argue that no jury of laymen has the ability to render "satisfactory" verdicts. They claim that unlike other complex institutions in contemporary society, the jury continues to make decisions on matters in which specialized knowledge and training have, in most instances, replaced common sense knowledge and lay experience. These critics would like the jury replaced by a body of men selected on the basis of their expert knowledge of the particular issues raised in a given case; or by a bench trial in which the judge would be free to seek the advice and guidance of experts.

Some critics would replace the jury only when the complexities of a contract dispute, an antitrust action, or the medical questions involved in a plea of insanity case are, to their mind, beyond the purview of the general public. But those who would abolish all jury trials argue that the application of law is too difficult for laymen. They believe that the court's instructions to the jury concerning the rule of law, the testimony of expert witnesses, and the distinction between evidence and opinion are beyond the comprehension of a jury; and that the jurors come into the courtroom too burdened with the weight of their own biases to listen to the evidence.

Carl Becker, a noted historian and able student of American history and institutions, had this to say about the jury system:

Trial by jury as a method of determining facts is antiquated and inherently absurd—so much so that no lawyer, judge, scholar, prescription-clerk, cook, or mechanic in a garage would ever think for a moment of employing that method for determining the facts in any situation that concerned him.[7]

Osborn, a noted legal scholar and observer of many jury trials, wrote in 1937:

When a group of twelve men, on seats a little higher than the spectators, but not quite so high as the judge, are casually observed it may appear from their attitude that they are thinking only about the case going on before them. The truth is that for much of the time there are twelve wandering minds in that silent group, bodily present but mentally far away. Some of them are thinking of sadly neglected business affairs, others of happy or unhappy family matters, and, after the second or third day, and especially after the second or third week, there is the garden, the house-painting, the new automobile, the prospective vacation, the girl who is soon to be married, and the hundred and one other things that come to the mind of one who is only partly interested in the tedious proceeding going on before him. There is probably more woolgathering in jury boxes than in any other place on earth. . . . It is plainly said by those whose opinions command the utmost respect that the administration of the law in this land is on a lower plane than other phases of government and is unworthy of the civilization it poorly serves.[8]

Some critics suggest that a panel of specialists trained in criminal law, psychology and/or criminology, etc., should determine the defendant's guilt.

An empirical study of the American jury system has been conducted for some time at the Law School of the University of Chicago.[9] In conducting the study, the Jury Project used a variety of methods of investigation, including: analysis of historical documents about the origins of the jury system; intensive interviews in the homes of each juror on panels that had deliberated together; comparison of judge and jury verdicts over a range of cases; and presentation of recorded trials (based on real cases) to jurors on their regular period of jury duty.

# Trial by Jury: A Critical Assessment

The effects on verdicts and participation of the jurors' sex, socioeconomic status, education, personality characteristics, and geography, have at various times been reported.[10] In this paper, we shall examine some general findings on the competence of the jury to assess the facts of a case, and to render a verdict in keeping with the facts and with the instructions of the court.

I shall draw most heavily on the materials available from the recorded data on jurors' reactions to two criminal trials, both involving a defense of insanity. The first trial, based on a housebreaking case,[11] was replicated before 30 juries in Chicago, St. Louis, and Minneapolis. The second case involved a defense of insanity to a charge of incest. This trial was played before 68 juries in the same three cities. In addition to obtaining the reactions of individual jurors before and after the deliberations, each deliberation was recorded and subsequently analyzed. For reasons that we had stated many times, we have considerable confidence that these recorded deliberations are remarkably akin to the jury discussions that occur in actual cases.[12]

## Selective Findings From the Jury Study

### A. HOW MUCH WEIGHT DOES THE JURY ATTACH TO THE EVIDENCE?

Many critics believe that jurors argue from their own particular associations and prejudices; and that the members of the jury make little attempt to recreate the evidence presented during the trial. From a sample of the juries' deliberations on the housebreaking case, we did a content analysis of the deliberations by counting the number of references that the jurors made to the various topics in the category scheme. We found the distribution shown in Table 1.

### Table 1—Relative Content Usage in July Deliberations[a]

| Content Category | Per cent |
|---|---|
| References to Instructions | 8 |
| References to Evidence | 45 |
| Opinions Based on Personal and Daily Life Experiences | 23 |
| Procedural Comments | 24 |
| Combined | 100 |

[a] These data are based on ten juries. The total number of acts was 5357 and the mean number of acts per jury was 536.

Most of the jury's time was spent recreating the trial. This is not to say that the jurors systematically reviewed each piece of evidence in the order

*297*

that it arose. Rather, their tackling of a case is like the piecing together of a jigsaw puzzle. The jurors may jump from the testimony of witness A, to a discussion of witness X, who appeared much later in the trial, because of a comment by one of the jurors emanating from his own experiences. They may then continue to discuss witness X for some time. In the majority of instances, however, they do return to witness A. Before the deliberation is over the jurors generally succeed in assembling all the pieces of the puzzle.

It is an interesting side-note that when one of the jurors makes an incorrect statement, it is usually corrected, but not immediately. Rather, the pattern seems to be that the misinformation will stand for several minutes. Most frequently, another juror will return to the previous discussion and make a correct restatement. For example, in one of the deliberations based on the housebreaking case, a majority of jurors wished to acquit the defendant on grounds of insanity. One juror, arguing for a guilty verdict, claimed that the defendant was a teenager. In fact, he was 25 years old. The juror said:

If we find him guilty, since he is a teenager, the judge will be very reluctant to sentence him to prison for, at the very most, a year.

About a half hour later, another juror, reviewing the defendant's background, mentioned that at the time the act was committed the defendant was 25 years of age.

### B. WHAT FACTS DOES THE JURY CONSIDER IMPORTANT IN DETERMINING GUILT OR INNOCENCE?

The jurors emphasize the events surrounding the commission of the crime. They ask this question: Does the defendant in the case fit the picture of the typical criminal, whose aims, the jurors believe, are rational and understandable. If the crime is an offense against property, then the jury assumes that a criminal will attempt to steal objects that are valuable, easy to dispose of, and readily carried away. They consider the strategy that the defendant used in breaking and entering, and the possibility that he would have been detected. The jurors in the housebreaking case tended to evaluate the defendant's sanity or insanity by the similarity of his behavior to that of an ideal criminal.[13] The defendant's motivation, childhood experience, and unconscious factors had much less impact on the jury's ultimate decisions, than did his behavior at the scene of the crime.

Even in the incest case, a crime that many laymen would say, by definition, could only be committed by a person who is mentally deranged, the jurors examined the specific details of the commission of the act. They looked for such cues as the contraceptive precautions that the defendant took to avoid pregnancy, his ability, over a long period of time, to maintain a responsible job, and his efforts to prevent exposure of his deviant sexual behavior. The jurors' detailed discussions of each of these matters do not support Mr . Broeder's expectations:

The increased emotion attendant upon criminal trials probably warps the jury's fact-finding abilities in roughly the same degree as does the complexity of the issues involved in civil suits.[14]

## C. DOES THE JURY UNDERSTAND AND ATTEMPT TO IMPLEMENT THE COURT'S INSTRUCTIONS ON THE RULE OF LAW?

The stereoptic criticism is that jurors do not understand the instructions which they have received from the court and, therefore, ignore them. Indeed, Judge Jerome Frank observed:

To comprehend the meaning of many a legal rule requires special traning. It is inconceivable that a body of twelve men . . . could, merely from listening to the instructions of the judge, gain the knowledge necessary to grasp the true import of the judge's words. For these words have often acquired their meaning as the result of hundreds of years of professional disputation in the courts. The jurors usually are as unlikely to get the meaning of those words as if they were spoken in Chinese, Sanskrit or Choctaw.[15]

From a quantitative assessment, that 8 per cent of all comments in the deliberation refer to the instructions,[16] we know that the instructions are far from ignored. But jurors do sometimes misinterpret or reinterpret instructions.

At the present time, for criminal cases involving a defense of insanity, the courts are likely to offer the jury two sets of instructions for arriving at its verdict. There is the traditional *M'Naghten* instruction which has as its major premise the ability of the defendant to distinguish right from wrong; and the recently formulated *Durham* criterion of mental disease and the behavior emanating from such disease.[17] The *M'Naghten* instruction emphasizes cognitive factors almost to the exclusion of any other considerations. In the *Durham* rule an attempt is made to integrate cognitive, volitional and emotional factors. Many jurors believe that cognition is the crucial issue in the determination of responsibility. Some of the juries that deliberated under *Durham* managed to construe the *Durham* instruction so as to make it similar to the more generally known *M'Naghten* rule with its emphasis on cognition.

If we turn for a moment to an experiment that was conducted with a civil case, we find the following interesting phenomenon. The recorded trial was an automobile negligence action in which a passenger in the struck car was suing the driver of the other car. Three versions of the trial were recorded. In *version A*, the jury heard that the defendant had no insurance. In *version B*, when the defendant stated that his insurance agent instructed him to return to the scene of the accident, the defendant's attorney called for a mistrial. The judge refused to grant a mistrial but instructed the jury to disregard the defendant's mention of insurance. In *version C*, the defendant made the same reference to insurance, but the jury received no instruction to disregard it.

Did the jury abide by the court's instructions to disregard the information they heard about the defendant's insurance? If we examine the figures shown in Table 2 it is clear that the jurors make noticeably fewer refer-

**Table 2—Insurance Mentions[a] by Treatment and Implication for Award**

| | IMPLICATIONS OF INSURANCE MENTION | | | | |
|---|---|---|---|---|---|
| Defendant's Insurance Status | Raise | Neutral | Lower | Total | Per Cent Neutral |
| A. No Insurance | 41 | 51 | 27 | 119 | 43 |
| B. Insurance but Instruction to Disregard | 7 | 25 | 4 | 36 | 69 |
| C. Insurance and No Instruction to Disregard | 28 | 24 | 9 | 61 | 39 |
| Total | 76 | 100 | 40 | 216 | 46 |

[a] An insurance mention is one consecutive burst of speech on the part of a single participant; these mentions are recorded and then classified according to their tendency to raise, lower, or have no effect upon the award.

ences to the defendant's insurance status when they are instructed to disregard it, and those references that are made are much more likely to be neutral in their implications for verdicts. In Table 2A we compare the verdicts with the version of the trial that the jury heard. Even though the

**Table 2A—Defendants' Insurance Status vs. Group Verdicts**

| Defendant's Insurance Status | Group Verdicts[a] (mean value) |
|---|---|
| (A) No Insurance | $33,000 |
| (B) Insurance, but instruction to disregard | $46,000 |
| (C) Insurance, and no instruction to disregard | $37,000 |

[a] In each version, there were ten juries.

jurors made fewer references to insurance they awarded $46,000 to the plaintiff in Version B and only $37,000 and $33,000 in Versions A and C.

# Trial by Jury: A Critical Assessment

Did the jury abide by the judge's instructions to disregard the defendant's insurance status? If we looked only at the number of explicit references that were made during the deliberations, it would seem that they did. But, when we compared the verdicts that the juries reported in Versions A, B and C, they suggest that the judge's statement to disregard had the effect of emphasizing the defendant's insurance status.

## C. HOW DOES THE JURY EVALUATE EXPERT PSYCHIATRIC TESTIMONY?

For almost as long as there has been a jury system, courts have called experts to advise them on matters not generally known to the average person. At first, the experts served as technical assistants to the court rather than as witnesses. The judge summoned experts to inform him about technical matters; and he then decided whether or not to pass the information to the jury. By the middle of the 17th century, the practice of the court-appointed expert reporting to the judge was changed to the present system. The court then, as it does today, instructed the jury along these lines:

You are not bound as jurors to accept the testimony of expert witnesses. You should certainly consider carefully the qualifications of the witnesses, their experience, their observations of the defendant and all the factors they told you in their lengthy testimony. Then evaluate their testimony, with full recognition of the fact that while you shouldn't arbitrarily disregard the testimony of any witness, yet, if you are satisfied that you don't accept the testimony of expert witnesses, you are not bound to do so.

Expert witnesses are privileged to give opinions as well as facts. In these opinions they are freer than lay witnesses to draw upon ideas that are more abstract than the specific circumstances of a given trial. Many critics claim that the expert's testimony is utterly lost upon the average jury.

Our observations of jurors' reactions to expert testimony are based only on psychiatric testimony in criminal cases.[18] We see no reason, however, why our conclusions should not generalize. We did not collect quantitative data on the amount of time the jurors spent discussing expert testimony. But our observations impress us that they considered it heavily. Furthermore, over 75 per cent of the jurors reported in a questionnaire following the trial that they considered expert testimony very important.[19] But, the expert's testimony is not crucial in determining verdicts. How do we explain this rejection at the verdict level if we discount such factors as ignorance, confusion and bias on the part of the jury?

We think that jurors take very seriously the distinction that the court makes between the function of a witness, even an expert witness, and the function and responsibility of the jury. But the jurors recognize that the responsibility for the final decision rests with them. They understand that they are free to accept or reject, in part or in full, the testimony of any witness. Many jurors are willing to grant the psychiatric expertise and general learnedness of the psychiatrists' testimonies but they do not feel that they are obliged to accept their testimony as directives for their own actions. Some jurors regard psychiatrists as special pleaders who advocate policies that are generally not practical for adoption by the courts.

A finding of insanity in a criminal trial is not a medical determination. Under the traditional *M'Naghten* rule the court instructs the jury that not every mental aberration or defect excuses the defendant from responsibility. Even in the more recent and widely acclaimed (especially in psychiatric circles) *Durham* rule, the jury is instructed:

If you believe the defendant was suffering from a diseased or defective mental condition when he committed the act but believe beyond a reasonable doubt that the act was *not* the product or result of such mental abnormality, you may find the defendant *guilty*.

In deciding whether or not to exempt the defendant from responsibility, one factor which the jury should (but is not bound to) consider is the psychiatrist's opinion of the defendant's mental condition at the time of the crime. But the jury acts within the tradition of the court when it behaves as if the assessment of responsibility is determined by moral and social standards.

In our opinion this attitude on the part of the jury is well illustrated by the jurors' responses to one of the items on the post-trial questionnaire.

Which to you is the best way of deciding what should be done with a person who has committed a crime and pleads that he is insane?
    The jurors were given the following choices:
        —He should be tried before a jury just like anyone else.
        —He should be turned over by the court to psychiatrists and they should determine what is to be done with him.
        —He should be tried before a judge.

In each case, only about 5 per cent voted for a judge. In the housebreaking case, 65 per cent of the jurors indicated that they believed psychiatrists should decide criminal cases involving a plea of insanity. In the incest case, only 33 per cent of the jurors were willing to delegate authority to the psychiatrists.[20] These findings suggest to us that for relatively minor crimes, and in cases in which there is clear evidence of mental illness, jurors are more willing to allow the medical experts to make the final disposition.

But, for more heinous crimes, acts that threaten the basic moral order of society, and/or with an equivocal medical diagnosis, the jury is not nearly as willing to be relieved of its traditional responsibility.

To summarize: jurors seem to listen attentively and with considerable understanding to the testimony of the expert witnesses. In arriving at their verdicts, however, they generally choose not to allow the opinions of experts to determine the decision which the court has placed in their hands.

### E. IS THE JURY PREJUDICED BY LACK OF INFORMATION ABOUT DISPOSITION OF THE DEFENDANT?

In many jurisdictions, in plea of insanity cases, the jury is given no information about the disposition of the defendant if it should find him not guilty by reason of insanity. Many lawyers believe that jurors assume the defendant will go free. They argue that this lack of information interferes with the defendant's right to acquittal. They reason that the jury could not tolerate a decision that would set free a man who had committed, albeit unknowingly, an act that violated the legal and moral code of the community; and who might repeat the act.

In point of fact, in almost all jurisdictions, the defendant is committed to a mental institution for some period of time. Some members of the judiciary have recommended that before beginning to deliberate the jury be informed that if the defendant is found not guilty by reason of insanity, he will be committed until the medical authorities authorize his release.[21] This information, they believe, would increase the likelihood of the jury returning a verdict of not guilty by reason of insanity.

A few years ago, we ran an experiment in which half the juries were given commitment information by the judge and half were not. The distribution of verdicts was almost identical in the two sets of juries, as shown in Table 3.

#### Table 3—Commitment Information by Jury Verdicts

| Jury Verdicts | COMMITMENT INFORMATION | |
| --- | --- | --- |
| | Present | Absent |
| Not Guilty by Reason of Insanity | 9 | 8 |
| Guilty | 2 | 3 |
| Hung | 4 | 4 |
| Total | 15 | 15 |

From listening to the deliberations we also know that the juries that received *no* commitment information discussed possible alternatives and decided that the court would not allow such a person to be released. On the post-trial questionnaire more than 90 per cent of the jurors in both treatments stated that they believed that a defendant acquitted on grounds of insanity would be kept in custody until medical authorities authorized his release.

## Concluding Remarks

We have suggested in this paper that when a group of laymen of diverse backgrounds are brought together as a jury, they function and arrive at verdicts in a manner unexpected by many persons. We think that the ritual of the law, the solemnity of the court, and the dignity of the bench have a profound effect on a group of laymen who become collaborators in the mysterious and awesome process of justice.

The jurors manifest a new-found ability to discuss matters that they would probably find extremely embarrassing in almost any other social context. The intimate details that must be retold in an incest case are not topics that a group of persons are likely to discuss during an evening with friends; or at least, not in a clinical manner. Yet, within the context of the courtroom, a group of strangers, men and women together, discuss rape, incest, homosexuality as objectively as they might consider an automobile negligence action or a contract dispute. We believe that this occurs because the law imposes a universalistic and impersonal set of expectations which the jurors internalize, even within as short a period of time as their first trial.

Authors and actors dramatize a jury of a group of twelve angry, vengeful citizens seeking to punish the accused for the misconduct that they repress in themselves. This picture gains little documentation from our study. A British jurist wrote some 70 years ago:

I think it is highly desirable that criminals should be hated, that the punishment inflicted upon them should be so contrived as to give expression to that hatred and to justify it as far as the public provision of means for expressing and gratifying a healthy natural sentiment can justify and encourage.[22]

We doubt that juries often follow his recommendation. This is not to say that emotions find no expression in the jury room, that feelings of disgust, anger, annoyance and a desire to punish are all checked at the door, and that the jurors proceed with their deliberations, as a computer might, to find the most efficient solution. Our data suggest that these feelings become socialized. They are redefined so as to be functionally responsive to the expectations of the judicial system and of popular sentiments.

# Trial by Jury: A Critical Assessment

Jurors develop a sense of collective responsibility. They think of themselves as representatives of the public; and it is in this role that they are concerned about reaching a verdict that is in accordance with the rule of law and with their understanding of public sentiment. Jurors do not see themselves as individuals deciding private issues. They assume the role of statesmen, and in the performance of that role, seek to discharge a dual responsibility: toward the constituency that selected them and toward the law that they are pledged to uphold.

## NOTES

1. Many states have introduced similar provisions in their constitutions.

2. Extensive bibliographies of jury materials have been collected by Hill, *Selected List of Materials on Juries,* 4 Record of the Bar Association of N.Y. 139 (1949); Johnsen, *The Jury System,* 5 Reference Shelf No. 6 (1928), 11 *University of Cincinnati Law Review,* 119 (1937); Hunter, "Law in the Jury Room," 2, *Ohio State Law Journal,* 1 (1935).

3. A few of the devices that have been introduced are the special verdict, the polling of the jury on the process of reaching the verdict, either before or after its technical rendition and the taking of notes by the jurors.

4. Glasser v. United States, 315 U.S. 85, 86.

5. See Dale Broeder, "The Functions of the Jury," 21 *University of Chicago Law Review* (Spring 1954), p. 390.

6. As a case in point, Mr. Broeder cites the Illinois exemption statute which he claims is typical. Under that statute, the following persons are exempt from serving as jurors: The Governor, Lieutenant Governor, Secretary of State, Auditor of Public Account, Treasurer, Superintendent of Public Instruction, Attorney General, members of the General Assembly, all judges, all clerks . . . sheriffs, coroners, postmasters, mail carriers, practicing attorneys, all officers of the United States, officiating ministers of the Gospel, school teachers, practicing physicians, registered pharmacists, ferrymen, majors, policemen, members of the Fire Department, embalmers, undertakers and funeral directors . . . and all persons actively employed upon the editorial or mechanical staffs and departments of any newspaper. . . . [and] all legally qualified veterinarians. *Ill. Rev. State.* (1953), c.78, 4.

7. From Jerome Frank, *Courts on Trial,* Princeton: Princeton University Press, 1950, p. 124.

8. *Ibid.,* p. 124.

9. The Jury Project is under the direction of Harry Kalven, Jr., Professor of Law, University of Chicago. Professor Fred L. Strodtbeck of the Sociology Department was primarily responsible for the experimental jury studies, the data on which this paper is largely based. The ideas discussed in this paper are largely on the materials accessible from the author's own research on the project which will appear in book form under the title, *The Jury and the Plea of Insanity.* Professors Kalven and Strodtbeck are presently working on a volume in which many of the issues raised in this article will be treated in greater detail. In addition, substantive volumes by other members of the project will be forthcoming.

10. The following is a list of some of the articles that have been published on

these matters by persons associated with the Jury Project: Strodtbeck and Mann, "Sex Role Differentiation in Jury Deliberation," *Sociometry*, 19, pp. 1–11 (1956); Strodtbeck, James & Hawkins, "Social Status in Jury Deliberations," *American Sociological Review*, 22 (1957), pp. 713–719; James, "Status and Competence of Jurors," *American Journal of Sociology*, 64 (1959), pp. 563–670; Kalven, "The Jury, The Law and Personal Awards," 19 *Ohio State Law Journal*, 19 (1957); James, "Jurors' Assessment of Criminal Responsibility," *Social Problems*, 7 (1959), pp. 58–69; Zeisel, Kalven and Bucholz, *Delay in the Court*, Boston: Little, Brown and Co., (1959).

11. The housebreaking case was based on the celebrated test case *United States v. Monte Durham* heard in the District and Circuit Courts of the District of Columbia in 1954.

12. A brief summary of the experimental procedure appears below.

(1) A transcript is obtained of an actual case that has been decided by the courts. The transcript is edited and condensed from a trial that lasts, generally, two or three days, to one that can be heard in about 60 to 90 minutes. The experimental transcript contains the lawyers' opening and closing statements and the judge's instructions to the jury; as well as the testimony of all the witnesses.

(2) The "experimental" trial is then recorded, with the parts of the attorneys, witnesses, principals in the case, and the judge, usually performed by faculty members at the Law School of the University of Chicago.

(3) With the co-operation of local bar associations and presiding judges in three jurisdictions, Chicago, St. Louis and Minneapolis, subjects for the experiment are drawn by lot from the local jury pools. The jurors are *assigned* to these recorded trials by the court. A judge explains their duties and the court's interest in this comprehensive study of the judiciary. He also tells them that although their verdicts on the case can have no immediate practical consequences, the judges of this court are very interested in the results of the study. A juror's service on the recorded trials is not voluntary; it is part of his regular period of jury duty.

(4) Before listening to the trial, each juror fills out a questionnaire which is comparable to a trial lawyer's extensive *voir dire*, or pre-trial examination of prospective jurors. There are questions about the juror's age, occupation, marital status, ethnicity, religion, income, etc., and a series of general attitude items.

(5) The jurors then listen to the recorded trial until it is time for lunch. Before leaving the court the jurors are instructed not to discuss the case among themselves. When the jurors report back to the jury room the trial continues.

(6) After the trial, but before the deliberations, each juror is asked to fill out a brief questionnaire in which he is asked to state how he would decide the case at this time.

(7) The jury is ready to deliberate. It has been told before the trial began that its deliberations will be recorded. Everyone (the bailiff, the experimenters, etc.) leaves the jury room except the twelve jurors, who have been instructed to select one of their members as foreman.

(8) When the jury has reached a verdict, the foreman reports it to the experimenter. The jurors are then given a final questionnaire in which they are asked about their reactions to the trial and to the deliberation. Each juror is also asked if, sitting as a one-man jury, he would have found as the group did.

(9) The jury is then taken to the judge and reports its verdict. The judge thanks the jurors for their service and either dismisses them or sends them back to the jury pool.

13. Sir James Stephen wrote in 1883: "Juries care very little for generalities. In my experience they are usually reluctant to convict if they look upon the act itself as upon the whole a mad one, and to acquit if they think it was an ordinary crime." (Quoted from Henry Weihofen, *The Urge to Punish*, New York: Farrar, Straus & Cudahy, Inc., 1956, pp. 46–7.)

14. Broeder, *op. cit.*, p. 417.

15. Frank, *op. cit.*, p. 16.

16. See Table 1, based on the *Housebreaking* case.

17. In the experimental design of the two trials, an equal number of juries were exposed to the *M'Naghten* instructions and to the *Durham* instructions. The *M'Naghten* rule which was formulated in England in 1843 and adopted in the United States a few years later states:

> To establish a defense on the grounds of insanity, it must be clearly proved that, at the time of the committing of the act, the party accused was laboring under such a defect of reason, from disease of the mind, as not to know the nature and the quality of the act he was doing: or if he did know it, that he did not know he was doing what was wrong. *M'Naghten Case*, 10 Cl 8, Fin. 200, 210, 8 Eng. rep 718, 722 (H.L. 1843).

The *Durham* rule, formulated in the Circuit Court of the District of Columbia in July, 1954, states:

> If from all the evidence in the case you believe beyond a reasonable doubt that the defendant committed the crime of which he is accused in manner and form as charged in the indictment, and if you believe beyond a reasonable doubt that the accused was not suffering from a diseased or defective mental condition at the time he committed the criminal act, you may find him guilty. If you believe he was suffering from a diseased defective mental condition when he committed the act, but believe beyond a reasonable doubt that the act was not the product of such mental abnormality, you may find him guilty. If you believe he was suffering from a mental disorder at the time he committed the act and the criminal act was a product of mental abnormality, you must find the accused not guilty by reason of insanity. *Durham v. United States*, 214 F.2d 862 (D.C. Cir., 1954).

18. For a fuller discussion of jurors' reactions to expert testimony, see Rita James, "Jurors' Evaluation of Expert Psychiatric Testimony," 21 *Ohio State Law Journal* (Winter 1960).

19. In the incest trial, the defense relied wholly on the testimony of two psychiatrists. In the housebreaking case, the defense kept the two psychiatrists on the stand longer than any other witness, save the defendant himself.

20. In the housebreaking trial, the defendant was described as being psychotic; as having a long history of internments in mental institutions; and as having made several suicide attempts. In the incest case, the diagnosis was that of psychoneurosis, with no previous history of mental disorder or internment in mental institutions.

21. In recent years, many more jurisdictions have made it mandatory to provide commitment information to the jury.

22. Quoted from Weihofen, *op. cit.*, p. 137, from a statement made by the eminent British jurist of the 19th century, Sir James Stephen.

*Part IV*

*APPLIED SOCIOLOGY*

*AND*

*GENERAL SOCIOLOGY*

# 24.    Are the Aged a Minority Group?

GORDON F. STREIB

Sociologists face the perennial problem of semantics. Often their words have both a professional and an everyday meaning. This creates confusion not only in the minds of laymen but of sociologists themselves. An example of this confusion over terminology is found in the terms "aging" and "aged." By applying the concept of "minority group" to the aged in American society, sociologists have used the image-producing meaning of the term as if it were a technical term.

## The Concept, Minority Group, in Sociology

The literal meaning of minority is "the smaller number." In this sense most societies have many minority groups. In a complex society such as the United States the number of these groups is limitless. If less than 50 per cent of the population have a particular trait, that trait characterizes them as a "minority group." Less than 10 per cent of the total population are over age 65. In the statistical sense, therefore, the aged may be considered

This paper is part of a current program of research on aging and retirement conducted by the Department of Sociology and Anthropology of Cornell University. The research was initially supported by a grant from the Lilly Endowment, Inc. The work has also received financial assistance from the National Institute of Mental Health, United States Public Health Service under grant M-1196 and from a research grant of the Social Security Administration, Department of Health, Education, and Welfare, Washington, D.C. I would like to acknowledge the help of Rose K. Goldsen, Martin U. Martel, and Robin M. Williams Jr., who read a draft of the paper and made many valuable suggestions. I also want to thank Nona Glazer for her research assistance.

a minority group. If this were the only criterion, or even the principal one, we would also view as minority groups collectors of antique dolls, persons with incomes over $35,000 per year, or sociologists interested in problems of aging. This numerical or statistical approach to the aged as a minority group cannot yield analytic clarification, for it focusses attention on the frequency or incidence of a characteristic, rather than on its functional social meaning.

Sociologists define "minority group" not only in terms of frequency of characteristics, but also of the objective and subjective features of a group, and of its way of fitting into the social setting. Wirth, for example, stresses the reciprocal dominance-submission patterns between groups, the sense of identification, actual deprivation or exclusion from privileges, and frustrated expectations. In the case of the aged, the dominant group is a constantly changing one, for as people grow older, they presumably move from the dominant-young category to the old-submissive category. Wirth has defined a minority as ". . . a group of people who, because of physical or cultural characteristics, are singled out from the others in the society in which they live for differential and unequal treatment, and who therefore regard themselves as objects of collective discrimination. The existence of a minority in a society implies the existence of a corresponding dominant group with higher social status and greater privileges. Minority status carries with it the exclusion from full participation in the life of the society."[1] (It can be noted that this definition does not even mention frequency of incidence.)

Sociologists who have viewed the aged as a minority group rarely test their assumption by referring to all the elements of Wirth's definition. Breen, for example, makes a plausible case when he writes: "In many respects the aged show characteristics of a minority group. They are subject to categorical discrimination, they have relatively high visibility, and, in many parts of our society, they constitute a functioning subgroup. Stereotypes are held about the group, and individuals are judged thereby. Prejudice is not uncommon, especially in industry, where persons over age 40 are discriminated against in employment practices. Thus, the ingredients necessary to the development of minority group status are present for the aged. The characteristics commonly attributed to minority groups as a result of such categorization may be expected to develop among older persons."[2]

And yet it can be argued just as plausibly that the aged are not a group in a true sociological sense. They have little feeling of solidarity, consciousness of kind, or group spirit. Moreover, the aged do not have any distinct cultural traits, and usually do not operate as a distinct group. *In a strict sociological sense the aged are a statistical aggregate or a social category, not a genuine group.* Age is a biologically determined status of the life cycle which every member of society can expect to achieve if he lives long enough. Minority group members, on the contrary, are so defined through all stages of the life cycle. Membership is exclusive and permanent.

It has been claimed that the aged are similar to women as a minority group.[3] The work of Helen M. Hacker has been cited to support this contention, but a careful reading of her work indicates that she is cautious in drawing the analogy. Hacker writes: ". . . Few women believe themselves to be members of a minority group in the way in which some Negroes, Jews, Italians, etc., may so conceive themselves."[4] At another point, she is careful to point out: "It has been indicated that women fail to present in full force the subjective attributes commonly associated with minority groups. That is, they lack a sense of group identification and do not harbor feelings of being treated unfairly because of their sex membership."[5]

Simone de Beauvoir, denying that women constitute a minority group in society, makes similar points. Indeed, her comments on women can be neatly paraphrased: The aged are not a minority group for they have no past, no history, no religion of their own, and unlike the proletariat, they have no solidarity of work and interest. They are not herded together in the way that creates community feeling among the American Negroes, the ghetto Jews, the workers of Saint-Denis, or the factory hands of Renault. They usually live dispersed among the young, attached through residence, housework, economic conditions and social standing to other people—husbands, wives, children, friends—more to family than to other old people. If they belong to the bourgeoisie, they feel solidarity with the old of that class, not with proletarian old people; if they are white, their allegiance is to white men, not to Negro old people.[6]

## Specification of the Minority Group Concept

In considering the aged as a minority group it is useful to spell out the dimensions of the concept. We have pointed out that the everyday statistical meaning does not apply to the aged; nor does the traditional concept of minority group which emphasizes a dominant majority, because the dominant group is a constantly changing one. The present paper tests the evidence for considering the aged as a minority group. First, we specify the criteria for defining a minority group and then examine the evidence relevant to each criterion.

Let us turn to the criteria for specifying minority group characteristics.

*1.* Members of the group possess identifying characteristics with accompanying status-role expectations throughout the life cycle.

*2.* There is a prevailing sentiment that this status characteristic makes group members less deserving of respect and consideration (as Negroes, Jews, ethnic groups, etc.) This is often discernible in current stereotypes and clichés about (*a*) work performance and (*b*) appropriate activities.

*3.* Possession of the status characteristics is associated with a sense of group identity.

*a.* There is intragroup identity, or a sense of consciousness-of-kind.

*b.* There is intergroup identity in that the status provides others with an absolute criterion for group identification.

*4.* There is a readiness to organize as a political pressure group.

*5.* The possession of the status characteristic leads to differential access to power, privileges and rights.

*a.* Civil rights are sometimes denied.

*b.* Group members may not be found among the elite and influential members in the society.

*c.* There may be restrictions on political roles and activities.

*6.* Possession of the status characteristic may lead to: *a.* less economic and social security; *b.* unequal access to work; *c.* residential segregation; *d.* social isolation.

With the above criteria in mind, we shall examine a variety of empirical data to determine the degree of correspondence between the aged in the United States and the concept of minority groups.

## 1. DOES THE CHARACTERISTIC IDENTIFY ALL WHO POSSESS IT THROUGHOUT THE LIFE CYCLE?

Clearly this is not so for the aged. It would be equally justifiable to study children as a minority group. They too are a statistical minority. They possess distinct physical traits, their age defines their cultural role; they would consider themselves (if they could articulate their feelings) deprived by adults, and objects of adult prejudice and discrimination. They are a source of social conflict. Yet to analyze "the young" as a minority group would only hinder understanding their social role.

## 2. DOES THE MAJORITY GROUP HOLD STEREOTYPES AND CLICHÉS ABOUT THE AGED?

(*a*) *Work performance*—One way to test whether the aged constitute a minority group is to ascertain whether other categories of persons in the community think they deserve less respect and privilege than others. Let us begin with attitudes to their work. Do people relate the fact of age (like the fact of race) to less adequate work performance?

Recently, Breen and his associates at Purdue conducted an interview study of attitudes and opinions about older persons. They chose a random sample of over 700 persons from age 20 to 80 in a county in Indiana. These investigators report that all age categories are more likely to say that the old are better workers than younger persons. However, the Purdue investigators found some differences of attitude between the two groups. For example, there is a tendency for older persons to maintain that the old are better workers than the young. But younger persons in the study were more likely to say that there are only individual differences in the quantity and quality of work produced by various age groups. Perhaps what is of greatest interest, when we consider the aged as a minority group, is that only 7 per cent of the respondents from age 20 to 40 display any negative attitude toward older workers. This Indiana study shows clearly that older workers are not held in low esteem[7] by younger age categories in the community.[8]

On the other hand, in an Iowa study of self-appraisal of working ability, an overwhelming majority of men sixty and over stated that they could not do their regular work as well as when they were in their 30's and 40's.[9] Unfortunately, the investigators limited their questioning on this point to men who had already changed from their regular job to some other kind of employment. Thus, a crucial category of employed older persons was excluded.

Studies conducted at the University of Illinois in which supervisors rated the effectiveness of older workers suggest a need to reappraise the effectiveness of older workers in a variety of jobs. The general conclusion, based upon studies of 3,000 workers, is that they are useful and productive workers. However, caution is required in interpreting the findings, and the author's conclusions are instructive: "While the findings of this study are highly favorable to older personnel we must avoid the tendency to infer more than is actually indicated. There is a suggestion, for example, that older people tend to become more efficient by virtue of their age alone. This, of course, is not true because it fails to consider that the older personnel in this survey represent a selective group in several senses: only those with motivation have continued to work, only those with the best apparent capabilities were selected for employment, and only the fittest have survived dismissal."[10]

Thus, when we examine the evidence on work performance we find varying judgments by younger workers, older workers, and by supervisors. As might be expected, persons in each of these categories view work performance from different perspectives; but the over-all rating tends to be favorable.

(b) *Appropriate activities*—The Purdue study offers additional evidence that younger people do not hold more stereotyped notions about appropriate activities for the old than the old themselves. Respondents were asked to indicate which social activities they thought "improper or unfitting" for older persons (if the respondent was over 60, the interviewers were instructed to insert an age decade ten years older than that of the respondent). While all age groups agree that "Sedentary-Social" activities are appropriate for persons over 65, persons in the younger age categories were *more likely* to suggest activities for older persons which are socially more vigorous than the older respondents believed appropriate for their age group.[11]

### 3. GROUP IDENTITY

(a) *Self-Image*—Another important way to distinguish a minority group is the group's own sense of identification. To what extent do the aged view themselves as a separate and distinct group possessing its own sociological identity?

Do older persons look upon themselves as elderly, middle aged, or old? In four different surveys of persons over sixty years of age, conducted over a period of years at Cornell University, we found that the majority of persons considered themselves to be "middle-aged." Only among those over 65 is there any noticeable tendency to identify themselves as "old" or "elderly." The crucial age break is somewhere between 65 and 70. We found, for example, that among a large population of persons approximately 64 years old, and gainfully employed, about two-thirds classified themselves as "middle-aged" and another 20 per cent as "late middle-aged."[12] Only 10 per cent identified themselves as elderly, and about 3 per cent as old. These survey data tend to support the claim that older persons do not think of themselves as members of an "old" or "elderly" subgroup.

(b) *Absolute criteria for group identification employed by others*—The Indiana study conducted by the Purdue group reports that people in all age categories identify "middle age" and "old age" not by an absolute criterion, but by a relative one. Most respondents said, "It depends upon the individual."[13]

Researchers have had difficulty establishing absolute criteria for identifying the aged as a group. Some investigators have chosen sixty as the beginning of old age and others sixty-five, because it is a common retirement age. The question is this: does chronological age determine when a person is old? Cumming and Henry, for example, state, "The most important criterion was age. . . . Thus, in order to follow a panel, people whose youngest members were entering middle age and whose oldest were entering old age, we decided upon a twenty-year range, from fifty to seventy."[14] It is pertinent to add that these same investigators found it necessary to undertake a special analysis of "The Very Old," those persons in their eighties whom the researchers considered to be members of "a biological, and possibly psychological, elite."[15]

#### 4. READINESS TO ORGANIZE AS AN IDENTIFIABLE PRESSURE GROUP

Among minority groups (e.g., Negroes, Puerto Ricans) in American society, this internal sense of identity, or self image, reinforced by the external definition of separateness that society applies to the subgroup, is often translated into attempts at political action as a pressure group.

Since the time of the Townsend Movement, there have been appeals to the aged to act as a cohesive pressure group. A study of the California Institute of Social Welfare (the McLain movement) reveals how the weak sense of group identity among the aged inhibits such efforts.[16]

In recent years, the McLain movement has been one of the most effective in organizing older persons. The most radical proposal of the McLain organization was to eliminate the means test in the Old Age Assistance Law. McLain and his organization purported to advance the interest of approximately 273,000 Californians over 65 who were recipients of Old Age Assistance. These people constituted 30 per cent of those 65 and over. In 1952, about 23 per cent of the persons on OAA were on the membership roster of the California Institute of Social Welfare. At the peak of their activity, the membership of the CISW constituted about 7 per cent of the population over age 65 in the state of California.

McLain achieved his greatest political success in 1948 when the voters of the state passed a proposition changing the administration of the Old Age Assistance law and raising the amount of money for the recipients. The victory was due to a slim majority of 1 per cent of the total vote cast. The following year in a special election the proposition was repealed; the margin of loss in this second election was 13 per cent of the total vote. Although the political climate of California is somewhat idiosyncratic, it is relevant to note that even at the peak of the success of the McLain movement this group never constituted a cohesive political unit. This was due mainly to the lack of group identification among the aged. Pinner and his associates stress this point in their analysis of the organization. They report that pensioners hesitated to identify themselves as aged or pensioners, and preferred to be called "citizens." Moreover, open-ended interviews of a subgroup of McLain followers revealed no evidence of "we-feeling" (sense of group identification).

A large majority of the respondents in the survey favored organizations to protect the needs and "rights" of the aged because they cannot take care of themselves. *But a small number (12 per cent) thought the aged should defend themselves against a hostile world.* Pinner and his associates report that the older persons felt that the need for a group stemmed from their bewilderment about the problems of dependency. "In their view, organizations will either do for them what they cannot do for themselves, or enable them to manage their own affairs more actively. *It is not identification with older persons, or a general desire for political action that impels participation in organizations.*"[17]

That the aged lack a sense of identification as a minority group is also illustrated in the California study. Questions were designed to determine who the pensioners thought should be included in the organization. Members of the Institute are more likely than nonmembers to express a preference for mixed groups.[18] The authors emphasize that older persons regard organizations like the McLain Institute as "groups *useful to* the aged, not as groups *of* the aged."[19]

### 5. DIFFERENTIAL ACCESS TO POWER, PRIVILEGES AND RIGHTS

(a) *Civil rights*—Are the property rights of the aged restricted? No. Are the aged denied equal protection of the law? No. Are they deprived of suffrage? No. Excluded from public office? No. If these people are deprived of such rights, it is because they are members of ethnic, racial, or religious minorities, not because they are old.

Readiness to organize as an identifiable pressure group is related to the realization that their group characteristic denies them equal access to power, privileges, and rights.[20] The Pinner study indicates that the aged supported the McLain movement more because of their bewilderment about the privileges due them than because of their interest in a political demand for privileges denied them.

There is no evidence that older people are denied civil rights because of their age. Indeed, the evidence suggests that the aged are more likely to exercise their right to vote than younger people.[21] Schmidhauser has made an interesting analysis of voting patterns in Iowa. He found in that state, as in a number of others, that the rural areas have a larger proportion of representatives in the state legislature than their numbers warrant. "Because they constitute so great a proportion of the population of the over-represented rural areas, the aged have the strategic political advantage of being concentrated where their numbers are most effective in state legislative election."[22] Moreover, since the long-range national trend is for the aged to settle in rural areas, they will continue to have a disproportionate voice in state legislative bodies.

(b) *Elites and influentials*—Possession of the group characteristics "justifies" denial of equal access to economic, social, and political opportunities to minority groups. They are, therefore, over-represented among the less-privileged, and under-represented among the elites. Studies of local elite systems suggest that the aged are over-represented among elites. In Hunter's study of Regional City, a financial and industrial city of 500,000 population in the Southeast, the men of power in the community tend to be the wealthy businessmen and bankers.[23] This seems to hold for other communities which have been studied. Although the top power group in Regional City is divided into the older and younger group, the *older* group ultimately exercises the most influence in the community. As Hunter says, "In most instances decision-making tended to be channeled through the older men at some point in the process of formulation . . ."[24] Because the chief power wielders are older persons in Regional City, I suspect that power policies there and elsewhere, are dictated by the economic interests of the power groups. *Older men may exercise a pivotal function in decision-making even though they do not operate as a gerontocracy.*[25]

Although we find greater complexities in the national power structure than in the local scene, the evidence suggests that older persons exercise considerable influence.[26] Harvey Lehman conducted an exhaustive study of the relation of age to achievement and leadership.[27] His work indicates that the elderly acquire positions of leadership more frequently in contemporary society than was true in earlier periods in our history. He offers evidence that U.S. Senators and Representatives, U.S. Supreme Court Justices, Secretaries of State, heads of federal bureaus and services tend to be older when one compares periods like 1900–1940 and 1789–1874. Donald Matthews reaches a similar conclusion in his study of political decision-makers.[28] It was an old man—G. Stanley Hall—the eminent psychologist and retired president of Clark University, who at age 75 noted in his book, *Senescence: The Last Half of Life:* "Perhaps the world is a little too much in the hands of people who are a little too old, but this is being rapidly remedied."[29] Hall made this provocative assertion in 1923, but the ensuing years have not borne out his prediction.[30]

(c) *The political role of the aged*—The political role of the aged is related in a complex manner to many other factors. The aged, for example, have a high sense of political duty as is evidenced by their voting behavior, but other age groups rate higher in their belief that individual political action can affect the political process. On the other hand, the investigators who conducted a detailed study of voting behavior and political processes in one urban community (Elmira, New York), reported that younger adults tended to show respect for the political opinions of their elders.[31] Moreover, the authors of this study stated that over a tenth of the workers of both major parties were from the retired or widowed categories.[32]

Weighing the various elements in the political process, it appears that the aged are not viewed as a minority group in political affairs nor do they act as one. Schmidhauser summarized his review of the literature by saying: "Virtually all of the foregoing discussions of the growing population proportions of older people—their strategic location for state legislative politics in certain states, their high voting record in presidential elections and probable high participation record in non-presidential general and primary elections, their higher motivation toward political participation, their possible roles as public affairs leaders—all these underscore the real as well as potential influence oldsters have in American politics."[33]

### 6. DEPRIVATION

(a) *Economic and social security*—Many of the aged, like many of the minority groups, are underprivileged. This is the principal reason for the minority group analogy. Consider health, for example: The aged are sicker, spend more time in hospitals, and are less likely to recover from chronic illnesses than younger persons. But the fact of neediness does not warrant viewing the aged as a minority group. Nor does focussing attention on providing for their medical and health needs as if they were a homogeneously sick group.[34] Shanas has pointed out, "The current public discussion of the health needs of the older people, which tends to classify all persons 65 and over as a homogeneous group, has obscured rather than clarified the differing requirements for medical care of various groups of the aged."[35]

There are many aged people who are economically underprivileged. But these people, for the most part have been underprivileged throughout their life cycle. The neediness of the aged is concentrated among Negroes, the lower educated persons, the foreign-born, etc.—in short, the groups who generally suffer the greatest economic pressures. Old age compounds these pressures for them. One of the major subgroups of the aged whose economic security is lowest, is the widowed female over 75 years of age.[36] Many of the aged are underprivileged in several ways and suffer deprivations. But that is not the problem for this paper. Age, as a status characteristic, compounds multiple deprivations for many groups, including minority groups. But a "deprived group" is not synonymous with a "minority group."[37]

Economists who study the economic status of the aged tend to concentrate on the objective or financial aspects of the problem. Sociologists have looked at the economic needs of the aged, not only in objective terms, but also in the subjective terms of the older persons themselves. In the Iowa survey, for example, the investigators asked questions about satisfaction with standard of living and adequacy of income. The results indicate that most of the respondents were reluctant to complain about their economic situation. The authors conclude: "From the various statements made by the interviewees concerning income adequacy, it appears that more than a third were well-satisfied financially, perhaps another 50 to 60 per cent saw their position as adequate, and one out of ten was seriously dissatisfied. Considering the income levels reported by the survey population, (annual average of $2,400 for the men and $1,500 for the women), it appears that a good many were fairly well-adjusted to living on incomes that would rate very low by the standards of younger American adults."[38]

(b) *Equal access to jobs*—Workers are often denied jobs solely because of their advancing age. Here is the first genuine equivalent between "the aged" and other minority groups. Indeed, evidence that such practices are widespread is found in the laws in seven states which forbid discrimination in employment on the basis of age.[39]

Yet even here the analogy breaks down. The age range covered in these laws varies from state to state, but, in general, they refer to persons of 40 to 65.[40] Thus it is the rights of the middle-aged, and not of the old, that are being legally protected against discriminatory practices.[41] If this criterion justifies the minority group concept, it is the middle-aged, not the old, who constitute the minority group.

(c) *Residential segregation*—Does being aged result in residential segregation as it does sometimes for ethnic and racial minorities? One might cite the segregation of the ages in institutions; but fewer than 5 per cent of older persons are in institutions. Many older persons live alone, but they are not ghettoized. Most surveys have found, moreover, that older persons would rather live by themselves than with children or other relatives.[42] This kind of residential segregation is clearly of a different type than the kind imposed upon Negroes, Puerto Ricans, and other ethnic minorities.

(d) *Social isolation*—Even if advanced age does not in fact lead to spatial segregation, one might argue that it results in segregation in a psychological sense: that the aged are not necessarily ecologically isolated, but are socially isolated from personal and community contacts.

This claim, however, would be difficult to support. Studies both in the United States and in Great Britain have shown that the aged have a high degree of social contact with their children and other relatives.[43] The data from the Iowa survey are illustrative. The investigators report, for example, that less than ten per cent of the men and less than five per cent of the women say, "I wish my family would pay more attention to me." Moreover, almost forty per cent of both sexes report that they have more friends now than ever before.[44]

Writers who argue that the aged are a minority group claim that the old are lonely, isolated, unhappy people.[45] Our point is not to deny that there are isolated older persons; (indeed it is quite likely that the proportion of the lonely and unhappy is greatest among the old: but it does not follow that because some aged face these social circumstances, they therefore constitute a minority group. In a study of two small upstate New York communities, Taietz and Larsen found that their data do not support the notion that the aged are less integrated in the community than other age categories. The older heads of households participated less in employment activities because some were retired. However, in three general areas used to index community integration (behavioral factors, attitudes, and situational) the aged did not display the characteristics of a minority group.[46]

A report on an urban area (Kansas City) by Havighurst, which employed different indices of community integration, offers evidence which supports the findings of the New York study. He found that for men "role performance goes down consistently but slightly with age . . ." and for women he found that "there is no relationship between age and role performance."[47] The analysis of what Havighurst defined as role patterns (role performance scores characteristic of eight or more persons in the study) showed little or no relationship to age. Another study conducted in an urban setting (San Francisco) offers corroboration that age is a less important variable than economic level as a correlate of community integration and participation in formal associations. Bell and Force found: "In the high economic status neighborhoods the percentage of frequent attenders increases with increasing age, but in the low economic status neighborhoods no such trend exists."[48]

## The Concept of "Disengagement" of the Aged

We might ask whether the aged are denied access to educational opportunities or admission to voluntary clubs and associations. The evidence indicates that the aged use both types of facilities infrequently. But this is not due to denial of access[49] but rather, to older people's definition of such activities as inappropriate or undesirable. (Older people say that they think members of their families and friends would consider them unusual if, for example, they return to school.[50]

The data on these points lend more support to the concept of disengagement as a social psychological accompaniment of advancing age than to the concept of the aged as a minority group.[51]

In brief, the idea of disengagement suggests that the aged individual may be described "as participating with others in his social systems in a process of mutual withdrawal, rather than being deserted by others in the structure."[52] Usually, the disengagement process begins in the sixth decade of life and is marked by a reduction in interaction. This results in a more self-centered style of behavior among the aged who are ambulatory. The authors of the theory of disengagement have called it a tentative theory.[53] However it suggests new insights and a reasonable explanation for some kinds of behavior and interactions, previously represented as minority group reactions. The theory suggests, for example, that what some writers have described as stereotyping of the old by the young and social isolation of the old may result from individual and societal withdrawal and changes in the expectations of both young and old.

## Summary

In summary, viewing the aged as a minority group does not clarify their social role in our society. The aged do not share a distinct and separate culture; membership in the group defined as "aged" is not exclusive and permanent, but awaits all members of our society who live long enough. As a result, age is a less distinguishing group characteristic than others such as sex, occupation, social class, and the like. True, many aged persons possess distinctive physical characteristics. But even here there is a broad spectrum, and these "stigmata" do not normally justify differential and discriminatory treatment by others. The aged have little feeling of identification with their age group: they have a low degree of collective consciousness; hostility towards a depriving out-group is exceptional. The aged are not organized to advance their own interests and are not particularly attracted to such organizations. Nor are they systematically deprived of power and privileges. They are not herded in ghettos, deprived of civil rights, excluded from public facilities, or from jobs they are qualified to perform. That they are often underprivileged economically and have more frequent health problems is more the result of handicaps that often accompany aging, than of social organization or group structure.

From the standpoint of conceptual clarity and empirical fact, the notion of the aged as a minority group does not increase understanding. It obscures it.

## NOTES

1. Louis Wirth, "The Problem of Minority Groups," in Ralph Linton, editor, *The Science of Man in the World Crisis,* New York: Columbia University Press, 1945, p. 347.

2. Leonard Z. Breen, "The Aging Individual," in Clark Tibbitts, editor, *Handbook of Social Gerontology,* Chicago: The University of Chicago Press, 1960, p. 157. Barron was among the first to use the term in this manner. See Milton L. Barron, "Minority Group Characteristics of the Aged in American Society," *Journal of Gerontology,* 8 (October, 1953), pp. 477–482, and reprinted as chapter 3 in *The Aging American,* New York: Thomas Y. Crowell, 1961, pp. 55–68. See also Milton L. Barron, "Attacking Prejudices Against the Aged," in *Growing With the Years,* New York State Legislative Committee on Problems of Aging, Legislative Document No. 32, 1954, pp. 56–8.

3. From the statistical standpoint, women are, of course, *not* a minority group.

4. Helen Mayer Hacker, "Women as a Minority Group," *Social Forces,* 30 (October 1951), p. 61. Myrdal preceded Hacker in discussing women as a minority group. In Appendix 5, "A Parallel to the Negro Problem," he writes, "In every society there are at least two groups of people, besides the Negroes, who are characterized by high social visibility expressed in physical appearance, dress, and patterns of behavior, and who have been 'suppressed.' We refer to women and children." Gunnar Myrdal, *An American Dilemma,* New York: Harper and Bros., 1944, vol. 2, p. 1073. Quoted from p. 1073.

5. Hacker, *op. cit.,* p. 62. The low degree of group identification by women is not to be confused with feelings of personal and sexual identity as women.

6. Adapted from Simone de Beauvoir, *The Second Sex,* p. xix.

7. That older workers are not held in lower esteem should not be confused with the unemployment of many older persons. About one man in five between ages 60 to 64 was not working according to a study conducted by the National Opinion Research Center; a random sample of all older persons not in institutions was

# Are the Aged a Minority Group?

interviewed. The same survey reports that among men 65 and over about six in every ten were not in the labor force (*i.e.*, retired). This cannot, however, be considered evidence of "under-employment" and discrimination without determining how many of these older people withdrew voluntarily from the labor force, or were retired because of a realistic handicap. There is evidence that *employers* do discriminate against older workers. See: Fred Slavick and Seymour L. Wolfbein, "The Evolving Work-Life Pattern," in *Handbook of Social Gerontology* edited by Clark Tibbitts, Chicago: The University of Chicago Press, 1960, pp. 306–10. Ethel Shanas, *Meeting Medical Care Costs Among the Aging,* Research Series No. 17, New York: Health Information Foundation, 1960, pp. 1–3. Shanas reports that her findings are comparable to those of the Census Bureau. The findings on the employment or lack of employment of older persons should also not be confused with the sources of income of older persons. We note, for example, a report which lumps all older persons together and shows that employment constitutes a source of income for only 24 per cent of all persons over age 65. See "Health and Economic Conditions of the American Aged," Committee Print of the Special Committee of Aging, United States Senate, 87th Congress, 1st Session, Washington: U.S. Government Printing Office, 1961, p. 14. In terms of employment and income, a substantial number of older persons are deprived, but this does not mean that they constitute a minority group.

8. Leonard Z. Breen et al., *The Adult Years,* Lafayette, Indiana: Department of Sociology, Purdue University, 1961, p. J15.

9. Martin U. Martel and W. W. Morris, *Life After Sixty in Iowa.* Institute of Gerontology, State University of Iowa, 1961, pp. 33–4.

10. Robert L. Peterson, "The Effectiveness of Older Office and Managerial Personnel," *Business Management Aids* (BMA 10) College of Commerce and Business Administration, University of Illinois, (no date) p. 8. See also Robert L. Peterson, "3,000 Older Workers and Their Job Effectiveness," *Business Management Aids* (BMA 15). Robert L. Peterson, "The Effectiveness of Older Personnel in Retailing," University of Illinois Bulletin, Vol. 50, No. 67 (May, 1953). Robert L. Peterson, "The Effectiveness of Older Personnel in Industry," University of Illinois Bulletin, Vol. 52, No. 3 (August, 1954).

11. Breen, *et al., op. cit.,* p. E6.

12. The tendency to rate oneself or one's group or social category in a more favorable manner has been observed in other contexts. When a person ranks his own or a similar occupation, his own evaluation is always considerably *higher* than the average appraisal of the position. See "Jobs and Occupations: A Popular Evaluation," National Opinion Research Center, in Reinhard Bendix and Seymour M. Lipset, editors, *Class, Status and Power,* Glencoe, Ill.: The Free Press, 1953, p. 415. See also the work of Landsberger and Hulin in which they report that labor leaders are more likely to rate officials higher than members. Henry A. Landsberger and Charles L. Hulin, "A Problem for Union Democracy: Officers' Attitudes Toward Union Members," *Industrial and Labor Relations Review,* 14 (April, 1961), pp. 419–31.

13. Breen, *et al., op. cit.,* p. D7. Tuckman and Lorge have reported that when one examines the responses by age category, there is a slight tendency for older persons to specify the beginning of old age at a higher age than younger persons. See Jacob Tuckman and Irving Lorge, "When Does Old Age Begin and a Worker Become Old?", *Journal of Gerontology,* 8 (October, 1953), pp. 483–488.

14. Elaine Cumming and William Henry, *Growing Old: The Process of Disengagement*, New York: Basic Books, Inc., 1961, p. 27.

15. *Ibid.*, p. 201.

16. Frank A. Pinner, Paul Jacobs, and Philip Selznick, *Old Age and Political Behavior*, Berkeley: University of California Press, 1959.

17. *Ibid.*, p. 90. Italics added.

18. *Ibid.*

19. *Ibid.* (Italics by Pinner, *et al.*)

20. It would be instructive to ascertain the special privileges for the aged in the form of tax exemptions, lower or nonexistent admission charges, etc. Mohawk Airlines, for example, has recently inaugurated a Golden Age Club with one third reduction in fare.

21. John R. Schmidhauser has summarized some of the pertinent literature in his article, "The Political Behavior of Older Persons, A Discussion of Some Frontiers in Research," *The Western Political Quarterly*, XI (March, 1958), p. 115. He is careful to point out that a number of political studies employ age 55 for the older age group, rather than age 65, the common age used in private retirement programs and for the male eligibility for benefit under OASI. This discrepancy in definition does not detract from the pertinence of the findings on the voting patterns of the aged.

22. *Ibid.*, pp. 116–17. Some minorities, such as Jews and Negroes, may have strategic voting power when they live in concentrated areas in a city.

23. Floyd Hunter, *Community Power Structure*, Chapel Hill: University of North Carolina Press, 1953. More recent investigations question Hunter's generalizations about the power structure. See Morris Janowitz, ed., *Community Political Systems*, Glencoe: The Free Press, 1961.

24. Hunter, *op. cit.*, p. 80. See also pp. 29–30; 40–1.

25. West reports that the older members of the small community he studied had a "stranglehold" on most of the wealth in the county. James West, *Plainville, U.S.A.*, New York: Columbia University Press, 1945, pp. 110–111. He also noted that older women exerted considerable social control in a small town. He writes: "Certainly through the dread and fear of them which exists, *old women* exert a great restraining influence against deviation from stricter and older moral patterns." *Ibid.*, p. 105, italics added.

26. For example, in 1961 16 United States Senators were between 60 and 64 years of age and 31 were 65 or older. Also, only two members of the United States Supreme Court were under 60. Yet no one claims that older Senators or Justices act as representatives of the old. It shows, however, that older persons occupy positions of power and influence in a youth-oriented society.

27. See Harvey C. Lehman, *Age and Achievement*, Princeton: Princeton University Press, 1953, pp. 269–88. Lehman's statistical series varies from one occupational category to the other. The interested reader should consult Lehman's work for the pertinent details and qualifications.

28. Donald R. Matthews, *The Social Background of Political Decision-Makers*, New York: Doubleday and Co., Inc., 1954, p. 33.

29. G. Stanley Hall, *Senescence: The Last Half of Life*, New York: D. Appleton and Company, 1923, p. 135.

30. The election of President John F. Kennedy confirmed Hall's prediction.

31. Bernard R. Berelson, Paul F. Lazarsfeld, and William N. McPhee, *Voting*, Chicago: The University of Chicago Press, 1954, p. 104.

32. *Ibid.*, p. 164. The local leadership of the minority party in Elmira (Democratic) was held by six men, all over seventy years of age. *Ibid.*, pp. 160–2.

33. Schmidhauser, *op. cit.*, p. 120.

34. If we consider only those older persons living in the general community, and exclude the estimated 3 to 5 per cent in institutions, we find that only 10 per cent of a nation-wide probability sample of persons 60 and over are classified as "very sick." See Ethel Shanas, "The 'Very Sick' in the Older Population," *The Journal, Michigan State Medical Society*, 58 (May, 1960), pp. 752–3.

35. Ethel Shanas, *Medical Care Among Those Age 65 and Over*, New York: Health Information Foundation, Research Series, No. 16, 1960, p. 29.

36. The complexity of the economic situation of the aged has been cogently discussed by Peter O. Steiner and Robert Dorfman, *The Economic Status of the Aged*, Berkeley and Los Angeles: University of California Press, 1957. There have been changes in the income status of the aged since the Steiner and Dorfman study was published. Gordon states: "There is considerable evidence that both the money and the real income status of the aged have improved . . ." Margaret S. Gordon, "Aging and Income Security," in *Handbook of Social Gerontology* edited by Clark Tibbitts, Chicago: The University of Chicago Press, 1960, p. 225.

37. If home ownership is considered a mark of privilege and affluence, the aged are more privileged than other segments of the population. However, home ownership presents financial disadvantages as well as advantages. For a discussion of the subject, see John J. Corson and John W. McConnell, *Economic Needs of Older People*, New York: The Twentieth Century Fund, 1956, pp. 89–91.

38. Martel and Morris, *op. cit.*, p. 41. Another study supporting the point of view of the Iowa study is Wayne E. Thompson and Gordon F. Streib, "Situational Determinants: Health and Economic Deprivation in Retirement," *The Journal of Social Issues*, XIV, 1958, pp.

18–34. The Iowa investigators, it should be noted, believed that their findings tended to underestimate feelings of economic deprivation.

39. Milton L. Barron, *op. cit.*, 1961, pp. 63–6.

40. For details on these laws see *The Aged and Aging in the United States—A National Problem*, Report No. 1121, U.S. Senate, 86th Congress, Second Session. Subcommittee on the Problems of the Aged and Aging, Washington: U.S. Government Printing Office, 1960. See inserts between pages 50–1.

41. The effect of these anti-discrimination laws has not been thoroughly studied. However, one piece of research made before New York had such a law, showed that New York placed a higher percentage of older workers than Massachusetts, which had a law at the time. See *Good News for Later Life*, Legal document #8, New York State Joint Legislative Committee on Problems of the Aging, 1958, p. 23. Barron reports that during the first year of the law's operation in New York, 148 complaints were initiated and 54 were settled; nine cases were sustained on the basis of discrimination. Barron, *op. cit.*, 1961, p. 66.

42. The careful survey conducted in Iowa is informative on this point. The investigators asked: "Which of the following living arrangements would be acceptable to you, if circumstances led you to seriously consider them?" Six alternative arrangements were mentioned and about two-thirds of the respondents said that living alone was the most acceptable. The next alternative selected by almost a third was living in a project for elderly people (with separate apartments or cottages for each where you had to do your own cooking). Martel and Morris, *op. cit.*, p. 46.

43. For data on the British urban, working class see Peter Townsend, *The Family Life of Old People*, Glencoe, The

Free Press, 1957, pp. 31–40. For a summary of American data see Gordon F. Streib and Wayne E. Thompson, "The Older Person in a Family Context," in Clark Tibbitts, ed., *Handbook of Social Gerontology*, Chicago: The University of Chicago Press, 1960, pp. 476 ff. The Iowa survey can be cited in this connection: ". . . most parents in the sample did maintain regular contacts with at least some of their children and grandchildren, and derived important satisfactions from these relations. Well over half said they had visited with a son or daughter during the week preceding the survey, and more than 40 per cent had spent time with a grandchild. Nearly 75 per cent saw one or more of their children at least once a month, and about 38 per cent said they visited with all their children at least that often." These investigators added that about five per cent of the parents in the study "complained of neglect by their families." Martel and Morris, *op. cit.*, p. 52.

44. Martel and Morris, *op. cit.*, p. 90.

45. Again the Iowa study offers interesting evidence on this point. It was reported that 73 per cent of the men and 83 per cent of the women state that their lives are still busy and useful. There is, however, a sharp decline in this feeling after age 75. *Ibid.*, p. 86.

46. Philip Taietz and Olaf F. Larsen, "Social Integration of the Older Person in the Rural Community," Unpublished manuscript, Ithaca, N.Y.: Department of Rural Sociology, Cornell University. The study included only male heads of households, and the age categories were under 45, 45 to 65, and over 65 years of age. There were 215 males over 65 who were interviewed.

47. Robert J. Havighurst, "The Social Competence of Middle-Aged People," *Genetic Psychology Monographs*, 56, 1957, p. 321. In the Kansas City study 234 persons were in the age range 40 to 70. It might be argued that this was not a study of the aged. Indeed the author refers to his study as one of the middle-aged.

48. Wendell Bell and Maryanne T. Force, "Urban Neighborhood Types and Participation in Formal Associations," *American Sociological Review*, 21, February, 1956, p. 34.

49. Clark Tibbitts, "A Regional Approach to Social Gerontology," in Carter C. Asterbind, ed., *Aging, A Regional Appraisal*, Gainesville, Fla.: Institute of Gerontology Series, X, 1961, pp. 8–9.

50. See Breen, *et al.*, *op. cit.*, p. H-6

51. Elaine Cumming, Lois R. Dean, David S. Newell, and Isabel McCaffrey, "Disengagement—A Tentative Theory of Aging," *Sociometry*, 23, March, 1960, pp. 23–35.

52. *Ibid.*, p. 35.

53. In conducting the study of disengagement, the investigators included only the middle strata of the class structure. The highest and lowest strata were excluded. Hence, the theory and the data may have a class bias. See: Elaine Cumming and William E. Henry, *Growing Old: The Process of Disengagement*, New York: Basic Books, Inc., 1961, pp. 232–3.

# 25.    The Study of Mental Illness

JEROME K. MYERS

*Introduction*

                                          SOCIOLOGICAL STUDY OF MENTAL ILLNESS IS A NEW
but rapidly expanding field.[1] Since its boundaries are not as clearly defined
as those of more traditional subfields of sociology, there is confusion about
its exact nature. Research covers a wide range of topics from clinical
studies of etiology to mass surveys of attitudes and knowledge about mental
illness and its treatment. Consequently, some definition of the field is desirable before undertaking a discussion of sociological theory within it.
Clausen's definition is most pertinent for our purposes. According to him,
the sociology of mental illness is, "the study of the social norms and processes which have a marked bearing upon the production or course of various forms of psychic disturbance (especially as such disturbance impairs
the individual's ability to carry out usual roles), or which govern the ways
in which disturbed persons are perceived, defined and dealt with during
and after phases of acute disturbance."[2] Although this definition stresses
psychic disturbance, its lack, i.e., mental health, is not excluded.

    Sociological study of mental health and illness can be called "applied"
because it has arisen to considerable extent in response to a social problem.
During the past fifteen years there has been an increasing demand from the
mental health professions for sociological research on a wide variety of
practical problems. In their initial research sociologists treated mental
illness and its perception, definition, and treatment as dependent variables
to be "explained" by a variety of independent social and cultural factors.
Through this approach sociological concepts, theories, and research techniques have been applied to the study of psychiatric problems.

## Jerome K. Myers

For this reason, the sociology of mental illness has developed as a substantive field defined by its subject matter. There are no sociological "theories" of mental illness in the sense that there are theories of stratification, social organization, or social change. Rather, concepts and theories, proved useful in the traditional subfields of sociology, have been applied to the study of psychiatric illness. Frequently, an important aim of this application of theory has been to advance our practical knowledge of mental health and disease; at other times, it has been to test in a new area of behavior hypotheses and conceptual formulations developed in the more traditional areas of sociological investigation. As mental health research has developed, however, it has become apparent that many such studies have theoretical as well as practical importance.

Although the distinction between "applied" and "general" sociology is useful for some purposes, it can lead easily to confusion about the nature of sociological theory. Principles about the structure and functioning of groups and their influence upon man's behavior can be derived as easily from the study of mental illness as from any other form of human behavior. The study of a mental hospital or clinic, for example, is no more "applied" than the study of a factory, university, family or community. General sociological theory develops from the study of all types of groups and varieties of human behavior; it does not exist in a vacuum sealed against contamination by empirical data. Theory has developed through the gradual accumulation of concepts, principles, and hypotheses derived from all the subfields of sociology. In fact, some of the most fruitful work has come from "applied" research, such as the enrichment of reference group theory resulting from the American Soldier studies.[3]

Because of the large amount and variety of sociological research in mental illness during the past fifteen years it is impossible to cover the field adequately in a short paper. Suffice it to say, its contributions to sociological theory have been uneven. For example, research in mental health has added little to our theoretical knowledge of social and cultural change, whereas it has enriched immensely our understanding of complex organizations. Our procedure will be to present examples in two areas where the theoretical contributions have been significant: social organization, and the relationship of the individual to his social environment.[4] Other areas might have been chosen, but because of space limitations selection was necessary.

### Social Organization

Studies of mental hospitals have been particularly illuminating in specifying the importance of informal structure in the operation of a complex organization.[5] Currently, the theoretical conditions are being delineated for the informal social organization which arises when the formal structure of the hospital fails to meet the needs of its members and to provide stable goals and expectations for them. Although the informal structure is essential for the operation of a mental hospital, it results in a large number of informal communications and authority networks which are frequently covert and hard to identify.[6] The flow of communication, therefore, is difficult to trace and is confusing, leading to many types of communication problems detrimental to the hospital's adequate functioning.

The rigid authority structure of hospitals and the existence of a sharply defined status hierarchy also lead to a number of organizational and communications problems. Under ordinary circumstances personnel can advance only within their own level so that status levels are "mobility blocked."[7] For example, an attendant cannot become a nurse, nor can a nurse become a doctor. Such a social structure results in the development of different values, goals and perceptions of hospital life at the various levels. Interpersonal relations between levels are formalized; the consequent effects upon the flow of communication is of theoretical as well as practical significance.

The existence of a system of dual control in mental hospitals has increased our theoretical knowledge of decision-making and social control. The formal administrative lines of authority seldom operate the way they are supposed to because of the informal but very real power of the physicians who carry out the clinical work. The theoretical significance of this dual system of control for other types of organizations, such as universities or industrial research organizations, is just beginning to be worked out.

The importance of role conflict has not only been demonstrated clearly in hospital studies, but the concept itself has been refined greatly. An important feature of the formal structure of a hospital is the extent to which it relies on what Henry has termed systems of "multiple subordination," where one worker is under the authority of several independent chiefs.[8] Consequently, one worker, such as a ward nurse or attendant, may have a difficult time resolving conflicting orders. In fact, such confusion may arise that the efficient operation of the entire organization is threatened. The utility of this concept for organizational theory is quite clear.

The disrupting influence of hidden or covert staff disagreement upon the clinical course of the patient has been demonstrated dramatically in hospital studies.[9] For example, such conflict has been found to be related to pathological excitement, incontinence, and collective disturbances. Although some staff disagreement is due to psychological or personality factors, much of it stems from inevitable role conflict due to the nature of the hospital's social structure. The theoretical significance of such covert disagreement upon not only patient behavior but upon the entire operation of an organization, represents a significant contribution to sociological knowledge.

The above examples are representative of the contributions made to organizational theory by studies of mental hospitals. They are by no means exhaustive nor necessarily the most significant. For instance, Goffman's concept of the total institution, developed in his study of the mental hospital, is having a significant impact upon organizational history.[10] All of the above examples are illustrative of findings of mental hospital studies which have theoretical applicability to many other hierarchical structures, such as schools, industries, prisons, and business organizations.

## The Individual and His Social Environment

Probably the greatest amount of sociological research in mental health has been concerned with social and cultural factors in the etiology of mental illness. The relationship between social factors and the development of mental illness is extremely complex, and much of the evidence is contradictory or inconclusive. Mental illness has been found related to upward and downward social mobility, to poverty and wealth, to migration and geographical isolation, to rapid social change and to lack of change, to mention only a few.[11] Perhaps most consistent is the inverse relationship between social class and rates of psychoses, especially schizophrenia.[12] Attempts to interpret these findings have utilized a variety of theoretical approaches. Faris and Dunham, for example, developed the social isolation hypothesis, emphasizing the lack of social interaction in areas of the community having high rates of schizophrenia.[13]

Other investigators have emphasized the subcultural aspects of social class, especially the role of the family in the socialization process.[14] Their attempts to develop functional linkages between social and psychiatric phenomena have theoretical relevance not only for the etiology of mental illness, but also for the relationship between social class and the socialization process.

Clinicians have long emphasized the importance of interpersonal relationships within the family upon the child's personality development, but have neglected the study of the family within its broader social context. Sociologists have demonstrated, however, that the larger social structure influences significantly intrafamilial role relationships.

Independent studies in Hagerstown, Maryland and New Haven, Connecticut, for example, discovered similar class-related patterns of authority structure in parental families of schizophrenics. In Hagerstown, Kohn and Clausen studied a sample of former schizophrenic patients and a matched control group to determine their perception of parental authority while they were growing up.[15] Both lower and middle class schizophrenics saw their mothers as their primary authority figure. In contrast, respondents from the lower social control group of nonpatients saw their mothers as the principal authority figure more frequently than did middle class controls. Stated another way, former schizophrenics in both classes and controls of the lower class reported a strong authority role for their mothers. In contrast, higher status controls more often reported a weak authority role for their mothers.

In New Haven, a group of lower-middle and lower-class schizophrenics were compared with neurotics from the same social levels by Myers and Roberts.[16] They discovered that the mothers of schizophrenic patients were the central figures in the home in both classes, while the fathers were ineffectual, passive, and uninvolved in family affairs. Since most fathers were not only inadequate, but generally unconcerned about the patient's activities, the responsibility of the patient's rearing fell almost entirely upon the mothers. This type of maternal responsibility and authority was also common in the families of lower-class neurotics, although to a lesser degree than among schizophrenics. However, it was virtually absent in the families of middle-class neurotics.

Psychiatrists have long recognized the influence of child-rearing practices upon personality development and have carried out extensive research on the subject. However, they have seldom examined systematically the basic relationship between social structure and child-rearing. Sociological research on this subject, such as the Miller and Swanson study of child-rearing and social class in Detroit, has theoretical significance for psychiatry as well as sociology.[17] Their evidence suggests that the relationship between social class and child-rearing practices can be understood more fully if we take into account another dimension in the social milieu—the family's integration setting as determined by the type of occupation. According to their evidence, families differ in their way of life depending upon whether the breadwinner's occupation is entrepreneurial or bureaucratic in nature. Furthermore, on the basis of this classification of family integration they discovered significant differences in child-rearing techniques both within and between classes.

For example, they found that the relation of mother and child in the lower classes was not significantly different in the entrepreneurial and the bureaucratic situation. In the middle classes, however, their set of experiences did differ. The increased security of the bureaucratic middle class has led to a lesser emphasis on the importance for the child to develop self-control, internalize his desires, and take an active and individualistic approach to the world. Consequently, child training in the bureaucratic middle class appeared similar to that of the lower classes. Miller and Swanson emphasize that this finding does not mean that the child care of the bureaucratic middle class is exactly the same, since the reasons for choosing similar techniques of rearing children are probably different for people of the bureaucratic middle class and those of the entrepreneurial and bureaucratic lower class. However, in their interview schedules they were not able to detect significant differences. The important theoretical point of the research is that child-rearing practices can be understood better by classifying families on the basis of the entrepreneurial or bureaucratic nature of their occupation as well as their social class position.

The relevance of the above studies for psychiatry is clear; they attempt to link social and psychiatric phenomena to increase understanding of deviant personality development. At the same time, the problem they are studying is central to sociological theory as well: the influence of social class position upon the socialization process, and the influence of the dynamic structure and functioning of the family on personality development.

## Methodological Problems

Studies of the etiology of mental illness reveal the inadequacies of current research methodology for much sociological research in the area of social psychiatry. Future theoretical developments in this field will depend, to a significant degree, upon the emergence of a new level of methodology. Sociologists have pioneered in the use of quantitative methods for studying large numbers of cases and have perfected methodological approaches, such as survey research. However, it is becoming increasingly apparent that for a given case, such methods cannot produce sufficient materials of the type necessary to study the socialization process, intrafamilial role relationships, and similar problems central to etiological studies. Equally unsatisfactory is the intensive case method developed in psychiatry.[18]

The statistical survey provides well defined quantitative data on a large number of cases. It is a "macroscopic" approach, enabling the researcher to study a cross section of an entire community or other social unit. Materials can be collected systematically on standardized schedules, and analyzed statistically. However, the number of traits or characteristics studied in an individual case is usually limited. The survey provides a horizontal view which cuts across a vast surface of data, but furnishes relatively little depth material.

The case-study method, on the other hand, provides a vertical view of a small number of cases with few restrictions on the number of traits studied in any one case. It is a "microscopic" approach, permitting a detailed and dynamic study of any part of an individual's life cycle. Since materials are usually collected by free association or clinical interviews, they are not limited by prearranged plans. The researcher can collect a vast amount of unique data on his subjects, which he could not obtain by the survey method. Clinical experience and judgment are used in analyzing materials, and often provide greater insight than is possible in more standardized analytical procedures.

The very merits of the case-study method lead to serious limitations. Interest is focused on the uniqueness of a case and, as a result, problems of sampling are usually neglected. Since little is known about the sample's representativeness, generalizations are dangerous. The comparison of cases is also difficult because data are not collected systematically. Frequently, so few cases are studied that neither group comparisons nor objective analytic techniques can be undertaken, even if comparable materials on all subjects were available. Therefore, conclusions are usually impressionistic, based upon the investigator's subjective judgment; the replication of such studies is impossible.

What is needed is a research method somewhere between the two existing extremes, one in which the collection, analysis, and presentation of data are objective, but in which detailed materials of the life cycle can be obtained. Admittedly, the development of such methodology is difficult, but it is crucial for the further extension of etiological theory based upon empirical data.

### NOTES

1. See the following for excellent summaries of developments in this field: John A. Clausen, "The Sociology of Mental Illness," in Robert K. Merton *et. al.* (ed.,), *Sociology Today: Problems and Prospects*, Basic Books, 1959, pp. 485– 508; John A. Clausen, *Sociology and the Field of Mental Health*, Russell Sage Foundation, 1956; and H. Warren Dunham, "The Field of Social Psychiatry," in Arnold M. Rose (ed.,), *Mental Health and Mental Disorder: A Sociological Ap-*

proach, W. W. Norton and Co., 1955, pp. 61–86.

2. Clausen, op. cit., 1959, p. 486.

3. Samuel A. Stouffer et. al., The American Soldier: Adjustment During Army Life, Princeton University Press, 1949; Stouffer et. al., The American Soldier: Combat and Its Aftermath, Princeton University Press, 1949; Carl I. Hovland, et. al., Experiments on Mass Communication, Princeton University Press, 1949; and Stouffer, et. al., Measurement and Prediction, Princeton University Press, 1950.

4. See Clausen, op. cit., 1959, for a more general discussion of sociological contributions to the field of mental health. Also, see William Caudill, The Psychiatric Hospital as a Small Society, Harvard University Press, 1958, pp. 1–18 for an excellent summary of studies of hospital social structure. The influence of these two sources will be seen clearly in the following discussion.

5. See, for example, Alfred H. Stanton and Morris S. Schwartz, The Mental Hospital, Basic Books, 1954; Caudill, op. cit.; and Ivan Belknap, Human Problems of a State Mental Hospital, McGraw-Hill, 1956.

6. Caudill, op. cit., p. 8.

7. Harvey Smith, Sociological Study of Hospitals, unpublished doctoral dissertation, University of Chicago, 1949. See also Albert F. Wessen. The Social Structure of a Modern Hospital, unpublished doctoral dissertation, Yale University, 1951; T. Burling, E. M. Lentz and R. N. Wilson, The Give and Take in Hospitals, G. P. Putnam's Sons, 1956; and Belknap, op. cit.

8. Jules Henry, "The Formal Structure of a Psychiatric Hospital," Psychiatry 17 (1954), pp. 139–51. See also Caudill, op. cit.; and Stanton and Schwartz, op. cit.

9. See, for example, Stanton and Schwartz, op. cit.; and Caudill, op. cit.

10. Erving Goffman, Asylums, Doubleday, 1961.

11. See the following for a detailed discussion of this problem: Lawrence S. Kubie, "Social Forces and the Neurotic Process," in Alexander H. Leighton, J. A. Clausen, and R. N. Wilson (eds.), Explorations in Social Psychiatry, Basic Books, 1957, pp. 77–104; Clausen, op. cit., 1959, pp. 487–90.

12. See August B. Hollingshead and Frederick C. Redlich, Social Class and Mental Illness, John Wiley, 1958, for a summary of such studies.

13. Robert E. L. Faris and H. Warren Dunham, Mental Disorders in Urban Areas, University of Chicago Press, 1939.

14. See, for example, Jerome K. Myers and Bertram H. Roberts, Family and Class Dynamics in Mental Illness, John Wiley, 1959; Melvin L. Kohn and John A. Clausen, "Parental Authority Behavior and Schizophrenia," American Journal of Orthopsychiatry, 26 (1956), pp. 297–313.

15. Kohn and Clausen, op. cit.

16. Myers and Roberts, op. cit.

17. Daniel R. Miller and Guy E. Swanson, The Changing American Parent, John Wiley, 1958.

18. See Myers and Roberts, op. cit., pp. 23–39 for a detailed discussion of this problem and an attempt to develop a more appropriate methodological approach.

# Part V

# APPLIED SOCIOLOGY

# AND PUBLIC POLICY

# 26. Social Science and Juvenile Delinquency

CLARENCE C. SHERWOOD

THERE HAVE BEEN MANY COMPLAINTS ABOUT THE failure to integrate social science findings with action programs aimed at the solution of social problems. Complaints have come from both sides; the social sciences complain that action programs are not based upon sound principles derived from social science research and theory; action-programmers and policy-makers, on the other hand, complain that the social sciences do not tend to produce the kind of findings that are applicable to social action programs.

Much less often, however, have there been detailed examinations of the issues involved: in particular, examinations of what is meant by "known in the social sciences"; of the "kinds" of knowledge of findings; and of the "relationships" among these various types of knowledge and their applications—in the present analysis, to the solution of the problem of juvenile delinquency.

The notion of "the applicability of social science knowledge" has at least two different meanings. It can refer to the application of knowledge to the solution of individual or social problems (that is, the formulation of policies or action programs based upon relevant social science knowledge). It can also refer to the idea that the research findings in the laboratory—the principles used to describe or explain some phenomena—should apply to (that is, to be true for) those phenomena when and where they occur or exist outside the laboratory. It is the former meaning

*339*

of applicability, as it relates to efforts to solve the problem of juvenile delinquency, which is explored in this paper.

## Differential Applicability of Different Types of Knowledge

A distinction among the various kinds of knowledge on at least two different dimensions is relevant to this analysis: (1) Levels of knowledge (2) A specificity—generality dimension in terms of the source of the knowledge of the subject matter. The levels-of-knowledge dimension includes: (a) descriptive data, (b) relationships, (c) theories. "Descriptive data" refer to the raw data—that is, the facts and events, the more-or-less immediately observable data which have been recorded.

"Relationships" refer to the specific empirical relationships which have been found to exist among relatively directly observable, measurable variables—that is, the correlations which have been found in statistically controlled studies involving the association of two or more variables.

"Theories" refer to the explanations which attempt to provide an understanding of the observed descriptive data and relationships.

The term "subject matter source" refers to the question of whether or not the knowledge has been derived from studies of the social problem and pertains specifically to it. In the present instance, the problem is juvenile delinquency.

The above types and combinations of types of knowledge are, or will be, important in the application of social science knowledge to action programs. However, the types of application, and the degree to which social science findings can provide implications for social action programs vary for each kind of knowledge. There is a different relationship for each, between the content of the knowledge and of the action program with which it may be connected. It is believed that the mutual complaints referred to at the beginning of this paper have centered almost exclusively on what can be called "specific," "descriptive" (factual) and "relationship" knowledge. This is the type of knowledge which has been pursued in social scientific studies of delinquency, but which may also be the type of knowledge least easily translated into *directives for action*.

For example: descriptive, specific findings about increases in delinquency suggest that action is needed but contain no directives for it. Thus, data collected by the United Nations[1] provide a valuable source of descriptive materials on the size of the juvenile delinquency problem in various parts of the world, as well as on new forms of delinquency, but contain no clues for the action programs required. Descriptive data are particularly useful in predicting trends and thus in evaluating the time, money, and effort needed for prevention and/or treatment purposes. In addition, even if no preventive action is taken, trend analysis is useful in determining the size of the facilities and personnel required to deal with the problem. Thus, for example, based on data collected on the changes in the population under 21, the proportions within this age group tending to become delinquent, and the knowledge of administrative changes in commitment, probation and parole policy, Rose and Weber were able to predict the future population in institutions for delinquent children and youth in Minnesota.[2] In Florida, the Parole Commission was successful in its attempt to increase appropriations through legislative action by a presentation of carefully gathered descriptive data about juvenile delinquency trends in Florida.[3]

Relationship-type knowledge tends to suggest more specifically than descriptive-type knowledge the content of action programs. Relationships, such as: boys are more likely to get into trouble with the law than girls and urban areas tend to have higher delinquency rates than rural areas are valuable in focusing attention on particular aspects of the problem, but often contain little or no direct implications for action. We cannot necessarily expect to eliminate delinquency by eliminating the conditions which correlate with delinquency. For example, what implications for action can we derive from the finding that boys are more likely to get into trouble with the law than girls? The elimination of boys can hardly be regarded as a practical suggestion for an action program.

As another example, it has been found that children from low socioeconomic areas are more likely to become delinquent than children from high socioeconomic areas. True or not, we cannot go back and change the residential circumstances or the delinquent's early childhood; nor, for that matter, can we hope, at the present time at least, to eliminate low socioeconomic areas.

Nonetheless, action programs have been undertaken on the basis of such relationship-type knowledge. The Gluecks' prediction studies are cases in point.[4] They are also examples of the limitations of relationship-type knowledge when the effort is made to apply such findings directly without consideration of the implications of such findings. Based on a scale which combines a number of observed correlations between certain family background factors and juvenile delinquency, the Gluecks are attempting to identify potential delinquents and concentrate efforts on preventing these children from becoming delinquent. Setting aside the complex, unresolved questions of the validity of these findings and of the ethics and potential effectiveness of their application to delinquency prevention programs, the Gluecks' prediction scales are an example of social science findings which have been adopted by the world of social action. Definite efforts are being made in New York City, for example, to utilize these scales in actual programs of delinquency prevention.[5] However, the scales are being used only for prediction, on the assumption that the scales will identify youngsters who will become officially involved in delinquency-patterned behavior. Whatever general implications the actual content of the scales may have, they are not being utilized in the development of the prevention program. In other words, the social science knowledge involved, in the form of relationships among variables, is being used simply as a measuring or identifying instrument. Disregarded are the contents of the scale, the nature of the questions, the issues explored, all of which have undeveloped, general implications.

The instrument is used only to select youths for community attention. The content of the action is independent of the content of the knowledge which initiated the action. To be meaningful, the specific content for the action programs must be deduced from the content of the knowledge and its implications.

As suggested by the above analysis, relationships may give clues and insights, and thus have implications for the content of action programs of social agencies. But whether the content is formulated specifically to explain delinquency, or is drawn from the total body of social science knowledge, we must turn to the theories which explain these observed relationships. Only then can we formulate specific, detailed, and organized programs for changing behavior. When the goal of social agencies is to change behavior, their attempts at social action will, at best, be piecemeal, haphazard, and relatively trivial—unless these agencies program their efforts systematically in terms of some general theories of behavior (1) which have implications for social action, and (2) which reasonably order the recorded data and observed relationships.

Seen in this light, there can be no question but that social science knowledge has been frequently applied—that is, used—by practitioners. On the simplest level, knowledge concerning increases in the volume of delinquent behavior, for example, may set off a whole series of efforts by people responsible for dealing with the problem. It can also be seen, at this point, that the validity of the knowledge and the use of the knowledge are fundamentally separate issues. On the scientific level, they are distinctly separate, for the degree of validity is in no way dependent on the practical usefulness of the theory. On the reverse level, there is no relationship between the degree of validity of the knowledge and its amenability to application. "Knowledge" that the earth was flat, for example, was definitely amenable to translation into action.

Probably at the root of the mutual criticism of social scientists and practitioners is the recognition by both that, in spite of the efforts being made to combat the problem—

1. The juvenile delinquency problem in the United States is an enormous and increasing one. Without delving into the problem of official against unofficial delinquency, the problem extends far beyond the limits described by our official delinquency statistics.

2. In general, present-day efforts by our society to deal with the problem of delinquency are woefully ineffective. There seems to be very little evidence that any real impact is being made on the problem.

## Suggested Directions: Deriving Social Action Directives from General Social Science Propositions

It can be seen, therefore, that social science knowledge must be explored more carefully for the neglected findings which may have implications for social action. What are vitally needed here are basic break-throughs in emphasis and effort. A perusal of some of the well-known social science studies, concepts, theories, etc. have led us to the position:

1. that although the emphasis at present has tended to be on the search for specific findings which may be directly applied in action programs, a much greater attempt should be made to put some of the more theoretical—usually less precise—findings of the social sciences to work;

2. that most fruitful types of knowledge for solution of the delinquency problem need not necessarily be findings which have been derived from studies aimed at that problem.

For example, "delinquency" studies may not provide the most valuable suggestions for action. From the scientific point of view they are unquestionably necessary for checking and verifying theories, etc. But it may be that the more general kinds of findings, not specifically oriented toward the problem of delinquency—such as general findings about mobility—will be even more useful, or at least necessary to combine with the more specific kinds of findings.

To serve as examples of how directives for social action can be gained from social science knowledge, we will analyze two sociological propositions. Both have tended to be neglected in terms of their implications for, and relevance to, action programs. These propositions are representative of what has been termed general-type knowledge, that is, knowledge pertaining to our total society and system rather than specifically to the delinquency problem. The examples to be discussed are residential mobility and urbanization. The first is of a relatively factual, or descriptive nature. The second is representative of more theoretical social science findings.

### EXAMPLE 1—RESIDENTIAL MOBILITY

A distinctive and significant feature of American society is the high and increasing rate of residential mobility. Upon examination, this generally known finding is clearly relevant to the problem of delinquency. However, it has not been utilized to any significant degree, if at all, in the formulation of delinquency action programs. Probation programs are perhaps an exception. They have faced the fact of the potential mobility of their probationers by restricting their movement and by requiring them to appear periodically at the probation office.

The extremely high residential mobility of the American population—and the clear trends toward even greater mobility—emphasizes the distinction which must be made between dealing with (1) the problem of delinquency from the point of view of a given neighborhood or community and (2) the problem of dealing with delinquents. As an example, any neighborhood of New York City can attempt—and perhaps succeed to a reasonable degree—to deal with the youth and delinquency problems in its area. It can observe and identify major troublemakers, provide mass recreation programs to get the youngsters off the streets, work out effective communication systems to report behavior, and elicit responses from the relevant community agencies, including the police, etc. It can even attempt to screen out or eliminate from the neighborhood as many of the misbehaviors as possible. But these tend to be much more in the nature of programs dealing with delinquency rather than delinquents.

There are areas where agency programs attempt to deal with either the preventive aspect of the delinquency problem and/or the treatment of already known delinquents (in many instances, returned to the community from institutions). However, the tremendous mobility of the population guarantees the futility of a long range program of attempting to deal with individual delinquents, or even potential delinquents, on a narrow geographic basis. Before any real impact can occur, the delinquents will have moved and been replaced by others. Delinquents must be dealt with on as broad a community basis as possible; the programs must follow them—or the youngsters are, at best, merely brushed lightly as they pass through.

At present, when a youngster who has been worked with—before or after actual delinquency has occurred—moves out of the community, the program ends for that individual. Even if some headway has been made, seldom, and then only by accident, will support of the previous efforts be continued. Everything that has been learned about him goes into the proverbial wastebasket. The same principles hold, in reverse, when a similar individual moves into the community. The point is that the potential co-ordination and continuity which would constitute inherent features of a program in a residentially stable community must be artificially provided under conditions of high residential mobility.

Recognition of the high mobility of population is a basic and very significant implication for action programs. It introduces another dimension of the problem of translating findings into action. Previous mention was made of the notion of the content of the action program and the influence of findings on such specific content. Mobility data appear to have implications for what we might call the form—as distinct from the content—of an *action* program. That is, rather than suggesting specifically what is to be done (casework, recreation programs, employment programs, psychotherapy, etc.) it suggests continuity of whatever is done, of the movement of the subjects. This is a big order, unquestionably, but a necessary one.

### EXAMPLE 2—URBANIZATION

Another distinctive and significant feature of American society is the increasing trend toward an urban pattern of life. There is evidence that this does not inevitably occur in all cities. In Indonesian cities, for example, migrant villagers moving into the city tend to settle in urban *kampongs* according to original residence or area. Within these kampongs, "social control does not differ much from that in the rural areas . . . In fact, these subdivisions of kampongs, designated by serial numbers, form the real social units. Their inhabitants form a typical primary group, they know each other by sight and through local gossip have simple information as to each other's doings."[6] This suggests that an urban way of life is not inevitable in all cities.

It is significant that: (1) in cities where rural family patterns have persisted, delinquency rates are very low,[7] and (2) in the United States, rural patterns *do not tend to persist* under the forces of American city life. Therefore, it is not simply the fact of living together in crowded situations that produces delinquency, but something about the changed dynamic relationships among people which are the important variables.

In terms of the significance of the implications of such findings as these, the question is: What is there about these dynamic relationships among people which creates the difference between urban and rural life, and the consequences of these differences? One generally agreed major difference is the anonymity of urban life. As has been pointed out many times, two rural farm families separated by miles of wheat fields are much more likely to know each other well than two city families living across the hall from one another. If it is true in our society that the higher delinquency rates in urban areas are a function of inherent features of urban life, and that anonymity is one of those significant inherent features, then the implications for action are clear. In some way, the anonymity of the urbanite must be reduced, but this will not occur without deliberate intervention. That is, a natural feature of rural life, apparently so crucial to social control must, under urban circumstances, be provided artificially.

From the point of view of the individual or of the community, social control is a function of what have been called "internal" and "external" influences. In a sociological sense, as individuals become members of their society, they learn the rules and values of their system on two levels:

1. They become aware (in a cognitive sense) of the rules and values of their society and of the sanction systems which may be invoked when infractions occur; and,

2. They become aware of the need to conform to, or internalize rules and values of their society.

Nearly everyone learns most of the important rules and values in the first sense; learning on the second level varies greatly from individual to individual, and differently for the many rules and values.

Anonymity as a factor in the breakdown of social control is relevant only for the first level of learning. An example of this is the individual who has learned of, but has not internalized, particular rules and values of his society. For such a person, there are external controls via the threat of imposition of sanctions. The community should know who the individual is, and if and when he has committed an infraction. Anonymity reduces the possibility of both.

There is one practical implication of this analysis for reducing the anonymity of the young people in an urban community. Professional youth center programs must be street oriented not only to reach new and needy members, but also to affect the existing membership. To function as part of the community's external control system, such programs must attempt to be aware of, and influence, their members when they are not in formal attendance. At the present time, youth center programs tend to operate primarily within the building itself and to focus on affecting the internal control systems for the individual—character, personality, emotional adjustment, citizenship programs, etc. Whether or not they are equipped to, or, in terms of the high mobility of urban populations, have the time to make a real impact on this level is at least questionable. However, such agencies represent, in terms of staff, skill, and interest, one of the few possibilities for a comprehensive *external control* system for the youth of an urban community.

Also, it can be seen that the rejection from the center program of misbehaving members—a common practice in many of these centers—only increases the anonymity of such individuals, individuals who clearly need external control pressures. If, for the sake of an inbuilding program, it is necessary to exclude such individuals, they must be carefully and intensively worked with out in the community. Furthermore, this same analysis questions very directly 9 A.M. to 5 P.M. or even 9 to 9, five-day week youth programs.

But external control systems represent only one part of the total social control system.

If there is one general, basic finding in the social sciences, it is that social order is highly dependent upon the system's ability to inculcate a significant proportion of its members with a need to conform to its basic rules and values. It is generally agreed that no society can survive for long if its only means of gaining conformity from its members is its set of external controls. The key concept involved is the idea of internalization; the key societal process is socialization.

Though tentative, present knowledge indicates that the child is likely to accept as part of his response system the values of individuals with whom he strongly identifies. Therefore, the content of the norms which the child does incorporate will depend upon the significance to him of the individuals with whom he interacts, the values they hold, the extent to which he associates with individuals who are significant to him, and the extent to which these significant individuals communicate their values to him. If, between parent and child, there is both an effective affectional tie and effective communication, the child is likely to identify strongly with his parents, incorporating into his response system their set of values.

This analysis suggests at least two significant dimensions of the socializing situation: (1) Whether or not the situation produces identification of child with parent, (2) Whether or not the parents tend to hold the generally accepted values of the society. This latter dimension has three categories: (a) parents with "no values"—the relatively unsocialized, (b) parents with many criminal, anti-social, unacceptable values, (c) parents with the prevailing values of the society.

*3 4 7*

Each of the possible combinations of these dimensions has different implications for action:

*1.* The child who identifies with the acceptably socialized parent. Presumably, this child will present no problem to the community. If he does become delinquent, the implication is that the problem is psychological in origin, and psychotherapy is the approach indicated. It would probably be agreed that clinics dealing with problem children tend to serve this type of child predominantly.

*2.* The child who has not identified with his unsocialized parents. If such situations can be recognized early, immediate removal from the family situation is clearly indicated. However, there are serious moral and ethical considerations involved, and our society is reluctant to take children away from parents. One alternative might be to work with the parents. The "socialization" of the parent involves the problem of education as well as motivation. At best, this is a long, laborious, if not impossible, task, under present conditions. And the question of what happens to the child, meanwhile, remains. Either the child must be removed from the parents or we must accept the almost certain consequences: behavioral deviance of the child.

There is an additional major imperative for direct action of this type— a sort of Malthusian version of a law of delinquency. "Unidentified," "unsocialized" members of society will increase in numbers geometrically from generation to generation. In addition, the ethics of removal in such cases are likely to be essentially academic. The child is almost certain to have been unwanted, accidental, and possibly illegitimate, and would be willingly given up by the parent or parents in many instances.

*3.* The child who has not identified with the anti-socialized parent. Again, removal is clearly indicated. The lack of identification of child with parent is, in this case, a factor suggesting hopeful prognosis. The ethics of removal would probably be most complicated and controversial in the case of the basically anti-social but legally unconvicted parent. Again, however, if procedures were established, the voluntary relinquishment of such children would undoubtedly provide more than enough cases to keep the authorities busy for quite some time.

*4.* The child who identifies with the anti-social parent. Here the prognosis is very poor. We can only hope that it does not happen too often. Social action programs attempting to deal with this type of situation would have to aim at either convincing the parent to change or at lowering the picture of the parent in the eyes of the child.

*5.* The child who has not identified with the acceptably socialized parent. This is the category where traditional family casework would seem to be most applicable. However, there is reason to question whether principles of family casework include methods of helping parents inculcate children with societal values.

At this point, however, a caution should be noted. The family casework approach seems to be based on the assumption that a solution of the personal or relationship problems of one or more members of the family will automatically lead to an improvement in parent-child relationships and in the ability of the family to train, influence, and control its younger members.[8] Although it is undoubtedly true that families with one or more members who have serious personal problems will tend to have difficulties in intra-family relationships, and that a solution to such problems may be a prerequisite to effective parent-child relationships, it may be that such a solution may not be sufficient to deal with the problem of the prevention of delinquency.

Further insights may be needed to help parents control their children effectively both in terms of (1) inculcating the desired norms into the youngster's response system (internal controls) and (2) controlling the youngster when he is not present (external controls).

## NOTES

1. See, for example: United Nations, General Reports, A/Conf. 17/3, Department of Economic Affairs, New York, 1960.

2. Arnold Rose and George H. Weber, "Predicting the Population in Institutions for Delinquent Children and Youth," *The Journal of Criminal Law, Criminology, and Police Science*, Vol. 50, No. 2, July–August 1959, pp. 124–31.

3. Joseph T. Cheney, "How Statistics Increase Appropriations," *NPPA* Journal, Vol. 3, No. 3 (July 1957), pp. 292–8.

4. See "Research in Delinquency at Harvard Law School," *Harvard Law School Bulletin*, Vol. 6, No. 2 (April 1955). For a detailed description of the social prediction scales, see: Sheldon and Eleanor Glueck, *"Unraveling Juvenile Delinquency,"* The Commonwealth Fund, New York, 1950.

5. See *Harvard Law School Bulletin*, *op. cit.*

6. J. J. Panakal, *Prevention of Types of Criminality Resulting from Social Changes and Accompanying Economic Development in Less Developed Countries, Part I*, New York: United Nations, 1960, p. 16.

7. *Ibid.*

8. It should be noted that no analysis is being made in this paper of social action implications to deal with children who identify with unsocialized parents, since it is believed that this combination is not likely to occur. More explicitly it is believed that the unsocialized parents' response would not be likely to include those acts which are necessary to the identification process—affection, concern, attention, etc.

# 27.     Community Issues

# and Their Outcome:

# How to Lose

# a Fluoridation Referendum

WILLIAM A. GAMSON

A NUMBER OF SOCIOLOGISTS HAVE SUGGESTED THAT students of community decision-making compare several communities on similar issues. This paper represents an informal assessment at the midpoint of such a study in 18 New England communities. Two issues from among such stalwarts as school bond proposals, zoning, parking, and sewerage are studied in each town, with a fluoridation controversy common to all. Fluoridation lends itself to this purpose because of its frequent occurrence and essentially "internal" character, i.e., most of the important determinants come from within the community.

In studying a community, we make use of documents and interviews. The documents include informal accounts in community newspapers, formal statistical data from the state and federal census, city planning reports, annual town reports, and various state manuals. The interviews are with active participants on both sides of each issue and with people named by these "issue leaders" as influential in the community. We call this latter group "reputational leaders" to avoid prejudging their actual influence on specific issues.

Systematic analysis of these interviews and other data has hardly begun, but several impressions have emerged. I am wary about stating these impressions, for they may not be our conclusions when the analysis is complete. However, with this caveat, I shall undertake the risk.

What I wish to say centers around fluoridation but applies, I believe, to other community issues as well. A major focus of this study is the set of conditions which determine whether political and other community leaders will become involved in an issue or will remain neutral. Originally, we reasoned that most community issues involved competing economic interests. Certain traditional alignments will arise around these issues and political leaders will draw their major support from among these segments. But if an issue upsets these alignments and offers no stable basis for new ones, we thought that political leaders would be under pressure to avoid involvement in the controversy. We reasoned that fluoridation was just such an issue, and that the failure of politically skilled individuals to exercise their influence on it paved the way for its defeat.

If this explanation is adequate then, as a minimum, we should find in studying the course of the controversy, first, that fluoridation divides the community in unusual ways, compared to other issues, and second, that it is not possible to identify most community leaders with either side on this issue.

We are discovering that these premises are true only in certain cases, and perhaps not even in a majority. Fluoridation often divides a community along cleavage lines similar to those of other issues—particularly school issues. This does not always bring strange bedfellows together. Instead, in some communities the controversy deepens and intensifies the cleavages partially formed by other issues.

Our evidence suggests that it is fruitless to ask if, in general, fluoridation follows conventional or unusual cleavage lines. Seen as a variable, the question becomes, "What conditions determine whether fluoridation divides the community along normal or unusual lines?" After answering this, we would also need to know how given strategies affect the outcome under each of these alternatives. Similarly, the second part of the original explanation—that community leaders will remain neutral—is also variable, and dependent on the distribution and functioning of power in a given community.

In short, neither fluoridation nor any other issue studied seems to follow some invariant pattern independent of the social structure and leadership patterns in the communities involved. Our hope is to be able to characterize certain modal patterns and to determine the conditions under which each occurs. I would like to describe my impressions of what now seems to me the most significant of these patterns.

# William A. Gamson

## Pro and Anti Voters

There has been a good deal of research on why people vote for or against fluoridation which suggests that both groups are heterogeneous. Among the active opponents are the disingenuous professionals, the sincere but rather emotional individuals, and the calm, rational citizens who object on grounds of individual rights or public policy. Among those who simply vote against fluoridation, are all of the above plus those who are confused and unconvinced by either side. The proponents of fluoridation are also varied; many confuse fluoridation with some water purification process such a chlorination. In short, it is difficult to predict that any given strategy will be effective without specifying the audience and the characteristics of the community involved.

But in spite of the variable character of both sides, a dominant theme runs through many of the findings. There seem to be substantial differences between the advocates and the opponents of fluoridation on the degree to which people feel able to control the important forces in their lives. This has been variously characterized as alienation, feelings of deprivation, and low sense of political efficacy. Essentially, those who vote against fluoridation have greater feelings of helplessness than those who favor it. Studies of voters in a predominantly lower-middle-class and working-class precinct in Cambridge, Massachusetts, and of a cross-section of voters in a medium-sized and a small city in the northeastern United States have yielded the same result. Those who voted against fluoridation were more likely to agree with such statements as "Public officials don't really care what people like me think," and "Sometimes politics and government seem so complicated that a person like me can't really understand what's going on." Additional data are needed to establish these differences conclusively for various populations. But I will assume at this time that these differences are valid and I will try to relate them to community decision-making on fluoridation.

One further contrast between the two groups of voters is worth mentioning here. Some proponents have incorrectly argued that opponents are anti-scientific. This assumes that opponents perceive scientific unanimity on this issue and refuse to respect it. There is evidence that many who vote against fluoridation see the "experts" as divided on the merits of the proposal. How, one might ask, can they continue despite endorsement by the United States Public Health Service, the American Medical Association, and the American Dental Association?

To answer this, it is necessary to make a distinction between "experts" and "authorities." Many active opponents point out that the doctors and dentists in their community have done no special research on fluoridation. They perceive such organizations as the American Medical Association and the American Dental Association, not as technical experts, but as medical *authorities* with the power to punish individual doctors and dentists who do not follow their policies. Furthermore, they frequently do not believe that these organizations use their power in a disinterested fashion. They may easily interpret the self-interested attitude of the American Medical Association on medical care for the aged as evidence for such a belief. On the other hand, when an occasional doctor or dentist opposes fluoridation, they may see him as a technically qualified "expert" with the courage to oppose the "authorities." These partisan opponents, then, will see the authorities as united, but the experts as divided. In a less explicit fashion, many ordinary voters may be unconsciously making this kind of distinction.

## A Hypothetical Campaign

To explain why a fluoridation referendum passes or fails, it is not sufficient to simply point out differences between opponents and proponents. In some way, the fluoridation campaign in a community must make these differences salient. The description which follows of a campaign in the hypothetical town of "Fluoradale" suggests how the actions in a campaign can make feelings of political helplessness relevant. While my hypothetical community is "purer" than any actual community through the omission of extraneous complicating factors, it is not simply a straw town designed for easy criticism. The actions I will describe have all been done in one or more actual communities studied.

The health officer in Fluoradale is a conscientious, intelligent, but somewhat rigid person. He is aware that fluoridation has been a controversial issue in many places, but he sees no reason why it can not be adopted in Fluoradale if it is handled correctly. In his view, opposition in these other communities has come from a handful of "crackpots" who have managed to scare or hoodwink a gullible populace.

The health officer goes to other health officials and finds that they also favor fluoridation. He contacts various physicians and dentists in town. One of the dentists points out that fluoridation does poorly on referenda and that it would be wise to try to have fluoridation adopted directly by the town council. Up to this point, no opposition has developed and everyone concerned is optimistic.

The council is sympathetic, although one member has some doubts, and they decide to hold a public hearing on the proposal. In response to a notice in the paper, an unexpectedly large number of people attend the hearing and most of them are hostile to fluoridation. Proponents are heckled and asked hostile questions from the floor. One opponent, a retired chiropractor, asks to be allowed to testify. The health officer argues that he is unqualified. "There is no sense in letting a lot of scientifically un-trained people shoot their mouth off about this," he tells the council. Several people in the audience loudly object and the meeting threatens to get out of hand. One of the councilmen most sympathetic to fluoridation makes a short speech about democracy. "This is a public hearing and anyone here who wishes to speak may do so," he announces.

The retired chiropractor makes a moderate plea: "There is a lot of controversy about this question of fluoridation and I think we should study it thoroughly before we adopt it. In a lot of places, they've tried to rush it through and suppress the opposition. I hope the people of Fluora-dale will be given a chance to hear both sides and decide for themselves on this question."

The health officer is annoyed at the response of the partisan audience. He reacts by reasserting the technical nature of the question and the lack of qualifications of the average citizen to pass judgment on a scientific matter. *He* is willing to take the work of reputable scientific organizations on faith. Why should those so much less qualified than he insist on exer-cising their own judgment?

After lengthy discussion the council decides to place the question on the ballot at the next town election and to set up a study committee to pub-lish an impartial report. The health officer, another physician, and a dentist are appointed along with the chiropractor and another opponent, a house-wife.

The active proponents begin mobilizing quickly. They contact all the dentists and physicians except one, who is retired and rather senile. They publish advertisements over the names of most of the leading business and civic leaders, three of the five council members, the Chamber of Commerce, and a service club.

By misreading the operation of community power (a misreading which many sociologists have helped to perpetrate), they believe that they have followed the politically realistic strategy of enlisting the "community powers" on their side. In the community where there is no "ruling elite" who can implement decisions at their collective will (and there are many such localities) this strategy backfires. Anti-fluoridation leaders, who have already begun to broadcast the message that something is being "put over" on the community, see this list of endorsements as additional evidence of the "power play" that is being conducted. "They" are beginning to turn on the heat.

The proponents see their campaign as "educational" rather than "political." They decide to hold a large public meeting to present their point of view. The active opponents bring in an anti-fluoridation "expert" from outside the community. The proponents charge that he is a "quack," that this is an educational forum, not a debate. Opponents claim that this is a deliberate effort to keep the people from being told both sides. Finally, the proponents consent to questions from the floor, and a free-wheeling, highly emotional debate ensues. Anti-fluoridation speakers repeatedly challenge the motives of the proponents.

As the controversy in Fluoradale grows more heated, several of the civic leaders among the original endorsers ask that their names be removed from the advertisements. They begin to let it be known that they are neutral on the issue, but intend to see that both sides are heard.

The opposition campaign begins to gather momentum. They point to the array of community leaders and medical people who endorse the proposal as evidence of powerful forces—not of scientific judgment. The defectors to neutrality are seen as men of conscience who are really opposed but do not have sufficient courage to buck the "powers." The elderly physician who was not contacted by the pro-fluoridation committee published a letter attacking fluoridation and the endorsing physicians. This is used as evidence of how an "expert" who is beyond the reach of sanctions will act. Any doubt privately expressed by a doctor or dentist is viewed as his "honest," unpressured opinion.

In the atmosphere of mistrust generated by the campaign, people whose normal skepticism would lead them to dismiss the usual flamboyant stories of pipe corosion, deaths from cancer, dying goldfish, stillbirths and what-have-you, are left in doubt. Furthermore, the pro-fluoridation partisans follow the policy of not responding to opponents' charges—"to avoid dignifying such hogwash."

On election day, fluoridation is beaten decisively. The nature of the campaign leaves most community leaders—active proponents—feeling that it would be a bad thing for the community to have the issue brought up again.

## Conclusion

It is an important characteristic of political debate in a democracy that proponents and opponents recognize the legitimacy of disagreement. When a person responds to an opponent by attempting to refute the logic of what he has said, we are implicitly accepting his "right" to express an opinion. When we respond with an *ad hominem* attack, we are asking people to ignore his opinions, not because they are wrong, but because he is not qualified to make them.

Fluoridation involves issues that go beyond the technical questions of effectiveness and safety. In many communities studied, proponents—irked by irresponsible and unqualified opinions on technical matters—have tended to challenge the legitimacy of opposition. They have done this by calling opponents "crackpots" (perhaps some are, but by no means all), refusing to debate the issue or answer charges, and doing other things which imply that this is not a fit subject for democratic political debate.

I am not interested in arguing here whether fluoridation is or is not an appropriate question for the citizenry to decide. I *am* interested in what, I believe, are the consequences of such a position. If I feel that some mysterious "they" make all the important decisions, if I distrust power as such, and find it difficult to distinguish between its use for selfish or for disinterested ends, I may easily misinterpret certain actions of the proponents.

I do not intend this unsuccessful fluoridation campaign to illustrate any specific tactical errors. I am not commenting on the general wisdom of getting endorsements from civic leaders, avoiding referenda, answering opponent charges, or any of the other specific acts which were performed. Such considerations are largely dependent on the conditions existing at a given time.

If I were to attempt listing "don'ts" they would center on certain characteristic attitudes among many active proponents in the fluoridation controversy:

Don't assume that all opponents are the same; that they are stupid, emotional crackpots. For every person this description fits, you'll convince several it doesn't fit to vote against it.

Don't assume that the mere multiplication of medical and political authorities will convince doubters that the experts agree. Attitudes of trust or distrust toward the influence held by such authorities may be decisive. Their endorsements of fluoridation may be given a different meaning by potential opponents.

Don't assume that those who are influential on some types of issues will necessarily be influential on fluoridation. An individual who wields a great deal of power on a sewerage or new school proposal may or may not be able to influence the outcome of a fluoridation vote.

Don't be annoyed that your role as expert is challenged. Some active proponents, by allowing themselves to be "baited" by hostile questions, seem to confirm opposition charges of high-handedness or concealment.

I wish to illustrate a more general criticism which grows out of the earlier discussion on the sources of opposition. Many people have feelings of political helplessness. This in itself does not turn them against fluoridation. That differences exist on this issue between voting proponents and opponents seems to indicate that there is something about fluoridation which arouses these feelings. This "something" may be inherent in the nature of the issue (its technical quality or some other feature) and beyond the control of anything proponents do in a campaign. On the other hand, it may be the partisans' attitude which stimulates these reactions. I have tried to illustrate in my hypothetical example how well-intended actions in a fluoridation campaign can have such unintended consequences.

Most of us are annoyed and self-righteous when an unqualified person challenges our opinion on a subject on which we feel we are to some degree an expert. This kind of legitimate "arrogance" is more refreshing than false humility. But legitimate or not, it is a poor posture to take on fluoridation or any other issue which will be decided by the voters of a community.

# 28.    The Policy-Maker
## and the Social Sciences

VINCENT P. ROCK

TIMES CHANGE AND SO DOES THE IMPORTANCE OF
the roles men play. In the 1930's the overriding problem was economic—
putting people to work. The result was that economists were accepted as
policy-makers, and policy makers became their own economists. It was
thought that if full employment were restored our major problems would
be solved and we could look toward the sunlit uplands of inevitable growth
and human progress.

But the way was hard and difficult. Why was it so difficult to find the
solution to be a fitting problem for political psychiatry? Not until World
War II was far advanced did the backlog of unemployed disappear. By then
the attention of policy-makers had turned elsewhere. They had become sol-
diers and strategists. Their great task was to defeat the enemy and re-
establish peace. With this accomplished, many believed that a single system for maintaining world order could be created and human progress
rapidly resumed. But hardly had peace been restored by the soldier-
strategists than conflict began again in new forms.

Today, we are deeply aware that neither economics nor military
strategy can, by themselves, provide solutions to the problems facing society. We are coming to recognize that our society is a highly complex
structure in the midst of an even more complex world. The policy-maker
has inevitably had to assume the role of sociologist or social scientist.
Lacking adequate tools for his new tasks, he is beginning to look more and
more to the whole range of social science for assistance.

In the 1960's, the major problems for the U.S. policy-maker are these:

First, how to influence, or at least avoid inhibiting the changes occurring within the Communist nations and particularly within the USSR, which are in the interest of their people, and not contrary to ours. Second, how to maintain the military security of the U.S. so that the Soviet Union could not destroy or overwhelm us. Third, how to guide or simply comprehend the vast socio-political changes occurring in third areas—that is, outside the communist block or the industrial West—so that our interests will not be jeopardized. Fourth, how to accelerate the integration of marginal groups within our own society, both to improve our image abroad, and reduce the sense of alienation and injustice at home. These groups comprising perhaps 14 to 20 per cent of our population are in our society, but not of it. They include many Negroes, the migratory farm workers, the Puerto Ricans, and others.

There are, of course, other questions that concern the policy-maker. How to curb juvenile delinquency, reduce crime, or accommodate the increasing number of older members of our society. But for the moment these are distinctly of a second order of importance to the policy maker at the national level.

If our country is to cope with the four great policy problem areas effectively and rationally, it requires a vast and organized contribution from the social sciences. Today the issues of public policy require all of us to a degree, to be social scientists just as in the thirties we were all economists.

Looking at the world today we are filled with a sense of bewilderment. We do not adequately understand what is happening, nor what should be done. We face the miracles of science and the persuasive fantasies of modern ideology, yet feel that neither science nor religion can provide adequate explanations or guidance. But more is known than is understood, and we hope that with time, talent, and resources more can be known and applied.

Viewed topically, our world gives rise to deepening pessimism. With study, however, we may find the basis for a reaffirmation of our historical belief in human progress. More men are literate, are educated in the scientific method, and have a degree of control over their own destiny than ever before in human history. But the change we desire will not come automatically. It requires a commitment to action, the avoidance of apathy. In acting, we must be aware of the complexity of society and the variety of human desires. To this end a full partnership between the policy-maker and the social scientist is required. Yet it is often difficult to achieve a fruitful alliance of social science and policy. Why is this so?

There appear to be four main reasons:

## Vincent P. Rock

*1.* Widespread lack of understanding of the nature of the policy process and the scope of research support it requires.

*2.* Both a critical imbalance and, in some areas, a gross deficiency in the allocation of funds among the various disciplines which could make a contribution to policy.

*3.* Confusion and conflict about the respective roles of the policymaker and the social scientist.

*4.* Lack of adequate institutional arrangements for linking social science with policy.

Let us now examine each of these problem areas.

Our understanding of the nature of policy-making is ambiguous. There is a widespread belief that policy decisions may be very broad and general in character. A President or head of a great department may, and indeed must, limit himself to setting general objectives and indicating broad directions for the country or department. After this, lesser hands implement the broad "policy" decisions. However, to be effective, policy decisions must have a substantial instrumental aspect. They must arise out of a vast effort of research, analysis, investigation, and discussion in which each of the large number of means and ends must be tested or examined in terms of some major means-ends relationship. For effective application, policies must be "engineered" in detail as well as agreed upon in general.

Many choices are open to us to influence Soviet power and performance in ways that may in the long run, contribute to the American ideal of a just and lawful world community. Today there is a vast gulf between the investment in research and development of a choice of weapons systems and the investment in research in all other areas of national life.

In the field of weapons development, vast funds are available for research. Seldom does one hear a figure of less than $100,000,000 for the basic and applied research on a new weapon. Even a small "widget" in such a weapons system may require and get ten or twenty million dollars in research funds. In any major weapons system there may be scores of such "widgets," each flowing from a major stream of research funds requiring the efforts of a large number of scientists and engineers throughout the country. As these "widgets" are conceived, designed, and tested, the possibilities and limitations of the weapons system begin to take shape.

At some point in this process an evaluation is made of the feasibility and cost-benefit relationships of producing the weapon and introducing it into the armed services. The purpose is to estimate the probable effectiveness of these weapons compared with those the enemy may be developing during the same period. In part, the evaluation is useful and reasonably

*360*

sound because the "widgets" and the subsystems have been developed by systematic and widespread research and each has been subjected to its own subsystem evaluation. The final product is a summary conclusion on the relative effectiveness and cost of the weapon in a period six to ten years beyond the time of the evaluation. Based on this evaluation and taking into account certain other factors, such as the state of the domestic economy, the policy-maker decides whether or not to proceed.

Such a decision may result in the expenditure of billions of dollars. The new weapon will be produced, the armed forces retrained and, if necessary, reorganized for its effective use. In a few years, however, frequently before actual combat use, the estimation of what the enemy is doing will suggest that the weapon is no longer valuable, or at least as valuable as it was estimated to be. When this occurs, the process may begin again with a new weapon system. Whether or not this process is valid can be tested only in war, and war is what we seek to avoid.

Yet, if war is to be avoided it would seem important to develop other capabilities. For this purpose I believe that similar investments in research and development of other capabilities are required. But they are not being made. Outside the areas of weapons and space competition, funds for research are limited to a few thousand or at most, a hundred thousand dollars in support of many major decisions.

Resources—money—available for social science and other research which may contribute to our survival and progress is grossly inadequate. If the social sciences are to have more than a marginal influence on policy and their conclusions treated as more than opinions about what should be done, there must be a major increase in the resources for research. While there is no doubt that the Federal Government is today more research minded than ever before, the funds available for research are unevenly distributed.

According to the National Science Foundation, research and development expenditures of the Federal Government in 1961–62 constituted about ten per cent of the national budget. This amounted to more than $9,500,-000,000 and the figure is growing rapidly. In the preceding year over $1,600,000,000 was allocated for research alone, excluding related development expenditures. Of the proportion spent for research, the vast bulk was concentrated in the natural sciences with only a small amount devoted to the social sciences. Almost $1,100,000,000 was spent in the fields of physical, mathematical and engineering sciences. Approximately $450,-000,000 was directed toward the life sciences, biology, medicine and agriculture. Only $58,000,000 went to the social sciences.

As might be expected, there was a heavy concentration of funds in the departments related to military security. About 1.1 billion dollars went to three agencies: Defense, $700,000,000; Atomic Energy Commission, $200,-000,000 and the National Aeronautics and Space Agency, over $150,-000,000. About one-third of the funds was allotted for the "improvement of our domestic welfare." The major recipients were the Department of Health, Education and Welfare—to help us live longer and better, and the Department of Agriculture—to help us use our growing food surpluses more effectively.

Almost nothing was directed to the major task of building a more viable world community. The Department of State, for example, received less than $1,000,000 for research on problems it was attempting to solve. In ludicrous contrast, the Department of Interior assigned approximately $8,000,000 for research "to insure the conservation of the nation's wild birds, mammals and sport fish, to encourage their maximum present use . . . compatible with their perpetuity." A praiseworthy objective, even if man is not included among the mammals.

Looking at the allocation of federal research resources from a somewhat different perspective one finds that in 1962 the Department of Defense had research and development contracts of more than $100,000,000 each with ten major business corporations. In addition, it is estimated that the Department of Defense assigned between $350,000,000 and $500,-000,000 to nonprofit research organizations. Within the government, the Department of Defense, the National Aeronautics and Space Agency, and the Atomic Energy Commission support 90 per cent of all research and development. This is not to suggest that such a massive research program is an unhealthy development. It is undoubtedly inevitable and necessary if our military security is to be maintained and the space race won in an age of rapid scientific and technological advance. The point to be stressed is that investments in other policy areas are likely to result in comparable ratios of benefits to costs.

But questions of roles as well as resources affect the contribution of social science to public policy. The social scientist is primarily concerned with the collection, analysis, and integration of knowledge which will enable him to understand society as it is, and perhaps even how to change it. His role is that of an observer and recorder. In contrast, the policy-maker is concerned with influencing or directing society, either his own or another, so that its behavior will be more compatible with the objectives of the U.S. as he sees them.

Since the policy-maker must act, he wants to know how his actions will affect the behavior of some group, either at home or abroad. He seeks answers to questions such as: (*1*) How can I influence the actions of a group within another nation or the nation as a whole in ways that will benefit the United States? (*2*) Is the group or nation accessible to the actions I may take? If not, how can it be made accessible? (*3*) What are the attitudes and trends within the other nation or group which are susceptible to influence by my action? (*4*) How can I use differences among opposing groups to serve the interests of my nation or, conversely, how can I strengthen cohesion and elicit cooperation in the objectives I seek to accomplish?

To illustrate further: if a policy-maker is concerned with the revolutionary movements throughout the world, it is not sufficient for him to have a complete and systematic description of past revolutions. He must know the conditions and circumstances for preventing revolution, the actions and the probability of their success in retarding or accelerating social change, and the best way of relating the instrument he has to the issue before him.

U.S. policy-makers do not have the knowledge that would increase the effectiveness of their actions on such questions. Nor is it likely to spring from the current interests and resources of social science. In the absence of sure knowledge, a policy-maker relies on intuition to judge the consequences of his acts. Unfortunately, as soon as a policy-maker makes one decision, he must turn to other problems. As a result, he seldom has time to evaluate the consequences of his acts and perhaps develop a more reliable basis for future action.

The imperative to act, to manage, which governs the policy-maker's view of his problems, is hard for many social scientists to accept. There are examples of social scientists, employed by the government to conduct research, whose contribution has been of limited utility because of a misunderstanding. To the policy-maker, the social scientist appears to have a neurotic reluctance to engage in the kind of research that would help him in his most important function—namely, the management of people and events to achieve national objectives. Obviously, some policy-makers may view society as more malleable, or at least more predictable than it is. Nevertheless, the essence of policy is to deal with the environment as though it were both perdictable and malleable while providing for the fact that it may be recalcitrant and unyielding to the methods used. Social science research, if it is to make its full contribution, must be sensitive to this point of view. Is it unfair to suggest that many social scientists consider it undemocratic or immoral to seek to manage people and that this view limits their contribution to policy?

More important may be the social scientists' belief that their disciplines are not ready to provide the tools the policy-maker requires. The social scientist prefers to spend his life gathering facts and presenting a rounded picture of society as a whole or aspects of it which interest him most. He becomes reticent when asked to reverse this process—to distinguish and study those phases of society which can be changed and modified by the policy-maker. The social scientist is reluctant to risk misusing his science. He recognizes the danger of premature application of social theory and experiments. Undoubtedly there is a risk. But in the end, the resolution of any great policy issue requires a significant injection of value judgments not open to experimental verification. One must also recognize the urgency of the times and the importance of the issues. Given the power of nuclear weapons, civilization may not have forever to find improved solutions to some of its basic problems.

Many years ago, P. S. Florence illustrated the problem of social science in his remarkable book, *Sociology and Sin*. He used the following example: suppose a government has built roads in the territory of a savage tribe and expects to be repaid by taxes. However, they resist paying the taxes. A military expert may advise the government to subdue the tribesmen by dropping bombs on the area. If the government continued to believe that savages must be made to pay their taxes, and relied on the advice of its military expert, the action would then be to drop bombs from airplanes.

However, if a social scientist were also advising the government, he could suggest that some parts of this argument can be tested. In the past, bombs encouraged tribesmen to pay their taxes promptly. But this statement will not apply to all tribes or all times. Unfortunately, from the point of view of the contribution of social science to policy-making, the second step, namely, that savages must be made to pay their taxes, is probably non-experimental. It embodies someone's sentiments in terms of national, or other interests.

Is social science to be excluded because of the second element of the problem? Hopefully, no, if the problem can be restated. Perhaps if the culture and value system of the tribe were adequately understood, alternative means could be devised which would rely less on force, and might even be more effective in getting the men to pay taxes. Or perhaps the sentiment of national interest could be broken down into its components to show that only under certain circumstances would it be prudent to resort to force.

This example illustrates the practical consequences of the lack of involvement of the main body of social scientists in national policy. Natural scientists, engineers and military officers have markedly different attitudes toward such involvement. They have had to enlarge their role to deal with policies which have as their central issue man and society rather than nature or technology. Of course, the law and similar vocations continue to provide the sturdy backbone of our professional political policy-makers.

The natural scientists, as a group, seem to have less anxiety about maintaining the independence of their scientific effort and are more at ease than the social scientists in contributing to federal policy-making. At the same time, the natural scientists have been able to maintain and substantially enlarge, the area of basic, undirected research in their fields financed by the federal government. In contrast, from the point of view of government, a break with the social sciences as a group began in the early 1950's, perhaps in part because of the McCarthy era. Until recently, many social scientists have continued to be sensitive about becoming involved in the federal policy process. Oddly enough, and perhaps connected with these attitudes, is the phenomenon that despite the dramatic difference in funds available to natural scientists and social scientists, spokesmen for the latter group have been inclined to say that resources for social science research are adequate.

Many federal agencies and even the executive office of the President are inadequately organized and staffed to make effective use of social science research. On the other hand, social scientists working alone are not able to organize their effort in a way that will provide results that are directly relevant to policy.

The issue posed by the policy-maker is frequently not directly susceptible to research. It must be redefined and perhaps even narrowed. However, this must be done in a way that will make the results of research relevant to the issue confronting the policy-maker. To provide the necessary linkage with policy, social scientists must organize and train men to perform at least three different roles. First, there is a requirement not only for individual but interdisciplinary group research on a large scale. Second, there is a need for policy innovators—men whose creative imagination and wide knowledge of research findings enable them to visualize the relevance of research findings to policy problems. Third, there is a necessity for men trained in the social sciences whose function in both research and in the policy process is to broaden and sharpen the communication between policy-maker and researcher. Thus, social engineers are required to observe the policy process, formulate questions for research and communicate these to individuals or groups prepared to undertake the research. In turn, they must translate the findings of research into terms that the policy-maker can understand and use.

*365*

## Vincent P. Rock

In conclusion, in dealing with the problems of competition with the Communist nations, social and political change in the emerging areas, and sheer survival in the nuclear age as well as with the further integration and development of our own society, the contributions of social science are urgently needed.

More than ever before, policy making at the national level faces a complex, changing environment, both international and domestic. It is confronted by almost overwhelming scientific and technological change. It must deal with more than a hundred sovereign nations whose cultures and values, in many cases, it only imperfectly perceives. It must cope with the implications of a gigantic flow of new information from every field of knowledge. Confronted by a vast range of problems, one would expect that research which has been found so useful in other fields would be consistently used to conserve the time and supplement the judgment of the policy-maker. The facts are otherwise. Research to support this nation's policy-making is only partially organized and its use fragmentary in character.

The reasons for the present state of affairs include (1) an inadequate understanding of the policy process both within and outside the government, (2) inadequate resources, (3) lack of clarity in the respective roles of the policy-maker and social scientist and (4) insufficient institutional provisions for linking policy and social science.

The cooperative effort of those in government and those in social science is needed to insure that research in all the disciplines and for a variety of purposes makes its appropriate and valuable contribution to policy.

The policy-maker's task is to choose among competing alternatives. The function of research is to provide him with a rational basis for his choices, within the broadest framework of information, analysis, and theory.

# 29.  Social Research and Social Action
# in Prevention of Juvenile Delinquency

EVA ROSENFELD

M OST WORKERS IN THE FIELD OF JUVENILE DELIN-
quency are painfully aware of the wide gap between the amount of past
and ongoing research in this area, and the difficulty in translating our
knowledge into effective preventive action. No doubt there are many reasons for this difficulty, some of them inherent in the very complexity and
scope of the problem. But it is becoming increasingly clear that some, and
perhaps major, reasons are methodological: the tradition of our research
approach seems to be remarkably sterile.

The following discussion concerns itself primarily with these methodological reasons for the notorious deficiency in our knowledge of how to
prevent juvenile delinquency. The analysis of the problem will be illustrated by a case study, the problem of prevention of narcotics use among
juveniles.

To begin with, let us briefly consider how much have we learned about
the problem of juvenile delinquency in the past thirty years of empirical
study.

*What We Knew in the 1920's and What We Know Now*

In 1925 an English psychologist and educator, Cyril Burt, published a
book on "The Young Delinquent"[2] which (in England at least) is still

mentioned as a classic in the field. In this 600-page classic, Burt, who had been working with juvenile delinquents for many years, carefully evaluated available evidence concerning the variety of factors contributing to juvenile misbehavior and concluded that crime springs from a "multiplicity of . . . converging factors" . . . "a concurrence of subversive factors." "The nature of these factors and of their varying combinations differ greatly from one individual to another and juvenile offenders, as is amply clear, are far from constituting a homogeneous class."

In spite of this variation, however, Burt listed a number of "major" background factors which he found discernible in about 96% of the several hundred cases he studied. Among them we find poverty, defective family relations—especially the absence of a father and defective discipline—a family history of vice and crime, and emotional and intellectual disturbances in the personality, especially "mental dullness" and "temperamental instability."

In 1953, almost 30 years after the publication of this classic, the Youth Board of the City of New York, a most forward-looking agency, undertook a four-year study in two elementary schools to test the validity of a prediction-of-delinquency scale developed, after many years of intensive research, by Sheldon and Eleanor Glueck. This scale is composed of three basic variables: parental discipline and supervision, parental affection, and family cohesiveness. A preliminary report indicates that the predictive use of the scale is likely to be validated with a high degree of significance.

The juxtaposition of these two theories of causal factors in juvenile delinquency would indicate that not much new has been added, but, rather, that the understanding already available three decades ago has been tested, narrowed down, and specified.

But how about prevention? Certainly the goal of most, if not of all, of our investigations into the causes of juvenile crime was to learn how to prevent it. Here, unhappily, our achievements are even more modest.

Writing 30 years ago, Cyril Burt recommended the following six basic pillars of a prevention and rehabilitation program[2] (pp. 584–87):

1. All young persons who show delinquent tendencies should be dealt with at the earliest possible stage. Parents should be taught that the pre-school period is a period vitally decisive. . . . Teachers should be urged to watch, and when necessary to report, all who show antisocial inclinations . . . When the school period is over, after-care workers should be persuaded to extend their supervision to the social conduct, as well as the industrial efficiency, of children who have just left; and, above all, special efforts should be made to meet the transitional phase of adolescence.

2. The problem of delinquency in the young must be envisaged as but one inseparable portion of the larger enterprise for child welfare. Crime in children is not a unique, well-marked, or self-contained phenomenon, to be handled solely by the policeman and the children's court. It touches every side of social work. The teacher, the care committee worker, the magistrate, the probation officer, all who come into official contact with the child, should be working hand in hand not only with each other, but with all the clubs, societies, and agencies, voluntary as well as public, that seek to better the day-to-day life of the child.

3. The delinquent himself must be approached individually as a unique human being with a peculiar constitution, peculiar difficulties, and peculiar problems of his own. . . . The court, therefore, and whatever authority has to grapple with such cases must at all times regard not the offense, but the offender. The aim must not be punishment, but treatment; and the target not isolated actions, but their causes. . . . Such authorities must have access to all available information and possess means to make for every case intensive investigations of their own. . . . A social investigator must report upon home circumstances; a medical officer must inspect the child for physical defects; a psychologist must be at hand to apply mental tests, to assess temperamental qualities, and to analyze unconscious motives. A psychological clinic embodying all these different workers studying the same cases scientifically, side by side, is the most pressing need of all.

4. The remedies, in the same way, will be adapted, not to the nature of the offense, but to the nature of the factors provoking it. Probation should be employed with a larger freedom, and at the same time with finer discrimination; it should include, for each separate case, not merely passive surveillance, but active and constructive efforts. . . . After-care, in particular, calls for further extension; to lavish a hundred pounds upon the intensive training of a youth in an institution and then suddenly to fling him loose into the old environment, sparing neither time nor trouble for further aid and following-up, is not economy but waste.

5. Fuller knowledge is urgently wanted: it is wanted both in regard to the causation of crime and in respect of the relative efficacy of different remedial measures. Only from the organization of research can this fuller knowledge come, and organized research means an established criminological department. The fruits of such research should be made immediately accessible to the practical officer, and courses of instruction should be arranged where all who have to deal with the young offender may learn the latest and best accredited results of modern criminal psychology.

6. Finally, society must aim at prevention as well as at cure. Housing, medical treatment, continued education, the psychological study of children in schools, improved industrial conditions, increased facilities for recreation, the cautious adoption of practicable eugenic measures, and above all, sustained investigation into all the problems of childhood—these are but a few of the

countless needs to be supplied, if delinquency in the young is to be not merely cured as it arises, but diverted, forestalled, and so far as possible wiped out.

This, let us remember, was said on the basis of the available research evidence of over 30 years ago. Let us now take a look at our current accomplishments in the field of preventive action.

We have very few studies on *what* can be done to arrest the rising tide of juvenile delinquency, *how* it might be done, and *how effective* the efforts are. Consider research reported in the *Current Sociological Research* series for the past three years. About 30 to 40 studies on criminology and sociology of law are studied each year. Most of these studies deal with the description of the ongoing practices in criminal procedure, or statistical description of crime rates and areas of high delinquency, or a refinement of analysis of background factors. Of the over one hundred studies reported in the past three years, only 10 have anything to do with the evaluation of some way of handling some aspect of the problem, and of these, eight deal with evaluation of treatment in correctional institutions, that is, at the end of the line, after the crime has been committed. Only one research project dealt with an evaluation of a preventive program in the community.

Neither was there much activity in this area in the past years. We have available a survey of delinquency prevention programs in this country and of the measure of their success. The survey was recently prepared by Helen Witmer and Edith Tufts of the Children's Bureau.[8] There have been a number of preventive programs in various parts of the country, some of them carried on over a period of many years and evaluated—in a manner. One striking characteristic of all these programs is that each is focused on *one* simple aspect of the supposed multiple causal factors: better recreational facilities *or* detached group workers *or* better community facilities *or* friendly counselling *or* child guidance treatment *or* an "area" approach stimulating grass-roots responsibility and neighborhood feeling. We may add that not even the New York City Youth Board, which includes many approaches in its program, pursues any of these in an integrated fashion in any one area of the city; in effect, its program consists of a congeries of programs rather than of one program.

Another characteristic of these programs is that those who had set them up truly believed that their particular program would make a significant difference in delinquency rates, and were genuinely disappointed when evaluation in those terms showed no results whatsoever. The authors of the survey sum up by asking, "What does it all add up to in knowledge about how to prevent or reduce delinquency?"—and their answer is, "With certainty, rather little."

## Research and Action in Prevention of Delinquency

When we compare this sad state of affairs with Cyril Burt's six points, we are faced with a most embarrassing situation. Not only have we not learned anything in the past 30 years, but we seem to have proceeded on premises which common sense, logic, and available knowledge would declare to be most naive. What, then, interferes with the progress of applied and applicable knowledge in this field?

Let us take a case in point: the problem of understanding and controlling narcotics use among juveniles. By looking at it, we will obtain a clear picture of most of the difficulties in the general field of delinquency prevention.

## A Case Study: How to Prevent Narcotics Use by Juveniles

### 1. THE FIRST STEP: UNDERSTANDING THE NATURE OF THE PROBLEM.

When the most recent wave of juvenile drug use hit the headlines some five years ago and the staff of the Research Center for Human Relations started its investigations at the request of the National Institute of Mental Health,* we were exploring a virtually unknown territory. Available information was for the most part unsystematic or unreliable or both. Consequently, in planning a series of studies, we felt compelled to obtain, first, a bird's-eye view of each of the many aspects of this phenomenon which might be likely to play a role as a contributing factor. Using the customary methods, we pinpointed the New York City areas where the greatest juvenile users live and investigated the distinguishing characteristics of these neighborhoods; we looked into the backgrounds and past histories of the juvenile drug-users; we studied their family situations and their relations with peers; we tried to understand the general climate of values and attitudes which is hospitable to a favorable attitude to drug-use; we studied the role of the street gang in the spread of drug-use and the relation between drug-use and other forms of delinquency. We worked closely with a psychiatrist who had done studies of the personality of juvenile addicts and is currently engaged in therapeutic work with addicts.

Thus, we arrived, after several years of research, at a general understanding concerning the social and psychic dynamics behind the problem. The picture that emerged is, briefly, as follows:

The adolescent boy who becomes involved with drugs, continues to use

---

* A series of studies have been conducted since 1952 by Donald L. Gerard, Robert S. Lee, Eva Rosenfeld, and Daniel M. Wilner, under the general direction of Isidor Chein. See 3, 4, and 6.

371

them regularly, and eventually reaches the stage of being "hooked" is, usually, a member of a deprived racial or ethnic group, often a native-born son of immigrant parents, whose family lives in one of the poorest and most disorganized areas of the city, though their own social and financial standing is often higher than what is typical for the area. His family is a source of special strain and deprivation. Relations between parents are seriously disturbed. The father is absent or hostile or weak. The mother's attitude to the son is extreme: either passionate and consuming, or cool and distant. Parental discipline is either overindulging or extremely harsh. Parental standards and expectations are unclear and unrealistic— too high or too low. Their general attitude to life and to society is pessimistic and distrustful.

The boy's personality is seriously damaged. He might be suffering from overt or incipient schizophrenia. Whatever the form of his disturbance, however, he is almost certain to have a weak, inadequate ego and a poorly functioning superego. He also has serious problems in sexual identification, distrusts authority and has a poor sense of reality, especially regarding his own future. As he reaches young adulthood at the age of 16, 17, or 18, he enters situations with which he cannot cope. He faces failure and loneliness of which he is deeply afraid.

He is likely to be more or less loosely attached to one of the street gangs in the neighborhood. Unlike his well-adjusted neighbor, he has made no efforts to stay away from the aggressive, delinquent "cats," though their violent "hell-raising" may not be quite to his taste. But he stays in their orbit. He gains some measure of support from a sense of belonging to a group. In this group, he becomes exposed to drugs, marijuana, and heroin, taken at parties for a kick, in a spirit of experimenting with danger. The drug has a pacifying effect—his sadness, loneliness, anxiety seem to vanish, and he experiences a pleasurable relief from unbearable tension. The gang frowns upon uncontrolled use of drugs which leads to addiction. For a year, or even two, he may use the drug irregularly. But the time comes when the gang loses its cohesiveness, hell-raising becomes "kid stuff," and some of the less disturbed youngsters turn their minds to growing up in a man's world, going "steady," finding a good job. It is at this point that, having to face life alone, as a man, the anxious and inadequately functioning boy falls back on the pacifying and engrossing life of a habitual user. Enmeshed in the pattern of activities revolving around the purchase, sale, and use of heroin, and the delinquent efforts to get money to meet the exorbitant cost of the drug, the young user can comfortably forget about girls, careers, status, and recognition in the society at large.

His sexual drive is diminished, he is able to maintain a sense of belonging to the immature, limited world of the addict. He can remain a child forever. He can give up all sense of responsibility for his life and conveniently project the blame for his shiftless existence on his "habit."

His chances for a cure are very small. Physical withdrawal does not take away the psychic need for some relief from inner tension, nor does it erase the memory of the relief brought by opiates. The road from the hospital or jail to the drug peddler is short, indeed. His resistance to psychotherapy is great; he feels that it offers nothing but increased anxiety and his tolerance of anxiety is, as we said, very low.

This is a bare outline of our knowledge. It satisfied our need for understanding and we took a pause for reflection.

### 2. THE SECOND STEP: DRAWING IMPLICATIONS FOR ACTION.

Our investigation was started with the general idea of learning something of relevance to the *solution* of a social problem. On the basis of our data, we regretfully find ourselves unable to recommend any specific action. Knowing the forces that *contribute* to a social evil tells us nothing about how to eradicate the evil. In fact, why should it? There is no logical reason why the weapon most effective in destroying a social phenomenon should be in a direct way related to the forces that make it grow. The general purpose of the type of exploratory studies we did is not so much to discover how to eradicate the evil but, rather, how *not* to try to eradicate it. For, by highlighting the enormous complexity of interdependent factors of which drug-use is a symptom, our studies in fact taught us that there is no simple and easy way of doing away with the symptom.

So far, we have not committed any methodological sins. What we did, had to be done. We now had a general picture of our target area. What next?

### 3. THE THIRD STEP: CREATING A FRAMEWORK FOR PREVENTIVE ACTION.

Clearly the next step was research on specific measures aimed at a reduction of drug-use by forestalling the pressures that appear to lead to it. And since so many of the pressures overlapped with those which had been discovered by experts in juvenile delinquency, we expected to profit from their experience. But in examining available research in the prevention of delinquency, we discovered—as I had mentioned—that very little had been done. There is, in fact, no conceptual framework for preventive action.

It is not difficult to understand why such a framework was slow in developing. Research in the causes of delinquency, as well as our own research in the causes of drug addiction, pointed, as we said, to a complex maze of interrelated personal and environmental pressures and deprivations. And theories based on empirical investigations stressed the fact that only a *convergence* of pressures and deprivations lead to delinquency. It was difficult, in fact impossible, to derive from this complex picture, by a process of reasoning, some reasonably manageable, manipulable prescription for effective prevention. A variety of things were to be recommended for the great variety of contributing factors: more financial help to deprived families, child guidance for the emotionally disturbed, recreation for the street gangs, a substitute father figure for the fatherless, grass-root participation, and so on. The multiplicity of these services adds up to a task which it is difficult for many an individual mind to grasp. And, as preventive programs were initiated as a rule by well-meaning individuals with limited funds at their disposal and acting in a framework of a single local agency, it would appear that good will and an urge to some action led them to substitute what was feasible for what reason and knowledge indicated was *necessary*. And in evaluating their one-pronged programs, it would seem that they were led by irrational hope: maybe it will make a difference.

Well, it did *not* make a difference. Profiting from their disillusion, we decided that in approaching the task of devising a preventive and rehabilitative program for youths in trouble, we will honestly consider all measures that, on the basis of our knowledge, appeared to be important, without worrying for the time being about the practicability of such a program. We consequently put down on paper all the measures that either available knowledge or, in its absence, common sense and intelligent guesswork suggested as remedies for the wide variety of personal and environmental deficiencies which appear to be at the root of the problem.

This task was not particularly difficult. Soon we had a list of preventive and rehabilitative measures, each backed by a specific rationale.

The general rationale of the project is to modify the youths' experience in their school and street environment so that it will counteract (rather than, as is now the case, reinforce) the early family experience of emotional deprivation, by giving multiple proof that the society *cares* about them and their future. More specifically, the aim is to: (1) expand their reference groups to include ever larger circles of people and, by thus giving them a more broadly-based sense of *belonging*, make it more difficult for them to deny guilt for hostile acts against persons perceived as strangers; (2) provide *constructive channels* for the expression of "free-floating energy" and, in general, to satisfy the adolescent need for new experience, exploration, and learning; and (3) offer special *help and support* to individuals who need it.*

### 4. THE FOURTH STEP: FROM SOCIAL THEORY TO SOCIAL ENGINEERING.

The chief difficulty in envisaging the program on a community basis was the nature and extent of coordination of all those efforts directed at youth, at their families, and at adults working with youth, such as teachers, police, recreation workers, parole officers, and the like.

We could say *what* we thought should be done, but when we started thinking about the *how*, we found that it was impossible to predict in advance what approach would be successful. It was, in fact, impossible to make safe guesses about the effectiveness of purposive social action. Why?

One way of answering this query is to say that, in general, purposive social action tends to lead to unanticipated consequences. In his classic analysis of this problem, Robert K. Merton suggests that *inability to foresee* all consequences of social action may derive—apart from the obvious reason, namely, simple ignorance—from the intrinsic inadequacy of knowledge of human behavior which is available to us. Human behavior in any situation is not a constant but, rather, is represented by a *range* of possibilities. This range increases with any variation in the *conditions* of the situation. In very complex situations, determined by many conditions, the range of behavior resulting from the interplay of all conditions is so immense that for all practical purposes the probable outcome of social action cannot be predicted.[7]

In addition, the effort at prediction is also contaminated by errors of judgment in appraising the conditions of the situation, by bias and by neglect, by an immediacy of interest in some one aspect of the problem, and by similar impedimenta.

For example, we recommended modifications in the policy of recreation centers and settlement houses, to one in which they would attempt to draw the anti-social gangs into some of the available activities. But how should they go about it? What approach, what steps are necessary to avoid a complete wreckage of the place?

In our wish to see this part of the program put into effect, we—in thinking out the techniques of approach—overlooked, as we were later told by no less an expert than Fritz Redl, the low "deviation tolerance" of the regular members of the community house or playground. Just as the "cats"

---

* This summary, by necessity so very brief, does poor justice to the original argument—in fact, it reduces it to a cliche. The analysis is developed in Isidor Chein, et al., *The Road to H.*

are thrown into a turmoil of emotions at the prospect of civil contact with the "squares," so the "squares" are likely to become anxious and disturbed by the prospect of admitting the wild "cats" into their regulated world. (And if the reader should think this oversight of ours was avoidable and that he would have thought of it, let me remind him that this is only one of the many factors that must be considered; each of us has some blind spots, somewhere.)

Besieged by these self-doubts concerning our ability to recommend the best course, we felt impelled to turn for help to experts in the field, people who have the actual "know-how." We felt that, even though so little of their work had been carefully evaluated, much could be learned from them. People who for many years continue in one type of work as a rule accumulate a wealth of intimate knowledge of the great variety of forces, pressures, interests, conditions that play a role in the situation in which they work. Every agency has an accumulation of past experience which could teach others if not how to do things better, or how not to approach certain problems, then at least what special conditions, usually overlooked, played a role in the failure of a given venture. A survey of such experience was, then, our next step. Through personal interviews with workers in the field, we tried to learn what they have learned.

5. THE FIFTH STEP: LEARNING FROM THE EXPERIENCE OF OTHERS.

The first difficulty in an experience survey is to dodge or get around the heads of the various agencies, who often are far removed from the work experience of field workers. The second difficulty is to get the field worker to feel free and unconstrained, to talk openly about his experience. In some cases—notably with the police, both obstacles are insurmountable in this type of a survey. In all cases, the tapping of experience is a slow and painstaking task. There are special reasons why this wisdom based on experience is not easily made explicit and available to the public or even to qualified research personnel.

One of these is the widespread reluctance to self-appraisal. This reluctance springs from a variety of sources. One is the common fear of change—a sense of security is derived from habitual routinized ways of doing things. It would take us too far afield to pinpoint all the elements in our social structure that contribute to this fear. But some of these contributors are based on misconceptions and misunderstandings of the function of research and those are of prime concern to us.

One such frequently encountered misconception is that only success is worth mention and mistakes are to be shamefully glossed over or covered up. Yet a careful analysis of how and why things have gone wrong can be extremely profitable. A good example is a survey of the accomplishments and failures of the Neighborhood Center for Block Organization, which functioned in Harlem in the mid-forties.[1] The survey spotlights the apathy of the tenants which made it so difficult to mobilize them effectively for self-help, and it provides some insight into the nature of this "apathy."

In fact, one might point out to those shy of their failures that these failures, if recorded and analyzed, are more rewarding for applied social science than successes. In terms of the logic of scientific method, interpretation of successes may easily lead to the "fallacy of affirming the consequent." If some theory of delinquency leads to some program of action, the success of the program does not confirm the theory—it merely demonstrates that it is not yet untenable.

Furthermore, an attempt to reproduce the conditions of success has at least two pitfalls: (1) it may include spurious or irrelevant factors or (2) it may easily overlook an important ingredient of it. But failures at least enable us to disprove a current hypothesis or focus the need to revise it. Specifically in the field of social action, failures point to the need for re-examining the premises of action more carefully and often pinpoint an important but overlooked condition in the situation. It is clearly our duty to explain these truths to heads of agencies and their financial backers and convince them that by keeping adequate records and periodically analyzing their mistakes and failures, they will provide a most enlightened and forward-looking attitude which will reflect most favorably on their management of their agencies.

Another reason why the learning value of failures receives so little publicity is related to our academic tradition of research. Our colleges and even graduate schools apparently fail to tell social science (and social work) students about this "royal road" to action-relevant knowledge and in general to scientific discovery. For while they carefully design laboratory experiments to disprove a hypothesis at great cost and effort, few students and few scholars are encouraged to avail themselves of the blunders, the mistakes, the failures in social action as a means for challenging and disproving commonly accepted premises on which this action was based. It may be true that such research, which evaluates retrospectively the causes of failure, can hardly be rigidly exact and lead to validated conclusions. Formal, traditional, academic research, very rigid, very exact, is oriented to neglecting the golden mine of hunches, hypotheses, insights.* But,

* Another aspect of the tradition of academic research contributes to this under-evaluation of failures as sources of discoveries, and that is the attitude that negative

surely, these are as valuable and as scarce as carefully validated tests of specific hypotheses.

But not only heads of social agencies and not only the academicians neglect to exploit real-life experience for the knowledge it hides—much of our non-academic research on social problems fails in this respect. And here again it is the tradition, the established, sanctified routines that are to blame—not the individual researchers. To take an example, a large youth agency in one of our cities recently designed a research project to evaluate and improve one of its casework services. The design called for an analysis of some 150 case histories by a statistician, to be followed by a more intensive study of a sample of cases. There was no mention of exploiting the years of experience of some dozen social workers and obtaining their impressions, hunches, opinions concerning their current methods of work and ideas for improvements.

Industrial sociologists and psychologists long ago pointed out that it pays to lend an ear to the worker on the lot and to his straw boss. Their recommendations apparently became generally accepted in modern, up-to-date industrial establishments. And listening to the consumer is, of course, the essence of marketing research. Yet in both academic and applied research this principle of listening to the grass roots is less explicitly stressed and seldom followed. Whence the difference?

The difference, I propose, derives from the different accounting principles of industrial research on the one hand and academic and applied social research on the other. In the former type of research *the client pays* the researcher. In the latter, the client—the person in whose interests the research is conducted—is the passive subject of research; researchers get paid by academic institutions (in degrees more often than in money), by foundations, by the local and federal government agencies. The researcher naturally has the interest of his client at heart. But he also has at heart his own interests which have to do with professional standards, with the recognition that is accorded a methodologically "clean" job, a neat conceptual framework which is safely derived from standard, prestigeful conceptual frameworks currently in fashion. There is no one, outside the researcher's own conscience, to put pressure on his work for more "action-orientation."

findings render a doctoral dissertation worthless as a means of getting a degree. The distinction is seldom made clear between "negative findings" (i.e., findings in which the hypotheses that have been advanced are shown to be untenable) and "equivocal" findings (i.e., findings which have no real bearing on the hypotheses: they neither confirm nor deny the consequent)—with the result that through a critical period in his training, many a Ph.D. candidate lives in dread of negative findings and learns to look upon them as worthless.

And in a peculiarly somnambulistic way, even the enlightened public often calls for "more research" (meaning more research on the causes of troublesome phenomena) than for more action. We have apparently succeeded in terrorizing this liberal public into the belief that much research has to be done before one may act safely. Yet in the slow progress from understanding to resolving social problems, action must precede full understanding, for much of the understanding comes from observing first attempts at remedial action fail.

It may be cogent to quote a conclusion of a committee of distinguished professional men after a survey of close to a thousand books and articles dealing with mental health activities and their evaluation:

The frequency in which research and service agencies in the same community operate in "isolated cells" is impressive. A research center may operate in an "ivory tower" and fail to include for research validation valuable exploratory leads in an applied field because of lack of such information, and with efforts limited to the pursuit of preconceived hypotheses which preclude other experimental approaches. Conversely, in an operating agency, experimental leads are discovered and attempts made at scientific validation with faulty conclusions and interpretations, as a result of inappropriate or inadequate methodology and in the absence of technical research "know-how." [5]

## What Must Be Done?

Further research into the origins of juvenile delinquency and of related symptoms of social and personal malfunctioning among our youth is not likely to produce much knowledge relevant to preventive and rehabilitative measures. What is needed now is a carefully recorded, analyzed, and evaluated trial-and-error method, using various approaches in various combinations in various conditions, learning all the while—unlearning and learning.

The need for such a "trial-and-error plus evaluation" approach is indicated not only by the uncertainty of our knowledge about prevention and by the difficulty of predicting in advance the effectiveness of any given program of action. This approach is also necessary to debunk the pessimism of those "experienced" workers who have become paralyzed by routine and have lost the daring for experimentation with new approaches.

Many types of services and methods of approach which appear to be vitally important as preventive measures for youths in deprived areas are now believed by many experts in the field to be either extremely difficult or totally impossible. Yet here and there an enterprising worker has tried and succeeded. In our own survey, we have learned that it *is* possible, though admittedly difficult, to draw anti-social gangs into a city recreation project. It *is* possible to teach many people who have work difficulties how to work in peace and productively. It *is* possible to establish good, friendly working relations with the police. Certain precautions must be taken, certain groundwork laid beforehand, certain resources made available for financial and spiritual sustenance and support. Not much cooperation should be expected initially from the largely apathetic, suspicious, frightened people in the deprived areas. Energy must be pumped into the area and this energy must be carefully sustained among the people who would become involved in preventive work, by tapping varieties of motivation, and by providing continuous rewards.

One source of motivation and of inner rewards that should be tapped and exploited to the full is the scientific interest in the principles of purposive social action. This interest should be stimulated both in our academic institutions and in operating agencies. This could be done in a variety of ways: encouraging more doctoral candidates to do their field work in social agencies; encouraging social workers to attend research seminars; publicizing among social agencies scholarly analyses of various experiences which stress the value of learning from failures; etc.

The responsibility for initiating such contact and stimulating scientific interest in social action rests with the social scientists.

## NOTES

1. Bowens, Marx G., "The Neighborhood Center for Block Organization," in *Group Work in Community Life*, ed. by C. E. Murray, M. G. Bowens, and R. Hogrefe, New York: Association Press, 1954, pp. 13–60.

2. Burt, Cyril, *The Young Delinquent*, New York: Appleton, 1925.

3. Chein, Isidor, "Narcotics Use Among Juveniles," *Social Work*, 1 (April, 1956), 50–60.

4. Chein, Isidor, and Eva Rosenfeld, "Juvenile Heroin Users in New York City," *Law and Contemporary Problems*, 22 (Winter, 1957).

5. *Evaluation in Mental Health*, U.S. Dept. of Health, Education and Welfare, 1955.

6. Gerard, Donald L., and Conan Kornetsky, "Adolescent Opiate Addiction: A Study of Control and Addict Subjects," *The Psychiatric Quarterly*, 29 (July, 1955), 457–86.

7. Merton, Robert K., "The Unanticipated Consequences of Purposive Social Action," *American Sociological Review*, 1 (December, 1936), 894–904.

8. Witmer, Helen L., and Edith Tufts, *The Effectiveness of Delinquency Prevention Programs*, Children's Bureau Publication No. 350, 1954.

*Part VI*

*ISSUES IN*

*APPLIED SOCIOLOGY*

# 30.   Values and Theory of Social Problems

## LLEWELLYN GROSS

Aᴄᴄᴏʀᴅɪɴɢ ᴛᴏ Hᴏʀᴛᴏɴ ᴀɴᴅ Lᴇꜱʟɪᴇ, ᴛʜᴇ ᴅᴇꜰɪɴɪ-
tion of social problems contains four distinct ideas: "(1) a condition affecting a significant number of people; (2) in ways considered undesirable;
(3) and about which it is felt something should be done; (4) through
collective social action."[1] The position of these authors is shared in whole
or in part by L. K. Frank, Fuller and Meyers, Cuber and Harper, T. L.
Smith, A. M. Rose and R. K. Merton, to mention a few.[2]

Although each of these authors has criticized aspects of this definition,
none has, to the writer's knowledge, proposed one that is less dependent
upon the responses of public spokesmen.[3] Despite serious misgivings from
other quarters, they have supported the principle that scientific conclusions
must be sharply separated from ethical conclusions. What, then, are the
possibilities of a program of scientific ethics directed toward the amelioration of social problems? But first, a brief critique of the principal ideas in
the preceding definition.

1. Attempts to specify the meaning of "a condition affecting a significant number of people" are handicapped by the absence of ethical
standards to guide decisions. Short of such standards, almost any question
produces theoretical dilemmas.

Perhaps every social condition affects a significant number of people.
For instance, can we claim that the unemployment of one million laborers
is more (or less) significant than the fatality rate from drugs, without
knowing how to evaluate human lives? Must we not have criteria for judg-
ing the privileges and privations of various families, classes and nations,
before estimating whether the Civil Liberties Union is numerically more
significant than a group of popularly acclaimed beatniks? Is the disbanding
of a group of volunteer firemen more significant than the demise of a group

*383*

of octogenarians? How large must a minority be to be significant?[4] Obviously, we cannot answer these questions without general rules for defining standards of significance.[5]

2. The requirement that social problems refer to conditions deemed undesirable by a significant number of people, avoids entirely the ethical question of whether certain beliefs and practices may be "good" or "right" in spite of group opinion.

Some writers contend there may be group agreement on the undesirability of certain conditions such as murder and illness despite disagreement on solutions. But apart from the question of solutions is agreement on the undesirability of certain conditions scientifically meaningful without evaluation of their antecedents and consequences?[6] Even general rules of law allow for circumstantial exceptions by requiring judicial interpretation! From another standpoint, is not the widespread neglect, misguidance and alienation of children a "social problem" even though communication biases prevent awareness by a significant number of people? Cannot human slavery or deficient sanitation be social problems even though very few people regard them as undesirable? In the spectrum of history, free inquiry seems to have been a social problem for significant numbers of people. Can anyone in the academic community assess this problem without defining its conditionals, "if" and "since," or its consequentials, "then" and "therefore?" Before free inquiry can be viewed as undesirable we must know its sources and effects.[7]

3. The definition of social problems emphasizes the necessity of public feeling that something should be done to alleviate the condition. Implicit is the general belief, request, counsel, injunction, or command that the action taken should be the most appropriate or praiseworthy under the circumstances.

Unfortunately, social problems are aggravated by individuals who believe *definite* things should be done to realize their aims. Moreover, there is little evidence that *most* people desire to solve problems originating outside the visible confines of their immediate interests. (Consider, for instance, business corruption, drug addiction, and racial segregation.) Can we be sure our citizens are as strongly motivated by public concerns as by interest in self and family? Do we have substantial testimony that definitions of social problems reflect more than responses to personal distress or deprivation? Again, standards of evaluation are essential to adjudicate claims about the problematic status of social conditions.

4. The final ingredient in the definition of social problems includes the policy of collective action to support the feeling that some condition should be changed. Thus, the difficulty of agreeing on the undesirability of a so-

cial condition is compounded by the further difficulty of agreeing on the desirability of a particular course of action.

Cuber and Harper state that although there may be agreement on the existence of an undesirable condition, some may recommend that nothing be done because proposed actions would worsen conditions, be too complex, or go contrary to human nature. Others want the problem removed only in part.[8] These and the preceding circumstances suggest that "We cannot take for granted a reasonably correct public imagery of social problems: of their scale, distribution, causation, consequences and persistence or change."[9] If democratic solutions of social ills are to be more reliable than democratic solutions of physical ills, the diagnoses of social problems must be oriented to ethical principles. Prevalent conceptions of basic causes, effective actions, and long-run consequences must be reshaped to accommodate ethical standards.

## The Responsibility of Science to Define Social Problems

If most public groups lack sufficient resources to define social problems, greater responsibility must be carried by scientists with sociological competence and ethical values. On this assumption, the concepts and values of science can be used to guide public solutions to social problems. Granting this, we explore the likelihood that sociologists can contribute to the public's definition of what is ethically right, desirable, or good. This exploration rests on the following possibilities:

1. that valuational language implies and is implied by empirical language.

2. that socially meaningful facts imply valuational frameworks of conditions and consequences.

3. that socially meaningful values imply factual frameworks of conditions and consequences.

4. that ethical aims can be scientifically defined.

5. that sociologists must prescribe social values for laymen.

6. that laymen will ascribe social values to sociology.

7. that established views about science and values should be open to fresh inquiry.

Each of these possibilities will be reviewed in the following discussion.

### ARE VALUATIONAL AND EMPIRICAL LANGUAGES LINKED CONCEPTUALLY?

A future task for social problems theory is investigation of the linkage between valuational and empirical languages. For some laymen, right (or good) behavior is any activity promoting social innovations. For others, it is any procedure for allocating rewards consistent with the *status quo*. For still others, approval is given any activity which progressively elevates the standard of living of its less privileged members. Several possibilities apply to the nature of the bond between the two languages. First, the bond itself may be empirically derived and thus based on the appearance of repeated conjunctions between the languages. Even though the conjunctions are not uniform, limited regularities may occur, just as status may be associated in different places with occupation, income, education or genealogy. Second, the bond may be viewed as necessary in the same way that logical structure implies the truth of an analytical proposition. Third, the bond may be known in some intuitive sense not reducible to either empirical or analytical meaning. Finally, the bond may represent some combination of these or other alternatives.[10]

On the basis of empirical evidence favoring linkage between the two languages, theory construction can be introduced to resolve opposing interpretations. The resultant ethico-empirical generalizations may not embody direct observations but, for this very reason, they can provide useful standards for evaluating human conduct. Given such standards, any theorist's judgment could be taken as correct when he holds the appropriate ones, knows all the relevant facts, and makes no mistakes of inference. Beyond this, his first duty would be to unseat Schopenhauer's claims that "man can do what he will but he cannot will what he will."[11] Confronted with the scientific canon of unremitting appraisal, he would step beyond himself and the current state of sociology by seeking answers to the question, "Why should I choose these standards?" Led to appraise the very standards by which current appraisals are made his present knowledge would be seen as providing but one set of alternatives within a larger framework of choices, many of which are hypothetical. The exploration of untried alternatives would guarantee scientific decisions not encumbered by culture-bound creeds, options with powers to invert Schopenhauer by willing to will what they do. Only in this manner can scientists separate themselves from their prejudices and become critical objects to themselves.

### DO SOCIALLY MEANINGFUL FACTS IMPLY VALUATIONAL FRAMEWORKS OF CONDITIONS AND CONSEQUENCES?

We seriously doubt that facts can stand alone as discrete objects of observation in the pristine purity of value neutrality. They are tied by human nature to modes of evaluation rooted in private, public, and scientific concerns. Formed by perspectival and existential circumstances, their meanings vary with the categories and contexts of human experience. To see a fact, and describe its occurrence, is to appraise it through an angle of vision bound by personal experience, locality and cultural epoch. No person merely observes another's actions without considering their fitness or significance. If human actions were no more than physical motions of no consequence for the observer why should he not prefer to stare into space?

Just as observations depend upon intentions to be meaningful, so empirical facts depend upon values to be meaningful. The mere focussing of attention upon facts partially circumscribes their character, and as focus changes, character changes.[12] Therefore, facts are not notices without choice, conscious or unconscious; they reflect preferences and imply priorities; they are instruments of action, verbal or behavioral, and thus good (right or proper) for certain ends or objectives. In brief, empirical facts are meaningful by virtue of their conditions and consequences. Since the latter cannot be specified without choice, value elements are an ever present ingredient of the sources through which facts are identified and named.[13]

We have implied that facts without directional sense are transitory clues to the scientific study of social problems. Thus the simple occurrences of germ carriers (from which health or illness is diagnosed); the absence of work opportunities for groups of people (from which seasonal indexes of leisure and unemployment are estimated); the manifestation of idiomatic forms of expression (from which one is thought to be poetic or psychotic); the observed act of entering a building and carrying away its contents (from which social mobility or theft is inferred); the direct placing by one person of hands upon another (from which hate or affection is imputed); the plain act of sexual congress (from which love or rape is interpreted); are not social problems in and of themselves, apart from responses of the kind indicated. These become social problems when they are viewed as developing out of certain contexts and are credited to special kinds of outcomes. And this viewing and crediting is a result of cognitive judgment, with preferences playing a large role. Preference for one conditional emphasis over that, or this consequential outcome over another, are expressions of scientific value. Therefore, social problems cannot be seen as objects of human interest apart from the concerns which attend their occurrence.

### DO SOCIALLY MEANINGFUL VALUES IMPLY FACTUAL FRAMEWORKS OF CONDITIONS AND CONSEQUENCES?

The concept of values seems to have, at the very least, a dual reference. Values may refer to the behavioral fact of choice, preference or election among objects or events. In this sense, values can be observed when the individual or group strives to achieve, maintain or avoid an event or object. On the other hand, values may refer to the standards, criteria, or norms for appraising choice among objects or events. So construed, values do not refer directly to behavior, but to the ethical principles for assessing behavior.

So far as human behavior is neither entirely random nor expressive of fixed responses under fixed conditions it involves some degree of choice. Impulsive or drive-like reactions probably include minimal elements of choice, but with these exceptions, valuational behavior can be tested empirically in the sense that it may be joined at crucial points to observable choices. The status of values as ethical principles is less certain since they sometimes allude to subjective dispositions detached from systematic frameworks. To serve as generalized standards, such principles should express hypothetical sets of conditions and consequences which are applicable (though not equivalent) to descriptions of specific events. However, the requirement that ethical principles have transempirical validity is not met by claiming, as Kluckhohn does, that:

No society has ever approved suffering as a good thing in itself, as a means to an end (purification or self-discipline), yes; as punishment—as means to the ends of society, yes. But by itself—no.[14]

This interpretation of universal values, whether applied to punishment, killing, stealing, or lying within the in-group, is too undeveloped, analytically and empirically, to be scientifically useful. We cannot think or talk about punishment in communicable ways without using words that identify its attributes or compare it presumptively, at least, to like and unlike features of man's social experience. To speak of punishment, "in itself," is to speak without regard to who does what, when and how to whom. It is to speak without factual reference to types of personality, modes of social organization or categories of environmental situations.[15] If universal values are open to definition and application they must be stated as sets of conditions and consequences. Only by examining, analytically and empirically, the varied conditions and consequences within which a series of acts occurs can we be assured a value is universal for the range of phenomena to which it applies.

#### CAN ETHICAL AIMS BE SCIENTIFICALLY DEFINED?

We have said that all concepts, whether of fact or value, require empirical support but are not, in a technical sense, directly dependent upon sensory experience. For this reason, some of the alleged difficulties of deriving the "ought" from the "is" appear to apply with equal force to scientific laws. In the customary view, logical rules cannot be derived from experience. But this does not prevent construction of scientific laws by exhibiting correspondence between logical rules and observational statements. Why then shouldn't attempts be made to construct ethical laws by exhibiting correspondence between ethical rules and observational statements? If, on the other hand, ethical rules can be established by induction from experience, or from scientific laws, then statements about ethical aims should be possible because the validity of every induction rests upon deduction of consequences capable of some degree of confirmation. In short, if nature is orderly and values are an aspect of nature and thus subject to inductive study, then ethical aims can be scientifically defined.

Admittedly, we are assuming that people's actions ought to agree with what science reveals as the ethical aims of man. Can we provide an ethical justification for this ethical principle without a circular return to the reasons adduced in support of it? Are we saying that men ought to follow what we know from science to be the ethical aims of life, and that they ought to do this because such aims are scientifically grounded? Perhaps so, but before we regard this as a fatal defect we should be prepared to admit that circular reasoning is also found in the purely factual sciences. Isn't the scientific utility of both analytical and empirical propositions tested by reference to one another? Isn't every line of reasoning in science justified by other lines of reasoning which contain synonymous expressions? Don't we, as sociologists, sometimes attempt to achieve univocal designations by extracting common meanings from vague or ambiguous statements and then use these meanings to reinterpret the very same statements? When we defend methods of induction by pointing to regularities among events are we not using the inductive argument, one step removed, and thus presupposing the question at issue? For instance, don't we argue from the conclusion that inductive rules are valid to the observation that statistical samples converge toward a limit of probability (frequency) and then use this observation to support the rules? On other occasions, do we not use implicit rules of induction to show the absence of a limit of probability and then support the former on the basis of the latter?[16]

Why, we now ask, is circular reasoning about the possible place of values in social problems theory so distasteful to many sociologists? Is it because the circle of reasoning is narrower than in natural science? Or because there is little consensus about the validity of ethical "generalizations"? Is it because sociological judgments imply tendencies to action less frequently than value judgments? Or because sociological reasoning is more certain, more akin to logical deduction and thus less subject to unrelenting doubt? Research pointing to the clarification of these questions is scanty. Therefore, until we have more systematic knowledge about the ethical and scientific rules of human conduct, there will be a sharp separation of the two kinds of discourse in social problems theory. Can we be certain that systematic exposition and criticism of scientific results is entirely independent of the disposition of *all* people to act and talk in terms of right and wrong? Perhaps some sociologists are so accustomed to taking traditional views *about* science as gospel, they fail to realize that what they say may not *accord* with scientific practices. Given greater awareness of the use[17] and limitations of circularity in reasoning they might find ethical aims can be extrapolated from behavior and ultimately justified without sacrificing the enduring values of science.[18]

Narrow circularity can be avoided by constructing a metatheory extending beyond social problems theory, but even here presuppositions would be necessary. Moreover, the possibilities of contradiction would be greater, for then reasoning is more elaborate. Perhaps agreement on the legitimacy of research on the relation of scientific values to lay values would be sufficient for the present. Those who desire communication and conflict resolution should approve of such research, since a negative or indifferent standpoint is also a value position requiring justification. Otherwise there cannot be even a heuristic interest in social problems theory.

## MUST SOCIOLOGISTS PRESCRIBE SOCIAL VALUES?

Generally, sociologists uphold the viewpoint that value statements cannot be derived from factual statements. However, they often contend that values are subject to analysis by virtue of our ability to describe them. To be describable, values must have empirical properties, in which case it should be possible to assess them scientifically. For instance, consider the hypotheses that class and ethnic stratification are determined by historical or socio-cultural conditions, not biological superiority. If these hypotheses are probably true then every interpretation that contradicts them, without providing new evidence, is probably false. And from a scientific standpoint the statement that false hypotheses are true involves a breach of ethics. Can any scientist effectively resist supporting false hypotheses by professional colleagues and, at the same time, hold that it does not matter whether the public accepts them as true?

Moreover, if there are substantial scientific grounds for the further hypothesis that science arises only from an historical setting of political beliefs favorable to its growth, would it not be unscientific to deny this without adding to or reconstructing present evidence? Must not every scientist committed to values of integrity and consistency support political beliefs necessary for their survival? Can scientists believe that freedom of expression is a condition for scientific advance, and not oppose those who deny it?

Again, but nearer to our subject, if a significant number of people consider sociology undesirable and feel something should be done about it through collective social action we have a "social problem" in the usual sense. Would sociologists then insist that they are not to advise people on what to value but only on how they may achieve their values?[19] If we accepted this premise as the proper way to define our scientific role we would be putting ourselves out of work. On the other hand, if we refused to accept this premise we would, presumably, be compromising the role of objective scientist. In short, if we followed our present definitions of both a social problem and our proper professional role we would soon be defunct: it we did not follow these definitions we would be opposing public values.

Perhaps we can escape this dilemma by claiming that it is a hypothetical issue. Perhaps there will never be a significant number of people who consider sociology undesirable and feel something should be done about it. But if sociology proves so acceptable that few oppose it, or so strong that nothing can be done about it, would we not be compelled to recognize its alignment with public values? If few people oppose sociology it may be because it sustains established institutions or is ineffective as an instrument of social adjustment. If few people believe something can be done about sociology it may be because it is beholden to powerful social influences. Under these conditions it would be difficult to regard sociology as value neutral.

Similar dilemmas arise in appraising theories of social disorganization, social deviance, and social conflict as competing interpretations of social problems. Consider two theories, one attributing social problems to inadequate socialization and the other to social conflict. Can we base the differences between them entirely on factual criteria? We note that sociologists have written extensively on socialization without presenting conclusive evidence against competing interest in scarce values, the basis of conflict theory. If the data of social problems do not compel choice of one theory over another, from what sources do these theories arise? Can the two groups of theorists, looking at the same range of phenomena, see different things because their values are different? If this is a harsh hypothesis we should find sound ways of disproving it. It isn't enough to say that although both groups of sociologists used objective methods of observation and were guided by norms of disinterested inquiry they arrived at widely different conclusions. Presumably, objective methods of observation, objectively pursued, lead to agreement on results, and when results diverge someone has either slipped in the process of analysis or started from different value orientations.

Perhaps solutions to these questions will be found when sociologists admit that they begin with preconceived notions about the causes of social problems, when they accept the necessity of construing the properties of empirical phenomena in different ways for different purposes, and when they agree that modes of reasoning contribute substantially to the conclusions they draw.

## WILL LAYMEN ASCRIBE SOCIAL VALUES TO SOCIOLOGISTS?

So accustomed is the layman to confusing facts and values, that attempts to separate the two on grounds of "objectivity" are not likely to receive sympathetic support. Thus, if someone suggests a housing shortage can be met by selling surplus materials to low-income groups, or by subsidizing cooperative ownership, many laymen will regard these proposals as socialistic, if not idealistic. For most people, proposed solutions must be consistent with the framework of our legal and tax structures, which provide relatively free scope to private enterprise, individual initiative and the rights of personal property.[20] As a result many of the suggestions which scientists might offer people are not real possibilities for them. Innovative scientists would entertain conditions which do not now exist and for those who accept the current norms of society it is a "fact" that they cannot be made to exist. Consequently, any scientist who entertains new arrangements is assumed to believe[21] they are desirable and is held responsible for what lay people regard as signs of prejudice.[22] Of course, the label of prejudice may be escaped by suggesting arrangements which would operate within the existing framework of society, but laymen will view such proposals as favoring their solutions and conclude that their values and those of science closely correspond. In either case, we often find laymen construing the work of sociologists to include value judgments about the means and goals of social life.

The fact that sociologists differ widely in their choice and interpretation of problems indicates that they do, indeed, make value judgments. That they mirror conventional patterns of status and abide by the norms which govern other groups attests to the same processes of socialization which shape lay values. When sociologists become indifferent to these things or when they foster disinterested inquiry into cherished academic practices, stronger claims can be made for value neutrality. Will they learn to examine seriously social affiliations, prolific publications, or prestige of sponsors as measures of academic worth? Will they attempt to describe in detail the qualifications of college administrators, including their I.Q.'s, their personality limitations, and their sex lives as freely as they have done for students? Will they experiment with their social environment, as liberally as some physiologists have with their material environment, to increase understanding of the latent functions of deprivation? No doubt, many sociologists would feel research of this kind is foolish. But if value neutrality means that it does not matter what scientists do—because the consequences of their work are unimportant—why not engage in such studies? Do we have institutional evidence that these studies would impair the core values of science, truth and consistency? If such evidence is available then the central question of this paper can be quickly answered. The perceptive layman will see claims for value neutrality as mythical, enabling the sociologist to pursue what he wished including, of course, study of social problems which receive institutional acclaim.

## SHOULD SETTLED VIEWS ABOUT SCIENCE AND VALUES BE OPEN TO FRESH INQUIRY?

Perhaps in some societies public commitments prevent raising questions which might disturb social equilibrium. Free discussion is limited to the premises of each society. Far from increasing human freedom, the questioning attitude becomes a threat to every person's right to think as custom dictates. Do we have, then, an inverse relationship between social integration and freedom of inquiry? Is the scientific ethos immune to such a relationship? Is sociology freer than economics and less free than literature to affirm divergent values because of its closeness to science and society? Regardless of the answer, ancient perplexities have little chance of setting new lines of inquiry. At the risk of tedium we draw from a host of queries meriting fresh discussion:

Is there a need for scientific examination of the premise that values are beyond science, that science cannot choose among social values (or tell us which values to pursue)? Are there any *scientific* grounds for surrendering questions about ultimate values to custom, politic-legal decisions, revealed commandments or other nonscientific authorities?

Should public opinion, or expert opinion, or the acceptance of expert opinion by the public, or the acceptance of public opinion by the expert, be the basis for defining social problems? If sociologists help conflicting groups find a method for reconciling their differences do they not thereby support the value of compromise? Can sociology influence social values by scientific assessment of their implications and consequences without supporting certain social values at the expense of others? (Cf. views of Weber and Merton.)

Do we know how values are mixed or fused with empirical, logical and intuitional elements? Are not scientists better able than nonscientists to join established knowledge with conjecture and to draw the line between the two? If values have empirical content or grounding, as many scientists assume, can we base our scientific judgments about them on "degrees of evidence" rather than on exact demonstration? Can nondemonstrability be replaced by intuitional judgments, collectively validated? Can the problem of contradictory opinions be reduced to methodological obstacles which, if overcome, would show universal agreement on the right and the good?

Is every scientific investigation limited by objectivity in socio-historical or other existential types of situations: cultural period, class, generation, professional group, personal experience, dated decisions and scholarly maturity? Are some scientists afraid that recognition of the difficulties of objectivity would encourage others to take this value lightly or even to abandon it? If so, is this not an evaluation of human frailty? Paraphrasing Spranger, Brecht writes, "Although the *reality* of scientific work may always be influenced or prejudiced by various conditions, the *idea* of science never permits us to cultivate such partiality and peculiarity."[23] Why, then, can not scientists use the *idea* of impartiality to promote the achievement of universal values?

## Conclusion

The daily tasks of scientist and citizen alike require continuous commitment to the pursuit of both fact and value. Decisions in the determination of facts call for value judgments; decisions in the determination of values call for factual judgments. By minimizing the role of ethical standards in scientific research (either as means or ends) sociologists are unable to offer ethical leadership to laymen. By minimizing the role of factual standards in definitions of social problems laymen are unable to respond to what sociologists would offer. Were the sociologist to admit ethical judgments as essential elements in the construction of facts he could reconcile his role as scientist with his role as citizen. Mutual feedback and sharing of public and professional experiences would grow accordingly.

The thesis of this paper may be abbreviated as follows:

# Values and Theory of Social Problems

*1.* The sharp distinction between facts and values found in sociological literature will not bear close empirical or analytical scrutiny. Since facts and values require frameworks of conditions and consequences to be intelligible, they cannot, at the present time, be clearly distinguished.

*2.* The frameworks of conditions and consequences for both factual and valuational statements are similar in many essential respects:

*a.* Both require reconstruction of empirical observations to reveal underlying concepts and hypothetical principles.

*b.* Both demand choice and preference, and call for standards of judgment.

*c.* Both must be justified by ethical principles which cannot themselves be justified without circular reasoning.

*3.* Hence, the facts and values used for identifying and resolving social problems may be scientifically defined and prescribed.

## NOTES

1. P. B. Horton and G. R. Leslie, *The Sociology of Social Problems,* New York: Appleton-Century-Crofts, 1955, p. 4.

2. L. K. Frank, "Social Problems," *American Journal of Sociology,* 30 (Jan., 1955) pp. 462–73; R. C. Fuller and R. R. Meyers, "Some Aspects of a Theory of Social Problems," *American Sociological Review,* 6 (Feb., 1941) pp. 24–32; J. F. Cuber and R. A. Harper, *Problems of American Society: Values in Conflict,* New York: Henry Holt and Company, 1951, pp. 25–38; T. L. Smith, *Social Problems,* New York: Thomas Y. Crowell Company, 1955, p. 4; A. Rose, "Theory for the Study of Social Problems," *Social Problems,* 4 (Jan., 1957) pp. 189–99; R. K. Merton, "Social Problems and Sociological Theory" in R. K. Merton and R. A. Nisbet, eds., *Contemporary Social Problems,* New York: Harcourt Brace and Co., 1961, esp. pp. 701–18.

3. Several writers begin their definition of social problems by referring to the relevance of group awareness. A few include scientific experts among those groups concerned with solving social problems. Others explicitly emphasize the lag or disparity between social ideals and actual behavior or, less commonly, the occurrence of social conflict.

4. The concept of majorities is not, of course, a simple notion. See R. Bierstedt, "The Sociology of Majorities," *American Sociological Review,* 13 (Dec., 1948) pp. 700–10.

5. Merton has described several difficulties that block procedures for estimating the magnitude of social problems. As he suggests, when adequate measures of the discrepancy between shared standards and actual behavior are absent, the relative importance assigned to social problems will reflect the values of those occupying different positions in the social structure. Therefore, different groups will have conflicting judgments on whether a particular state of affairs constitutes a problem. Merton would supplement the subjective definition of 'a significant number of people" with reports about the latent values and consequences which accompany social problems. He insists that such reports would not involve imposition of sociologists' values but merely call people to account for consequences of

policies they advocate. See R. K. Merton, *op. cit.*, pp. 706–11.

6. We assume that adequate accounts of social problems must rest upon evaluation of the conditions and consequences through which any state of affairs is scientifically known. Needless to say, these accounts will usually include evaluations of a logical, causal and empirical character. Cf. L. Gross, "Theory Construction in Sociology: A Methodological Inquiry" in L. Gross, ed., *Symposium on Sociological Theory*, Evanston, Illinois: Row, Peterson and Co., 1959, pp. 531–64.

7. However, some sociologists seem to reason as follows: "Definitions of social problems depend upon agreement of many people. The causes of social problems (according to social disorganization theory) stem from inadequate socialization (or group differentiation of values and meanings) resulting in failure of communication." Are we to conclude that consensus accounts for definitions of social problems and lack of consensus accounts for the causes of social problems?

8. Cuber and Harper, *op. cit.*, pp. 33–4.

9. Merton and Nisbet, *op. cit.*, p. 712.

10. Were we writing a monograph we might inquire about the diagnostic position of other determinants entering into various statements of this bond. Consideration of linguistic contexts prompts questions concerning the artful, expressive, advisory, decisional and stipulative bases of the bond. Consideration of behavioral processes prompts questions concerning the role of volitional, willful, intentional, operational and habitual elements in the formulation of the bond. Consideration of subject-domain prompts questions concerning the place of phenomenal, nativistic, biopsychological, sociocultural and metaphysical constancies in illuminating the bond. Pervading these nonexclusive categories are the "good reasons," ethical or not, of experience, cause, logic and belief.

11. For opposing interpretations see C. D. Broad, "Some of the Main Problems of Ethics" in H. Feigl and W. Sellars, eds., *Readings in Philosophical Analysis*, New York: Appleton-Century-Crofts, Inc., 1949, pp. 547–63; and A. Rapoport, *Science and the Goals of Man*, New York: Harper and Brothers, 1950, pp. 214–24.

12. Cf. C. Kluckhohn's citation of the "Heisenberg effect" from the Cornell Value Study in "Values and Value-Orientations" in T. Parsons and E. A. Shils, eds., *Toward a General Theory of Action*, Cambridge: Harvard University Press, 1959, p. 408.

13. A more detailed analysis of sources of values in science would follow from dissecting conditions and consequences into such processes as deliberations, options, claims, bestowals, certifications and policy adaptations. This kind of formulation would highlight the precept that scientific descriptions of past actions must be directed toward the ethico-technical resolution of future actions.

14. *Ibid.*, p. 418.

15. Unless we wish to support the case for intrinsic malignity, an invariant state of being which obtains regardless of social circumstances, including all forms of humanly produced conditions—a possibility not to be completely dismissed—disapproval of punishment *per se* is little more than verbal utterance with tonal effect and psychic solemnity.

16. Though apparently not conscious of the process, many sociologists of functionalist persuasion engage in circular reasoning. A social system is said to be maintained because of certain functional consequences and these consequences are, in turn, explained by their contribution to social equilibrium. The final step of explaining social equilibrium by referral

to the maintenance of society returns to the starting point of analysis.

17. The more rigorous the circularity, the nearer premises and consequences approach mutual implication, the closer one comes to realizing necessary and sufficient conditions, the ideal of a complete system.

18. S. S. West has questioned the idea of classical scientific values, especially their persistence after 1920. Interviews with 57 researchers in the science departments of a major university revealed that less than $\frac{1}{2}$ felt it indispensable for scientists to have unlimited choice of research problems. Only $\frac{1}{3}$ believed in complete neutrality and about $\frac{1}{4}$ felt they could separate their roles as scientists and citizens. Less than $\frac{1}{4}$ said they appraised facts impersonally and im-

partially without regard for other considerations. For a brief summary see *The American Behavioral Scientist*, March, 1961, p. 35.

19. Among the countless statements of this viewpoint, perhaps the best known is G. Lundberg's *Can Science Save Us?* New York: Longmans, Green & Co., 1947.

20. See L. K. Frank, *op. cit.*

21. Like social role, belief is a synthesizing concept in which value and fact are blended.

22. Compare the studies discussed by G. Allport in *The Nature of Prejudice*, Boston: The Beacon Press, 1954, pp. 9–12.

23. A Brecht, *Political Theory*, Princeton: Princeton University Press, 1959, p. 299.

# 31.     Social Problems and Social Theories:

# Dilemmas and Perspectives

MABEL A. ELLIOTT

*Dilemmas in the Nature of Conceptions of Social Theory*

In MAKING PREPARATION FOR WRITING THIS PAPER, I began by reading the new textbooks in social problems, re-reading a number of the old, and by reviewing current materials in social theory. On the whole it was a discouraging process because there was so little sociological theory in many of the problems' textbooks and so little empirical data in those on theory. This situation poses one of the major dilemmas of sociology generally, as well as for the area of social problems, and is largely responsible, I presume, for some of the scurrilous attacks made on social scientists, including that of Russell Kirk.[1] A great deal of modern so-called sociological theory consists in sociologists thinking on a common sense and *a priori* fashion aided and abetted by varying degrees of empirical data in the background of their minds, but without any substantial amount of verification to back up their conclusions. Often they have thought deeply. Their conclusions, meanwhile, are sometimes befogged by abstruse terminology and a general lack of facility in their sentence structure. It seems to me therefore that C. Wright Mills is justified in some of his attack on contemporary sociologists.[2]

This article obviously is not to decry either imagination or thinking on the part of sociologists. A great deal of what is wrong with sociology may be attributed to failing to employ the perceptive and rational processes of the far-reaches of the mind in the exploration of the complexities of our social structure. Frequently we become convinced solely by the logic involved in the thinking.

## Social Problems and Social Theories

Extensive ruminations about how people act in developing, reorganizing and rebelling against a social structure which they inherited from their forebears who also engaged in the same processes is scarcely scientific, however. The codifications of human activity and of the social structure thus produced have provided some very useful tools for further exploration it is true. Nevertheless, sociology is only in the process of becoming a science—if by science we mean principles based upon tested and verified empirical data. A closely reasoned analysis of how society is organized and how it functions is certainly superior to a loosely reasoned conception of society, if only because it attempts to test the validity of the conceptions by critical judgment, by common sense observations, and on occasion by empirical data. All effective thinking involves close reasoning and we shall never wish to discard it. Close reasoning is a tool which must always be employed in any analysis of social data. Many years ago when Francis Merrill and I were working out the approach to the first edition of our book *Social Disorganization*,[3] my maid (after listening to our thinking out loud on the subject) said to me—"Miss Elliott, when you write a book you just have to concentrate and imagine, don't you?" That, I submit, is a fair description of much social theory.

If, however, social theory is left in the "concentration and imagination stage," what seems so logical, so true and so apparent may disregard the fact that many truths are yet to be discovered. Consequently much sociological theorizing had better be classified as intellectual gymnastics rather than science.

### Dilemmas in Empirical Research in Social Problems

Much of the dilemma of the social theory which pertains to social problems arises from the unscientific but determined effort of sociologists to find one cause, or one simple unifying concept to explain all social deviation of a particular variety. Thus we have special theories which would explain all delinquency in terms of cultural conflict, or in terms of frustration, class, subculture, and bad neighborhood or of "body type." (I shall use many illustrations from criminology and delinquency in this chapter because this is the area of my concentration.) There is some validity in these various approaches but none is a complete explanation,—least of all the "body type." Mesamorphs have been held to be the major group of delinquents by the Gluecks, but there are too many mesamorphs who are not delinquents to give this factor significance except in association with other factors. The desire to find a single explanation to social phenomena has plagued the minds of men since the days of the ancient philosophers. Aristotle thought the physical world was made up of earth, air, fire, and water, and he built up a closely reasoned argument which was not successfully disputed until man began a more detailed analysis of the chemical elements. Today there are more than 91 recognized elements but no chemist will say that "this is all, there are no more". And through the penetration of the elements (by modern physicists), they, too, have been found to be complicated organizations of matter.

Today, it seems to me, we are at the beginning of a new day in sociology. During the twentieth century research methods in sociology have been so refined and developed that we have been able to explore social situations and analyze relationships to a degree undreamed of by the founders of the American Sociological Association, much less by their nineteenth century predecessors. At the same time, we still have much to do in penetrating the subtleties of social relationships with any degree of precision. Studies of the American family during the depression, for example, indicated that some families were torn apart by the husbands' failures to make a living. Other families were cemented by the united attack of the family members on the problem of securing sufficient income. Presumably the emotional bonds were closer and monetary considerations were not a factor in such marriages.[4] Nevertheless family pride and the intellectual capacity and training of the wives and children may also have had an effect on family stability. Reasoning must always give us leads in new directions and put a check on exaggerated interpretations of data.

## Dilemmas in Definition

Obviously, any discussion of social problems and social theories should not proceed further without a few definitions. What specifically do sociologists mean by these two terms, "social theories" and "social problems"? Unfortunately, sociologists, and for that matter other social scientists do not always mean the same thing when they discuss social theory —nor are all social problems germane to the subject of sociology. Obtaining a pure water supply may be a social problem but is primarily a matter of sanitary engineering.

Social theory is often defined as a scientific explanation of social phenomena. This definition in turn hinges on what is "explanation" and what is "scientific." In modern terminology, science consists in the conclusions drawn from empirical data, and such an "explanation" is reasonably acceptable to most of us when it is a statement of cause and effect which permits social prediction. Much social theory, unfortunately, does not fit this definition. Many social theories are hypotheses concerning social organization and social interaction. Such hypotheses are built out of what seem to be logical analyses of reality but without any counting, sorting or correlating of facts. A still further variety of social theory is the hypothesis projected from an examination of facts without any demonstrable evidence that the coexisting data have a cause and effect relationship. The recent research of Sheldon and Eleanor Glueck, in their book *Physique and Delinquency*, is a case in point.[5] They found that mesamorphs constituted the preponderate body type among 500 delinquents in the Cambridge-Somerville area and that the 500 nondelinquents had a much lower percentage of mesamorphs. What they did not show was why a well-built athletic boy is more apt to become delinquent than the ectomorph or endomorph. The fact that some of the delinquents were ectomorphs and some were endomorphs pointed to a hazard in their conclusion and makes it impossible to accept physique as a basic explanation for delinquency. We need also to know what percentage of the population is mesamorphs, and what percentage of the mesamorphs become delinquent. Defects in the environment of the mesamorphs may be the basic explanation for their delinquency. Meanwhile, no satisfactory reason for ectomorphs and endomorphs becoming delinquents is posited by this theory.

When we turn to the definition of a social problem this presents somewhat less a dilemma. Although there are some disparities in their conceptions of social problems, the majority of sociologists appear to define a social problem as a situation or condition which disturbs society to the extent that society tries to do something to ameliorate the situation.

What constitutes a social problem may be analyzed still further and the majority of sociologists recognize that the concepts of social disorganization and social deviation both provide further insight into the nature of social problems. Both of these concepts are related and in many instances one seems to produce the other, but they are nevertheless separate concepts. According to Elliott and Merrill,[6] social disorganization may be defined as the process by which group relationships are disturbed or broken. Their definition does not vary greatly from Merton and Nisbet who restrict social disorganization to the failure of institutions to meet human needs. Other disturbances which involve individuals failing to conform to norms Merton calls "social deviation." However, what Elliott and Merrill classify as individual disorganization is termed "social deviation" by Merton and Nisbet[7] (and their colleagues), and this is likewise true of Clinard.[8] Both classifications are essentially concerned with persons who have violated group norms and have defied or rebelled against or failed to observe accepted social values. Social deviation is thus generally recognized only when it produces social disorganization and the same thing is true in recognition of the disorganized individual as employed by Elliott and Merrill. That is, the disorganized individual is usually recognized as such only when he violates behavior norms and by so doing harms the functioning of the group.

Both individual and social disorganization in turn tend to be produced by social problems. When the terms are understood the conflict in viewpoint thus is not great. Merton and Nesbit say that moral values are always involved in social problems. Elliott and Merrill would agree that moral values are usually involved in individual disorganization. In cases of social disorganization caused by social change the moral value involved may or may not be so apparent, but, by and large, we would accept this premise for social disorganization. Merton and Nisbet go so far as to include a discussion of traffic problems as moral problems.[9] When traffic ceases to be a civil engineering problem and becomes a moral problem we may presume what happens when the policeman takes over; seriously, there are times when we would all admit that traffic problems are disturbing. Heavy traffic is not necessarily immoral, however, in this sociologist's view.

On the question of what a social problem is—sociologists have to face the fact that there are social problems which are only indirectly social problems, and are rather more significantly sanitary engineering problems, as in the case of sewage, and economic problems, as in the case of stock market manipulations. A ballistic missile problem similarly may be considered rightly a problem of physics and chemistry. Nevertheless, these all may have a definite influence in producing social disorganization. Obviously it is difficult to establish limits as to what is a social problem for sociologists.

On the other hand, the social problems which the sociologist believes to be his area of concern are not *solely* his province. Many social problems in which the sociologist has done the most and the earliest research have now become the concern of his fellow social scientists. Thus, the problem of unemployment is not only a matter of the social disturbances created by men out of work, it is the concern of the economist in his analysis of the business cycle and of marketing and production. It is a problem for the political scientist as a lag in the state's plans for public works and legislative action and for the psychologist in terms of the personality adjustment involved. Problems of the family are likewise no longer a matter of academic interest solely to sociologists. Anthropologists, economists, psychologists, and home economists are also studying the family. Do the various social sciences have boundaries in these areas? This is presently a real dilemma. When is an anthropologist a sociologist? The questions entailed are virtually endless. Social workers and other persons whose professional or job interests are basically concerned with the treatment of social problems have also developed a sizable amount of data in published form about the nature of social problems. The training of social workers has been greatly extended and most professionally educated social workers now have some understanding of the developments in sociology, anthropology and psychology. Some of the training of social workers has been superficial and faddish, however. Social workers have been accused of going through stages when they belonged to (1) the "tonsil and adenoid school", (2) the Freudian School and, in later years, (3) the anthropological-cultural approach to social work problems. Whatever their orientation, most social workers have generally attempted to help their clients adjust to the status quo. Little effort is directed toward any frontal attack on the environment producing the problems, or toward an analysis of the social structure in relation to social problems.

Practical politicians (whether they be Presidents of the United States, members of the state legislature, judges or local politicians) likewise are often involved in varying degrees of depth in the implementing of methods developed for dealing with social problems, whether the problem is crime, race relations, unemployment, or public health or some other area. Occasionally social scientists are consulted about such problems as is witnessed in the sociologists who testified in the Supreme Court case on school segregation, and in the important part Edwin Witte and his associates played in writing our Social Security Act adopted in 1935.

The implementation of social theory in dealing with social problems would seem to be the goal of social theory, and sociologists may later develop responsibility for this. Smoothing out social conflicts, attacking social problems at their source, would seem to be a legitimate goal of the empiricists bent on answering the question as to why such situations exist.

Many sociologists spurn any such end to their work, however, and why they take such a stand would in itself be an interesting research project. Some sociologists apparently are distressed about the application of social theory to social problems because they are not sure of their theory, —much less the results. To many sociologists, however, any concern with such problems is distasteful because of temperament or previous conditioning. Their major concern is for discovering the uniformities of social behavior which they regard as normal. To be concerned with social problems, with social disorganization, and social deviation is considered "messy". In this, they have absorbed popular prejudice. Why should sociologists be involved in studying social problems, they reason, when the far-reaches of complex social organization are so much more pleasant to contemplate. Any interest in social disturbances, to be of concern to such sociologists, must be stated in abstract terms, uncontaminated by concrete details of how women become prostitutes, men become criminals, or political corruption invades the city hall. Some of their attitude might be summarized by the small placard I saw in a plumber's office the other day. "Don't just do something about a problem," it charged, *"Stand there."*

Doing something about a problem without proper understanding of its nature obviously may be even more disastrous in social relations than in a plumbing job. All attempts to work out a solution to a social problem should be based on an adequate examination of the facts by trained and competent persons. This requires time, intelligence, and techniques in structuring the necessary research projects. At the same time, many problems such as those occurring in times of natural disaster or in time of war have to be met somehow on the basis of existing knowledge or on occasion by untried methods. Sometimes valuable social data can be derived from such a necessity but there are dilemmas!

In 1946–1947 I was Consulting Sociologist to the American National Red Cross. During this time, I conducted a special research project on their disaster services.[10] One of the appalling things about flood disasters to me was their continual recurrence. Certain families were helped year after year, or every few years whenever the house where they lived or the business where they worked was ten, twenty or sometimes more feet under water. The Red Cross has excellent social workers (who take over and work with the victims) as well as technicians, architects and administrators who assess the loss, restore the damaged buildings, sometimes set up a new business for those "washed out" and, in general, lend a helping hand to the people in distress.

I was assured by the Red Cross that the perennial victims are tied to their flood-prone homes. They *want* to live by the river where they have spent so many years. Such persons have even developed techniques for removing the mud, which makes a permanent stain if allowed to dry on furniture or wall paper. Floods are a part of their pattern of facing the hazard of living. To a research sociologist interested in the goal of social theory this is a nonsensical end to the very fine humanitarian service of the Red Cross.

Why should not the Red Cross provide data to the army engineers who deal with floods on our rivers? Why should not a program for resettling of victims of flood disaster be developed? The position of flood victims is certainly more hazardous than that of the farmers on marginal land who are in line for resettlement.

Resistance to the application of intelligent solution to a social problem is thus another very real dilemma in applied sociology. People become attached to a hazardous home site, but it would seem desirable to remove either the hazard or the home site. Eventually, social theory must be extended to an analysis of the problem faced in applying social theory. The importance of social change in producing problems has long been recognized by sociologists and other social scientists and presumably will always remain a stumbling block to social theory—since *social theory must always be in the "process of becoming" in order to keep up to date.* Society is never finished in any final sense—it is always in a state of becoming, with no complete road map for the route ahead, despite the relative rigidity in the rules previously established.

## Dilemmas and Perspectives in Social Theory

In retrospect, earlier social theory, including that of American sociologists at the turn of the twentieth century, was based on reasoning without much reference to empirical data, largely because no extensive body of empirical data existed. I shall not review early theories because of lack of space, but there have been many attempts to develop some simple but consistent explanation for society's functioning as it does and for "the human condition" which we call social problems.

These simple explanations have been made presumably out of the sociologists' hunger to understand life and to state their understanding in comprehensible terms. So far as I am concerned, these simple explanations are virtually no explanations at all. Some sociologists have dealt with local data or with a small segment of a social problem in a local community, or have made a study of certain factors hypothesized as significant in producing a given problem and have made startling statements from the relationships they believed they had established. The dangers of such an approach are obvious when confined to a specific area of research, as may be illustrated in the case of criminology.

Bad housing, low economic status, immoral parents, membership in a subculture, ineffective schools, physique, and various other factors have been all studied and advanced as separate basic explanations for delinquent behavior. The research sociologist has often compiled empirical data without much extended or perceptive thinking about his data. Surely any theory which will give an adequate explanation of criminality or delinquency must piece together the various researches and find the missing links. Any acceptable theory must also recognize *that there is no necessary single cause underlying a wide variety of antisocial acts merely because they may be subsumed under the category of delinquency.* A child can be punished for "delinquent" acts not considered criminal for adults, as, for example, truancy. Is something which is not a crime for adults caused by the same factor as that which induces an adult to murder, or to rob or rape? One might equally well argue that pneumonia and a broken bone, because they are human ailments, must be traced to the same source—yet the search for one cause persists.

In recent years, Roman Catholic sociologists have promoted the doctrine of natural law as a social theory which, they hold, explains all social problems. This explanation is consonant with their acceptance of Thomas Aquinas' disquisitions on the subject, but offers no real explanation of what is responsible for crime, delinquency, or political corruption. Crime, delinquency, political corruption and other manifestations of deviant behavior or disorganization may thus be said to be social problems (they hold) because they subvert the purposes of society, which are built upon moral laws established by the Creator. Actually, the moral concepts of Catholics are approximately the same as the moral values of the rest of Christendom since they were derived from the same sources—the *Old Testament* and the teachings of Jesus.

To say that particular social problems subvert the purposes and goals of the group would appear to be acceptable to most sociologists, without reference to religious belief. But this in no way explains the factors responsible for the subversion of moral or social values. The natural law theory assumes that social problems are a function of the way things are, whether one makes this a matter of religious belief or not, but it is not a scientific explanation. Scientific sociologists must examine the factors which have precipitated deviating behavior and social disorganization before they can explain a particular disturbance with any degree of specificity.[11]

The fact that social problems involve moral values which are also of concern to the theologian likewise presents dilemmas if one accepts a broad theologically oriented explanation. Theological explanation cannot be scientific. The natural law theory is not anti-scientific,—it is merely too simple to be meaningful on a scientific basis. Measles are the result of natural law, too, in a sense, but it is a disease scientifically known to be the result of a specific bacterial infection.

### FUTURE PERSPECTIVES

The quiet work on the accumulation of social data from which social theory may be derived and for which scientific treatment of social problems may be developed is, I believe, one of the major tasks of sociologists. I agree with Robert Merton that this "middle-level range" for developing social theory offers the best hope in the long run for developing a tenable over-all theory.

### THE GRAND SCHEME OF TALCOTT PARSONS IN PERSPECTIVE

Some sociologists, notably Talcott Parsons, have decided to work out an all-encompassing social theory by attacking the problem intellectually and proceeding on a basis of coldly reasoned logic from observations about society which are not rigidly outlined nor analyzed according to research methods. In so doing, Parsons has tried to develop a social theory far-reaching enough to be acceptable to all social scientists. Other social scientists in various ways have tried to give a rational explanation of man and the social order,—although such explanations have been slanted toward their particular division of the social sciences. Influenced by the conceptual theories of J. S. Mill, Karl Marx, Durkheim, Weber, Pareto, as well as those of Freud, (to mention some of his most important precursors), Parsons, with the assistance of his colleagues and graduate students, has worked strenuously to develop his over-all conception of the way the social organization and man (the actor) functions, by attempting to integrate social theories of the various areas. Whether the structure and functioning of modern society can be dissected and analyzed within the interior and internal processes of the mind is a question which has not been settled. In any event, Parsons' theories have been built up into a grand scale scheme for explaining man's behavior and the social order. These theories have acquired a large following, and many of Parsons' concepts have provided tools for other sociologists to employ in developing their research and writing. I refer especially to his concepts of "status," or "roles" and "expectations" as they affect the relations of members of groups and the larger society

Because of the extensive ramifications of his theories I can at best make a partial and somewhat superficial analysis. How much his abstruse and complicated diagrammatic explanations of social organization will stand the test of empirical research is a question. My comments here must be restricted to the meanings of his concepts as applied to the nature of social problems.

Parsons himself has done very little to apply his theories to social problems,[12] nor has he drawn much of his conceptual analysis from any direct interpretation of existing empirical research. His chief claim to being scientific is in the Marxian sense of the term "scientific." That is, Parsons' theories are based on careful and precise reasoning and like Karl Marx' writings are perhaps better defined as "scientism."[13] Parsons' concepts are "verified" by careful logic rather than by painstaking research into facts. Parsons is, of course, no Marxian revolutionist, but he admits his intellectual indebtedness to Karl Marx, as well as to Weber, Durkheim, Pareto, Freud, and others.

Parsons insists that his theories also codify empirical data, although their direct relationship to such data is often not obvious to his critics. Max Black and his colleagues at Cornell University have raised some serious questions about the validity of a theory of the social system which is based so little on empirical data.[14] Parsons does not give much recognition to social problems or social disorganization, as we have mentioned. His social theory (which he admits has changed with the passing years),[15] is basically concerned with order, integration, and equilibrium as they have been developed in the social organization. Nevertheless, he holds that much of the functioning of social order is not primarily concerned with meeting individual needs, hence, human beings often are inclined to "deviance" and "alienation." In consequence, society builds up mechanisms of social control and socialization in order to check threats to the equilibrium of the social system. Within the social system differentiated subsystems develop. These likewise pose threats to the social system's equilibrium. Mechanisms for controlling the incompatible elements of the differentiated subsystems must therefore be developed. Certain accommodations must be made at the same time to resolve "head-on" conflicts. Thus segregation may resolve race conflict (albeit on a precarious basis). Further threats to equilibrium also arise out of the failure of institutional structures to serve basic functional, biological, or psychological needs.

Such unmet needs are not only a threat to the social order; they are at the same time an affront to the group dominant values. Consequently, ways of meeting incompatible elements are thus illicit; hence *sub rosa* patterns of behavior spring up which are permitted yet condemned. Thus, prostitution and gambling become institutionalized deviant patterns of behavior. According to Parsons, the threat of prostitution and gambling to the social structure are presumably less than not permitting such institutions.[16] Unfortunately, Parsons does not examine the extent to which such deviations threaten the social structure. There are many other ramifications of Parsons' theories of the social structure and social action but these particular points have a major reference to social problems. Thus, certain actions such as theft and murder are controlled through mechanisms of the court and the exacting of penalties. Other actions by their nature cannot be effectively suppressed, hence are socially disapproved, but are tacitly winked at in order to prevent greater threats.

## Social Research in Social Problems

While Parsons and others have been building up their theories, most of the empirical research in sociology has been concerned with the problems which threaten the stability of the social order. Thus, a great amount of detailed empirical data has been accumulated about juvenile delinquency, illegitimacy, crime, problems of the worker in industry, mental illness, and suicide. Similarly, family disorganization, community disorganization, racial and religious conflict, revolution, totalitarianism, and war have been subjected to research. Since these problems are the ones which vex and disturb the public, many philanthropic foundations, the federal government, city officials, and universities themselves have granted large sums for such research, as we all know. From the area of social problems research a body of generalizations has been developed, some of which have been tested and retested; others are still in the hypothetical stage. Thus, many varieties of social research, whether involving interviews, examination of case studies, or acquiring data by questionnaire and schedule, have been motivated by a desire to explain the reasons for a problem or to explore the nature of a problem.

Out of these discrete and separate projects certain hypotheses and certain conclusions with reference to the social order may now be made. Out of the projected research projects of the future some further light on social structure and social processes will be possible. Normative behavior must also be further studied and analyzed in greater detail. This the psychologists (notably Gesell and his associates) have already attempted with considerable success in studying the behavior of children at successive age levels until they can say fairly safely that certain behavior is characteristic of any one-year-old child. They have not, however, studied the relation of the social milieu to such normative behavior.

# Mabel A. Elliott

In summary, the extensive research in social problems has given us new insights into the nature of society. Such research has also made possible a great increase in the number and type of college courses offered in sociology. Thus, as stated above, we know a great many facts about the various problems. We know a great deal about the social factors which produce such problems and the imperfections in the social structure which have produced them. Meanwhile, sociologists are no longer alone in conducting these researches. Anthropologists are now investigating juvenile delinquency and family and community disorganization, as witnessed by the work of Walter B. Miller and Alexander H. Leighton, to mention but two.[17] Psychiatrists have published extensive tomes on criminal behavior, which has been explained by nonsocial factors. According to Robert Lindner, criminals are "rebels without a cause".[18] Philip Q. Roche, on the other hand, holds criminals to be synonomous with the mentally ill.[19] At the same time, sociologists are lending penetrating insights to mental illness as illustrated in the important work of August B. Hollingshead. Hollingshead has made it clear that class status is related to the prevalence of mental disease, with the two upper classes having the lowest rate, the lower class having the highest rate and the two middle classes lying between.[20]

The current over-lapping of the research by sociologists, anthropologists, the psychologists (and in certain instances by historians, economists, and political scientists) is at once provocative and stimulating to the sociologist.[21] He is challenged by these fresh insights and sometimes perturbed by their sociological naiveté. He has also been required to reexamine and on occasion revise his concepts and his social theory. This direction toward the integration of the social and psychological sciences is bound to continue and may result in social scientists and psychologists understanding each other. Out of their coordinated efforts it seems likely that there will be new developments in social theory.

## NOTES

1. Russell Kirk, *"Is Social Science Scientific?" New York Times, Magazine* Section VI, Sunday, June 25, 1961, p. 11 and p. 15.

2. Cf. C. Wright Mills, *The Sociological Imagination,* New York: Oxford University Press, 1959, for an incisive attack on certain sociologists.

3. Mabel A. Elliott and Francis E. Merrill, *Social Disorganization,* New York: Harper & Brothers, 1934 (Fourth Edition, 1961).

4. Cf. Robert C. Angell, *The Family Encounters the Depression,* New York: Charles Scribner's Sons, 1936, for a discussion of these points, and Katherine Howland Ranck, *The Family and the Depression,* Chicago: University of Chicago Press, 1938, Chapter V.

5. Sheldon and Eleanor Glueck, *Phy-*

*sique and Delinquency,* New York: Harper & Brothers, 1956.

6. Cf. Elliott and Merrill, *op. cit.,* (Fourth Edition), 1961, Chapters I, II and III.

7. Robert C. Merton and Robert A. Nisbet, *Contemporary Social Problems,* New York: Harcourt, Brace and World, 1961, Chapters I and XV.

8. Cf. also Marshall Clinard, *Sociology of Deviant Behavior,* New York: Rinehart and Company; 1957, Chapter I and II.

9. Merton and Nisbet, *op. cit.,* Chapter XIII.

10. Mabel A. Elliott, "Disaster Services of the American National Red Cross," 1947, unpublished mss., available for consultation at the Historical Division of the ANRC, Washington, D.C.

11. Cf. Mary Elizabeth Walsh and Paul Hanly Furfey, *Social Problems and Social Action;* Englewood Cliffs, N.J.; Prentice-Hall, Inc., 1958 for a Catholic text presenting the "natural law" theory as a basic explanation for social problems. Actually, the Stoics developed the theory of natural law which was expanded by Aristotle and the latter's teachings were incorporated in Roman Catholic doctrine by Saint Thomas Aquinas.

12. Cf. Talcott Parsons and Edward A. Shils, eds., *Toward a General Theory of Action,* Cambridge; Harvard University Press, 1951.

13. Cf. J. F. Talmon, *The Rise of Totalitarian Democracy,* Boston; Beacon Press, 1952, for an interesting discussion of "scientism" in Parts I and II. Talmon also includes a discussion of the theorists whose "scientism" provided the rationale of the French Revolution.

14. Edward C. Devereux, Jr., *"Parsons' Sociological Theory"* in Max Black, ed., *The Social Theories of Talcott Parsons,* Englewood Cliffs, N.J., 1961, pp. 1–63.

15. Talcott Parsons, "Pattern Variables Revisited," *American Sociological Review,* pp. 457–483, August 1960.

16. Cf. Devereux, *op. cit.,* for an illuminating discussion on Parsons' theories with reference to action threatening order.

17. Cf. Alexander H. Leighton, *My Name is Legion,* New York: Basic Books, 1959; Walter B. Miller has served on the recent National Education Association committee on delinquency and has done extensive research in delinquency in Boston, as is well known.

18. Robert M. Lindner, *Rebel Without a Cause,* New York: Grune and Stratton, 1944.

19. Philip Q. Roche, *The Criminal Mind,* New York: Farrar, Straus and Cudahy, Inc., 1958.

20. Cf. August B. Hollingshead and Frederick C. Redlich, *Social Class and Mental Illness,* New York: John Wiley & Sons, Inc., 1958, especially pp. 202–210.

21. Arnold B. Toynbee has given a sociological slant in his study of history. Cf. *A Study of History,* New York, Oxford University Press, 1959.

# 32.    Social Science and Public Service

ROBERT BIERSTEDT

$A$s SOCIAL SCIENTISTS WE COULD HARDLY ARGUE
the irresponsibility of our discipline at the same time that we meet frequently to consider its responsibilities. Our discussions prove by reflexive
logic the validity of the contention that the social scientist is willing to
"accept" responsibilities whether or not anyone thinks he "has" them, or
owes them. Irresponsible persons would hardly assemble in great numbers
and with high frequency to consider their own responsibilities.

The notion that social scientists have social responsibilities, however,
and are willing—even eager—to accept them, is not one that helps us along
very far in the answer to our central questions. For there are many kinds
of responsibility. Some of them are relevant to the pursuit of social science
and some of them are not. It is perfectly clear to everyone, I think, that
there are certain responsibilities with which we are not here concerned.
We are not concerned, on the one hand, with the public responsibilities
that the social scientist shares with other citizens. The responsibilities of
citizenship include such obligations as the payment of taxes, service in the
armed forces, and a range of others depending upon the community in
which one resides. From duties of this kind no one, of course, would want
the social scientist to be exempt. These are the public responsibilities that
the social scientist has because he is a citizen of a politically organized
society and they have nothing to do with our present problem. Whatever
the responsibilities are that social scientists have, their range would be inclusive of these as well.

We are not concerned, on the other hand, with those responsibilities
the social scientist assumes because he represents a certain kind of enterprise—the enterprise of science and of scientific inquiry. This enterprise

has its own rules and regulations—its own norms—and these he has the moral obligation to obey. I refer in this connection to the ordinary norms of intellectual discipline—the discipline, in the other sense of that word, that makes of scientific inquiry a regulated and orderly kind of procedure. These are the *mores* of science, the responsibilities that the social scientist owes to the discipline itself. They include such things as his obligation to satisfy appropriate canons of evidence, to exhibit a proper energy in the search for negative instances, to dissipate his biases as far as possible, to allot a condign credit to his predecessors, to enclose his quotations in quotation marks, to entertain his premises with scepticism, and to offer his conclusions with humility. These, however, have to do with what might be called the morality of the intellect and of intellectual endeavor. They require only this brief mention because we are concerned here, I take it, not with the responsibility of the social scientist to his discipline, but rather with his responsibility to society.

## *Wertfreiheit*

There is, however, in this area, one issue that causes a bit of difficulty, and that is the issue of *Wertfreiheit*. It becomes an issue here because in a curious way it touches upon the responsibilities we have both to science and to society. I have just said that it is a responsibility of the scientist to dissipate bias as far as he humanly can. The adverb is necessary because, if to err is human, human too is the tendency to treasure certain prejudices of our own, certain private points of view, and these we can never wholly eradicate from our hypotheses, our precedures, and our conclusions. In language that is perhaps sesquipedalian one might say that absence of bias is at once a methodological desideratum and a psychological impossibility.

I should like to insist, however, that it *is* a methodological desideratum. The scientist and the propagandist cannot live in the same house; the laboratory and the advertising agency are different institutions; and, although the same circle may encompass them, the social scientist and the social philosopher dwell on different diameters. Many minds have sought a scientific basis for ethics, in our century as in others. The effort is doomed to failure, not because of the limitations of the human mind but because, by definition, science and ethics are two different enterprises and two different kinds of inquiries. Categorical judgments are not normative judgments, and just so long as one wishes to maintain a distinction between a proposition that asserts what is and a proposition that asserts what ought to be—

between, that is, a proposition that states and one that urges or recommends—just so long will it be impossible to gather ethics into science and, correspondingly, social philosophy into sociology.

There is, unfortunately, no logic of the normative, no table of valid syllogisms in the normative mood, no argument to refute the apothegm that, in the realm of values as well, *de gustibus non disputandum est*. It is always, and perhaps tiresomely true that, as Bertrand Russell has said, normative judgments are not only outside the realm of science, they are equally far outside the realm of knowledge. They are solely matters of taste and preference, either personal or social. It is true as a matter of formal deduction that the square on the hypotenuse of a right-angled triangle is equal to the sum of the squares on the other two sides, and it is true as a matter of empirical confirmation—unfortunately—that energy equals mass multiplied by the square of the velocity of light. But by what logic can we prove that monogamy is good, illiteracy bad, atheism wicked, and capitalism virtuous? Just so long, I say, as one wants to preserve a distinction between one kind of judgment and another kind of judgment, just so long will we have to maintain, in consequence, that science is one thing and ethics another. The question is not, therefore, one that minimizes the capabilities of the human mind but one rather that utilizes these capabilities in order to make an important and indeed a necessary distinction.

But what, you may ask, is the relevance of this to our problem. The relevance is that no social scientist may support on scientific grounds even the most meritorious public policy without at the same time violating the basic canons of scientific inquiry. He may do this as a citizen, of course, and his civic conscience will tell him that frequently he must do it. But it is important not to confuse a moral judgment or a political preference on the one hand with a scientific conclusion or an empirical proposition on the other. So also is it important not to confuse the status of citizen with the status of scientist. To do so is to do a disservice both to science, and to society. To do so, in fact, is to do a double disservice to science, once in violating its own rules and twice in defacing the standard by which it is publicly judged.

*Wertfreiheit*, in short, is itself a responsibility. It is an obligation the soical scientist owes to society in return for such privileges as freedom of inquiry, freedom of thought, and freedom of expression. It is the final rationale, in fact, of academic freedom. It is often thought—parenthetically speaking—that academic freedom is a discriminatory privilege granted with reluctance to a special (and especially vociferous) group of citizens who call themselves professors and teachers in order that they may, by attacking the ideological foundations of their society, make public nuisances of themselves. Academic freedom, on the contrary, is a responsibility that society lays upon this special group in order to assure that its own defects will be under continuous and critical scrutiny and subject to the kind of objective examination that makes correction and improvement possible.

It is sometimes difficult, even for some of us, to recognize that the norms of science and the norms of citizenship may be in conflict and that the norms of citizenship require what the canons of science forbid. Citizenship requires commitment and even advocacy on matters of public policy; science requires neutrality and objectivity. Citizenship requires value-involvement, science requires value-freedom. The reason this is difficult to acecpt is that the scientist, of course, is also a citizen. One of his statuses conflicts with another; their norms are contradictory; and they thus may not be occupied by the same person at the same time—although they may, of course, be occupied by the same person at different times. But this phenomenon is a commonplace of sociology and should therefore occasion no difficulty. A man may handle large sums of money that do not belong to him when he occupies the status of company treasurer, let us say, and not in his other statuses. A man may banish a player from a baseball game in the status of umpire but not in the status of spectator. And similarly, a man may be an advocate on an issue of public policy in the status of citizen and also of course, *a fortiori*, in the status of voter, statesman, and political adviser. But science, including social science, dispenses with this kind of advocacy. There is no science that can tell us whether or not to take an intransigent or an accommodating stance on Berlin, whether or not to give socialized medicine a fair trial, or whether or not to test atomic weapons.

A social science can certainly exhibit, in hypothetical propositions, the consequences of alternative lines of action and estimate the costs of different decisions. But this is the limit of its powers. It cannot itself decide.

I began this section by suggesting that *Wertfreiheit* presents a special problem to the social scientist. I hope that in concluding it I have convinced you that it is a special responsibility as well, that to abandon the principle would be itself an abdication of responsibility, and that to preserve it intact—even in time of turmoil—is an especial obligation. When we do this we strengthen—not weaken—our social science, and make it in the long run a more useful instrument for the society that supports it

## Wisdom

There is yet another reason, apart from *Wertfreiheit*, why the social scientist need be chary about an immediate commitment of his discipline to the vicissitudes of the social scene and to the changing arenas of political controversy. We may assume, I think, that the social scientist is a man of a rather high order of intelligence and that, in the course of this training and in the pursuit of his profession, he has acquired a good deal of knowledge. Are we permitted to assume that he is also wise? Unfortunately, there is no discoverable correlation between intelligence and wisdom or between knowledge and wisdom. Wisdom seems to be an independent and random variable, keeping only vague and irregular communion with these other attributes. It seems to have a rather special suspicion of knowledge. Indeed the Germans have a proverb—directed mainly at professors, one presumes —which says, *"Je gelehrter desto verkehrter"* (the more learned they are the crazier they are). However that may be, no one would claim, I think, that there is any particular unanimity among social scientists on the resolution of contemporary political issues. There may be sizeable majorities, of course, on certain questions, but even a small minority would refute the notion that agreement is in any sense a function of the knowledge that social scientists have. Where there is agreement it may easily be due to a selective factor, which induces some people and not others to become social scientists, people with a prior similarity of motive and opinion, and not to the knowledge they acquire in the pursuit of their calling.

## The Liberal Arts

What then is the ground for the suspicion of the social scientist that one so frequently encounters in the public press and in other public relationships? One factor almost certainly involved is that social scientists in general and sociologists in particular tend, as citizens, to range themselves on the liberal side on social and political issues. Lazarsfeld and Thielens have offered a certain amount of evidence to support this view and it conforms to many common observations. My own experience induces me to believe that not only social scientists, but members of liberal arts faculties in general align themselves on the liberal side, in contrast to those in law, medicine, theology, agriculture, commerce, and engineering. Why should this be so?

I suggest that the answer to this question is not difficult to find. The liberal arts and sciences, in loyalty to the adjective that describes them, are in truth liberating disciplines. They liberate those who pursue them from the provincialisms of time and place and social circumstance. They are disciplines in which truth is never given but is always a matter of inquiry, and in which inquiry itself is untrammeled by doctrine, creed, or preconception. Contrast this situation with that which obtains in law, for example, where truth is largely a matter of tradition, where the practitioner, that is, seeks not new truths but rather old precedents, and where the function of the professor is instruction in what is already established rather than inquiry into what is still unknown. Compare with theology, where exegesis and *explication des textes* take the place of inquiry, where one seeks the ramifications and implications of a pre-established certainty rather than moving with scepticism to examine assumptions and premises long and possibly erroneously entertained. And compare with medicine, where we have again a professional school concerned with the transmission of mental and manual skill rather than with the expansion of scholarship and of scientific research. Compare, finally, the faculties of commerce, agriculture, and engineering, which are all applied sciences and practical arts depending, respectively, upon economics, genetics, and physics, and which again offer training in the sense in which training may be contrasted with education.

These comparisons suggest that the liberal arts and sciences—including, it goes without saying, sociology—differ profoundly in content and method from these other disciplines and that these differences will be reflected in the temper of those who pursue them. For it is in the liberal arts and sciences that truth is a terminus—never quite reached—to which inquiry leads, rather than a starting block from which training proceeds. In the former truth is the goal, scepticism the method. In the applied disciplines proficiency in the goal, practise the method. Scepticism belongs in the biology laboratory; it is out of place in the anatomy classroom. Scepticism belongs to sociological inquiry; it ill becomes the lecturer in torts or contracts in the school of law. The lawyer has his precedent, the theologian his dogma, and the physician his anatomical fact. The member of the faculty of philosophy, however, which embraces all the liberal arts and sciences, has only his scepticism which, as George Santayana has reminded us, is the chastity of the intellect and something to be preserved therefore through a long youth.

But the difference is more than one of method. It is also one of mood. The man in arts and sciences—whether he be physicist, sociologist, or poet—is apt to carry over into his political life those principles that he has learned to use in his discipline. He sees nothing so sacred that it can escape criticism, nothing so sacrosanct that it is immune to change, nothing so established that it is resistant to inquiry. Merit, rather than precedent, becomes the criterion of decision, in political as in intellectual affairs. The man of science, anxious to seek new truths, does not confer prestige upon old ones and as a result, conservatism in any sphere has little appeal.

His mood in addition gives him larger loyalties than those circumscribed by class, race, or nation. Indeed, it is one of the virtues of science and of scholarship that it transcends these barriers. There is no such thing, as I have written elsewhere, as a Russian genetics, an English mathematics, a Chinese chemistry, a Negro botany, a Republican physiology, a Socialist meteorology, a Catholic physics, or a Protestant sociology. Prejudice and patriotism (which is a form of prejudice) are both transcended in the pursuit of truth. And this, perhaps above all, makes the man of science an object of suspicion in the community. Because he subscribes to no provincial loyalties he is accused of having none at all. Because his vision is cosmopolitan rather than local he arouses the distrust of his neighbors. And because he is a humanist rather than a patriot, he attracts the ire of those who are patriots rather than humanists.

What does this have to do with responsibility? I think it has this much to do with it—that it has increased it. I have suggested that neither knowledge nor intelligence is positively correlated with wisdom, or with "right" decisions on matters of public policy, and that *Wertfreiheit* is an attribute to be carefully preserved in our scientific approach to social questions. Our liberal inquiries as sociologists, however, have given us a certain stance, a certain cast of mind, a certain mood and temper, and this temper has as one of its consequences an increased responsibility to our society. Commitment requires only conformity; noncommitment, on the other hand, requires responsibility. We need reasons, and responsible ones, for delaying our political decisions, for viewing all sides of public questions, including the unpopular sides, and for withholding involvement until the evidence is in. All this is not an easy task in a polarized world, a world in which everything is all black or all white, a world in which "for" or "against" are absolute rather than relative terms. As social scientists we have this added responsibility—to show that not all contraries are contradictories, that the spectrum of opinion may be continuous rather than dichotomous, and that virtue, like vice, can sometimes appear in a strange disguise.

## Utility

We have other responsibilities. I should be far from supposing that immediate utility is the proper test of any scientific inquiry. Indeed, I am personally impressed by the observation of the late Morris R. Cohen, in defence of the ivory tower, that purely theoretical contributions to mathematics and astronomy, by increasing the precision of navigation, have saved more lives at sea than any possible improvements in the carpentry of lifeboats. I am perfectly willing to agree, in short, that the star-gazer can be ultimately more useful than the carpenter. But I should strongly disagree with the proposition that utility carries with it a certain taint and that conclusions are scientific only inversely as they are useful. Indeed, I should assert with some enthusiasm that the ultimate test of al knowledge is its social use and consequence. It is therefore incumbent upon the social scientist to attend in some measure, at least, to the problems his society sets for him. In a larger sense, of course, the sense of *Wiseenssoziologie,* he has no alternative. But he can, in a premeditated way, accept some responsibility for the flow of events in his own time, for the changes that give meaning to history, and thus create for sociology a place more enterprising and more important than any it has enjoyed in the past.

The feeling persists, finally, that in spite of such admonitions as I have expressed in this paper, the social scientist does differ in some degree from the ordinary citizen in the amount of civic responsibility he is expected to assume and the kind of public service he is expected to perform. He may represent a science that is still relatively undeveloped, he is almost certainly no wiser than other men, and he has only one vote. But he speaks with many voices. Each survey he completes, each article he writes, and each item he contributes to the sum of human knowledge is a voice of its own, and each has more influence than the votes of the inarticulate. Indeed, they help to determine the votes of the inarticulate. The social scientist, therefore, shares with other articulate citizens the responsibility that is the moral accompaniment of influence. It is clear that he lacks the power that is exercised by financial, political, or military authority. He belongs, if one may say so, to the powerless elite. But power is one thing and influence is another. There is the authority of power and there is also the authority of competence. Who can say which has had the greater impact upon the course of history? Spengler remarks in *The Decline of the West* that the unknown soldier who slew Archimedes at the gates of Syracuse has had a greater impact than the great classical physicist. Spengler conceals in this shocking statement what is doubtless a subtle and important insight. But his observation also sharpens the distinction between coercion and force on the one hand and influence and persuasion on the other. Whatever may be said of authority and power, influence requires its own special kind of responsibility and with the growth of the former there comes also an expansion of the latter.

## Robert Bierstedt

What I have said in this chapter reduces itself finally to the simple and quite unoriginal proposition that as social scientists we ought to stick to our last and try to do over more effectively and completely what it is our function to do; namely, to add as much as we can to the sum of knowledge about society. In observing this primary obligation to our science so also do we increase our influence in society. Our responsibilities, in short, are of two sorts, one to science and one to society. In the dedication of our endeavors to science, however, we perform a public service, for it is in this way that the two kinds of responsibility will finally coincide.

# 33.   Items for the Agenda
of Social Science

ALFRED MC CLUNG LEE

THE WORK OF THE SOCIAL SCIENTIST OFTEN
touches upon the changing techniques, devices, and conditions of control
in our society. Regardless of how abstract his interests may be, the social
scientist can scarcely fail to sense the increasing degree to which those
techniques and devices are entering into social integration, especially organizational integration, and are being used to manipulate society more
and more deliberately and precisely. If his interests are in the affairs of
the world rather than in the abstractions or methods of social science as
such, he often finds himself willy-nilly participating in efforts at integration and manipulation of a conscious and planned sort as well as in more
automatic social processes tending in a similar direction.

The character of this integration and this manipulation differs from
country to country. I am not speaking solely of the United States of America or even solely of the West. Americans can become much more sensitive
to the character of social manipulation in England, Ireland, Italy, or Sicily
than in our own country. We can see the organizational integration and
manipulation within the Soviet Union or Communist China more clearly
than in our own country. At the same time, I do not restrict myself wholly
to the contemporary situation. Every social scientist must try to understand
the historical contexts of his society, of his research problems and projects, and of himself. Even such a remote and different time and place as
the Spain of the Inquisition, of the victories of Ferdinand III over the
Moors, of the expulsion of the Jews and the Moors, and of the Great
Armada can shed bright flashes of light upon our own social problems and

especially upon our own politico-economic activities; for the institutional integration achieved by the ancient Spanish rulers placed their country in a straight-jacket from which its people have not yet succeeded in freeing themselves.

For a long generation the social scientist has seen less and less toleration for deviations in thought and action on the part of the media of mass communications, and of the leaders and other members of a great many social class groups. As a concomitant, those devoted to the maintenance of institutional controls without special and active concern for the human costs of such controls, have been riding higher and higher in our status hierarchies for at least a generation. Many a social scientist has turned from the rocky path of creative individualistic investigation and criticism to be embraced in the lush sympathy and support given those who deal "constructively" (i.e., protectively) with the problems of constituted authority, and who do not irritate their clients with critical analyses.

The social scientist today sees the findings of social scientists and the skills of their offspring, the social technicians, employed more and more successfully to create a new feudal order which is variously called—depending upon the country—capitalistic, democratic, socialistic, nationalistic, soviet, or communistic. "Free enterprise" used to be a synonym for "capitalistic," but the vast corporations, trade unions, civic and religious bodies, and governmental network that dominate our society make such a term too obviously a hollow one. A better term, "independent enterprise," has a tragic lack of appreciation both among intellectuals and men of action. The intellectuals appear to see greater virtue or at least profit in teamwork and thus make themselves into counterparts of the actionists' organization men.

In view of all this, the intellectual who remains a social scientist in fact as well as in name is curious as to his own present and future roles in human society. He often wishes to try to discover how social science and human creativity more generally, as well as other individualistic ways of contributing to human welfare, can survive today's overwhelming repressions and possibly even greater repressions of the future.

In discussing these and other selected problems to which social scientists might well now direct their attention, I am concerning myself here primarily with social science as a useful and creative intellectual endeavor and not as an area of entrepreneural business activity. I am concerning myself with the expansion of dependable and useful scientific knowledge and not with gimmicks for the raising of grants for so-called research or with other devices for maintaining organizational budgets. In other words, I am concerning myself with certain challenges of society to social scientists today and not, at this point, with the means by which persons may try to meet, to exploit, or to obscure those challenges. What items should be placed high today on the agenda of social science?

This emphasis was selected not only because it seemed to be one appropriate to the stated purposes for this symposium but also because the most important things to discuss in connection with means as such are negative—things to avoid. These negative things have often been discussed, and I have joined in doing so, but here I want to stress things to do rather than things not to do. A social scientist can see his colleagues become sterile scientifically often enough through their trying to satisfy their anxiety to participate more fully and directly in the legitimized structure of power in their society. This includes the search for the rewards of administrative recognition, of consultative busy-work, and of entrepreneurial opportunities. A social scientist can also often see his colleagues become sterile through entrapment in scientifically pointless games of scholarship or of methodology. At the same time, he becomes aware that the Marxes, Sumners, Cooleys, Freuds, and other highly productive social scientists as well as many more modest contributors, have defied the canons of research evolved by the institutional apologists, by those who seek to capture, to tame, and perhaps to automate the disturbing potentialities of social science. The Marxes, Sumners, Cooleys, Freuds, and a great many lesser contributors to social science are not even to be called scientists, as many of the respectable define such, and they would not care.

The very stimulating Robert Ezra Park often said that he did not know or care whether or not he should be called a scientist. He knew what stirred his curiosity, and he knew lines along which he could work. He thus kept his curiosity sufficiently fed for it to remain alert and involved and to stimulate and involve the curiosities of others. He always sustained his sense of discovering more and more dependable knowledge about society and of helping others to do so.

The social scientist, to be a social scientist, needs to know and apply to his tasks all he can about the nature of the processes by which knowledge is discovered, expanded, limited, transmitted, used, and rejected or abused —what is sometimes called the sociology of knowledge.

Let us now look briefly at some items which I propose might well be placed seriously and prominently on the agenda of social scientists to be given more substantial attention. These are items dealing with: (1) identity, (2) challenge, (3) social legitimacy, (4) science and democracy as symptoms of health in social process, and (5) the criticism of social data.

Alfred McClung Lee

## 1. IDENTITY.

Sociologists have given a great deal of attention to problems of seg-regation, assimilation, social mobility, and social stratification, but they have neglected a matter crucial to such problems, that of socially provided and permitted group identities. What kinds of identity are available in society to a given individual? Whether the bases of such identities are outworn, silly, or substantial is not nearly so relevant as many of our overly rational and moralistic social theorists apparently assume. What ranges of special identification with social categories should a democratic society provide for the purposes of individual security, of cohesiveness within use-ful groups, and of other social considerations? At what point do such iden-tifications become socially damaging? Social scientists see but rarely try to understand such American phenomena as a Legion Post, a col-lege fraternity or sorority, a local Grange, or a chapter of the Colonial Dames. It is too easy merely to dismiss those groups as inconsequential or unnecessary.

Sometimes I have had the impression that social scientists in the United States, especially sociologists and social psychologists, are of the opinion that we can and should evolve a society without noticeable differences in race, class, or ethnic background. Differences among occupational groups and neighborhoods (as derived chiefly from education and occupation) are conceded. How much social health (another neglected but necessary term for social vitality, adaptability, creativeness, drive) would such a homog-enized society enjoy? It is true that we also talk rather blandly about the virtues of a pluralistic society in the United States, but in doing so we can scarcely be oblivious to these facts:

*1.* that our pluralism is radically changing, with the emerging situation one of groups defined by class, occupational, and ethnoid factors;

*2.* that the homogenization of our population has proceeded to a point well beyond that of diminishing returns in at least certain segments in terms of social adaptability and certainly of productivity;

*3.* that the most influential contributors to the arts, to the sciences, and to leadership in social action in the United States today are typically per-sons identified with unassimilated groups which carry so-called "minority" racial and ethnic labels (overlooking the fact that we lack a "majority"); and

*4.* that popular commentaries upon the problems of our times are full of references to the searches our more vigorous young people are making for new or old identifications which will be satisfying and durable.

## 2. CHALLENGE.

As one studies a variety of primitive and contemporary societies, especially ones seen at first hand and in detail, and as one reads their social history, the overall differences and changes in their members' drive, adaptability, creativity, and productivity are striking. So many social scientists are preoccupied with conditions producing or preventing social equilibrium that they neglect the conditions under which a society's members may be challenged to contribute useful or dangerous deviations in its social process.

We have a growing scientific literature on artistic creativity, on scientific research, on the lives of especially useful and especially damaging men and women, and on leadership. This literature yields some conception of the social conditions making for such phenomena. I would like to see such studies broadened beyond a focus on the outstanding individuals and the exceptional events with which they are associated. Whole communities at certain periods appear to get caught up in a surge of creative or destructive activity. Periclean Athens and the Florence of the Renaissance are brilliant examples of communities in waves of creativity.

Great men are rarely isolated figures. Many times they stand with their heads only slightly above their productive competitors and colleagues. Historians and sociologists have suggested some of the conditions making for waves of creativity, of cultural deviation, of organizational expansion and exploitation, and of other forms this sort of thing may take; but such scientists have not yet pried into the social aspects of challenge deeply enough. We are somewhat aware that American fine arts—painting, the theater, poetry, sculpture, and fiction—flowered in the 1930's and languished since. Many specialists are of the opinion that what creativity we now have in the fine arts got its impetus from the 1930's and from imports. We are also aware of the veritable domination of the literature of England during this century and part of the last by writers born in Ireland—James Joyce, George Moore, Sean O'Casey, George Bernard Shaw, Oscar Wilde, William Butler Yeats, and many others.

But, beyond vague generalities and rather imprecise and even inaccurate historical analyses of such situations, what do we actually know about the conditions of popular challenge out of which such flowerings arise? Could we indicate to United States policy-makers today the kinds of conditions of challenge that would help us to solve our great and pressing national needs for creativity so often discussed in these days in governmental, business, educational, and scientific circles?

Certainly the creativity in literature and in the theater one sees everywhere in Ireland today is not a product of Institutes and Bureaus or even of an educational organization or a lack of suppression. James Joyce, Bernard Shaw, and Sean O'Casey are popular heroes but are greeted with no enthusiasm, to say the least, by officials of church and state. Ireland is in a social situation of the opening of minds; individuals are developing imagination and drive, and are seeing and feeling challenges to personal expression. The writers are saloon keepers, farmers, air lines hostesses, governmental clerks, housewives, and others from many parts of the country, and it is a tiny country with only three million inhabitants, one-eighteenth of those who live in the British Isles. Literary expression, like Gaelic football and the Little People, is in the air and pervades many minds.

### 3. SOCIAL LEGITIMACY.

I am referring here to the mystique or charisma and influence possessed by the individuals and social organizations which appear to participate in socially sanctioned social power. Associated with the term are discussions of orthodoxy, agitation, apparent social structure, apparent system.

Legitimacy is a personal problem to a great many social scientists. Its psychological hold derives from its sources in parental approval, support, and power. Those who have been raised to excel in the sibling-type rivalry of our classroom educational procedures often regard social legitimacy as a thing given, a thing to be assumed, rather than as a phenomenon to be subjected to impolite examination. In society, the more revered and stable a phenomenon may appear, the more social scientists need to probe it deeply—with as great freedom from preconceptions as possible.

As I see it, there is not such a thing as a single "system" of legitimacy or even a series of such "systems." The word "system" involves an untenable analogy to either the mechanical or the biological. At any rate, many views of what are popularly thought to be systems of legitimacy are held in a society and by its members. The matter is complex, and I have discussed it elsewhere. Others have been concerned with it in a variety of ways, but few appear to be able to break through their own psychological needs to view social legitimacy and legitimation objectively and with greater penetration. Until more social scientists can effectively learn how to do so, important break-throughs in social science here must wait.

### 4. SCIENCE AND DEMOCRACY AS SYMPTOMS OF HEALTH IN SOCIAL PROCESS.

Social historians have concluded variously as to the etiology and consequences of science and democracy in social process. Some treat our few centuries of relative democracy as a transitional interlude between two dark ages, the second of which may be as dark as Orwell and Huxley predict. Some try to distinguish between the conditions of which science and democracy are symptomatic. Such pundits as George Lundberg are of the opinion that science can flourish under any system of government. The regimentation of scientists and the limitation of democracy for an assortment of plausible expediences are common developments of our day. The exigencies of the West's struggle with the Soviet Union provide a major premise for many such rationalizations in the United States, and I gather that Soviet apologists similarly make use of the American threat to maintain their own autocratic procedures and controls.

Rather than merely creating a pseudo-scientific facade for polemics about science and democracy, indefinitely or chauvinistically defined, we are urgently in need of studies of behavior and of social history which will indicate clearly the nature of these phenomena as aspects of social process before policy-makers have helped impair them further.

### 5. THE CRITICISM OF SOCIAL DATA.

When the Kennedy Administration failed to use the accurate social data concerning Cuba which were available to them, the crucial role of objective, disinterested criticism of data by scientifically oriented and trained professionals again became dramatically apparent. But every time one criticizes social data, one analyzes and possibly deflates materials of propaganda useful to a special interest, possibly to powerful special interests as in the case of the Cuban situation. It was easy—in fact it was cheap—for *Time* newsmagazine to speak up candidly about those interests and about the strategically relevant facts of the situation *after* the invasion fiasco had taken place. *Time* did not provide its readers such data before the aborted attempt was made.

Perhaps the greatest contribution social scientists could make in our time would be to reassess social data of social importance and to make their conclusions available. The nonsense in public opinion polls, the silly and contradictory statements of interested parties about business trends and conditions, and the unwarranted generalizations of political leaders and lobbyists about the consequences of a Berlin development, a public electric power project, the further breaking down of the separation between church and state, and the rest require objective analysis. Issues raised in *The Ugly American* are deadly serious even though its authors may or may not have misstated or caricatured them.

Our profession owes society a far higher level of candor and far less

Alfred McClung Lee

double talk than we now give. Many social scientists are intimidated by the thought of being called unscientific, in other words by a threat to their legitimacy, their respectability. Those who wish respectability should be encouraged to seek a comfortable cult, rather than permitting themselves to help convert what is called social science into a ritual-ridden secular order. Scientific innovation of a fundamental sort has never been legitimate—even though it may later be legitimated. It is always unorthodox, agitational, irreverent.

# 34. Moral Obligations of the Scientist

RALPH ROSS

## I

I CAN SEE NO DIFFERENCE IN PRINCIPLE BETWEEN the responsibilities of the natural and of the social scientist, so I shall treat them together.

The standard, or purist, belief about the scientist is that his responsibilities, obligations, and values amount to neither more nor less than doing good scientific work. Sometimes that itself is spelled out in detail: the scientist ought to value truth; he should not fake his research; he should listen to all qualified opinion; and so on. But the heart of the matter is that the responsibility of the scientist is to science, and nothing else.

There may be a few differences in the way people would state the purist's underlying, or presupposed, argument, but its main line, I think, is this: (1) Values and obligations cannot be established by reason or evidence; they are personal preferences. (2) Scientists have expressed a value (or preference) they all happen to share, by the very act of becoming scientists. (3) That value is science. (4) Science is an activity of a certain sort, whose end is truth. (5) Therefore, the responsibility of the scientist is to pursue truth by means of that activity.

In this argument there is the tacit assumption that people who express a value ought to realize it if they can; at least people ought to do a good job of what they do. If one objects to even so minimal an "ought," he can do away with it by saying that number five in the argument is just another way of stating the meaning of "value." That is, to say that a man values x means that he wants x, and to want x is to be willing to do something to get it. And even that may be pared down further by some. After all, a man

429

may want x and be unwilling to do anything to get it. He may even want x only if he can get it without doing anything. But, one might answer, if x is truth and the man who values x is a scientist, he is committed both to the end and the means. On the other hand, if x is science, as in our argument above, then the man who values x may be willing to accept truth as a product of science but have no *direct* commitment to it; he may simply love the activity, science, but have no passion for the truth. This is far from an impossible attitude; indeed, it is a common romanticism to love the chase and care nothing for the fox.

It is possible to go still one step further in limiting the scientist's responsibility, and that nearly eliminates it. One can object to proposition number two in the argument by denying that the act of becoming a scientist implies any serious commitment to science as a value. A man may be a scientist in order to earn a living. Since there are many other ways of earning a living, his choice may imply that the work of science is relatively easy or pleasant for him, or that it was the line of least resistance, granted his abilities and opportunities. Thus, he has as much commitment to science as a ditch-digger has to ditch-digging, and no more.

The responsibilities of the scientist, then, are found somewhere on a scale from the ditch-digger type of commitment and responsibility to proposition number five, the conclusion of the original argument. And no more can be claimed, according to this purist belief, because of the truth of proposition number one. There is no way of establishing that anything is more valuable than anything else, or that people ought to do one thing rather than another. We must start with what a man, in fact, finds valuable for himself, and then we may analyze the meaning of that commitment.

In talking to the purist, one may wish to quarrel with his first proposition, which is stated naively, to say the least. But as a tactic of persuasion, that would be a great mistake. For the purist-scientist may very well refuse to discuss what he regards as a philosophical question, while resting content with his own philosophical conclusion. Indeed, his quickest way of absolving himself of responsibility and of the need for philosophical questioning is by saying, as he does, that science is value-free. Since he regards science as the guarantor of knowledge, it follows that we have no knowledge of what is valuable. All we can do, in consequence, is to act in terms of what we happen to value.

This is as good a point as any from which to start considering the purist argument. What does it mean to say that science is value-free? It may mean that there are no sentences affirming or denying values which are, or can be, the result of scientific investigation. And that is true. Does it follow that the scientist *qua* scientist makes no value judgments, explicit or implicit? Well, in the sentences he writes, he makes no value judgments.* But of course he also does the work that culminates in those sentences, and although that work does not conclude in value judgments, doing the work may reveal some.

I am not talking about the honesty and impartiality of the investigation; they are a function of efficiency. The purist-scientist agrees that they are values of science; but that is as far as he goes. I am talking about a consequence of the kind of work science is. It is not, except at some particular stages of an investigation, mechanical and necessary. Especially at the outset of an inquiry, when the problem is chosen, it is quite open. Indeed, the choice of problems differs from the rest of science in an important respect: the problem is the spot at which society impinges on science most significantly. Once an inquiry is under way, it can scarcely be influenced by extra-scientific matters without being injured as science. Of course, the money spent on research, the equipment provided, the number and caliber of assistants are extra-scientific. But they help or hinder the work, they do not substantially alter its direction or conclusion. At the level of problem-selection, however, social pressures may determine choice. And the money to be spent, the equipment and assistance provided, which would not alter an ongoing inquiry, might very well dictate what inquiry is to be started. That depends on the decision of a man, a scientist, who is going to conduct an inquiry. And his decision may have a moral element.

The issue is not so simple as resisting social pressures and choosing problems of some significance in science. It may be, on occasion, that one should resist the pressures of scientists and choose problems of some significance to society. Nor is the effect of society on the problems chosen by science always, or usually, one of direct pressure; the social context of the moment has a profound indirect effect. And that effect is discoverable in physical, as well as social, science. V. F. Lenzen, for example, wrote:

In the period preceding Newton and contemporary with him, the chief problems of physics were, first, the properties of simple machines which are the subject matter of statics; second, the motion of falling bodies and the trajectory of projectiles; third, the laws of hydrostatics and atmospheric pressure; fourth, the mechanics of the heavens and theory of the tides. The foregoing physical problems were determined by the needs of industry, war and transport. The principles of statics contributed to the improvement of the

---

* Although he makes such judgments, implicitly, by writing the sentences instead of doing something else.

lifting and conveying equipment used in mining and building. The theory of motion contributed to the improvement of artillery. The laws of hydrostatics and aerostatics were important for the design of ships, the building of canals, and the ventilation of mines. The mechanics of the heavens was of value to navigation in war and peace. . . . It appears to me a justifiable conclusion that the scheme of physics was mainly determined by the technical tasks set by a rising capitalism and nationalism.[1]

Whether or not the "scheme" of physics was "determined" by a rising capitalism and nationalism, it seems to have been much influenced by them. For if every conclusion of physics rested on the methods of physicists, every conclusion was still the answer to a particular problem. And the set or pattern of physical laws was a body of conclusions about some things (the concerns of the society) and not about others.

In addition to the massive, sometimes indirect, influence of social context on scientific problems, there are many direct influences and extra-scientific motives. One can make a list of possible reasons for the choice of a problem in science, and can appraise each, without too much difficulty, in moral terms.

*1.* Personal advancement as the sole criterion (a popular subject, or one that will receive publicity, and/or one for which money is available, etc.).

*2.* Quick results and equally quick publication (problem easy to solve, though trivial).

*3.* Currying favor with superiors by choosing a problem that interests them but not the worker.

*4.* A problem that has current interest, though for the wrong reasons.

*5.* Solution of problem that would have social value.

*6.* Solution of problem that would contribute significantly to science, open new areas of research, etc.

*7.* Selecting a problem that deeply interests the worker.

The machines of academic life grind slowly but effectively. What attracts graduate students to a science often has little to do with the scientific work they do ten years later. What a young academic wants to work at is often forgotten in the pressure for publication, especially since publication may mean keeping his job, being promoted, and getting more money. Fashions in science, whether good or bad for the science in question (e.g., neobehaviorism in psychology, behavioral study in political science), may make the difference between national recognition if they are followed, and relative neglect if they are not. These are extra-scientific factors that bear on the work of science and influence the "scheme" of science at any time. To resist such pressures requires courage, not only because of the consequences of resistance but also because it is almost impossible to convict any scientist of yielding to them. It is too easy for him to say, to others and to himself, that he is doing only what he believes. In any event, the moral dimension, with its responsibilities and obligations, is clearly evident in the scientist's work at this level.

## II

The purist's argument rests, as we have seen, on a mistaken assumption that the work of science does not at any point touch society in such a way that it must be influenced by extra-scientific considerations. But there is another mistaken assumption, equally damaging to the argument, hidden in the discussion of the scientist *qua* scientist. Here the purist admits that the scientist as a citizen has the same responsibilities that any other citizen has, and, of course, as husband, father, friend, religious communicant, takes on many more. But, he insists, the scientist as scientist has responsibilities only to science (what I have called responsibilities of efficiency), namely, to do what is needed so that scientific work is done well. This assertion has already been disposed of, but the underlying assumption must be examined, for its denial opens still another realm of responsibilities for the scientist.

The assumption is that we are talking about *someone* whom we designate as scientist *qua* scientist. But we are not; we are talking about a status and role. And statuses are related to more or less systematic and stratified social structures which give them whatever warrant they possess; they have no independent existence, as men do, but are ways of characterizing relationships within the structure. If we are entitled to hypostatize "scientist as scientist," we are entitled to do the same for "Indian Chief" and "ditch-digger." And so we may argue that the ditch-digger *qua* ditch-digger has responsibilities only to ditch-digging, and that his only obligation is to dig well. The same argument can be applied to the lawyer as lawyer, the doctor as doctor, the businessman as businessman. And these occupations, when they are not related to anything else, are no less value-free than science.

What, then (to continue with the consequences of such an argument) is not value free? There is ditch-digging, and law, and medicine, and business, and science, and how they are related to social welfare. Whose responsibility is it to decide whether there should be such things? Obviously, the citizen's. In our society that means almost everybody's, but only in one of his capacities. And a responsibility that is almost everybody's is almost nobody's, especially if we bear equally, as we do, the responsibility for all public decisions and acts. Ordinary good sense tells us that, although every citizen is responsible for stopping crime, the apprehension of criminals is more a job for the police than for other people. Equally, the responsibility for continuing the existence of science is more that of scientists than of ditch-diggers.

A man may choose his vocation (in societies where there is such choice) in order to earn a living, or to have pleasant work, or some such reason. Often there is little actual choice of vocation, because what some men can do is limited. So the ditch-digger's stake in the existence of ditch-digging may be only his desire for the continuance of an occupation which permits him to work. But this is either not true of the scientist or should not be, as it is not or should not be, true of the professor. Society cannot afford people in these occupations who place little value on them. Indeed, even the purist assumes the truth of this when he contends that the scientist has a responsibility to science.

If a man values something enough to want its continued existence (and every scientist ought thus to believe in science, or at least his science), then he has an obligation to do some things to bring it about. But if there were such a creature as a scientist *qua* scientist (i.e., a creature who was a scientist and only a scientist) there would be nothing he could do. He would have to leave it to others, chiefly the citizen *qua* citizen, to ensure that science exists. It is precisely because the scientist is a person, usually a citizen, working at science, that he can do many things to help science. And it is because he is, as scientist, more devoted to science than other men are, that he bears more responsibility for its existence than they do.

As is so often the case, it is one thing to know there is an obligation to bring something about, but quite another thing to know what to do to bring it about. Here we need to know the social conditions under which science is most likely to continue. Indeed, since the scientist not only wants science to continue but also to prosper, there are many things to know: under what conditions is science likely to appear in a society without science; under what conditions will it languish or disappear; under what conditions will it flourish? When he knows the conditions, the scientist ought to create or maintain them. That is his obligation.

Since the conditions are many and varied, the scientist may have to choose those for which he can be most effective. Some scientists will argue at once that they are too busy as scientists to take on other activities. But farmers are busy, too, and yet they may have to fight for their countries and their farms. If scientists are too busy to fight for their science, they may cease altogether to be busy as scientists. And they may have to bear witness before authority to explain their failures. Political conditions may bear on science in many ways; at the least, equality and inequality of opportunity have to do with recruiting scientists, the lack of opportunity for some reduces the size of the group from which scientists come. Economic, educational, and cultural conditions are often relevant. Sociologists and historians of science have done less work on this subject than they might; when more is known it may turn out that some democratic conditions are necessary to the health of science, and a scientist would then be committed to aspects, at a minimum, of a particular political form.

It is at this point in thinking about the matter that a scientist should realize the extent to which, as scientist, he is involved with the rest of society's institutions and activities. For he must, if he values science, be committed to some things in society and, in consequence, opposed to others. But he must also ask himself whether he can, in all conscience, be committed to those things. Should it prove the case that conditions necessary to scientific welfare are abhorrent to him (inimical to other, more cherished values), then he may have to reconsider his evaluation of science, and decide, indeed, whether he wants to remain a scientist. If there were such a being as the scientist *qua* scientist, he would have one fundamental value, science, and it would be absolute. But since scientists are only men who practice science, their evaluation of science is dependent on their evaluation of other things. Indeed, their evaluation of science should change as they learn more about the social conditions necessary for science, and the consequences to man and society of the existence of science. Should it be discovered that unless scientific activity is stopped there is a high probability that the world will be destroyed within ten years, the ultimate scientific purist could scarcely argue that his only responsibility is to science, and that what happens to the world is not his concern. For, of course, science would come to an end either way, but in one way the world—and the erstwhile scientist—might survive.

## III

There are two more types of obligations that fall on the scientist *qua* scientist. First, he has obligations to other scientists and to his employers. No scientist has created science, nor does he sustain it, by himself. To those who make available to him their ideas and research, he owes a return in kind. If isolated from the world of scientists, his work might be rendered fruitless or repetitious. This obligation may be thought of as one of efficiency, like the obligation not to tamper with the facts, but it has a wider range. It requires encouragement of others, offering one's own work as help in another's enterprise, subordination of one's ego to the welfare of one's science.

The obligation to "employers" (universities, foundations, business concerns) is an obligation to those who provide the immediate conditions of scientific work. The scientist is normally employed as scientist to do some sort of work, and to do it under particular circumstances. He is always a bio-chemist, a rural sociologist, a nuclear physicist, one particular role, and not others. In addition, his problems and scientific interests must be guided somewhat, perhaps greatly, by the concerns of his employers. If he objects, he should resign.

The second type of obligation is a little like obligations to employers, but is even more important. Society supports science. Even if it merely tolerated the existence of science, that would be on the tacit assumption that science was not destructive of society's ends. But millions and millions of dollars are now spent on the conduct of science and the training of scientists. We make the stronger assumption that science is of value to society. Obviously, the fact is that the conclusions of science have been used extensively and in countless ways, from technology to community planning, and society is more than amply repaid for its support of science. But support of science rests on the presumption that either science will benefit society, or that the knowledge it yields is so valuable in itself or for other purposes that society should support science. Thus another obligation is created. If one accepts the support of society, one incurs the obligation to support society in return: (1) to do the sort of work expected; (2) to have some care for the welfare of the society whose support one accepts.

The purist might accept the first of these obligations to society, yet reject the second. The work expected of him, he might say, is the science he normally does. But as scientist, what other concern for social welfare need he have? If we say, concern for the uses of science, for example, he disagrees; this point he will not concede. The uses of science are not, he will assure us, the business of the scientist. The purist, driven from every other position, will maintain this one to the end. And to some extent he is right. As scientist, it is not his business to try to determine the ends of society, nor is it his business to play the engineer and use science for practical ends. But we cannot let him stop with an idea so little analyzed, because it is just as scientist that he often has a special responsibility for the uses of science. Suppose a physicist learns that a new weapon is being constructed so that when used, it will blow up and kill the user. Shall he say that it is none of his business *qua* scientist and that he need not tell anyone about it? Suppose a sociologist knows that under conditions A, B, and C, violent race conflict will ensue. If he discovers that, thoughtlessly, the city fathers are actually bringing A, B, and C about, does he, as scientist, have no obligation to speak out?

The purist would, surely, deny that as scientists the physicist and the sociologist, in these instances, have any obligation to call attention to the situation. He would probably add that if they did not, they would be sorry specimens of man. But he would want to cling to his distinction. Yet to do so would require a rapid change of hats for the scientist. After all, it is *because* he is a physicist that he knows the dangers of the weapon. No one else can tell us. Even if he rushes out in a citizen's hat to sound the alarm, it is not *qua* citizen but *qua* scientist that he has the information to divulge (and *qua* scientist that he will be needed).

Then (a lesser point), if the scientist as scientist has a responsibility to science and a part of that responsibility is to keep science in existence, does he not harm science if his sin of omission becomes known and is then defended by him as proper conduct? Will society put up with an activity that breeds men who reject ordinary moral duties because of a special code of their own, that of scientist *qua* scientist? And if we are told it is not a code prescribing and limiting conduct, but merely an intellectual distinction between what a man does as scientist and what he does as citizen and member of a community, then we are entitled to answer that it is indeed used as a code, again and again, when scientists excuse themselves for not thinking about nonscientific matters.

More important, though, is the first point: if the scientist does argue that, as scientist, he has no responsibility to say or do anything about the weapon or the race conflict, he has ruled out the possibility of anybody else doing what ought to be done in those matters. Because nobody else can. It is folly to talk about obligations to do what one cannot possibly do. So it is not just as man or citizen that one has a responsibility to help in these situations, for he cannot help without scientific knowledge. And it is not just as man or citizen that the scientist has the responsibility, for it is only as scientist that he knows what is indispensable for any effective intervention. Perhaps again we must recognize that "scientist *qua* scientist" is not a term referring to anybody, but only a name for status. And a man who is a scientist has a special obligation in these instances *because* he is a scientist, not in spite of it.

The problem of the scientist's conduct in the cases of the weapon and the race conflict has a further complication. It is not necessary that the scientist do anything to rectify those situations. He is neither an engineer nor a municipal official. He has to say something, and what he has to say is scientific information. He would probably regard it as his duty to make that information public to other scientists. Does it cease to be his duty when the recipients of the information are laymen and the information is relevant to practice? If so, he does not understand what it means to be a member of society, or what the relation is between any vocation and its social context.

Finally, there is a practical question about the way to meet this last obligation. For the scientist to learn about the weapon or the possibility of race conflict might be sheer accident. For him to inform the people concerned might seem gratuitous or arrogant. The problem is one of regular and regularized communication between laymen and scientists. What is needed is a channel of communication that is efficient, and that does not take the scientist from his work for prolonged periods of time. Fortunately, the machinery already exists, it has been created by scientists, and it needs only to be extended. I am referring to the professional scientific associations which meet annually, or more often, and publish technical journals. Almost every scientist is a member of one or more of these associations; the associations are used for communication with other scientists, not only about scientific matters, but even about filling jobs.

It is time for scientific associations to design the means by which social problems which science can help are brought to the attention of scientists, and whatever in science is relevant to those problems is brought to the attention of the appropriate laymen. There are always scientific administrators and statesmen to do such work. If it is done well, it could be one of the most effective social acts ever performed by scientists as scientists.

## NOTE

1. Adams, Dennes, and Pepper, eds., *Civilization*, University of California Publications in Philosophy, Volume 23, University of California Press, 1942, p. 12.

# Part VII

# CONCLUSION

# 35.  Prospects: The Applied Sociology
## of the Center-City

S. M. MILLER

APPLIED SOCIOLOGY HAS GROWN ENORMOUSLY IN recent years. As the papers in this volume indicate, the applied sociologist functions as researcher, consultant, and social critic in many different settings. I believe that in recent years applied sociologists have made substantial contributions to sociology and to society. I am impressed, however, that the potential contribution is much greater, particularly in two ways that are increasingly emergent.

In recent years, an applied sociology of the center-city and applied sociology as social criticism have appeared. Sociologists have assumed posts in the new planning and action organizations that are involved with the problems of center-cities. Within these organizations, sociologists have done a great deal more than research. A parallel but independent trend has been the reemergence of social criticism by sociologists. I shall concentrate on these two developments, ignoring the great expansion of applied sociology in medical, industrial, educational, and other settings. My stress will be on the strains and difficulties encountered in the course of applying sociology, rather than on the gains and growth that have been achieved. My purpose is critical examination of applied efforts, rather than self-congratulatory celebration.

---

My collaboration with Martin Rein has shaped many of the ideas presented here. I am also grateful to the following for comments: Louis Kriesburg, Irwin Deutscher, Robert Hardt, and Frank Riessman. None of them is responsible for the present formulation. I am indebted to Alvin W. Gouldner for editorial pruning.

*441*

# S. M. Miller

## *The Applied Sociologist of the Center-City*

A new social mechanism has emerged to deal with the proliferating problems of the center-cities of large metropolitan areas, especially in their slum areas. This device commonly takes the form of a community organization which plans and carries out a comprehensive and interrelated set of programs to improve education, employment, housing, social service, and other conditions of center-city residents. The financing for these programs has come from several sources. Most important have been local funds, the Ford Foundation in their gray area projects, and the President's Committee on Juvenile Delinquency and Youth Crime in their support of coordinated plans for reducing delinquency and increasing opportunities in slum areas. The "war on poverty" will greatly expand such activities. The geographic scope of the planning and action agency varies: Mobilization for Youth and HARYOU, for example, deal with two neighborhoods of New York City, the Lower East Side and Harlem; the Youth Opportunities Board of Los Angeles has the city and county as its province. In some programs the residents of the area are involved in various forms of self-help, in political action and in decision-making bodies.

In these new community planning and action agencies, as well as in older organizations, the applied sociologist has played many roles: planning consultant, basic researcher, advisor on the course of the program, and evaluator of the impact of the program. In these quasi-governmental agencies, new demands have been placed on the applied sociologists. The agencies are attempting to change communities, or sections of them, in drastic ways; the sociologist is suggesting ways of effecting change as well as evaluating the outcomes of the interventions. The sociologist is now playing a more central role in planning operations, along with conducting research.

An important political consequence of the sociologist's involvement has been the increased pressure which he brings to bear on the clarification of goals. Many evaluations of action programs founder on administrators' unwillingness or inability to provide concrete and useful description of the outcomes they seek. For example, a work-training project can be aimed at increasing the "employability" of youth or the actual employment of youth. The former would focus study only on the quantity and quality of training programs; the latter forces attention to what actually happens to the graduates of the programs.

While the clarity of goals is frequently low, the technical interests of

*442*

the applied sociologist involved have resulted in increasing the precision with which they are formulated, for he cannot evaluate the organization's effectiveness unless he knows what it is trying to do. Indeed, in many cases the researcher has provided the rationale for a project whose goals and plans were initially vague and diffuse.[1]

In a number of the planning-action projects, the applied sociologist has developed a subtle, continuing role by helping to choose and improve programs. He has provided and interpreted information useful in deciding on the kinds of programs to adopt and adapt. Sociological consultants, for example, have often provided counsel on the most appropriate ways of conducting programs for low-income youths, emphasizing the importance of concrete, visible, and ready results which are defined as useful by low-income youth.

Despite the diverse activities of sociologists in these center-city projects, the major emphasis has been in evaluating their outcomes. Many of the programs are listed as "demonstration projects" or "pilot programs," implying a tentativeness in continuity and a concern for tested results. The "research-evaluation" component is frequently an ingredient necessary to secure funding. Alvin Gouldner has pointed out to me that parliamentary committees in an earlier day used research as a way of forestalling action, while today research often becomes the socially acceptable front for undertaking action.

As a result, evaluation research has become one of the popular forms of applied social science activity in recent years. In part this reflects our anxieties about the efficacy of current practices in education, training, and social welfare. It also mirrors the growing courage and technical competence of sociologists in pursuing difficult tasks. Ten years ago, many sociologists, touchy about maintaining progressional standards, would not have undertaken many of the current evaluations. With new and powerful techniques and more precise instrumentalization, applied sociology has moved into fresh realms.

#### THE NARROW EVALUATION FOCUS

The roles of the applied sociologists of the center-city are novel and changing. The agencies which employ them are young. (And perhaps that is why they can use sociologists in new ways.) Despite the short experience, it is possible to discern some characteristic difficulties in the uses of applied sociology in the center-city.

The basic orientations of evaluation designs are often limited. The applied sociologist has frequently failed to assess adequately the operating possibilities of his research, and to plan research that would maximize his contribution to the processes of urban life. He has often tended to adopt uncritically the conventional norms and outlook of traditional sociological "scientific" practices. For example, utilizing traditional tests of significance with small samples leads to the rejection of "too many true hypotheses because of a concern not to accept false ones." Where "minimal efficacy is really all that can be hoped for" the wisdom of this statistical strategy is dubious.[2] New aims, methods and practices would develop sociology itself, as well as deepening its contribution to policy.

The courage of sociologists' initial commitment has often not been sustained in practice. Traditional practices are followed even where the conditions to make them useful do not actually exist, although these conditions were specified in the original design. The exigencies of operations have frequently disrupted effective and rigorous evaluation dreams and designs.[3] The investigators are promised a control group by the administrators of the programs; in practice, however, this is extremely difficult to deliver. Selective and separate program inputs are planned initially by the administrators, so that the impact of each program (e.g., pre-kindergarten, employment training, family casework), can be measured individually. In practice, however, saturation programs—with many simultaneous inputs—occur so that it becomes impossible to discern which, if any, program is having what effects.

As is frequently the case in social research today, we have the know-how for doing a study under ideal conditions. We lack, however, a readily codified set of directions for those disturbing (and frequent) situations where we cannot pursue procedures which are methodologically desirable.[4]

Even if the needed conditions are present, it might still not be advisable to maintain the restricted perspectives of many evaluators. The questionnaire and the interview have been the primary—often the exclusive—instruments of the applied sociologist of the center-city, supplemented by statistical compilations like rates of juvenile delinquency. These obviously useful instruments screen out many exciting events which are taking place in the new community planning organizations. *Social usefulness has frequently been subordinated to sociological respectability.*

These projects are unusual social experiments. They are in the middle of powerful competing political groups, professional and organizational interests and ideologies, and local history and traditions. They are laced by great controversies. They frequently are deeply involved in the strategy of obtaining change in the established institutions of educational and social services in the United States.[5] Little of this is reflected in the evaluation research that is taking place. The process of this great and ongoing change is ignored.

What is needed is the willingness to adopt another focus of work—a concern with social change and social history. Here, less "hard" data may be necessary to get at the swift interplay of events. Social chronicles and analysis, based on observation and records, would be extremely useful in studying social change in general and organizational change in particular. It would provide sharp insights into community life.[6] The sociological study of organizations would be enhanced by the analysis of conflict over changes in social agencies.[7]

The unit of evaluation is also important. If only the new special services are studied, we do not develop an estimate of the operation of the total social service network in a community. The fit of social services to social needs is left unappraised and a crucial aspect of the life of the poor is unexplored. By taking a restricted and fragmented view of what should be evaluated, the applied sociologists of the center-city have not provided the broad, integrated benchmark measurements of urban life that are needed.

The widening of perspective would also be important for improving measures of output and input. Greater attention might be paid to these issues if we recognized more profoundly the technical limitations of input and output measurements.

The evaluation of *output* requires measures that are sensitive to movement and that cover a wide range of possible changes. Often, we know of useful types of such measures but cannot obtain the actual measurements. For example, an innovation in school policies may have had a primary impact on teachers' attitudes but school authorities will not permit the study of the changing attitudes of their personnel. Frequently, we are assessing new types of activities with competing goals and activities, and we do not know the full array of potential change. An instance might be a social program to involve residents of a slum area in political action; the impact of this activity might spill over into intra-family relations, increased job-searching, relationships to the Welfare Department, and the like. The limitation here is not the operating barrier to the collection of adequate data but an ignorance dimension. Higher technical competence will not reduce ignorance.

Similarly, in the measurement of *input* (the program of intervention—the independent variable) the researcher is faced with ignorance. Indeed, frequently, systematical input measurement is overlooked, and practitioners' statements about what they have done or are doing are taken at face value. The programmatic outline of activities is used as the description of input. Closer examination all too often reveals that what occurs in a program is far different from what is planned, perceived, or reported.

The following is frequent: An innovation is planned; the outcomes of the program to test the innovation are measured and show little impact. Actually, the original innovation was quite debilitated in practice; quality control was low. Consequently, a negative report on the innovation as originally discussed is inappropriate. And, of course, many positive evaluations are misleading because special factors other than those intended were those that produced the change.

Further, if movement does or does not occur, we have little basis for understanding the causes of failure or success. Few evaluation programs are sufficiently concerned with what goes on *inside* a program to explicate the reasons for the outcome. Where we have ambiguity of goals and where goals change—as frequently occurs—the analysis of the forces affecting outcome are especially necessary. The observational approach will not readily provide answers to all these issues, but it can provide additional understanding of the succession of events.

### THE PRESSURE FOR RESULTS

The agency's pressure for results is an important source of stress for the applied sociologist of the center-city. Basic information for developing programs are urgently needed. The reports of research evaluation are required to obtain further funding. Information and results are needed *now;* many applied sociologists have met incredible bureaucratic deadlines only by their unrelenting devotion.

Difficulties that ensue are the hasty design of a study, especially of the instruments used in it, inadequate quality control in the collection of data, and skimpy or inflexible analysis of data. Narrow concerns in data interpretation are joined to limited perspectives in design. The larger implications of the data are usually ignored.

There is no guarantee, of course, that research pursued under less strenuous circumstances will not suffer from the same set of inadequacies. Nor should it be ignored that pressure for results may also produce certain advantages. As Morris Rosenberg once expressed it to me, there is no finite end to research. Without strong pressure to end a research activity and write it up, many more studies would remain half-finished and half-baked.

Since more and more funds for research come from various kinds of outside agencies (grants from foundation and government agencies, contracts with other agencies), there is a constant need for reporting results in a given time period. The applied sociologist in an agency does not differ in that he has to make a report, but in that he usually has a shorter period in which to do it, has more direct pressure to produce, and has less scope and independence in his decisions.

### APPLIED SOCIOLOGY AND GENERAL SOCIOLOGY

Another area of difficulty is the inadequate contribution of applied sociology to general sociology. In surveying the work of the center-city applied sociologists, I have been impressed with the potential theoretical implications of the current work. But almost no effort is expended to feed these back into general sociology and to develop their implications for theory and further research. These applied sociologists seem to have the same difficulties in their relation to general sociology as do applied sociologists in other situations.

In general, there is little attention to sifting the findings and analyzing applied sociological investigations so that they build general sociology. In developing the symposia which led to this volume, we encountered great difficulty in getting papers that explored the contribution of applied sociology to general sociology. While we were fortunate in securing those published in this volume, we unsuccessfully solicited many more.

An important source of the difficulty is that not all social problems are sociological problems, nor are all sociological issues, social problems. Many important social problems cannot be readily formulated so that they are pertinent to the present or prospective expertise of sociologists and other social scientists. And any discipline has technical and internal problems that are important to resolve and deal with, if the field is to progress, but they may have no conceivable relationship to pressing social problems.

To ignore social problems and to act as though they have no value for study in a field is to surrender rich opportunities for intellectual development.[8] But a discipline cannot take a definition of its tasks automatically from the situations of society. To do so may leave a field rapidly barren of the technical developments needed to give power to its analyses. Further, if a discipline accepts society's definition of its problems and the sponsorship of established institutions, it can be made an adjunct to manipulation or suffer inadequate development, as has long been the case with rural sociology.[9]

Housekeeping research manifests the possibilities of stunted growth. Each of the center-city organizations employing sociologists requires the compilation of operationally useful data with little broader significance. For example, collecting data on the number of nonwhite, unemployed females in a given city may be a necessary task, but it is not exciting research. The sociologist cannot avoid such duties, but he cannot be content with them.[10] His independence is involved. I shall turn to this issue shortly, but I want first to discuss some things that might be done in the present context to broaden the intellectual value of applied sociology to sociology itself.

A single finding on a given city, such as that reported above, may have little general significance. Findings for a variety of cities may have some broad importance. The need is for a more effective communication and use of results than now prevails and for more effective cooperative activity among applied sociologists.

Effective communication is frequently limited by the nonavailability of reports and their haphazard, if not capricious, distribution. Because of the desire to keep to "professional standards," many reports are never available because they are not "finished" work.[11] Awareness of and access to privately circulated "ditto jobs" has become a source of inside-dopesterism. Work that should be widely known is frequently privileged information for selected acquaintances.

Despite these deprivations, the major difficulty is not the shortage but the proliferation of reports. We are in a publication explosion that overwhelms the eye and confuses the brain. While a great deal of value is issued, much nonsense is promulgated and false leads offered. A field develops in part by what it does not do as well as by what it does do. Although we like to look at science as cumulative and ever-developing, in practice many useful leads are thrown away or are long ignored. Other less useful leads are pursued for long periods, only to be abandoned after they have contaminated years of study. In more pessimistic moments, I believe that not to publish much of what is currently published would be a great contribution! Some "findings" and conclusions serve as detours rather than as intellectual highways.

Can the desire to contribute to general sociology also overcome the difficulties of communicating and using material? What is needed is a journal that can annually report on and systematically assess the many reports and working documents that are currently produced.

But we cannot establish czars who decide what is useful or potentially useful work. The editors and consultants of journals are gatekeepers, and frequently unimaginative ones, demanding allegiance to what is considered sociological good form. Perhaps the best that we can hope for is assessment and controversy. The multitude of research reports have to be shaken down periodically, evaluated, distilled for their useful residue. To prevent the acceptance of *ex cathedra* assessments as sociological gospel, other literature reviewers might comment on the review. In this way, it would be possible to get a more effective grasp of the abounding literature without tying it into a neat package which ignores issues, contrary findings, and controversial outlooks and positions.

The emphasis should be on a search for general significance in the reports. This progress might be aided by bringing applied sociologists together with sociologists of a more general orientation so that each might contribute to the other. For example, students of stratification theory might provide useful leads for analyzing the poverty "underclass" in the center-cities, while applied sociologists have much to offer in explicating the variations that exist among the new poor, requiring refinement of stratification theory. Perhaps those in applied sociology could move back and forth between university and other settings. In the former, hopefully, they may feel more unfettered or freer to develop the more general implications of what they have been discovering.

To raise the issue of the general contribution of applied sociology is not to deny that there is a current yield from the applied sociology of the center-city agencies. Perhaps their outstanding work along these lines is in the testing of existing propositions. This is especially true in the field of juvenile delinquency, where the formulations of Albert Cohen, Richard Cloward and Lloyd Ohlin, and Walter Miller are being assessed with data on attitudes of youth and in the evaluation of programs based on their theoretical conceptions.

Perhaps the most substantial long-term contribution of applied sociology, however, is made through thrusting forward new issues for sociological analysis. Applied sociological concerns heighten awareness of problems formerly ignored or underestimated. The recent concern of sociologists with poverty and inequality—which preceded President Johnson's much heralded war on poverty—was largely initiated by applied sociologists like Herbert Gans, who were actively concerned with various programs dealing with slum-dwellers.[12] In the course of their work they became acutely aware that small-scale programs were failing. This, in turn, led to a further analysis of the social arrangements and developments that impeded adequate help to the center-city population. Sociology's theoretical apparatus for analyzing poverty as a structural phenomenon is presently lacking, but the needs of applied sociologists (as well as those of policy-makers) are leading to its development.

### THE INDEPENDENCE OF THE APPLIED SOCIOLOGIST

Underlying many of these tensions is the degree to which the applied sociologist has independence of action—independence to analyze ade-

S. M. Miller

quately his data, to contribute to general sociology, to resist the distorting perspectives of organizational ideology.

The applied sociologist "can too easily become a 'servant of power' or lose his objectivity."[13] The center-city sociologist has a charter to produce work relevant to planning, policy and program, and this in turn exposes him to the ideology of his employing organization in a concentrated way. His data are expected to be immediately and unambiguously relevant to the activities of the agency. There frequently is a tacit assumption that the link between data and program is technical, not ideological. The sociologist frequently (and sometimes unwittingly) becomes caught in agonizing value dilemmas.

The applied sociologist can become the captive of the operating interests of his organization, analyzing everything in terms of its limited overarching assumptions. He may not think freshly about the issues and may end up providing the data and the interpretation which are needed to support the organization's commitments and to confirm its ideology. He runs the risk of becoming an ideologue parading his or his organization's values as sociological data. For example, after collecting data on rates of juvenile delinquency, should he suggest additional police service, the expansion of job opportunities, the elimination of discriminatory practices which affect the self-images of the discriminated, the spread of the Black Muslim movement or involvement in civil rights demonstrations, each of which does seem to reduce crime rates? The decision is not discernable from the data alone. Obviously, a diversity of data and, more importantly, values, affect the resultant proposals and advice he gives.

Again, the sociologist may ignore important areas of study—for example, the assessment of the social service network mentioned earlier—because they do not fit the narrow research charge laid down by the funder of the project or the project director. He may avoid crucial research because it might disturb the established institutions with which the center-city planning agency believes that it needs to work. The applied sociologist has frequently abdicated the responsibility of making the community planning agency aware of the appropriate set of problems to study.

The opposite danger also exists: The applied sociologist may choose to question his agency's ideology and may become a thorny but ineffectual pressure within the organization. In general, however, he rapidly moves to the first position—not out of venality but from familiarity with the agency's staff and sympathy with their problems as well as from the desire to be relevant and useful.

The applied sociologist is in tension between his role as employee and his commitment as professional. As employee, he performs a defined task with a relatively clear-cut function for his organization. As professional, he wishes to have an independent stance, to relate his work to the ongoing body of work of fellow professionals, to make them aware of his findings and to develop the implications of his materials for his professional field.

Some argue that if the applied sociologist is to be effective he has to fit into the perceptions and needs of his organizational superiors; he should adopt a stance which abates anxieties about his activities and maximizes his relevance to the organization.[14] This view assumes that most organizations hiring applied sociologists have a clear perspective on what they want from their sociological employees. A good deal of the time, however, this must be forged in the interaction within the organization and does not exist in the beginning of their relations.

But a more fundamental assumption is involved: The applied sociologist is an employee and has to work within the confines and perspective of his organization. Throughout all organizational life, this is a general issue—What degree of independence do employees have? How much criticism of the organization is permissible? How much raising of uncomfortable issues is acceptable? The boundary between legitimate and illegitimate activity is unsettled, particularly in many bureaucracies which are really warring "fiefdoms" operating under one corporate identity.

Is the contribution of the professional best when he takes a narrow definition of his role? I do not believe it is. There should be a constant effort to move the boundary so that it protects the independence of the professional. One can, of course, fall into the trap of becoming irrelevant to one's organization, but there are many contrasting ways in which to be relevant. The acceptance of *multiple identities* is important in the development of applied sociology.

The tension between organizational commitments, on the one hand, and professional and societal allegiances on the other, is never fully resolved. Ideological issues constantly intrude in decisions about work. They cannot truly be avoided; they can only be ignored.

The struggle to expand the autonomy of the applied social scientist is of little avail if he does not take advantage of whatever independence he has. The earlier comments on the reluctance to adopt new norms and goals for applied sociological investigations are pertinent here. Internal professional restraints can be more effective than external bureaucratic constraints. Applied sociology should not only be housekeeping research writ large, nor general sociology writ pertinently. Its need for independence is particularly great because of the necessity of developing approaches which are suitable to the research tasks, which contribute both to policy and to sociology, and which teach us how to deal effectively with an expanding range of problems.

## Social Criticism

The sociologist has also expanded his role in the direction of social criticism. The work of C. Wright Mills and David Riesman did not readily fit into what had come to be the methodological and theoretical style of modern sociology, although it came closer to the reformist bent of early American sociology. Current empirical research reports keep close to the data, although the last chapter might indeed discuss the wider ramifications of the data. To be treated seriously, less directly empirical research has had to be defined as "theoretical," applying fairly specifically to the accumulating band of sociological theorizing.

Today, however, there is increasing development of sociological analysis as social criticism. Mills and Riesman have not only been raising questions about the operation of American society, but they have also been evaluating it. Implicitly setting up a set of guidelines to judge society, social critics have taken applied social science into new directions. In this work, specific sociological concepts are not dominant. What sociology has provided for these social analysts is a sensitivity to new issues and problems.

Obviously, we have long had social criticism and social critics. Obviously, too, sociologists, like others, have at various times played a role as social critics. But until recent years, there was a diminution of sociological effort along these lines. Today a new attitude has emerged. Sociologists like Daniel Bell and Nathan Glazer see social analysis and criticism as a central and legitimate part of their *professional* role and not as an activity performed as citizens, separate from their professional activities. In their view, social criticism is not in conflict with professional orientations. The sociologist *cum* social critic sees his professional activity not as incidental to but as providing the basis for his social criticism.

This is partly due to the growing diversity of issues in American public life, so that the concerns of sociologists are now perceived of as useful and relevant to American life. This change also results from the new kinds of experiences sociologists have had in varying capacities with various action organizations, in schools, training programs for jobs, welfare programs, or public housing. Another factor has been the personal dismay that many sociologists feel over the ways things are going in American society so that they feel themselves propelled to do something about them. This was especially true of the possibility of nuclear war, which led a number of social scientists to become concerned with international tensions and to develop an understanding of competing nuclear strategies.[15]

Social criticism is presently taking several forms. Examination of American values and a diagnosis of the basic character of modern society are under way. Paul Goodman's work, for example, takes mass society rather than class society as the central concern. Basic values, especially about education, are discussed. The issues attacked and the mode of analysis often lack a political strategy for change. The need for fundamental change is the theme and an apocalyptic view frequently prevails. At the other extreme is an incrementalist social criticism where the basic social structure and established institutions are taken for granted. Here, the effort is to make them succeed more effectively in their conventional directions. Should the minimum wage be $1.50 or $1.75 an hour? The political strategy for change is frequently obvious even if tacit, for political choices are readily coordinated to certain problems, for example, of spurring economic growth or reducing unemployment.

Between Paul Goodman and George Meany, a middle-level of social criticism is emerging. It is concerned with political relevance, but it also attempts to go beyond the conventional terms of public discussion. An example of such criticism are those discussions of poverty which question the notion of a fixed poverty line and which formulate the issue in terms of inequality seen as characteristic of industrially advanced societies.[16] We expect such middle-range criticism to grow with the increasing concern for the structural causes of center-city strains.

### STRAINS IN SOCIAL CRITICISM

One difficulty with social criticism as applied sociology is that one has to run a narrow course between proving a case and developing a position. Since the social critic is talking about objectives, he must assert a position about goals and cannot confine himself to a criticism of the means used to secure goals which are taken on faith. Frequently, social criticism is a response to negative feelings about the status quo. Less pronounced and less clear are statements of what the critic wishes to move toward. In part, Mills' criticism of power reflects his ambiguous views.

A similar difficulty arises when an orientation hardens into a stance. A general point of view can be powerful in providing leverage for examining problems and in looking for certain kinds of issues. When it becomes a rigid stance, the social critic tends to close off new experiences and emerging issues. He may issue "pronounciamentos" which are more likely to reflect his stance than social circumstances. The social critic's usefulness comes from his unique way of viewing events, but this can become blinding idiosyncracy rather than an enlightening perspective.

Accompanying these difficulties is the danger of becoming negative, compulsively and bitterly illuminating the vice in virtue and the failure in promise. Since the social critic's role is largely cautionary, he tends to emphasize defects rather than achievements. By criticizing, he hopes to spur change. Sometimes, however, he may denigrate real advances, for they are small relative to the scope of the problems and to the depth of his yearning. If the critic runs the risk of becoming a yes-man to every act of professed amelioration, he also faces the danger of becoming irrelevant to the issues of the day by an all-embracing nay–saying.

In his zeal to affect policy, the social critic may not do his "homework," the tedious accumulation and detailed analysis of relevant data. Where data are sparse and difficult to collect, it is easy to skip this strenuous stage and leap to positions. To demand that the social critic be armed with systematic data is unreasonable when they do not exist. But to become "expert" without conscientiously attempting to acquire available data can transform social criticism into personal fantasy.

Frequently, the social critic consumes intellectual capital without replenishing it. The process of criticism may not force rethinking of issues, particularly for sociology as an intellectual discipline. Old issues are analyzed or reanalyzed *ad nauseam*, but there is little feedback into sociology as well as little improvement in practical policy.

It is difficult to be a social critic within a social movement, and it is difficult to be one without it. The responsible social critic today lacks an effective arena of discussion, a sophisticated public that converses with him, raising questions of intellectual substance and practical policy relevance. I believe that this public is emerging, sparked by the civil rights movement. Increasingly, the quality of programs to improve the conditions of the poor will be under constant surveillance by civil rights and other groups; the inadequacies of public policies and programs will be assessed and the goals and directions of society questioned. In this process, the social critic and the center-city sociologist should be increasingly aligned. They have much to give to each other.

### CENTER-CITY AND SOCIAL CRITICISM

The poverty and inequality which ramify through the problems of center-city life are leading to increased criticism of the entire fabric of American society. Increasingly, our difficulties are seen as structural and not as peripheral, as permeating the basic operations of our economic and social institutions. Social criticism is forcing us to pay closer and more penetrating attention to the basic character of our society. The applied sociologist of the center-city is collecting fundamental data and assessing the effectiveness of public policy.

As yet, however, we lack an adequate conceptual apparatus for dealing with these data. Applied sociologists need new directions in their work if they are to be effective. Direction may be provided by that strand of social criticism which is raising questions about growing inequalities in the distribution of income, wealth and services. The search for data and for explanation of the distribution of amenities in society will infuse the applied sociology of the center-city with direction and significance. And it will provide the data and analysis for knowledgeable social criticism about the drift of our society and for a sociology informed and informing on the social issues of our time.

## NOTES

1. Frequently, however, the rationale has little to do with what goes on and the researcher is disturbed by the gap between purported goals and irrelevant or limited means. For example, the major educational goal of many projects is to reorient schools so that they deal more effectively with disadvantaged youth. The main educational program is, however, the provision of remedial activities. Little effort is directed at changing the internal, day-by-day operations of the schools.

2. Howard E. Freeman, "The Stratgey of Social Policy Research," Social Welfare Forum, Columbia University Forum, 1963, pp. 153–4.

3. These and other research problems of large-scale demonstration projects are discussed in Martin Rein and S. M. Miller, "The Demonstration Project as a Strategy of Change," paper presented at the Training Institute of Columbia University School of Social Work and Mobilization for Youth, April 30, 1964. The following remarks have been influenced by discussions with Peter Marris.

4. Social research training, it has long seemed to me, might more directly face the operating difficulties of conducting research. The training of students might be concerned with coping with the exigencies of practice as well as with the demands of rigorous methodology.

5. Mobilization for Youth's difficulties with school principals in the Lower East Side of Manhattan and the later attack on it as harboring "sociological subversives" are indicative of the conflict net which envelops these projects.

6. One reason that there has not been more of the kind of research suggested here is that many of the applied sociologists who do the evaluation have certain specific skills or interests. To move in new directions would require that they expand their interests and skills or that new kinds of researchers become interested or be acceptable for activities in the evaluation field.

7. Many organizational studies of change have been narrowly concerned with enhancing productivity or reducing personal conflict arising from personality

clashes. The impact of changes in policy have seldom been investigated. For one such study, see Alvin W. Gouldner, *Patterns of Industrial Bureaucracy*, Glencoe: Free Press, 1954.

8. Cf. Alvin W. Gouldner, "Explorations in Applied Social Science," *Social Problems*, 3 (1956), pp. 169–81, and "Theoretical Requirements of the Applied Social Sciences," *American Sociological Review*, 22 (1957), pp. 92–102. The first article is reprinted in this volume. Eric Trist takes the strongest position in favor of following what he calls "the professional model": "In a sense, therefore, the social scientist begins in practice, however imperfect scientifically, and works back to theory and the more systematic research which may test this and then back again to improved practice." "This . . . is proper when a science (and this is the case in many areas of the social sciences) has not yet advanced to the point where there is a large body of fully attested empirical knowledge related to generally accepted theories. For if at this stage the problem is determined too exclusively by the scientist himself, the hypotheses to be tested will tend to be doctrines rather than true theories, or, as a reaction against this, investigation will become artificially restricted to what can be measured exactly. One may expect both too much formal conceptualization of a shallow kind and too much secondary manipulation of meager primary data." Eric Trist, "Social Research and a National Policy for Science," London: Tavistock Institute of Human Relations, June, 1964, appendix 1, mimeo.

9. There is a conflicting as well as a converging interplay between a profession and society. At various points, it is desirable to have closer ties and more immediate concerns with social problems. At other times, it may be less desirable to do so, particularly if social problems cannot be defined in ways which allow scope for broader concerns and interests.

10. Rose has strongly attacked this type of narrow research in a review of work on race and housing. Arnold Rose, "Race Relations in Housing: An Essay–Review," *Social Problems*, 12 (1964).

11. Many reports are unavailable because of their supposed "confidentiality." The push of most professionals, however, is always to reduce the realm of the suppressed.

12. Herbert Gans, *The Urban Villagers*, New York: The Free Press, 1963.

13. Warren S. Bennis, "A New Role for the Behavioral Sciences: Effecting Organizational Change," *Administrative Science Quarterly*, 8 (1963), p. 163.

14. Cf. Howard E. Freeman, *op. cit.*

15. Despite considerable writing, the role of social science knowledge and training in the analysis and criticism of nuclear strategy remains murky. Presumably, social science training does contribute to this type of thinking and provides a basis for questioning the rationality assumption implicit in much of strategic writing. In other respects, however, social science does not appear to have a special contribution to make in this field. See Frank Riessman and S. M. Miller, "Social Change Versus the 'Psychiatric World View' ", *American Journal of Orthopsychiatry*, XXXIV (January, 1964), p. 38.

16. Richard Titmuss, *Social Change and Income Distribution*, Toronto: University of Toronto Press, 1962, Chapter 9; S. M. Miller and Martin Rein, "Poverty and Social Change," *American Child*, March, 1964.

# Name Index

# Name Index

Cohen, Albert K., 196, 198, 201, 202, 449
Cohen, Morris R., 418
Cook, Stuart W., 283n
Corson, John J., 327n
Coser, Rose L., 106, 113n
Cressey, Donald R., 58, 59, 73n, 177n, 205n
Cuber, J. F., 383, 385, 395n
Cumming, Elaine, 317, 326n, 328n

Dahlberg, G., 250, 258n
Dalton, Melville, 111n
Davis, F. James, 51n
Davis, James A., 110n
Davis, Kingsley, 251, 252, 258n
Davison, W. Phillips, 145n
Dean, Lois R., 328n
Dederich, Charles E., 59, 70, 73n
Dentler, Robert, 162n
Deutsch, Morton, 282n, 283n
Deutscher, Irwin, 441n
Devereux, Edward C., 110n, 411n
Dewey, Richard, 161n
Dickson, William J., 10, 22n, 236n
Dorfman, Robert, 327n
Dunham, H. Warren, 332, 335n, 336n
Duplessis, G., 248, 258n
Durkheim, Emile, 19, 189, 194, 205n, 271, 407, 408
Dykeman, Wilma, 161n

Eaton, Joseph W., 111n, 113n
Ekman, Paul, 282n
Ekstein, Rudolf, 98, 110n, 111n
Elliott, Mabel A., 401–02, 410n, 411n
Etzioni, Amitai, 281n
Eulau, Heinz, 293n
Evan, William M., 292n, 293n

Faris, Robert E. L., 332, 336n
Fenchel, Gerd H., 111n
Festinger, Leon, 287, 293n
Firey, Walter, 214n
Firth, Raymond, 21n
Fitzgerald, Stephen E., 110n
Florence, P. S., 364
Force, Maryanne T., 322, 328n
Forde, Darryl, 6, 21n
Foster, George, 7, 21n, 116
Fox, Renée C., 113n
Frank, Jerome, 299, 305n
Frank, Lawrence K., 111n, 383, 395n, 397n
Frankfurter, Felix, 177n
Freeman, Howard E., 455n, 456n

Freeman, Linton, 252, 258n
Freire-Martin, N., 250, 259n
Freud, Anna, 21n
Freud, Sigmund, 9n, 41, 271, 407, 408
Fuller, R. C., 383, 395n
Furfey, Paul Hanly, 411n

Gadourek, I., 255, 259n
Gans, Herbert, 449, 456n
Gay, Eleanor, 111n
Gerard, Donald L., 371n, 380n
Gerard, Harold B., 292n
Gesell, Arnold, 409
Gillin, John P., 116
Glazer, Nathan, 452
Glazer, Nona, 311n
Glick, P. G., 250, 259n
Glueck, Eleanor, 341–42, 349n, 368, 399, 401, 410n
Glueck, Sheldon, 341–42, 349n, 368, 399, 401, 410n
Goffman, Erving, 332, 336n
Goffman, Irwin W., 111n
Goldsen, Rose K., 311n
Goldstein, Joseph, 177n
Goode, William J., 7, 22n
Goodman, Paul, 161n, 453
Gordon, Margaret S., 327n
Gordon, William E., 112n
Goss, Mary E. W., 111n
Gouldner, Alvin W., 281n, 283n, 441n, 443, 456n
Greer, Scott, vii, 246n, 247n
Gross, Edward, 51n
Gross, Llewellyn, 396n
Guetzkow, Harold, 283n

Hacker, Helen M., 313, 324n
Hagedorn, Robert, 51n
Hajnal, Jan, 249, 259n
Hall, G. Stanley, 319–20, 326n
Hardt, Robert, 441n
Harper, R. A., 383, 385, 395n
Hartley, Eugene L., 111n
Hatt, Paul K., 7, 22n
Havighurst, Robert J., 322, 328n
Hawley, Amos H., 246n
Hayner, Norman, 59
Henry, Jules, 331, 336n
Henry, William, 317, 326n, 328n
Herzog, Elizabeth, 110n
Hill, R., 251, 252, 259n
Holden, Matthew, 247n
Hollingshead, August B., 336n, 410, 411n

# Name Index

# Name Index

Miller, Daniel R., 333–34, 336n
Miller, Delbert C., 51n
Miller, Justin, 179n
Miller, S. M., 205n, 455n, 456n
Miller, Walter B., 205n, 410, 411n, 449
Millis, Walter, 273, 283n
Mills, C. Wright, 112n, 161n, 398, 410n, 452, 453
Mitchell, Howard E., 94, 110n, 112n
Mogey, John, 255, 259n
Moles, Oliver, Jr., 202, 206n
Monahan, T. F., 251, 259n
Monderer, Jack H., 111n
Moore, Barrington, 22n
Moore, Wilbert E., 22n
Moreno, J. L., 56
Morgan, Arthur E., 161n
Morris, W. W., 325n, 327n, 328n
Mudd, Emily H., 94, 110n, 112n, 113n
Murray, Henry A., 205n
Myers, Jerome K., 333, 336n
Myrdal, Gunnar, 148, 160–61n, 324n

Naegele, Kaspar D., 96, 110n
Newell, David S., 328n
Newman, Donald J., 179n
Newman, Russell W., 22n
Niederhoffer, Arthur, 205n
Nisbet, Robert A., 395n, 396n, 401–02, 411n
Noel, R., 283n
North, Robert C., 283n

Ohlin, Lloyd E., 179n, 189, 190 ff, 205n, 449
Orwell, George, 427
Osborne, Thomas M., 59, 73n
Osgood, Charles E., 281n, 282n, 283n

Panakal, J. J., 349n
Pareto, Vilfredo, 407, 408
Park, Robert Ezra, 423
Parsons, Talcott, 8, 9n, 11, 22n, 205n, 252, 253, 272, 282n, 283n, 407–09, 411n
Paul, Benjamin, 116
Pellegrino, Roland J., 111n
Perez, Leander, 139
Perry, Stewart E., 107–08, 113n
Peterson, Robert L., 325n
Peterson, Virgil, 177n
Pinner, Frank A., 318, 326n
Podell, L., 255, 259n
Pollak, Otto, 96, 110n
Polsky, Ned, 72

Poston, Richard, 161n
Pound, Roscoe, 177n
Preiss, Jack J., 41, 51n
Putney, Snell, 282n

Radcliffe-Brown, A. R., 6, 21n, 106, 113n
Ranck, Katherine H., 410n
Rapoport, Anatol, 268, 282n, 396n
Rapoport, Robert N., 112n, 113n
Reader, George C., 111n
Reckless, Walter C., 187n, 188n
Redl, Fritz, 375
Redlich, Frederick C., 336n, 411n
Reimer, Hans, 59
Rein, Martin, 441n, 445n, 456n
Remington, Frank J., 177n, 178n, 179n
Riesman, David, 236n, 452
Riessman, Frank, 197, 205n, 441n, 456n
Ribbins, Richard, vii
Roberts, Bertram H., 333, 336n
Roche, Philip Q., 410, 411n
Roethlisberger, F. J., 10, 22n, 236n
Rose, Albert, 96
Rose, Arnold M., 160n, 292n, 293n, 341, 349n, 383, 395n, 456n
Rosenberg, Morris, 446
Rosenblum, Victor G., 177n, 178n
Rosenfeld, Eva, 371n, 380n
Rossi, Peter H., 145n, 162n
Ruesch, Jurgen, 111n, 113n
Russell, Bertrand, 414

Sand, Mary, 139
Santayana, George, 417
Sawyer, Jack, 282–83
Schanck, Richard L., 145n
Schelling, Thomas C., 275, 282n
Schmidhauser, John R., 318–19, 320, 326n, 327n
Schmidt, William D., 102, 112n
Schopenhauer, Arthur, 386
Schramm, Wilbur, 18, 22n
Schrotel, Stanley R., 181
Schwartz, Mildred A., 293n
Schwartz, Morris S., 112n, 336n
Sellin, Thorsten, 176n, 177n, 181, 185, 188n
Sellitz, Claire, 283n
Selznick, Philip, 326n
Shanas, Ethel, 320, 325n, 327n
Shaw, Clifford R., 56, 154, 189, 191, 205n
Shils, Edward A., 20, 22n, 411n
Short, James F., Jr., 73n, 202, 205n, 206n
Siipi, J., 255, 259n
Silberman, Charles E., 162n

*460*

# Name Index

*461*

# Subject Index

# Subject Index

# Subject Index

Juvenile delinquency *see* Delinquency, juvenile

Labor-management relations, 11–12, 47–50
Labor unions, 86–92
Latin America, community studies, 12–13, 14, 47
  health studies, 7, 114 ff
Law, 285–307
  and administration of justice, 163–76
  authoritative sources of, 288–89
  and crime, 56–57, 165 ff
  and desegregation, 129 ff, 150
  educative role of, 288–91
  functions of, 286–87
  and labor unions, 87–88
  and psychiatry, 301–03
  resistance to, 287–88
  sanctions of, 290–91
  and social change, 285–92
  and trial by jury, 304–05
Leadership, 226–35
  in clinical agencies, 102
  in community programs, 207–14
  in Latin American community, 118
  in Negro community, 145n
  in organizations, 28–29
  and public opinion, 139, 146n
  typologies of, 227–32
Legitimacy, social, 423, 426

Market research, 7, 79, 83
Marriage, age at first, 248–49
McLain Institute, 317–18
Media, mass, 138, 146n, 422
Mental illness, 329–35, 410
Military institutions, 74–78
  and peace/war research, 273
  sociology of, 5
  *see also* U.S. Air Force; U.S. Navy
Minority groups, concept of, 311–23
  and deprivation, 320–23
  and differential access to power, 318–20
  and group identity, 316–17
  identifying characteristics of, 314
  as pressure group, 317–18
  stereotypes on, 314–16
Mobility, and delinquency, 344–45
Mobilization for Youth, 442
Motivation research, 79–80

National Association for the Advancement of Colored People, 129, 151, 160
National Institute of Mental Health, 371
Negroes, and desegregation, 129

and equality of opportunity, 148 ff, 161n
and labor unions, 91
leadership class, 145n
New York City Youth Board, 370
Normative theory, 241–44
  in child development, 409
  of cities, 241–44
  and social order, 409

Occupation, and community attachment, 217–19
  and marriage age, 249–50, 251, 253–55
Opinion, public, 127–45, 155
  *see also* Attitude study; Propaganda
Organization for the Southwest Community, 154
Organizations, 11–12, 23–28
  and consultant's role in, 79–85
  ideological bias of, 450–51
  and individual member behavior, 23, 26
  "informal," 10, 10n
  and social change, 445
  stresses in, 93–109
  structure of, in clinical agencies, 94–104
  structure of, in hospitals, 330–32
  and survey research, 23–28
  values of, 39–51
  variables in, 26 ff

Pan American Health Organization, 114 ff
Peace, and role of social science, 266–84, 360–62, 453
Personality, modal, and delinquency, 189, 194, 202–04
Political science, and peace/war research, 274–76
Politics, divergent international systems of, 260
  in metropolitan area, 208, 238–41
  in small commun'ty, 227, 350–57
Poverty, 161n, 449, 453, 454
Power structure, 453
  in community, 46–47, 127, 137–38, 141
  and legitimacy, 426
  in organizations, 26
  and role of social scientist, 423
President's Committee on Juvenile Delinquency and Youth Crime, 442
Prison, studies of, 59
Propaganda, 140
  research on, 5
Psychiatry, and crime, 301–03, 410
Psychoanalysis, 9, 20, 21, 41
Psychology, 9n, 20, 410
Public opinion *see* Opinion, public

# Subject Index

Race relations, 127–46, 147–60
RAND Corporation, 5, 267
Reference groups, and delinquency, 203, 204
  and legal norms, 289
Research, applied vs. basic, 5 ff
  approaches to, 11–15
  areas of, 5
  client's resistance to, 93–95
  in clinical settings, 93–109
  and communication patterns, 101–02, 448–49
  evaluative function of, 95–97, 443–46
  goals of, 24
  methodology of, 7, 400
  and role of researcher, 24
  in social problems, 399–400, 409–10
  as substitute for change, 16
  techniques of, 15–16, 19, 20, 23–28
  and values of clients, 39–51
  see also Social science, applied; Sociology, applied
Retreatism, and deviant behavior, 190–92
Role relations, concept of, 407
  and delinquency, 203, 204
  of researcher vs. client, 422
  of researcher vs. clinician, 95–101
  of researcher vs. policy-maker, 17–18, 21
  and role ambiguity, 31
  and role conflict, 107–08
  and value orientation, 49
Rural sociology, 447
  area studies, 215–25, 226–35
Russell Sage Foundation, 110n, 113n

Save Our Schools (SOS), 134, 139, 142, 145
Science, and democracy, 423, 426–27
Segregation  see Desegregation; Race relations
Services, social, vs. needs, 445
  see also Agencies, clinical; Health; Welfare, social
Sex, and community attachment, 220
  and leadership, 210
Slums, and community programs, 442
  and delinquency, 193–94
Social change  see Change, social
Social criticism  see Criticism, social
Socialization, theory of, 391, 408
Social Research, Inc., 79, 84
Social science, applied, 5–21
  basic vs. applied, 5–6
  and client-researcher relations, 422

and client's resistance, 15–17, 19–20
clinical model for, 12–13, 18–21
crucial problems in, 421–28
engineering model for, 11–12, 17–18
growth of, 5
and historical perspective, 421–22, 429–30, 445
independence of, 13
interdisciplinary research problems in, 402, 410
moral obligations of, 429–38
and policy-makers, 358–66
and public service, 412–20
and pure sociology, 6–11
role of, 17, 36–38
and social change, 8–11
and theory, 5–6, 7–11, 383–95, 398–400
utility vs. respectability in, 428, 444
value-free assumption in, 13–14, 430–31
  see also Research; Sociology, applied; Theory, sociological
Social structure, concepts of, 401–02, 407–09
  and desegregation conflict, 127–45
  and deviance, 401–02, 408–09
  and industrialization, 260–65
  and social disorganization, 401–02, 408
  stable vs. changing, 8, 453
  in underdeveloped areas, 117, 118–19
Sociology, applied, 5 ff, 439–56
  approaches to, 11–21
  and definition of social problems, 383–85
  ethical leadership of, 390–92, 394
  and general sociology, 311–36, 447–49
  growth of, 441
  independence of, 448, 449–52
  interrelation of fact and value in, 385–90
  and peace-war research, 274–76
  and public policy, 339–80
  and pure sociology, 6–11
  and social criticism, 427–28, 441, 442, 452–55
  utility vs. respectability in, 428, 444
  see also Research; Social science, applied
Society, analyses of, 453
  forms of, 128
  mass vs. class concept, 453
  pluralistic, 128, 150
  and social problems, 398–410
  see also Change, social; Social Structure
Society for the Study of Social Problems, 149
Southern Regional Council, 131

*465*

# Subject Index